50 Best College Majors for a Secure Future

Part of JIST's Best Jobs® Series

Laurence Shatkin, Ph.D., and The Editors @ JIST

Also in JIST's **Best Jobs** Series

- ❋ *Best Jobs for the 21st Century*
- ❋ *50 Best Jobs for Your Personality*
- ❋ *200 Best Jobs for College Graduates*
- ❋ *300 Best Jobs Without a Four-Year Degree*
- ❋ *200 Best Jobs Through Apprenticeships*
- ❋ *40 Best Fields for Your Career*
- ❋ *225 Best Jobs for Baby Boomers*
- ❋ *250 Best-Paying Jobs*
- ❋ *150 Best Jobs for Your Skills*

- ❋ *150 Best Jobs Through Military Training*
- ❋ *175 Best Jobs Not Behind a Desk*
- ❋ *150 Best Jobs for a Better World*
- ❋ *10 Best College Majors for Your Personality*
- ❋ *200 Best Jobs for Introverts*
- ❋ *150 Best Low-Stress Jobs*
- ❋ *150 Best Recession-Proof Jobs*
- ❋ *200 Best Jobs for Renewing America*

JIST
Works
America's Career Publisher®

50 Best College Majors for a Secure Future

© 2010 by JIST Publishing

Published by JIST Works, an imprint of JIST Publishing
7321 Shadeland Station, Suite 200
Indianapolis, Indiana 46256-3923

Phone: 800-648-JIST   Fax: 877-454-7839
E-mail: info@jist.com   Web site: www.jist.com

Some Other Books by the Authors

The Editors at JIST

EZ Occupational Outlook Handbook

Salary Facts Handbook

Enhanced Occupational Outlook Handbook

Health-Care CareerVision Book and DVD

Laurence Shatkin

200 Best Jobs for Renewing America

Quick Guide to College Majors and Careers

90-Minute College Major Matcher

Your $100,000 Career Plan

New Guide for Occupational Exploration

150 Best Recession-Proof Jobs

Quantity discounts are available for JIST products. Please call 800-648-JIST or visit www.jist.com for a free catalog and more information.

Visit www.jist.com for information on JIST, free job search information, tables of contents and sample pages, and ordering information on our many products.

Acquisitions Editor: Susan Pines
Development Editor: Stephanie Koutek
Cover and Interior Designer: Aleata Halbig
Cover Photo: Thomas Barwick, Getty Images
Interior Layout: Aleata Halbig
Proofreaders: Laura Bowman, Jeanne Clark
Indexer: Cheryl Lenser

Printed in the United States of America
14 13 12 11 10   9 8 7 6 5 4 3 2

Library of Congress Cataloging-in-Publication Data

Shatkin, Laurence.
  50 best college majors for a secure future / Laurence Shatkin, Ph.D., and the editors at JIST.
     p. cm. -- (JIST's best jobs series)
  Includes index.
  ISBN 978-1-59357-726-1 (alk. paper)
  1. Universities and colleges--United States--Directories. 2. College choice--United States. I. JIST Works, Inc. II. Title. III. Title: Fifty best college majors for a secure future.
  L901.S553 2010
  378.2'41--dc22
                              2009024378

ISBN 978-1-59357-726-1

This Is a Big Book, But It Is Very Easy to Use

If you want a career that's a steady ride and not a roller coaster, then this book will help you focus on the college majors that can provide your ticket.

The 50 college majors included in this book open the door to jobs that are considered secure because they meet needs that are not diminished even during hard times. And the majors are selected for and ordered on lists that emphasize those that can lead to jobs with the highest earnings and the highest demand for workers.

Specialized lists arrange these majors by the level of education required (a bachelor's or higher), by career clusters, by personality types, and by other useful characteristics of the related jobs.

Every major and every related secure job is described in detail later in the book, so you can explore the majors and jobs that interest you the most. For each major, you'll learn the typical college courses, the high school prerequisites, specializations, common career paths, and other majors that are related to the same jobs. For each related secure job, you'll learn the earnings, important work tasks, skills, educational programs, fastest-growing industries, personality type, and many other informative facts.

You'll also find tips about how to add security to your major and your job—ideas that can help you get ahead in both good times and bad.

Using this book, you'll be surprised how quickly you'll get new ideas for majors and careers that are good bets in an unsteady economy and can suit you in many other ways.

Credits and Acknowledgments: While the authors created this book, it is based on the work of many others. The occupational information is based on data obtained from the U.S. Department of Labor and the U.S. Census Bureau. These sources provide the most authoritative occupational information available. The job titles and their related descriptions are from the O*NET database, which was developed by researchers and developers under the direction of the U.S. Department of Labor. They, in turn, were assisted by thousands of employers who provided details on the nature of work in the many thousands of job samplings used in the database's development. We used the most recent version of the O*NET database, release 13.0. We appreciate and thank the staff of the U.S. Department of Labor for their efforts and expertise in providing such a rich source of data.

Table of Contents

Summary of Major Sections

Introduction. A short overview to help you better understand and use the book. *Starts on page 1.*

Part I: Add Security to Your College Major and Your Future Job. Explains what makes a major your ticket to a secure future and provides suggestions for how to find jobs with security or improve the security of an existing job. *Starts on page 15.*

Part II: The Best Majors Lists. Shows you the best majors that are linked to jobs with high employment security. Lists highlight the high-security majors with the best potential for earnings, job growth, and job openings. You can also see lists that classify the majors according to education and training required by related jobs and several other features, such as those leading to jobs with the highest percentage of women and of men and jobs with high rates of self-employment and many part-time workers. Although there are a lot of lists, they are easy to understand because they have clear titles and are organized into groupings of related lists. *Starts on page 21.*

Part III: Descriptions of the Best High-Security Majors. Provides descriptions of the 50 high-security college majors, plus 5 majors that are similar to our generic major called Graduate Study for College Teaching. Each description contains information on typical high school and college courses, specializations, common career paths, and related job titles, both high and low security. The descriptions are presented in alphabetical order, so you can easily look up a major related to a job that you've identified in a list from Part II and that you want to learn more about. *Starts on page 73.*

Part IV: Descriptions of Related Secure Jobs. Provides a brief but information-packed description of the 101 jobs related to the high-security college majors in Part III. Each description contains information on earnings, projected growth, education and training required, job duties, skills, related job titles, related knowledge and courses, and many other details. The descriptions are presented in alphabetical order, so you can easily look up a job related to a major that you've read about in Part III and that you want to learn more about. *Starts on page 137.*

Appendix: Resources for Further Exploration. Identifies Web-based and print resources for further exploration of college majors and careers. *Starts on page 329.*

Detailed Table of Contents

Introduction 1
How to Use This Book 1
Where the Information Came From 2
How the Majors in This Book Were Selected 5
A Sample Description of a Major 8
A Sample Description of a Related Job 10

Part I: Add Security to Your College Major and Your Future Job 15
Why Do Some Majors Provide More Security? 15
Getting a Secure Job After Graduation 17
Limitations of Forecasts 17
Work Habits That Can Save Your Future Job 18

Part II: The Best Majors Lists 21
Best High-Security Majors Overall: Majors Related to Jobs with the Highest Pay, Fastest Growth, and Most Openings 22
The 50 Best High-Security Majors Overall 24
The 20 High-Security Majors with the Best Income Potential 26
The 20 High-Security Majors with the Best Job-Growth Potential 27
The 20 High-Security Majors with the Best Job-Opening Potential 28
Best High-Security Majors by Demographic 29
Best High-Security Majors Related to Jobs with the Highest Percentage of Part-Time Workers 30
Best High-Security Majors Related to Jobs with a High Percentage of Part-Time Workers 31
Best High-Security Majors Related to Jobs with the Highest Percentage of Self-Employed Workers 33
Best High-Security Majors Related to Jobs with a High Percentage of Self-Employed Workers 34
Best High-Security Majors Related to Jobs Employing the Highest Percentage of Women .. 35
Best High-Security Majors Related to Jobs Employing a High Percentage of Women 36

Best High-Security Majors Related to Jobs Employing the Highest Percentage of Men 38

Best High-Security Majors Related to Jobs Employing a High Percentage of Men 38

Best High-Security Majors Related to Jobs Employing the Highest Percentage of Urban Workers 39

Best High-Security Majors Related to Jobs Employing a High Percentage of Urban Workers 41

Best High-Security Majors Related to Jobs Employing the Highest Percentage of Rural Workers 42

Best High-Security Majors Related to Jobs Employing a High Percentage of Rural Workers 43

Best High-Security Majors Sorted by Education or Experience Required by Related Jobs 44

The Education Levels 45

Best High-Security Majors Related to Jobs Requiring a Bachelor's Degree or Less 46

Best High-Security Majors Related to Jobs Requiring Work Experience Plus Degree 47

Best High-Security Majors Related to Jobs Requiring a Master's Degree 47

Best High-Security Majors Related to Jobs Requiring a Doctoral Degree 48

Best High-Security Majors Related to Jobs Requiring a First Professional Degree 48

Best High-Security Majors Sorted by Career Clusters of Related Jobs 48

Descriptions for the 16 Career Clusters 49

Best High-Security Majors in the Agriculture, Food, and Natural Resources Cluster 53

Best High-Security Majors in the Architecture and Construction Cluster 53

Best High-Security Majors in the Arts, Audio/ Video Technology, and Communications Cluster 54

Best High-Security Majors in the Business, Management, and Administration Cluster 54

Best High-Security Majors in the Education and Training Cluster 54

Best High-Security Majors in the Finance Cluster 55

Best High-Security Majors in the Government and Public Administration Cluster 55

Best High-Security Majors in the Health Science Cluster 56

Best High-Security Majors in the Human Services Cluster 56

Best High-Security Majors in the Information Technology Cluster 57

Best High-Security Majors in the Law, Public Safety, Corrections, and Security Cluster 57

Best High-Security Majors in the Marketing, Sales, and Service Cluster 58

Best High-Security Majors in the Science, Technology, Engineering, and Mathematics Cluster 58

Best High-Security Jobs Sorted by Personality Types 58

Descriptions of the Six Personality Types 59

Best High-Security Majors for People with a Realistic Personality Type 60

Best High-Security Majors for People with an Investigative Personality Type 61

Best High-Security Majors for People with an Artistic Personality Type 61

Best High-Security Majors for People with a Social Personality Type 62

Best High-Security Majors for People with an Enterprising Personality Type 63

Best High-Security Majors for People with a Conventional Personality Type 63

Best High-Security Majors by Level of Verbal and Math Skills 63

High-Security Majors Related to Jobs that Require the Highest Level of Verbal Skills 65

Best High-Security Majors Related to Jobs that Require a High Level of Verbal Skills 66

Best High-Security Majors Related to Jobs that Require a Lower Level of Verbal Skills 67

High-Security Majors Related to Jobs that Require the Highest Level of Math Skills 68

Best High-Security Majors Related to Jobs that Require a High Level of Math Skills 68

Best High-Security Majors Related to Jobs that Require a Lower Level of Math Skills 70
Bonus List: The Most Important Courses for a Secure Future 70
The Most Important Courses for a Secure Future 71

Part III: Descriptions of the Best High-Security Majors **73**
Actuarial Science 75
African-American Studies 75
American Studies 77
Anthropology 78
Archeology 79
Area Studies 80
Art History 81
Business Education 82
Chinese 83
Chiropractic 84
Classics 85
Communications Studies/Speech 86
Criminal Justice/Law Enforcement 87
Early Childhood Education 89
English 90
Environmental Science 91
Family and Consumer Sciences 92
French 93
Geology 94
Geophysics 95
German 96
Graduate Study for College Teaching 97
Health Information Systems Administration ... 100
Hospital/Health Facilities Administration 101
Humanities 102
Japanese 104
Journalism and Mass Communications 105
Library Science 106
Mathematics 107
Medical Technology 108
Medicine 109
Modern Foreign Language 111
Nursing (R.N. Training) 112
Occupational Therapy 113

Oceanography 114
Optometry 115
Pharmacy 116
Philosophy 117
Physical Education 118
Physical Therapy 119
Physician Assisting 120
Podiatry 121
Political Science 122
Psychology 123
Public Relations 124
Religion/Religious Studies 125
Russian 126
Secondary Education 127
Social Work 128
Spanish 129
Special Education 131
Speech-Language Pathology and Audiology 132
Statistics 133
Veterinary Medicine 134
Women's Studies 135

Part IV: Descriptions of Related Secure Jobs .. **137**
Actuaries 139
Agricultural Sciences Teachers, Postsecondary .. 140
Anesthesiologists 142
Anthropologists 144
Anthropology and Archeology Teachers, Postsecondary 146
Archeologists 148
Architecture Teachers, Postsecondary 150
Archivists 152
Area, Ethnic, and Cultural Studies Teachers, Postsecondary 153
Art, Drama, and Music Teachers, Postsecondary 155
Atmospheric, Earth, Marine, and Space Sciences Teachers, Postsecondary 157
Audiologists 159
Bailiffs 161
Biological Science Teachers, Postsecondary 162
Business Teachers, Postsecondary 164
Chemistry Teachers, Postsecondary 166

Table of Contents

Child, Family, and School Social Workers 168

Chiropractors 171

Clergy 172

Clinical Psychologists 174

Coaches and Scouts 176

Communications Teachers, Postsecondary 178

Computer Science Teachers, Postsecondary 180

Counseling Psychologists 182

Court Reporters 184

Criminal Investigators and Special Agents 185

Criminal Justice and Law Enforcement
    Teachers, Postsecondary 187

Curators 189

Economics Teachers, Postsecondary 191

Editors 193

Education Teachers, Postsecondary 195

Engineering Teachers, Postsecondary 197

English Language and Literature Teachers,
    Postsecondary 199

Environmental Science Teachers,
    Postsecondary 201

Environmental Scientists and Specialists,
    Including Health 203

Family and General Practitioners 205

Foreign Language and Literature Teachers,
    Postsecondary 207

Forestry and Conservation Science Teachers,
    Postsecondary 209

Geography Teachers, Postsecondary 211

Geoscientists, Except Hydrologists and
    Geographers 213

Graduate Teaching Assistants 215

Health Specialties Teachers, Postsecondary 217

History Teachers, Postsecondary 219

Home Economics Teachers, Postsecondary 221

Hydrologists 223

Immigration and Customs Inspectors 225

Industrial-Organizational Psychologists 226

Internists, General 228

Interpreters and Translators 230

Kindergarten Teachers, Except Special
    Education 232

Law Teachers, Postsecondary 234

Librarians 236

Library Science Teachers, Postsecondary 238

Marriage and Family Therapists 240

Mathematical Science Teachers,
    Postsecondary 242

Mathematicians 244

Medical and Clinical Laboratory
    Technologists 245

Medical and Health Services Managers 247

Middle School Teachers, Except Special and
    Vocational Education 249

Museum Technicians and Conservators 251

Nursing Instructors and Teachers,
    Postsecondary 253

Obstetricians and Gynecologists 255

Occupational Therapists 257

Optometrists 259

Pediatricians, General 261

Pharmacists 263

Philosophy and Religion Teachers,
    Postsecondary 265

Physical Therapists 267

Physician Assistants 269

Physicians and Surgeons, All Other 271

Physics Teachers, Postsecondary 272

Podiatrists 274

Police Detectives 275

Police Identification and Records Officers 277

Police Patrol Officers 279

Political Science Teachers, Postsecondary 281

Political Scientists 283

Postsecondary Teachers, All Other 284

Preschool Teachers, Except Special Education .. 285

Private Detectives and Investigators 287

Probation Officers and Correctional
    Treatment Specialists 289

Psychiatrists 291

Psychology Teachers, Postsecondary 293

Public Address System and Other
    Announcers 295

Public Relations Specialists 296

Recreation and Fitness Studies Teachers,
    Postsecondary 299

Registered Nurses.............................. *301*

Religious Workers, All Other........................... *303*

School Psychologists............................ *303*

Secondary School Teachers, Except Special and Vocational Education........................... *305*

Sheriffs and Deputy Sheriffs........................ *307*

Social Work Teachers, Postsecondary............. *309*

Sociology Teachers, Postsecondary.................... *311*

Special Education Teachers, Middle School..... *313*

Special Education Teachers, Secondary School... *315*

Speech-Language Pathologists *317*

Statisticians *319*

Surgeons *321*

Teachers and Instructors, All Other *323*

Veterinarians................................. *324*

Vocational Education Teachers, Postsecondary............................... *326*

Appendix: Resources for Further Exploration **329**

Index **331**

Introduction

Getting a bachelor's degree requires a considerable investment of time, money, and hard work. Most people who seek a bachelor's (or higher) degree expect it to pave the way to a good job that will make the investment worthwhile. And, in fact, workers with a bachelor's have an average of 30 percent less unemployment and 33 percent higher earnings.

But some college majors lead to careers that are much more secure than others and that pay better than others. Those are the majors highlighted in this book. To create the book, first we identified the majors linked to jobs that are least affected by economic downturns, and then we identified the 50 majors with the best potential economic rewards—again, based on the jobs linked to them. (The methods we used are explained later in this introduction.)

How to Use This Book

This is a book that you can dive right into:

⁕ **If you like lists and want an easy way to compare majors,** you should turn to Part II. Here you can browse lists of majors linked to secure jobs with the best pay, the fastest growth, and the most job openings. You can see these "best majors" broken down in various ways, such as by personality type or amount of education required by the related jobs.

⁕ **If you don't know what major might suit you,** you may want to look at the lists in Part II that organize majors by personality type or by career cluster. Or you might browse in Part III, looking for a major that interests you. When you find one, note its personality type and career cluster, find other majors in the Part II lists that share these characteristics, and read their Part III descriptions.

⁕ **If you have a major in mind but are not certain about it,** read the description in Part III and the descriptions of related jobs in Part IV. Also, see how it compares to other majors in the lists in Part II. It may be a good major for you even if it is not at the top of any "best majors" lists; remember that *all* majors in this book have been selected partly on the basis of their potential for good economic rewards.

❋ **If you have a job in mind but are not certain about it,** look for it in Part IV. If you can't find it in Part IV, that means that it either is sensitive to economic downturns or has low economic rewards. (It might also be a highly specialized job, in which case you should look for a related job.) If you do find it there, decide whether the economic facts match your expectations. For example, if you're interested in being self-employed, does the job offer many opportunities for that? Read the description and consider whether the work tasks, skills, knowledge, and work environment suit you. If the job seems like a good match, note the related major. Then turn to Part III and read the description of the major. Decide whether it appeals to you and whether you would find the coursework interesting.

On the other hand, if you like to do things in a methodical way, you may want to read the sections in order:

❋ Part I will give you useful background on how to **add security to your college major and your future job.** This advice can be useful even if you eventually decide on a major or job that isn't included in this book.

❋ **Browse the lists of "best majors"** in Part II and take notes on the majors that have the greatest appeal for you. If you're aware of your career-related personality type or if you've been aiming for a particular career cluster, you can start by looking at the lists that are organized around these characteristics. Or perhaps you'll focus on lists of majors with good potential for part-time work or self-employment.

❋ Look in Part III for the **descriptions of the majors** you found most appealing. Narrow down your list by asking yourself some questions: Do the required courses interest me? Can I do well in them? Is there a specialization and career route that might be a good direction for me?

❋ Then you can look up the **descriptions of related secure jobs** in Part IV and decide whether the work may be interesting and rewarding.

Of course, no single book can tell you everything you need to know about college majors and careers. That's why you will probably want to confirm your tentative choices by using some of the resources listed in the appendix.

Where the Information Came From

Because this book is about both college majors and the jobs they are related to, it uses information from a variety of sources.

The Classification of Instructional Programs, developed by the U.S. Department of Education, provided a standard title and definition for each major.

The information for the "Typical Sequence of College Courses" is derived from research in actual college catalogs. The courses are those that appeared in several catalogs and were commonly required for the majors. You may notice variations in the number of courses listed. Some majors have fairly standard requirements that can be listed in detail; in some cases, a professional association mandates that certain courses be included. For other majors, requirements are either so minimal or so varied that it is difficult to list more than a handful of typical courses.

The "Typical Sequence of High School Courses" sections are based on a general understanding of which high school courses are considered prerequisites for the college-level courses required by the major.

You should be aware that course requirements and prerequisites for majors vary widely from one college to another. The descriptions outline average requirements, but before you declare a major you need to be aware of *all* the courses that your college (or your intended college) requires. For example, most colleges do not require a course in introduction to forestry as part of their bachelor's degree program in geology. However, Sewanee: The University of the South does, and perhaps some other colleges do as well. Some colleges require *all* students to take certain core courses in writing, public speaking, math, or religion, and these core courses often are not reflected in this book's descriptions of majors.

The job-related information came from databases and books created by the U.S. Department of Labor and the U.S. Census Bureau. The definition, work tasks, personality (RIASEC) types, skills (including verbal and math), related knowledge, and work environment are derived from the Department of Labor's O*NET (Occupational Information Network) database, which is now the primary source of detailed information on occupations. The Labor Department updates the O*NET on a regular basis, and we used the most recent version available—O*NET release 13.

The information about earnings; growth; number of openings; level of required education; and workers who are part-time, self-employed, male, and female is based on figures from the U.S. Bureau of Labor Statistics (BLS) and the U.S. Census Bureau.

As you look at the economic and demographic figures, keep in mind that they are estimates. They give you a general idea about the number of workers employed, annual earnings, rate of job growth, annual job openings, and composition of the workforce.

When you see these figures, you may sometimes wonder how to interpret them: Is $60,000 a good yearly salary? Is 15 percent job growth considered slow or fast? What number of job openings represents a good job market? It helps to compare these figures for any one occupation to the national averages. For all workers in all occupations, the median earnings (half earned more and half less) were $31,410 in May 2007. For the 101 occupations linked to the majors included in this book, the average earnings were about $63,000. (This is a weighted average of the median earnings for the jobs, which means that jobs with bigger workforces were given greater weight. It is also not precise, because we lack accurate earnings figures for certain highly paid jobs, such as Anesthesiologists, whose income is reported only as "more than $145,600.")

The average projected job growth for all jobs over the 10-year period ending in 2016 is 10.4 percent, but for the 101 occupations in this book, the average is 16.9 percent.

For the 757 occupations for which job-opening figures are available from the Bureau of Labor Statistics, the average number of job openings each year is about 36,000, whereas for the 101 occupations in this book, the average is about 18,000. If that difference surprises you, think about the help-wanted advertisements you find in a typical newspaper. Most of those jobs require considerably less than a bachelor's degree, but most of them also are not as rewarding or fulfilling as you want; that's why they have high turnover, which creates lots of job openings. We presume you're reading this book because you want the kind of job you'll stick with for several years.

When you see figures in this book describing jobs, remember that they always describe an average and therefore have limitations. Just as there is no precisely average person, there is no such thing as a statistically average example of a particular job. We say this because data, while helpful, can also be misleading.

Take, for example, the yearly earnings information about related jobs in this book. This is highly reliable data obtained from a very large U.S. working population sample by the Bureau of Labor Statistics and is meant to reflect earnings levels in May 2007. For each job described in Part IV, we report three figures related to earnings:

* The Annual Earnings figure shows the median earnings (half earn more, half earn less).

* The Beginning Wage figure shows the 10th percentile earnings (the figure that exceeds the earnings of the lowest 10 percent of the workers). This is a rough approximation of what a beginning worker may be offered.

* The Earnings Growth Potential figure represents the ratio between the 10th percentile and the median. In a job for which this figure is high, you have great potential for increasing your earnings as you gain experience and skills. When the figure is low, it means you will probably need to move on to another occupation to improve your earnings substantially.

All of these earnings figures are national averages, and earnings of individual workers can vary greatly. For example, people who live in rural areas or who work for smaller employers typically earn less than those who do similar work in cities (where the cost of living is higher) or for bigger employers. People in certain areas of the country earn less than those in others. Other factors also influence how much you are likely to earn in a given job in your area. For example, dentists in the New York metropolitan area earn an average of $132,850 per year, whereas dentists in nine metropolitan areas in North Carolina earn an average of more than $145,600 per year. Although the cost of living tends to be higher in the New York area, North Carolina has only one dentistry school, and therefore dentists there experience less competition for patients and can command higher fees. So you can see that many factors can cause earnings to vary widely.

Also keep in mind that the figures for job growth and number of openings are projections by labor economists—their best guesses about what we can expect between now and 2016. They are not guarantees. A depression, war, or technological breakthrough could change the actual outcome.

Finally, don't forget that the job market consists of both job openings and job seekers. The figures on job growth and openings don't tell you how many people will be competing with you to be hired. The Department of Labor does not publish figures on the supply of job candidates, so we are unable to tell you much about the level of competition beyond a general statement of the economic factors involved. (In the Part IV job descriptions, look for the topic called "Other Considerations for Job Security.") Competition is an important issue that you should research for any tentative career goal. You should speak to people who educate or train tomorrow's workers; they probably have a good idea of how many of their graduates find rewarding employment and how quickly. People in the workforce also can provide insights into this issue. Use your critical thinking skills to evaluate what people tell you. For example, recruiters for training programs are highly motivated to get you to sign up, whereas people in the workforce may be trying to discourage you from competing. Get a variety of opinions to balance out possible biases.

So, in reviewing the information in this book, please understand the limitations of the data. You need to use common sense in making decisions about education and careers as in most other things in life. We hope that, using that approach, you find the information helpful and interesting.

How the Majors in This Book Were Selected

Open the catalog from any large university and you'll find dozens of majors listed, leading to a great variety of careers. We wanted to save you time by identifying the best commonly offered majors that are likely to lead to careers with job security.

Here is the procedure we followed to select the 50 majors that we included in the lists in this book:

1. We began with the descriptions of 120 college majors that were developed for an earlier book, *Quick Guide to College Majors and Careers* (JIST). These covered the most commonly offered programs. We identified the related O*NET occupations

by using the recommended major-to-job matches made by the National Center for O*NET Development, with one slight modification: We removed the postsecondary teaching jobs. Theoretically, students in *any* major can go on to teach the subject in college—for example, some statistics majors aspire to do what their professors are doing rather than work in the industry—but this number is difficult to determine and usually quite small, so it made more sense to create the pseudo-major "Graduate Study for College Teaching" as an option for those who want to use their education for that career goal. Another problem with the match-ups made by the National Center for O*NET Development is that it recognizes over three dozen different postsecondary teaching jobs, but job-outlook information is available only for a single job that combines them all (Postsecondary Teachers). Therefore, in the lists in Part II, we linked "Graduate Study for College Teaching" to one combined occupation, Postsecondary Teachers. (The 37 postsecondary teaching jobs are described separately in Part IV.)

2. From all of the jobs linked to college majors (after we eliminated a few jobs for which there was no economic information), we identified the jobs that are least likely to be affected by a recession. To do so, we followed the ratings given by an article in the *Occupational Outlook Quarterly* (OOQ), a BLS publication. It rates jobs on a four-point scale, from 0 to 3, for "economic sensitivity," which means how closely the jobs have, in the past, prospered or suffered along with the economy. For an additional check, we consulted the 2008–2009 edition of the *Occupational Outlook Handbook*, another BLS publication, focusing on the outlook statements given for the occupations. When necessary, we adjusted the sensitivity ratings for some jobs. Because many of the job titles are very diverse collections of jobs—for example, Actors, Producers, and Directors—we did not automatically assume that all the related specific titles deserve to share the same numerical rating for economic sensitivity. To determine separate ratings in these cases, we performed a statistical analysis comparing the historical ups and downs in the workforce size of occupations with the ups and downs in the national economy. For each job in these cases, we also considered the economic outlook projected between 2006 and 2016. (Our procedures for rating jobs on recession sensitivity are described in greater detail in *150 Best Recession-Proof Jobs* [JIST].)

3. We also flagged occupations that are at high risk for being offshored—meaning that the work can readily be handed over to workers in foreign countries. These jobs were identified in a 2006 BLS publication called *Occupational Projections and Training Data.* Some of these offshorable jobs have very good employment outlook through 2016, but their long-term security is questionable.

4. We then had a list of jobs we considered secure because (a) they were not easily offshored and (b) they were either rated 0 on economic sensitivity or rated 1 and had projected growth of greater than 23.5 percent.

5. We decided that a major promised a secure future if all the jobs it was linked to were secure. If a major was linked to more than one job, some of which were *not* secure, we compared the number of workers employed in secure jobs to the number employed in recession-sensitive jobs. If the secure jobs accounted for more than 25 percent of the total workforce, we considered the major high security, meaning that graduates have a reasonable chance of getting into a secure occupation.

6. At this point, we had a pool of 72 high-security majors. To determine the majors with the best economic potential, we assembled economic information about the secure jobs related to each major: the annual earnings, the job growth projected for a 10-year period ending in 2016, and the number of job openings expected annually during that same time span. When more than one secure job was linked to a major, we computed a weighted average for earnings and job growth in related jobs and computed the mean number of annual openings in related jobs. (The assumption was that a student is going to choose some specialization in the major and thus qualify for *one* of the linked secure jobs; therefore, it would be wrong to consider all occupations to be open to the student, and the average of the job-openings figures was appropriate.)

7. We ranked the majors in three different ways: by potential earnings, by potential job growth, and by potential job openings. We then added the numerical ranks for each major in each list to produce an overall score. To emphasize majors leading to jobs with the best economic rewards, we selected the 50 majors with the best numerical scores. These majors are the focus of this book.

For example, Physician Assisting is the high-security major with the best combined score for potential earnings, growth, and number of job openings—based on the related job Physician Assistants. Therefore, Physician Assisting is listed first in our "Best Majors Overall" list even though it is not the recession-proof major with the best earnings potential (which is Medicine), the best potential for job growth (which is Veterinary Medicine), or the best potential for job openings (which is Nursing [R.N. Training]).

All 50 of these majors appear not only in the lists in Part II of this book but also in the descriptions in Part III. Five additional majors are described in Part III but could not be included in the Part II lists because they are not linked to any particular job except college teaching, which is already represented in the lists by the pseudo-major Graduate Study for College Teaching. For example, American Studies is one such major that appears in Part III but not in Part II. People with a degree in this subject sometimes go on to careers in law, marketing, or politics, but this major is not the obvious one to link to these jobs, so it would be a mistake to calculate the economic rewards of the major on the basis of these or any other jobs. On the other hand, American Studies is a popular major and could be combined with postgraduate study in law, social work, library science, or several other fields covered by this book, so we decided that this major and four others—African-American Studies, Area Studies, Humanities, and Women's Studies—should be included in the Part III descriptions. Thus a total of 55 majors are described in this book.

A Sample Description of a Major

The 55 descriptions of majors in this book all have the same data elements. Following is a sample, together with explanations of how to interpret the information:

Title →

Environmental Science

Useful Facts About the Major →

Useful Facts About the Major

Focuses on the application of biological, chemical, and physical principles to the study of the physical environment and the solution of environmental problems, including subjects such as abating or controlling environmental pollution and degradation, the interaction between human society and the natural environment, and natural resources management.

Related CIP Program(s) →

Related CIP Programs: 03.0104 Environmental Science; 03.0103 Environmental Studies.

Specializations in the Major →

Specializations in the Major: Environmental education; environmental policy; environmental technology; land resources; natural history.

Typical Sequence of College Courses →

Typical Sequence of College Courses: English composition, college algebra, general biology, general chemistry, organic chemistry, oral communication, statistics, introduction to computer science, introduction to geology, ecology, introduction to environmental science, natural resource management and water quality, microbiology, introduction to economics, introduction to ground water/hydrology, regional planning and environmental protection, environmental impact assessment, environmental economics, environmental law, environmental chemistry.

Typical Sequence of High School Courses →

Typical Sequence of High School Courses: Biology, chemistry, algebra, geometry, trigonometry, computer science, English, public speaking, geography.

Career Snapshot →

Career Snapshot

Environmental science (or studies) is a multidisciplinary subject that involves a number of

sciences, such as biology, geology, and chemistry, as well as social sciences, such as economics and geography. It also touches on urban/regional planning and on law and public policy. With a bachelor's degree, you may work for an environmental consulting business or a government planning agency, or you may go on to get a graduate or professional degree in one of these related fields.

Other Programs Related to the Same Jobs

← Other Programs Related to the Same Jobs

Environmental Studies; Environmental Science; Physical Science Technologies/Technicians, Other; Science Teacher Education/General Science Teacher Education; Science Technologies/Technicians, Other.

Related Secure Job

← Related Secure Job(s)

(See Part IV for the full job description.)

Environmental Scientists and Specialists, Including Health. Conduct research or perform investigation for the purpose of identifying, abating, or eliminating sources of pollutants or hazards that affect either the environment or the health of the population. Using knowledge of various scientific disciplines, may collect, synthesize, study, report, and take action based on data derived from measurements or observations of air, food, soil, water, and other sources.

Related Recession-Sensitive Job

← Related Recession-Sensitive Job(s)

Environmental Science and Protection Technicians, Including Health.

Here are some details on each of the major parts of the descriptions you will find in Part III:

* **Title:** This is a commonly used title for the major. Sometimes the major may also be known by other names. For example, Humanities is sometimes called Liberal Arts.

* **Useful Facts About the Major:** This section begins with a definition of the major derived from the Classification of Instructional Programs (CIP), a database created by the U.S. Department of Education.

* **Related CIP Program(s):** This is the title of the CIP program or programs that provided the definition used in the previous data element.

* **Specializations in the Major:** These are the most commonly available concentrations that may be offered in the major. In some cases, these are job specializations rather than educational concentrations.

* **Typical Sequence of College Courses:** These courses are ordered roughly as they might be taken to complete the major. Survey courses and introductory courses, especially in supporting disciplines (for example, a writing course within an education major), are usually ordered near the beginning, whereas specialized and advanced courses are usually ordered near the end. Some of these titles may represent multiple-semester courses or even separate courses with different names collapsed into one title.

* **Typical Sequence of High School Courses:** These are the courses that are most commonly expected to provide secondary-level preparation for the college major. Additional courses are required by almost all high schools and are expected for college admission.

* **Career Snapshot:** This is an overview of the jobs that the major leads to. It usually indicates the level of education the employers expect for new hires, as well as the job outlook.

* **Other Programs Related to the Same Jobs:** This is based on a table of major-to-job matches prepared by the O*NET Development Center. If this major interests you but is not exactly what you want to study, this listing can help you identify other majors that help prepare for similar work. Some or all of these other majors may be uncommon or highly specialized and therefore not included in this book.

* **Related Secure Job(s):** These jobs are selected from all related jobs identified by the O*NET Development Center and are limited to those considered insensitive to ups and downs in the business cycle. The definition is from the O*NET database. For more detailed information about the jobs, see Part IV, where the jobs are ordered alphabetically.

Related Recession-Sensitive Job(s): These jobs are also identified by the O*NET Development Center, but this list is limited to those that are *not* considered to have the lowest level of sensitivity to fluctuations in the economy. These jobs are not described in this book, but you may find complete information about them in some of the sources listed in the appendix.

A Sample Description of a Related Job

The 101 job descriptions in Part IV cover the same data elements. Following is a sample, together with explanations of how to interpret the information:

Job Title →

Actuaries

Related Major →

Related Major: Actuarial Science

Data Elements →

* Education/Training Required: Work experience plus degree
* Annual Earnings: $85,690
* Beginning Wage: $48,750
* Earnings Growth Potential: High (43.1%)
* Growth: 23.7%
* Annual Job Openings: 3,245
* Self-Employed: 0.0%
* Part-Time: 5.9%

Industries with Greatest Employment →

Industries with Greatest Employment: Insurance Carriers and Related Activities (59.9%); Professional, Scientific, and Technical Services (21.1%); Management of Companies and Enterprises (8.5%).

Highest-Growth Industries →

Highest-Growth Industries (Projected Growth for This Job): Professional, Scientific, and Technical Services (75.7%); Securities, Commodity Contracts, and Other Financial Investments and Related Activities (44.1%); Management of Companies and Enterprises (38.3%); Administrative and Support Services (26.5%); Funds, Trusts, and Other Financial Vehicles (23.3%).

Lowest-Growth Industries →

Lowest-Growth Industries (Projected Growth for This Job): Federal Government (–5.5%); State Government (–1.9%); Insurance Carriers and Related Activities (5.4%); Credit Intermediation and Related Activities (10.8%); Local Government (12.0%).

Fastest-Growing Metropolitan Areas →

Fastest-Growing Metropolitan Areas (Recent Growth for This Job): Columbus, OH (176.5%); Providence–Fall River–Warwick, RI-MA (100.0%); Buffalo–Niagara Falls, NY (50.0%); San Diego–Carlsbad–San Marcos, CA (50.0%); Phoenix-Mesa-Scottsdale, AZ (44.4%).

Other Considerations for Job Security ←

Other Considerations for Job Security: Opportunities for actuaries should be good, particularly for those who have passed at least one or two of the initial exams. Candidates with additional knowledge or experience, such as computer programming skills, will be particularly attractive to employers. Most jobs in this occupation are located in urban areas, but opportunities vary by geographic location. Steady demand by the insurance industry should ensure that actuarial jobs in this key industry will remain stable through 2016.

Summary Description and Tasks ←

Analyze statistical data, such as mortality, accident, sickness, disability, and retirement rates, and construct probability tables to forecast risk and liability for payment of future benefits. May ascertain premium rates required and cash reserves necessary to ensure payment of future benefits. Ascertain premium rates required and cash reserves and liabilities necessary to ensure payment of future benefits. Analyze statistical information to estimate mortality, accident, sickness, disability, and retirement rates. Design, review, and help administer insurance, annuity, and pension plans, determining financial soundness and calculating premiums. Collaborate with programmers, underwriters, accountants, claims experts, and senior management to help companies develop plans for new lines of business or for improving existing business. Determine or help determine company policy and explain complex technical matters to company executives, government officials, shareholders, policyholders, or the public. Testify before public agencies on proposed legislation affecting businesses. Provide advice to clients on a contract basis, working as a consultant. Testify in court as expert witness or to provide legal evidence on matters such as the value of potential lifetime earnings of a person who is disabled or killed in an accident. Construct probability tables for events such as fires, natural disasters, and unemployment, based on analysis of statistical data and other pertinent information. Determine policy contract provisions for each type of insurance. Manage credit and help price corporate security offerings. Provide expertise to help financial institutions manage risks and maximize returns associated with investment products or credit offerings. Determine equitable basis for distributing surplus earnings under participating insurance and annuity contracts in mutual companies. Explain changes in contract provisions to customers.

Personality Type: Conventional-Investigative. Conventional occupations frequently involve following set procedures and routines. These occupations can include working with data and details more than with ideas. Usually there is a clear line of authority to follow.

Career Cluster: 06 Finance. **Career Pathway:** 06.4 Insurance Services.

Skills—Programming: Writing computer programs for various purposes. **Mathematics:** Using mathematics to solve problems. **Operations Analysis:** Analyzing needs and product requirements to create a design. **Complex Problem Solving:** Identifying complex problems and reviewing related information to develop and evaluate options and implement solutions. **Active Learning:** Understanding the implications of new information for both current and future problem-solving and decision-making. **Quality Control Analysis:** Conducting tests and inspections of products, services, or processes to evaluate quality or performance.

Related Knowledge/Courses—Mathematics: Numbers and their operations and interrelationships, including arithmetic, algebra, geometry, calculus, and statistics and their applications. **Economics and Accounting:** Economic and accounting principles and practices, the financial markets, banking, and the analysis and reporting of financial data. **Sales and Marketing:** Principles and methods involved in showing, promoting, and selling products or services. This includes marketing strategies and tactics, product demonstration and sales techniques, and sales control systems. **Computers and Electronics:** Electric circuit boards, processors, chips, and computer hardware and software, including applications and programming. **Personnel and Human Resources:** Principles and procedures for personnel recruitment; selection; training; compensation and benefits; labor relations and negotiation; and personnel information systems. **Law and Government:** Laws, legal codes, court procedures, precedents, government regulations, executive orders, agency rules, and the democratic political process.

Work Environment: Indoors; sitting; using hands on objects, tools, or controls; repetitive motions.

Here are some details on each of the major parts of the job descriptions you will find in Part IV:

❋ **Job Title:** This is the job title for the job as defined by the U.S. Department of Labor and used in its O*NET database.

❋ **Related Major:** This major (sometimes more than one) is described in Part III. It may be possible, although less likely, to enter this job with a different major.

❋ **Data Elements:** The information comes from various U.S. Department of Labor and Census Bureau databases, as explained elsewhere in this introduction.

❋ **Industries with Greatest Employment:** These are the industries that each employ more than 5 percent of the workforce, ordered with the biggest employers first.

❋ **Highest-Growth Industries (Projected Growth for This Job):** These industries are expected to show the greatest employment increases for this job through 2016. The figure in parentheses shows the projected amount of growth. The fastest-growing industries are listed first, and the list includes all industries offering more than 15 percent growth for the job. A few jobs are not growing at that level in any industry.

⊛ **Lowest-Growth Industries (Projected Growth for This Job):** We listed as many as 10 industries with projected growth of less than 15 percent for the occupation. The industries appear in ascending order of growth. Again, for some jobs, we could not list any low-growth industries here.

⊛ **Fastest-Growing Metropolitan Areas (Recent Growth for This Job):** These are the metropolitan areas in which the workforce for the job grew fastest between 2006 and 2007. (Unfortunately, it is not possible to obtain comparable figures for projected *future* job growth for all metro areas.) The percentage of growth appears in parentheses, and we list as many as five metro areas. Keep in mind that recent growth may not continue.

⊛ **Other Considerations for Job Security:** This information, based on the *Occupational Outlook Handbook,* explains the factors that are expected to affect opportunities for job-seekers. Note that these comments apply to the period of time from 2006 to 2016. They were written before the recession that began in 2008, and they are meant to apply to a longer period of time than that economic downturn is expected to last.

⊛ **Summary Description and Tasks:** The boldfaced sentence provides a summary description of the occupation. It is followed by a listing of tasks generally performed by people who work in this job. This information comes from the O*NET database but, where necessary, has been edited to avoid exceeding 2,200 characters.

⊛ **Personality Type:** The O*NET database assigns each job to a primary personality type, plus one or two secondary types. Our job descriptions include the names of all the related personality types as well as a brief definition of the primary personality type.

⊛ **Career Cluster(s):** This information cross-references the scheme of career clusters and pathways that was created by the U.S. Department of Education's Office of Vocational and Adult Education around 1999 and is now used by many states to organize career-oriented programs and career information. In identifying a career cluster and pathway for the job (sometimes more than one), we followed the assignments of the online O*NET database. Your state might assign this job to a different career pathway or even a different cluster.

⊛ **Skills:** For each job, we included the skills whose level-of-performance scores exceeded the average for all jobs by the greatest amount and whose ratings on the importance scale were higher than very low. We included as many as six such skills for each job, and we ranked them by the extent to which their rating exceeds the average.

❋ **Related Knowledge/Courses:** This entry can help you understand the most important knowledge areas that are required for a job and the types of courses or programs you will likely need to take to prepare for it. We used information in the O*NET database for this entry. For each job, we identified any knowledge area with a rating that was higher than the average rating for that knowledge area for all jobs; then we listed as many as six in descending order.

❋ **Work Environment:** We included any work condition with a rating that exceeds the midpoint of the rating scale. The order does not indicate their frequency on the job. Consider whether you like these conditions and whether any of these conditions would make you uncomfortable. Keep in mind that when hazards are present (such as contaminants), protective equipment and procedures are provided to keep you safe.

Getting all the information we used in the job descriptions was not a simple process, and it is not always perfect. Even so, we used the best and most recent sources of data we could find, and we think that our efforts will be helpful to many people.

Add Security to Your College Major and Your Future Job

Job security is always *one* of the factors that people consider when they make decisions about college majors and careers, but this factor takes on greater weight during and shortly after a recession. When you see people around you losing their jobs or having great difficulty finding work, you realize that if you don't have a job, you're not going to obtain any of the other satisfactions that a job can bring.

So, if you're making a decision about a college major after reading scary news about the economy for several months, you probably are thinking about the likely effects of your choice on your future job security. Consider this: No matter how prosperous the economy may be when you graduate, you are almost certainly going to experience a recession within your first 10 or 15 years out of college. Do you want to be in a job that is more secure than most? Do you want to avoid being in a job where opportunities melt away like snow in April? You can improve your odds of job security by choosing a high-security college major and, once you're employed, by taking steps to be the kind of worker who is least threatened by a recession.

Why Do Some Majors Provide More Security?

Political policy makers and the economists at the Federal Reserve Bank try their best to keep the economy growing smoothly and steadily. Despite their efforts, economic activity expands and contracts in a multi-year rhythm that is referred to as *the business cycle*. During years of expansion, consumers and businesses buy more and employers hire more workers to produce, distribute, and sell goods and services. When the economy contracts, consumers and businesses cut back on their spending and employers trim their workforces by hiring less and perhaps by laying off employees.

Although this pattern largely repeats itself, each recession is a little different from the one before. For example, the recession of 2001 followed the collapse of the technology bubble, so high-tech jobs were hit particularly hard. Construction jobs then recovered fairly quickly as a housing boom got under way, but that bubble popped in 2008 and started a recession that quickly affected jobs in construction, real estate sales, and finance—industries that had been propped up by mortgage loans and inflated home prices. Eventually the economic slowdown affected other industries as well, especially those that depend on discretionary purchases such as vacations and new cars.

It's impossible to predict what specific economic trends will trigger the *next* recession, so it's anyone's guess which specific parts of the economy will suffer the most. Nevertheless, certain industries and occupations are always sensitive to the ups and downs of the business cycle, and other industries and occupations are much less affected by it—they are much more secure. Although nobody's job has total security in a severe recession, labor economists have identified industries and occupations that are comparatively safe during recessions.

The secure industries and occupations tend to be those that serve fundamental human needs, needs that people always have and always seem able to pay for. For example, many health-care jobs have security because people will always get sick or frail with age and enough people have medical insurance to pay for care. Children have to go to school no matter how bad the economy gets, so education is comparatively secure. We expect electric power, natural gas, running water, mail delivery, television reception, telephone service, and Internet access to be totally reliable. Governments may shed some workers, but the law must continue to be upheld on the streets, at the borders, and in the courts. Religious and charitable institutions continue to offer guidance and comfort to a stressed populace. Death and taxes are certainties, and each has its associated workforce that is not left idle during recessions. People trade in their cars and replace their appliances less frequently when times are hard, so mechanics have many repair jobs to do.

Therefore, if you're looking for a job with security, you might want to consider choosing a major that can lead toward one of these secure industries or occupations—and that is the central theme of this book. Many secure occupations do not require a college degree—for example, the workers who change the linens of hospital beds, operate electric power generators, carry the mail, drive buses, or tune up cars. If you're planning to get a college degree, you might not be interested in these particular jobs, but you can obtain better-than-average security in a college-level job by aiming to work in one of the *industries* represented by these jobs, such as health care, utilities, government, or ground transportation. Other industries with security are education (especially postsecondary and adult education), the libraries, social assistance and other nonprofit organizations, repair and maintenance businesses, and insurance carriers.

So if you're attracted to a major that's *not* one of the 50 high-security majors profiled in this book—say you want to major in law, engineering, or business—you can increase your future job security by taking courses that will better position you to work in one of the secure industries. For a more detailed discussion, turn to the bonus list, "The Most Important Courses for a Secure Future," in Part II.

Getting a Secure Job After Graduation

Once you have your degree, in whatever field, you may want to consider job security when looking for employment, whether it's your first job or a mid-career shift. Location can make a difference; some parts of the country are more sensitive to downturns than others. As a general rule, the very large cities tend to be where the financial industry concentrates and thus tend to be sensitive. Other sensitive regions are those that are dominated by one industry, especially a sensitive industry. For example, the oil industry goes through cycles of boom and bust, so the economy of Texas fluctuates greatly. Nevada depends heavily on the gaming industry, which suffers when people are reluctant to risk money.

Another factor to bear in mind is the long-term economic health of any employer you're considering when looking for a job, although that can be very difficult to judge, especially from the outside or if it's a new business. You may be able to get a sense of how risky the business venture is—for example, if it's obviously based on a very unconventional technology or business model. Be wary if stock options are an important part of the compensation package. You may envy the early employees of Bill Gates, who were paid a small stake in Microsoft's business and eventually became multimillionaires, but consider that if the company goes under, you'll lose both your investment in its stock *and* your paycheck.

It may be easier to get a sense of the corporate culture regarding employees, especially by talking to workers. Ask whether the company tends to promote from within and whether it tends to invest in continuous training of employees, which is often a sign that employment there is not a revolving door.

Limitations of Forecasts

All of this book's forecasts of high-security majors are based on well-known economic trends, but economists know only what they know and tend to be unaware of what they don't know. One such unknown factor is a new technology that drastically changes the way people can do their jobs. For example, the invention of the phonograph severely reduced the number of jobs for musicians, musical instrument makers, and music teachers because live performance no longer was the only way to listen to music. On the other hand, the new technology also created jobs. Record companies formed, and for decades every downtown business district or shopping mall had at least one record store, providing jobs that didn't exist before Thomas Edison's invention. Now we're seeing a drastic loss of jobs in the music distribution business because the way we obtain music has changed again, this time the result of the Internet. The Internet will certainly destroy jobs in many fields, but it also will create many jobs.

The lesson to take away is that a recession is not the only economic event or trend that can threaten your job, and therefore even a high-security major is not a guarantee of lifetime employability. But this book focuses on the majors that appear to be best suited for the economic trends that currently are well understood.

Also, *even if every job-related prediction in this book turns out to be inaccurate,* the following tips will be useful because they can help you hang on to a threatened job or shift to a new job with minimal disruption to your life.

Work Habits That Can Save Your Future Job

Layoffs happen for various reasons, but you may be able to hang on to your future job *if you're irreplaceable.* You need to be so vital to the business that it can't go on without you. Here are some techniques to be the irreplaceable worker:

* **Focus on the core mission of the business.** Many businesses diversify and serve several functions, but usually there's a central mission that makes money and determines whether the business will succeed or fail. Identify that central function and play a role in it. Identify the skills the business needs for future development of this function and acquire them. If your first job with the business is in a peripheral function, plan to move toward a core function as soon as you can.

* **Be exceptionally productive.** This doesn't necessarily mean working longer hours. It's more important to find a task or role you can handle that goes beyond your job description. Maybe it's a task that nobody else wants to do. Here again, skills are important because they are the key to productivity.

* **Be visible where you work.** In many businesses, the person whose office is next to the boss's tends to get the best performance appraisals. If you don't have that office (and most new hires don't), find ways to make your accomplishments known; don't wait for performance-appraisal season. For example, start an in-house blog, newsletter, or bulletin board showcasing the project you're working on and soliciting suggestions from people outside the project. This will encourage them to buy into the project and make your efforts look not purely self-promotional. If you have a work-at-home arrangement, find reasons to show up at the office regularly or make lunch dates.

- **Be visible beyond your workplace.** Every occupation has a professional association, and every association is eager for volunteers to do committee work. Become active. Every industry has at least one blog where insiders share news and opinions. Become a frequent commenter on a blog or, if you have an unusual perspective, start your own blog. Besides the exposure it gives you, the discipline of following or writing a blog will also improve your knowledge of your industry. Having a reputation beyond your workplace can benefit you in several ways. It can provide a network of job contacts to tap into if you lose your job. (You may even get unsought job offers.) It can also make your employer more aware of your skills and more careful to keep you happy.

- **Acquire a mentor.** Find someone who really knows the business; be helpful; and ask a lot of very specific questions, including questions about how to improve your work. Give public credit to the mentor for the advice you get.

- **Be pleasant.** Back-stabbing may seem like a way to get ahead, but it can hurt you in the long run. Abrasiveness may make you stand out, but for the wrong reasons. If you really can't get along with some people in your work group, try to be transferred to one where you'll fit in better.

PART II

The Best Majors Lists

This part contains a lot of interesting lists, and it's a good place for you to start using the book. Here are some suggestions for using the lists to explore college majors linked to jobs that are likely to be less sensitive than most to economic slowdowns:

⊛ The Table of Contents at the beginning of this book presents a complete listing of the list titles in this section. You can browse the lists or use the Table of Contents to find those that interest you most.

⊛ We gave the lists clear titles, so most require little explanation. We provide comments for each group of lists.

⊛ As you review the lists of high-security majors, one or more of the majors may appeal to you enough that you want to seek additional information. As this happens, mark that major (or, if someone else will be using this book, write it on a separate sheet of paper) so that you can look up the descriptions of the major in Part III and its related jobs in Part IV.

⊛ Keep in mind that all majors in these lists meet our basic criteria for being included in this book, as explained in the Introduction. All lists, therefore, consist of majors that are offered at many colleges and universities and are linked to jobs that are considered not sensitive to recessions, with emphasis on majors with potential for high pay, high growth, or large numbers of openings. These measures are easily quantified and are often presented in lists of best jobs in the newspapers and other media, so we decided they would be useful for evaluating college majors. While earnings, growth, and openings are important, there are other factors to consider in your educational and career planning. For example, you may want to consider the availability of the major at a nearby college, your qualifications to enter the major (some have high entry requirements), and your comfort level with specific course requirements for the major. Many other factors that may help define the ideal major for you are difficult or impossible to quantify and thus are not used in this book, so you will need to consider the importance of these issues yourself.

❀ All data used to create these lists comes from the U.S. Department of Labor and the Census Bureau. In this book's introduction, you can read the full details about how we adapted information from these sources. The earnings figures are based on the average annual pay received by full-time workers in jobs related to the major. Because the earnings represent the national averages, actual pay rates can vary greatly by location, amount of previous work experience, and other factors. Projected job-growth rates are also national averages but can vary by location and industry. Many of the majors can lead to more than one career, and in some cases one career option may have much higher average pay or faster job growth than another option. In these lists we use the average pay, average job growth, and average job openings for all the related secure jobs, using a formula that gives extra weight to the jobs with the largest workforces. In Part IV, you can see the figures for average earnings, job growth, and job openings for *each* related secure job.

❀ Some majors have the same scores for one or more data elements. For example, Health Information Systems Administration and Hospital/Health Facilities Administration are both linked to the same job, Medical and Health Services Managers, and to no other jobs. Therefore, these two majors appear side by side in all lists, ordered alphabetically, and their order has no other significance. There was no way to avoid these ties, so simply understand that the difference of a few positions on a list may not mean as much as it seems.

Best High-Security Majors Overall: Majors Related to Jobs with the Highest Pay, Fastest Growth, and Most Openings

The four lists in this section are the most important lists in this book. The first list presents the majors related to secure jobs with the highest combined scores for pay, growth, and number of openings. This is a very appealing list because it shows majors with outstanding potential for economic rewards. The 50 majors in this list are the ones that are described in detail in Part III.

The next three lists present majors linked to secure jobs with the highest scores in each of three measures: annual earnings, projected percentage growth, and largest number of openings.

The 50 Best High-Security Majors

Most people want to see this list first. It shows the majors that can prepare you for a secure job with the highest overall combined ratings for earnings, projected growth, and number of openings. (The section in the introduction called "How the Majors in This Book Were Selected" explains in detail how we linked majors to jobs and rated the majors so we could assemble this list.)

A look at the list will clarify how we ordered the majors. Physician Assisting was linked to an occupation with outstanding figures for income, growth, and job openings: Physician Assistants. Nursing (R.N. Training), the second-place major, was linked to another high-reward job in the health-care field, Registered Nurses. More job openings are projected for Registered Nurses than for Physician Assistants, but the projected job growth for Physician Assistants is 3.5 percent higher than for Registered Nurses and the earnings are about $18,000 higher. Therefore, when all the rankings were added up, Registered Nurses came in at second place. The other majors follow in descending order based on their total scores. Several majors had tied scores and are simply listed one after another, so there are often only very small or even no differences between the scores of majors that are near each other on the list. All the other majors lists in this book use these majors as their source list. You can find descriptions for each of these majors in Part III, beginning on page 73. The related secure jobs are described in Part IV, beginning on page 137.

Remember that the figures for earnings, growth, and job openings are based on specific related secure jobs that are entered by many graduates of these majors; however, some graduates enter nontraditional jobs (for example, an English major who goes into advertising), and other graduates enter recession-sensitive jobs (for example, the journalism major who goes into broadcasting). Therefore, the figures do not indicate the economic rewards of *all* graduates of these majors. Figures on earnings in related jobs are sometimes limited; see the comments that precede the next list.

The top 10 positions on the list are dominated by jobs in health care, but if you look farther down the list you'll notice jobs in education, counseling, law enforcement, and the social sciences. Some fields aren't well represented, however, because they tend to experience layoffs and hiring freezes during hard times. Thus, you'll find few jobs in management, sales, or engineering.

The 50 Best High-Security Majors Overall

Major	Annual Earnings	Percent Growth	Annual Openings
1. Physician Assisting	$78,450	27.0%	7,147
2. Nursing (R.N. Training)	$60,010	23.5%	233,499
3. Physical Therapy	$69,760	27.1%	12,072
4. Pharmacy	$100,480	21.7%	16,358
5. Graduate Study for College Teaching	$56,567	22.9%	129,040
6. Medicine	$145,600+	14.2%	38,027
7. Health Information Systems Administration	$76,990	16.4%	31,877
8. Hospital/Health Facilities Administration	$76,990	16.4%	31,877
9. Veterinary Medicine	$75,230	35.0%	5,301
10. Actuarial Science	$85,690	23.7%	3,245
11. Environmental Science	$58,380	25.1%	6,961
12. Occupational Therapy	$63,790	23.1%	8,338
13. Public Relations	$49,800	17.6%	51,216
14. Geophysics	$75,800	21.9%	2,471
15. Religion/Religious Studies	$40,460	18.9%	35,092
16. Geology	$74,296	22.4%	1,579
17. Oceanography	$74,296	22.4%	1,579
18. Communications Studies/Speech	$48,648	17.3%	18,396
19. Philosophy	$38,821	18.9%	21,508
20. Chinese	$37,490	23.6%	6,630
21. Classics	$37,490	23.6%	6,630
22. French	$37,490	23.6%	6,630
23. German	$37,490	23.6%	6,630
24. Japanese	$37,490	23.6%	6,630
25. Modern Foreign Language	$37,490	23.6%	6,630
26. Russian	$37,490	23.6%	6,630
27. Spanish	$37,490	23.6%	6,630
28. Social Work	$40,373	17.8%	19,897
29. Medical Technology	$51,720	12.4%	11,457
30. Criminal Justice/Law Enforcement	$50,109	12.1%	15,535
31. Business Education	$49,420	5.6%	93,166
32. Optometry	$93,800	11.3%	1,789
33. Psychology	$62,449	15.9%	4,214
34. Family and Consumer Sciences	$48,920	8.6%	59,961

The 50 Best High-Security Majors Overall

Major	Annual Earnings	Percent Growth	Annual Openings
35. Early Childhood Education	$29,980	15.4%	88,989
36. Chiropractic	$65,890	14.4%	3,179
37. Physical Education	$46,990	8.6%	73,179
38. Secondary Education	$42,745	6.9%	127,178
39. Special Education	$49,350	11.6%	9,724
40. Podiatry	$110,510	9.5%	648
41. Speech-Language Pathology and Audiology	$60,567	10.5%	6,070
42. Library Science	$50,970	3.6%	18,945
43. Mathematics	$72,728	8.7%	1,953
44. Statistics	$72,728	8.7%	1,953
45. English	$48,320	2.3%	20,193
46. Anthropology	$53,080	15.0%	446
47. Archeology	$53,080	15.0%	446
48. Journalism and Mass Communications	$47,843	5.3%	11,406
49. Political Science	$91,580	5.3%	318
50. Art History	$41,228	18.3%	1,184

The 20 High-Security Majors with the Best Income Potential

In the following list you'll find the 20 high-security majors meeting our criteria for this book that have the best income potential. This is an appealing list, for obvious reasons.

It shouldn't be a big surprise to learn that most of the highest-paying jobs require advanced levels of education, training, or experience. In fact, the top four jobs (and several others on this list) require that you attend professional school, usually after earning a bachelor's degree.

Keep in mind that the earnings reflect the national average for all workers in the occupation. This is an important consideration because starting pay in the job is usually much less than the pay that workers can earn with several years of experience. Earnings also vary significantly by region of the country, so actual pay in your area could be substantially different.

The 20 High-Security Majors with the Best Income Potential

Major	Annual Earnings
1. Medicine	$145,600+
2. Podiatry	$110,510
3. Pharmacy	$100,480
4. Optometry	$93,800
5. Political Science	$91,580
6. Actuarial Science	$85,690
7. Physician Assisting	$78,450
8. Health Information Systems Administration	$76,990
9. Hospital/Health Facilities Administration	$76,990
10. Geophysics	$75,800
11. Veterinary Medicine	$75,230
12. Geology	$74,296
13. Oceanography	$74,296
14. Mathematics	$72,728
15. Statistics	$72,728
16. Physical Therapy	$69,760
17. Chiropractic	$65,890
18. Occupational Therapy	$63,790
19. Psychology	$62,449
20. Speech-Language Pathology and Audiology	$60,567

The 20 High-Security Majors with the Best Job-Growth Potential

From the list of 50 high-security majors that met our criteria for this book, this list shows the 20 majors that are linked to jobs projected to have the highest percentage increase in the number of people employed through 2016.

The very top of this list is dominated by majors in health care, but majors in language and the sciences can also be found here.

The 20 High-Security Majors with the Best Job-Growth Potential

Major	Percent Growth
1. Veterinary Medicine	35.0%
2. Physical Therapy	27.1%
3. Physician Assisting	27.0%
4. Environmental Science	25.1%
5. Actuarial Science	23.7%
6. Chinese	23.6%
7. Classics	23.6%
8. French	23.6%
9. German	23.6%
10. Japanese	23.6%
11. Modern Foreign Language	23.6%
12. Russian	23.6%
13. Spanish	23.6%
14. Nursing (R.N. Training)	23.5%
15. Occupational Therapy	23.1%
16. Graduate Study for College Teaching	22.9%
17. Geology	22.4%
18. Oceanography	22.4%
19. Geophysics	21.9%
20. Pharmacy	21.7%

The 20 High-Security Majors with the Best Job-Opening Potential

From the list of 50 best high-security majors, this list shows the 20 majors linked to jobs projected to have the largest number of job openings per year through 2016. Keep in mind that these figures for job openings are average yearly openings over a 10-year period. Although these jobs are considered not sensitive to economic fluctuations, the number of openings is likely to vary somewhat from year to year.

Majors linked to jobs with many openings present several advantages that may be attractive to you. Because there are many openings, these jobs can be easier to obtain, particularly when you first enter the job market after completing your degree. These majors may also create more opportunities for you to move from one employer to another with relative ease. Though a few of the majors lead to jobs with a moderate level of pay, most lead to jobs that pay quite well and can provide good long-term career opportunities or the ability to move up to more responsible roles.

The 20 High-Security Majors with the Best Job-Opening Potential

Major	Annual Openings
1. Nursing (R.N. Training)	233,499
2. Graduate Study for College Teaching	129,040
3. Secondary Education	127,178
4. Business Education	93,166
5. Early Childhood Education	88,989
6. Physical Education	73,179
7. Family and Consumer Sciences	59,961
8. Public Relations	51,216
9. Medicine	38,027
10. Religion/Religious Studies	35,092
11. Health Information Systems Administration	31,877
12. Hospital/Health Facilities Administration	31,877
13. Philosophy	21,508
14. English	20,193
15. Social Work	19,897
16. Library Science	18,945
17. Communications Studies/Speech	18,396
18. Pharmacy	16,358
19. Criminal Justice/Law Enforcement	15,535
20. Physical Therapy	12,072

Best High-Security Majors by Demographic

We decided it would be interesting to include lists in this section that feature high-security majors linked to jobs in which different types of people dominate. For example, what high-security majors are associated with jobs that have the highest percentage of male workers? We're not saying that men should consider these majors over others, but it is interesting information to know.

In some cases, the lists can give you ideas for majors to consider that you might otherwise overlook. For example, perhaps women should consider some majors that prepare for jobs that traditionally have high percentages of men in them. Although these are not obvious ways of using these lists, the lists may give you some good ideas about majors to consider. The lists may also help you identify high-security majors that work well for others in your situation—for example, majors that lead to plentiful opportunities for part-time work, if that is something you want to do at this stage of your career.

All of the lists in this section were created using a similar process. We sorted the 50 best high-security majors according to a demographic criterion and discarded those whose related secure jobs did not have a high percentage of that criterion. For example, we sorted the high-security majors based on the percentage of female workers in related secure jobs from highest to lowest percentage and discarded those with a figure less than 60 percent. This resulted in a list in which the majors meeting the cutoff were sorted by the demographic criterion.

We then ranked this subset of majors according to the usual economic criteria applied to related secure jobs—income, job growth, and job openings. This produced a second list showing which high-security majors (a maximum of 20) score best on these three economic criteria.

We used the same basic process to produce two lists for each of six demographic characteristics of the workers in related jobs: part-time, self-employed, women, men, urban, and rural. The lists based on demographic characteristics are very interesting, and we hope you find them helpful.

Best High-Security Majors Related to Jobs with a High Percentage of Part-Time Workers

In some cases, people work part time because they want the freedom of time this arrangement can provide, but others may do so because they can't find full-time employment in these jobs. (This is particularly common during a recession.) These folks may work in other full- or part-time jobs to make ends meet. If you *want* to work part time now or in the future, these lists will help you identify majors related to secure jobs employing 15 percent or more part-time workers. On the other hand, if you want full-time work, the lists may also help you identify majors related to secure jobs for which such opportunities are more difficult to find. In either case, it's good information to know in advance.

Best High-Security Majors Related to Jobs with the Highest Percentage of Part-Time Workers	
Major	Percentage of Part-Time Workers in Related Jobs
1. Early Childhood Education	34.0%
2. Occupational Therapy	29.8%
3. German	28.5%
4. Chinese	28.5%
5. French	28.5%
6. Spanish	28.5%
7. Japanese	28.5%
8. Russian	28.5%
9. Classics	28.5%
10. Modern Foreign Language	28.5%
11. Graduate Study for College Teaching	27.8%
12. Speech-Language Pathology and Audiology	25.0%
13. Psychology	24.0%
14. Podiatry	23.6%
15. Chiropractic	23.6%
16. Physical Therapy	22.7%
17. Nursing (R.N. Training)	21.8%
18. Secondary Education	21.8%
19. Library Science	21.2%
20. Optometry	20.8%
21. Political Science	20.1%

Best High-Security Majors Related to Jobs with the Highest Percentage of Part-Time Workers

Major	Percentage of Part-Time Workers in Related Jobs
22. Archeology	20.1%
23. Anthropology	20.1%
24. Art History	18.4%
25. Pharmacy	18.1%
26. Physician Assisting	15.6%

The following list shows the 20 high-security majors from the previous list with the best combination of potential economic rewards. Note that the earnings estimates in this list are based on a survey of both part-time and full-time workers. On average, part-time workers earn about 10 percent less per hour than full-time workers.

Best High-Security Majors Related to Jobs with a High Percentage of Part-Time Workers

Major	Percentage of Part-Time Workers in Related Jobs	Annual Earnings of Related Jobs	Percent Growth of Related Jobs	Annual Openings of Related Jobs
1. Physical Therapy	22.7%	$69,760	27.1%	12,072
2. Physician Assisting	15.6%	$78,450	27.0%	7,147
3. Pharmacy	18.1%	$100,480	21.7%	16,358
4. Nursing (R.N. Training)	21.8%	$60,010	23.5%	233,499
5. Graduate Study for College Teaching	27.8%	$56,567	22.9%	129,040
6. Occupational Therapy	29.8%	$63,790	23.1%	8,338
7. Chinese	28.5%	$37,490	23.6%	6,630
8. Classics	28.5%	$37,490	23.6%	6,630
9. French	28.5%	$37,490	23.6%	6,630
10. German	28.5%	$37,490	23.6%	6,630
11. Japanese	28.5%	$37,490	23.6%	6,630
12. Modern Foreign Language	28.5%	$37,490	23.6%	6,630
13. Russian	28.5%	$37,490	23.6%	6,630
14. Spanish	28.5%	$37,490	23.6%	6,630
15. Secondary Education	21.8%	$42,745	6.9%	127,178

(continued)

(continued)

Best High-Security Majors Related to Jobs with a High Percentage of Part-Time Workers				
Major	Percentage of Part-Time Workers in Related Jobs	Annual Earnings of Related Jobs	Percent Growth of Related Jobs	Annual Openings of Related Jobs
16. Psychology	24.0%	$62,449	15.9%	4,214
17. Optometry	20.8%	$93,800	11.3%	1,789
18. Library Science	21.2%	$50,970	3.6%	18,945
19. Chiropractic	23.6%	$65,890	14.4%	3,179
20. Early Childhood Education	34.0%	$29,980	15.4%	88,989

Best High-Security Majors with a High Percentage of Self-Employed Workers

About 8 percent of all working people are self-employed. Although you may think of the self-employed as having similar jobs, they actually work in an enormous range of situations, fields, and work environments that you may not have considered.

Among the self-employed are people who own small or large businesses, as many dentists and funeral directors do; people working on a contract basis for one or more employers, as many editors do; people running home consulting or other businesses; and people in many other situations. They may go to the same worksite every day, as commercial and industrial designers do; visit multiple employers during the course of a week, as many translators do; or do most of their work from home. Some work part time, others full time, some as a way to have fun, some so they can spend time with their kids or go to school.

The point is that there is an enormous range of situations, and one of them could make sense for you now or in the future.

The following list contains majors linked to secure jobs in which more than 8 percent of the workers are self-employed.

Best High-Security Majors Related to Jobs with the Highest Percentage of Self-Employed Workers

Major	Percentage of Self-Employed Workers in Related Jobs
1. Chiropractic	51.7%
2. Psychology	34.2%
3. Optometry	25.5%
4. Podiatry	23.9%
5. Japanese	21.6%
6. Chinese	21.6%
7. Spanish	21.6%
8. Russian	21.6%
9. German	21.6%
10. Classics	21.6%
11. Modern Foreign Language	21.6%
12. French	21.6%
13. Veterinary Medicine	17.1%
14. Medicine	14.7%
15. English	13.4%
16. Journalism and Mass Communications	12.7%
17. Early Childhood Education	10.8%
18. Speech-Language Pathology and Audiology	8.9%
19. Occupational Therapy	8.6%
20. Physical Therapy	8.4%
21. Health Information Systems Administration	8.2%
22. Hospital/Health Facilities Administration	8.2%

The following list shows the 20 high-security majors from the previous list with the best combination of potential economic rewards. Note that the earnings estimates in this list are based on a survey that *does not include self-employed workers*. The median earnings for self-employed workers in these occupations may be significantly higher or lower.

Best High-Security Majors Related to Jobs with a High Percentage of Self-Employed Workers

Major	Percentage of Self-Employed Workers in Related Jobs	Annual Earnings of Related Jobs	Percent Growth of Related Jobs	Annual Openings of Related Jobs
1. Physical Therapy	8.4%	$69,760	27.1%	12,072
2. Health Information Systems Administration	8.2%	$76,990	16.4%	31,877
3. Hospital/Health Facilities Administration	8.2%	$76,990	16.4%	31,877
4. Medicine	14.7%	$145,600+	14.2%	38,027
5. Veterinary Medicine	17.1%	$75,230	35.0%	5,301
6. Chinese	21.6%	$37,490	23.6%	6,630
7. Classics	21.6%	$37,490	23.6%	6,630
8. French	21.6%	$37,490	23.6%	6,630
9. German	21.6%	$37,490	23.6%	6,630
10. Japanese	21.6%	$37,490	23.6%	6,630
11. Modern Foreign Language	21.6%	$37,490	23.6%	6,630
12. Russian	21.6%	$37,490	23.6%	6,630
13. Spanish	21.6%	$37,490	23.6%	6,630
14. Occupational Therapy	8.6%	$63,790	23.1%	8,338
15. Early Childhood Education	10.8%	$29,980	15.4%	88,989
16. English	13.4%	$48,320	2.3%	20,193
17. Journalism and Mass Communications	12.7%	$47,843	5.3%	11,406
18. Optometry	25.5%	$93,800	11.3%	1,789
19. Psychology	34.2%	$62,449	15.9%	4,214
20. Chiropractic	51.7%	$65,890	14.4%	3,179

Best High-Security Majors Related to Jobs Employing a High Percentage of Women

To create the four lists that follow, we sorted the 50 best high-security majors according to the percentages of women and men in the workforces of the related secure jobs. These are our most controversial lists, and we knew we would create some controversy when we first included similar lists in our Best Jobs books. But these lists are not meant to restrict women or men from considering options for majors or jobs—our reason for including these lists is exactly the opposite. We hope the lists help people see possibilities that they might not otherwise have considered.

The fact is that jobs with high percentages (60 percent or higher) of women or high percentages of men offer good opportunities for both men and women if they want to do one of these jobs. So we suggest that women browse the lists of majors leading to jobs that employ high percentages of men and that men browse the lists of majors leading to jobs with high percentages of women. There are high-security majors in both lists that have high income potential, and women or men who are interested in them should consider them.

It is interesting to compare the two sets of secure jobs related to the best majors—jobs with the highest percentage of men and jobs with the highest percentage of women—in terms of the economic measures that we use to rank these lists. The female-dominated jobs have slightly higher average earnings ($50,530) than the male-dominated jobs ($48,023). On the other hand, the male-dominated occupations have potential for slightly greater job growth: 16.4 percent versus 15.2 percent. A much greater difference is in annual job openings: an average of 91,149 openings are projected for the male-dominated jobs compared to 28,503 openings for the female-dominated jobs. This difference is actually not as significant as it seems. Among the female-dominated jobs, the small occupation Interpreters and Translators gets counted eight times (it is linked to eight majors), so the small job-openings figure for this occupation drags down the overall average for women.

Best High-Security Majors Related to Jobs Employing the Highest Percentage of Women

Major	Percentage of Women in Related Jobs
1. Speech-Language Pathology and Audiology	93.7%
2. Nursing (R.N. Training)	91.3%
3. Occupational Therapy	90.3%
4. Library Science	84.2%
5. Special Education	83.5%
6. Art History	81.6%
7. Early Childhood Education	79.7%
8. Social Work	78.8%
9. Medical Technology	78.1%
10. Physician Assisting	71.7%
11. Chinese	69.3%
12. Classics	69.3%
13. French	69.3%

(continued)

(continued)

Best High-Security Majors Related to Jobs Employing the Highest Percentage of Women

Major	Percentage of Women in Related Jobs
14. German	69.3%
15. Japanese	69.3%
16. Modern Foreign Language	69.3%
17. Russian	69.3%
18. Spanish	69.3%
19. Health Information Systems Administration	68.3%
20. Hospital/Health Facilities Administration	68.3%
21. Psychology	67.7%
22. Family and Consumer Sciences	65.2%
23. Public Relations	64.6%
24. Communications Studies/Speech	64.0%
25. Physical Education	62.9%
26. Physical Therapy	62.7%

The following list shows the 20 high-security majors from the previous list with the best combination of potential economic rewards.

Best High-Security Majors Related to Jobs Employing a High Percentage of Women

Major	Percentage of Women in Related Jobs	Annual Earnings of Related Jobs	Percent Growth of Related Jobs	Annual Openings of Related Jobs
1. Physical Therapy	62.7%	$69,760	27.1%	12,072
2. Physician Assisting	71.7%	$78,450	27.0%	7,147
3. Nursing (R.N. Training)	91.3%	$60,010	23.5%	233,499
4. Health Information Systems Administration	68.3%	$76,990	16.4%	31,877
5. Hospital/Health Facilities Administration	68.3%	$76,990	16.4%	31,877
6. Occupational Therapy	90.3%	$63,790	23.1%	8,338
7. Public Relations	64.6%	$49,800	17.6%	51,216
8. Chinese	69.3%	$37,490	23.6%	6,630

Best High-Security Majors Related to Jobs Employing a High Percentage of Women

Major	Percentage of Women in Related Jobs	Annual Earnings of Related Jobs	Percent Growth of Related Jobs	Annual Openings of Related Jobs
9. Classics	69.3%	$37,490	23.6%	6,630
10. French	69.3%	$37,490	23.6%	6,630
11. German	69.3%	$37,490	23.6%	6,630
12. Japanese	69.3%	$37,490	23.6%	6,630
13. Modern Foreign Language	69.3%	$37,490	23.6%	6,630
14. Russian	69.3%	$37,490	23.6%	6,630
15. Spanish	69.3%	$37,490	23.6%	6,630
16. Social Work	78.8%	$40,373	17.8%	19,897
17. Communications Studies/Speech	64.0%	$48,648	17.3%	18,396
18. Family and Consumer Sciences	65.2%	$48,920	8.6%	59,961
19. Medical Technology	78.1%	$51,720	12.4%	11,457
20. Physical Education	62.9%	$46,990	8.6%	73,179

Best High-Security Majors Related to Jobs Employing a High Percentage of Men

If you have not already read the intro to the previous two lists about the best high-security majors leading to jobs with high percentages of women, consider doing so. Much of the content there applies to the following two lists as well.

We did not include these lists with the assumption that men should consider only majors leading to jobs with high percentages of men or that women should consider only majors leading to jobs with high percentages of women. Instead, these lists are here because we think they are interesting and perhaps helpful in considering nontraditional career options. For example, some men would do very well in and enjoy some jobs that have high percentages of women but may not have considered the associated majors seriously. In a similar way, some women would very much enjoy and do well in some jobs that traditionally have been held by high percentages of men. We hope that these lists help you consider high-security college majors that you previously did not consider seriously because of gender stereotypes.

Best High-Security Majors Related to Jobs Employing the Highest Percentage of Men

Major	Percentage of Men in Related Jobs
1. Religion/Religious Studies	87.2%
2. Criminal Justice/Law Enforcement	83.6%
3. Philosophy	82.7%
4. Environmental Science	78.0%
5. Geology	78.0%
6. Geophysics	78.0%
7. Oceanography	78.0%
8. Chiropractic	76.9%
9. Actuarial Science	71.6%
10. Medicine	67.8%
11. Podiatry	63.6%
12. Optometry	60.9%

The following list shows the high-security majors from the previous list with the best combination of potential economic rewards.

Best High-Security Majors Related to Jobs Employing a High Percentage of Men

Major	Percentage of Men in Related Jobs	Annual Earnings of Related Jobs	Percent Growth of Related Jobs	Annual Openings of Related Jobs
1. Medicine	67.8%	$145,600+	14.2%	38,027
2. Actuarial Science	71.6%	$85,690	23.7%	3,245
3. Environmental Science	78.0%	$58,380	25.1%	6,961
4. Geophysics	78.0%	$75,800	21.9%	2,471
5. Geology	78.0%	$74,296	22.4%	1,579
6. Oceanography	78.0%	$74,296	22.4%	1,579
7. Religion/Religious Studies	87.2%	$40,460	18.9%	35,092
8. Philosophy	82.7%	$38,821	18.9%	21,508
9. Chiropractic	76.9%	$65,890	14.4%	3,179
10. Optometry	60.9%	$93,800	11.3%	1,789
11. Criminal Justice/Law Enforcement	83.6%	$50,109	12.1%	15,535
12. Podiatry	63.6%	$110,510	9.5%	648

Best High-Security Majors Related to Jobs Employing a High Percentage of Urban Workers

Some people have a strong preference for an urban setting. They want to live and work where there's more energy and excitement, more access to the arts, more diversity, and better public transportation. On the other hand, some prefer the open spaces, closeness to nature, quiet, and inexpensive housing of rural locations. If you are strongly attracted to either setting, you'll be interested in the following lists.

We identified urban jobs as those for which half or more of the workforce is located in the 38 most populous metropolitan areas of the United States. These 38 metro areas—the most populous 10 percent of all U.S. metro areas, according to the Census Bureau—consist primarily of built-up communities, unlike smaller metro areas, which consist of a core city surrounded by a lot of countryside. In the following lists of high-security majors linked to urban jobs, you'll see a figure for each major that represents the percentage of the total U.S. workforce for the related jobs that is located in those 38 huge metro areas.

Best High-Security Majors Related to Jobs Employing the Highest Percentage of Urban Workers	
Major	Percentage of Urban Workers in Related Jobs
1. Political Science	72.8%
2. Public Relations	65.3%
3. Communications Studies/Speech	64.1%
4. Actuarial Science	63.7%
5. English	63.3%
6. Mathematics	63.2%
7. Statistics	63.2%
8. Journalism and Mass Communications	61.6%
9. Geophysics	58.2%
10. Geology	56.7%
11. Oceanography	56.7%
12. Medical Technology	56.4%
13. Chinese	54.6%
14. Classics	54.6%
15. French	54.6%
16. German	54.6%
17. Japanese	54.6%

(continued)

(continued)

Best High-Security Majors Related to Jobs Employing the Highest Percentage of Urban Workers

Major	Percentage of Urban Workers in Related Jobs
18. Modern Foreign Language	54.6%
19. Psychology	54.6%
20. Russian	54.6%
21. Spanish	54.6%
22. Environmental Science	54.0%
23. Occupational Therapy	53.1%
24. Art History	51.8%
25. Health Information Systems Administration	51.6%
26. Hospital/Health Facilities Administration	51.6%
27. Physical Therapy	51.6%
28. Family and Consumer Sciences	51.3%
29. Nursing (R.N. Training)	50.6%
30. Pharmacy	50.5%
31. Social Work	50.3%
32. Library Science	50.2%
33. Religion/Religious Studies	50.1%

The following list shows the high-security majors from the previous list with the best combination of potential economic rewards.

Best High-Security Majors Related to Jobs Employing a High Percentage of Urban Workers

Major	Percentage of Urban Workers in Related Jobs	Annual Earnings of Related Jobs	Percent Growth of Related Jobs	Annual Openings of Related Jobs
1. Physical Therapy	51.6%	$69,760	27.1%	12,072
2. Nursing (R.N. Training)	50.6%	$60,010	23.5%	233,499
3. Pharmacy	50.5%	$100,480	21.7%	16,358
4. Actuarial Science	63.7%	$85,690	23.7%	3,245
5. Health Information Systems Administration	51.6%	$76,990	16.4%	31,877
6. Hospital/Health Facilities Administration	51.6%	$76,990	16.4%	31,877
7. Environmental Science	54.0%	$58,380	25.1%	6,961
8. Occupational Therapy	53.1%	$63,790	23.1%	8,338
9. Public Relations	65.3%	$49,800	17.6%	51,216
10. Chinese	54.6%	$37,490	23.6%	6,630
11. Classics	54.6%	$37,490	23.6%	6,630
12. French	54.6%	$37,490	23.6%	6,630
13. German	54.6%	$37,490	23.6%	6,630
14. Japanese	54.6%	$37,490	23.6%	6,630
15. Modern Foreign Language	54.6%	$37,490	23.6%	6,630
16. Russian	54.6%	$37,490	23.6%	6,630
17. Spanish	54.6%	$37,490	23.6%	6,630
18. Religion/Religious Studies	50.1%	$40,460	18.9%	35,092
19. Geophysics	58.2%	$75,800	21.9%	2,471
20. Family and Consumer Sciences	51.3%	$48,920	8.6%	59,961

Best High-Security Majors Related to Jobs Employing a High Percentage of Rural Workers

The Census Bureau identifies 173 *nonmetropolitan* areas—areas that have no city of 50,000 people and have a total population of less than 100,000. We identified rural jobs as those for which 10 percent or more of the total U.S. workforce is located in these nonmetropolitan areas. In the following lists of high-security majors linked to rural jobs, you'll see a figure that represents the percentage of the total U.S. workforce for the related jobs that is located in nonmetropolitan areas.

You'll find a few majors, such as Nursing and Pharmacy, that are linked to both urban *and* rural jobs. These related jobs are well represented in all kinds of communities, so if you start your career in one of these jobs and tire of either the urban or the rural lifestyle, you can probably relocate to the opposite setting and still find job opportunities.

Best High-Security Majors Related to Jobs Employing the Highest Percentage of Rural Workers

Major	Percentage of Rural Workers in Related Jobs
1. Business Education	17.8%
2. Special Education	16.4%
3. Library Science	16.0%
4. Physical Education	15.9%
5. Secondary Education	15.8%
6. Social Work	14.1%
7. Family and Consumer Sciences	14.0%
8. Pharmacy	13.5%
9. Health Information Systems Administration	13.4%
10. Hospital/Health Facilities Administration	13.4%
11. Criminal Justice/Law Enforcement	13.2%
12. Early Childhood Education	12.9%
13. Veterinary Medicine	12.9%
14. Nursing (R.N. Training)	12.2%
15. Physical Therapy	12.0%
16. Speech-Language Pathology and Audiology	11.3%
17. Psychology	10.5%
18. Medical Technology	10.4%

The following list shows the high-security majors from the previous list with the best combination of potential economic rewards.

Best High-Security Majors Related to Jobs Employing a High Percentage of Rural Workers

Major	Percentage of Rural Workers in Related Jobs	Annual Earnings of Related Jobs	Percent Growth of Related Jobs	Annual Openings of Related Jobs
1. Nursing (R.N. Training)	12.2%	$60,010	23.5%	233,499
2. Health Information Systems Administration	13.4%	$76,990	16.4%	31,877
3. Hospital/Health Facilities Administration	13.4%	$76,990	16.4%	31,877
4. Pharmacy	13.5%	$100,480	21.7%	16,358
5. Physical Therapy	12.0%	$69,760	27.1%	12,072
6. Veterinary Medicine	12.9%	$75,230	35.0%	5,301
7. Early Childhood Education	12.9%	$29,980	15.4%	88,989
8. Social Work	16.1%	$40,373	17.8%	19,897
9. Business Education	17.8%	$49,420	5.6%	93,166
10. Psychology	10.5%	$62,449	15.9%	4,214
11. Medical Technology	10.4%	$51,720	12.4%	11,457
12. Criminal Justice/Law Enforcement	13.2%	$50,109	12.1%	15,535
13. Family and Consumer Sciences	14.0%	$48,920	8.6%	59,961
14. Physical Education	15.9%	$46,990	8.6%	73,179
15. Secondary Education	15.8%	$42,745	6.9%	127,178
16. Speech-Language Pathology and Audiology	11.3%	$60,567	10.5%	6,070
17. Library Science	16.0%	$50,970	3.6%	18,945
18. Special Education	16.4%	$49,350	11.6%	9,724

Best High-Security Majors Sorted by Education or Experience Required by Related Jobs

The lists in this section organize the best high-security majors into five groups based on the education or experience typically required for entry to related secure jobs. For each level of education or experience, we provide one list that includes *all* relevant majors—not just the best 5 or 10—ranked by their total combined score for the earnings, growth, and number of openings for related secure jobs.

These lists can help you when you plan your education. For example, you might be thinking about a particular college major because the expected pay is very good, but the lists may help you identify a major that interests you more and offers even better potential without additional required education.

Some of the jobs linked to these majors normally require less than a bachelor's degree for entry—for example, Coaches and Scouts (linked to Physical Education) requires only long-term on-the-job training and Detectives and Criminal Investigators (linked to Criminal Justice/Law Enforcement) requires only work experience in a related occupation. However, this book is based on the assumption that you intend to get at least a bachelor's degree, so if a related job requires less than a bachelor's degree, we grouped the major among the other related majors requiring a bachelor's.

You may notice that many majors appear in more than one list. These double listings occur when a major is related to two or more jobs that require *different levels* of education. For example, the Psychology major appears in the list for the master's degree because it is linked to the master's-level job Industrial-Organizational Psychologists, and it also appears in the list for the doctoral degree because it is linked to the doctoral-level job Clinical, Counseling, and School Psychologists.

We took care to sort each list in terms of the economic rewards of the related *jobs at that level*. So, to continue the example in the previous paragraph, at the master's level the Psychology major is sorted as if its potential earnings are $80,820 (which is true for Industrial-Organizational Psychologists), whereas at the doctoral level the same major is sorted using the wage figure of $62,210 (which is true for Clinical, Counseling, and School Psychologists). We followed the same procedure for employment growth and job openings.

As we did with all of the lists in this book, we considered only related secure jobs when we compiled these lists. The educational levels identified for the majors in the following lists include only the levels at which the related occupations are rated high on job security. For example, one of the jobs linked to the Mathematics major is Natural Sciences Managers, which usually requires a bachelor's degree plus work experience. This job, however, is low in job security, so you will not find Mathematics listed among majors at that level of education. On the other hand, there is high job security in another job linked to Mathematics at the master's level (Statisticians) and still another at the doctoral level (Mathematicians), so the lists for these two levels do include the Mathematics major.

The Education Levels

The U.S. Department of Labor defines the education and experience levels used in this set of lists as follows:

- **Bachelor's degree:** This degree requires approximately four to five years of full-time academic work beyond high school.
- **Work experience plus degree:** Jobs in this category are often management related and require some experience in a related nonmanagerial position in addition to a bachelor's or master's degree.
- **Master's degree:** Completion of a master's degree usually requires one to two years of full-time study beyond the bachelor's degree.
- **Doctoral degree:** This degree normally requires two or more years of full-time academic work beyond the bachelor's degree.
- **First professional degree:** This type of degree normally requires a minimum of two years of education beyond the bachelor's degree and frequently requires three years.

Best High-Security Majors Related to Jobs Requiring a Bachelor's Degree or Less

Major	Annual Earnings	Percent Growth	Annual Openings
1. Nursing (R.N. Training)	$60,010	23.5%	233,499
2. Public Relations	$49,800	17.6%	51,216
3. Business Education	$49,420	5.6%	93,166
4. Chinese	$37,490	23.6%	6,630
5. Classics	$37,490	23.6%	6,630
6. Communications Studies/Speech	$48,445	17.3%	18,396
7. French	$37,490	23.6%	6,630
8. German	$37,490	23.6%	6,630
9. Japanese	$37,490	23.6%	6,630
10. Medical Technology	$51,720	12.4%	11,457
11. Modern Foreign Language	$37,490	23.6%	6,630
12. Russian	$37,490	23.6%	6,630
13. Spanish	$37,490	23.6%	6,630
14. Criminal Justice/Law Enforcement	$49,919	12.1%	15,535
15. Family and Consumer Sciences	$48,915	8.6%	59,961
16. Social Work	$40,096	17.0%	26,869
17. Physical Education	$46,451	8.6%	73,179
18. Secondary Education	$41,338	6.9%	127,179
19. Special Education	$49,342	11.6%	9,724
20. Early Childhood Education	$29,693	15.4%	88,989
21. Graduate Study for College Teaching	$28,060	22.9%	20,601
22. English	$48,320	2.3%	20,193
23. Journalism and Mass Communications	$47,914	5.3%	11,407
24. Philosophy	$26,660	19.7%	7,924
25. Art History	$35,350	15.9%	1,341

Best High-Security Majors Related to Jobs Requiring Work Experience Plus Degree

Major	Annual Earnings	Percent Growth	Annual Openings
1. Actuarial Science	$85,690	23.7%	3,245
2. Health Information Systems Administration	$76,990	16.4%	31,877
3. Hospital/Health Facilities Administration	$76,990	16.4%	31,877

Best High-Security Majors Related to Jobs Requiring a Master's Degree

Major	Annual Earnings	Percent Growth	Annual Openings
1. Physician Assisting	$78,450	27.0%	7,147
2. Physical Therapy	$69,760	27.1%	12,072
3. Occupational Therapy	$63,790	23.1%	8,338
4. Environmental Science	$58,380	25.1%	6,961
5. Geology	$74,183	22.4%	1,579
6. Geophysics	$75,800	21.9%	2,471
7. Oceanography	$74,183	22.4%	1,579
8. Social Work	$43,600	29.8%	5,953
9. Philosophy	$40,460	18.9%	35,092
10. Psychology	$80,820	21.3%	118
11. Religion/Religious Studies	$40,460	18.9%	35,092
12. Speech-Language Pathology and Audiology	$60,690	10.6%	11,160
13. Mathematics	$69,900	8.5%	3,433
14. Statistics	$69,900	8.5%	3,433
15. Library Science	$50,970	3.6%	18,945
16. Political Science	$91,580	5.3%	318
17. Art History	$44,891	19.9%	1,106
18. Anthropology	$53,080	15.0%	446
19. Archeology	$53,080	15.0%	446

Best High-Security Majors Related to Jobs Requiring a Doctoral Degree

Major	Annual Earnings	Percent Growth	Annual Openings
1. Graduate Study for College Teaching	$59,040	22.9%	237,478
2. Mathematics	$90,870	10.2%	473
3. Psychology	$62,210	15.8%	8,309
4. Statistics	$90,870	10.2%	473

Best High-Security Majors Related to Jobs Requiring a First Professional Degree

Major	Annual Earnings	Percent Growth	Annual Openings
1. Medicine	$145,600+	14.2%	38,027
2. Pharmacy	$100,480	21.7%	16,358
3. Veterinary Medicine	$75,230	35.0%	5,301
4. Chiropractic	$65,890	14.4%	3,179
5. Optometry	$93,800	11.3%	1,789
6. Podiatry	$110,510	9.5%	648
7. Speech-Language Pathology and Audiology	$59,440	9.8%	980

Best High-Security Majors Sorted by Career Clusters of Related Jobs

This group of lists organizes the 50 best high-security majors into the 16 career clusters associated with their related secure jobs. By focusing on the clusters that align best with your interests, your past education, or your work experiences, you can use these lists to identify majors that might suit you. Within each cluster, majors are listed in order of their combined score for the earnings, job growth, and job openings of the related secure jobs, from highest to lowest.

The U.S. Department of Education's Office of Vocational and Adult Education developed these 16 career clusters around 1999, and many states now use them to organize their career-oriented programs and career information. Each cluster in this scheme is subdivided into several career *pathways,* and each pathway has several jobs assigned to it. (Pathways, as well as clusters, are identified for jobs described in Part IV, but in the following lists we consider only clusters.)

You should realize that assigning jobs to clusters and pathways is not a science; it is meant to serve the educational and economic needs of states and communities, and therefore some regional variations exist. We decided that the most definitive scheme to follow was the one used by the online O*NET database, and that scheme guided us both here and in Part IV. Career clusters are used most widely in education, especially secondary education, so the O*NET scheme is very generous in assigning jobs to clusters; that is, jobs frequently appear in two or more clusters. The rationale is that even after students choose a career cluster to focus on in secondary school, they should still have a wide variety of possible career goals open to them. That's why you'll find many majors appearing in multiple lists in this section.

For example, Statistics is linked to three career clusters: Business, Management, and Administration (through the job Statisticians); Human Services (through the job Mathematicians); and Science, Technology, Engineering, and Mathematics (through both Mathematicians and Statisticians). As in the previous set of lists, we included only related occupations high in job security and we sorted the majors on the basis of the economic facts for the related jobs *in that career cluster*. That's why, for example, you'll find different earnings figures for Statistics in the three places where it's listed: The figure in the list for the Business, Management, and Administration cluster is the earnings of Statisticians; the figure in the list for the Human Services cluster is the earnings of Mathematicians; and the figure in the list for the Science, Technology, Engineering, and Mathematics cluster is the average of the two other figures. (It's a weighted average, meaning that the job with the larger workforce, Statisticians, carries greater weight in the computation.)

Descriptions for the 16 Career Clusters

Brief descriptions follow for the 16 career clusters we use in the lists. Some of them refer to jobs (as examples) that aren't included in this book.

* **Agriculture, Food, and Natural Resources:** *Work with plants, animals, forests, or mineral resources for agriculture, horticulture, conservation, extraction, and other purposes.* In this cluster you can work in farming, landscaping, forestry, fishing, mining, and related fields. You may like doing physical work outdoors, such as on a farm or ranch, in a forest, or on a drilling rig. If you have a scientific curiosity, you could study plants and animals or analyze biological or rock samples in a lab. If you have management ability, you could own, operate, or manage a fish hatchery, a landscaping business, or a greenhouse.

* **Architecture and Construction:** *Work that designs, assembles, and maintains components of buildings and other structures.* You may want to be part of the team of architects, drafters, and others who design buildings and render plans. If construction

interests you, you might find fulfillment in the many building projects that are being undertaken at all times. If you like to organize and plan, you can find careers in managing these projects. Or you can play a more direct role in putting up and finishing buildings by doing jobs such as plumbing, carpentry, masonry, painting, or roofing, either as a skilled craftsworker or as a helper. You can prepare the building site by operating heavy equipment or installing, maintaining, and repairing vital building equipment and systems such as electricity and heating.

* **Arts, Audio/Video Technology, and Communications:** *Work in creatively expressing feelings or ideas, in communicating news or information, or in performing.* This cluster involves creative, verbal, or performing activities. For example, if you enjoy literature, perhaps writing or editing would appeal to you. Journalism and public relations are other fields for people who like to use their writing or speaking skills. Do you prefer to work in the performing arts? If so, you could direct or perform in drama, music, or dance. If you especially enjoy the visual arts, you could create paintings, sculpture, or ceramics or design products or visual displays. A flair for technology might lead you to specialize in photography, broadcast production, or dispatching.

* **Business, Management, and Administration:** *Work that makes a business organization or function run smoothly.* In this cluster, you can work in a position of leadership or specialize in a function that contributes to the overall effort in a business, a nonprofit organization, or a government agency. If you especially enjoy working with people, you may find fulfillment from working in human resources. An interest in numbers may lead you to consider accounting, finance, budgeting, billing, or financial record keeping. A job as an administrative assistant may interest you if you like a variety of tasks in a busy environment. If you are good with details and word processing, you may enjoy a job as a secretary or data-entry clerk. Or perhaps you would do well as the manager of a business.

* **Education and Training:** *Work that helps people learn.* In this cluster, your students may be preschoolers, retirees, or any age in between. You may specialize in a particular academic field or work with learners of a particular age, with a particular interest, or with a particular learning problem. Working in a library or museum may give you an opportunity to expand people's understanding of the world.

* **Finance:** *Work that helps businesses and people be assured of a financially secure future.* This cluster involves work in a financial or insurance business in a leadership or support role. If you like gathering and analyzing information, you may find fulfillment as an insurance adjuster or financial analyst. Or you may deal with information at the clerical level as a banking or insurance clerk or in person-to-person situations providing customer service. Another way to interact with people is to sell financial or insurance services that will meet their needs.

❀ **Government and Public Administration:** *Work that helps a government agency serve the needs of the public.* In this cluster you can work in a position of leadership or specialize in a function that contributes to the role of government. You may help protect the public by working as an inspector or examiner to enforce standards. If you enjoy using clerical skills, you could work as a clerk in a law court or government office. Or perhaps you prefer the top-down perspective of a government executive or urban planner.

❀ **Health Science:** *Work that helps people and animals be healthy.* This cluster involves working on a health-care team as a professional, therapist, or nurse. You might specialize in one of the many different parts of the body (such as the teeth or eyes) or in one of the many different types of care. Or you may want to be a generalist who deals with the whole patient. If you like technology, you might find satisfaction working with X-rays or new diagnostic methods. You might work with relatively healthy people, helping them to eat better. If you enjoy working with animals, you might care for them and keep them healthy.

❀ **Hospitality and Tourism:** *Work that caters to the personal wishes and needs of others so that they can enjoy a clean environment, good food and drink, comfortable lodging away from home, and recreation.* You can work in this cluster by providing services for the convenience, care, and pampering of others in hotels, restaurants, airplanes, beauty parlors, and so on. You may want to use your love of cooking as a chef. If you like working with people, you may want to provide personal services by being a travel guide, a flight attendant, a concierge, a hairdresser, or a waiter. You may want to work in cleaning and building services if you like a clean environment. If you enjoy sports or games, you could work for an athletic team or casino.

❀ **Human Services:** *Work that improves people's social, mental, emotional, or spiritual well-being.* Workers in this cluster include counselors, social workers, or religious workers who help people sort out their complicated lives or solve personal problems. You may work as a caretaker for very young people or the elderly. Or you may interview people to help identify the social services they need.

❀ **Information Technology:** *Work that designs, develops, manages, and supports information systems.* This cluster involves working with hardware, software, multimedia, or integrated systems. If you like to use your organizational skills, you might work as a systems or database administrator. Or you can solve complex problems as a software engineer or systems analyst. If you enjoy getting your hands on hardware, you might find work servicing computers, peripherals, and information-intense machines such as cash registers and ATMs.

❋ **Law, Public Safety, Corrections, and Security:** *Work that upholds people's rights or protects people and property by using authority, inspecting, or investigating.* In this cluster, you can work in law, law enforcement, fire fighting, the military, and related fields. For example, if you enjoy mental challenge and intrigue, you could investigate crimes or fires for a living. If you enjoy working with verbal skills and research skills, you may want to defend citizens in court or research deeds, wills, and other legal documents. If you want to help people in critical situations, you may want to fight fires, work as a police officer, or become a paramedic. Or, if you want more routine work in public safety, perhaps a job in guarding, patrolling, or inspecting would appeal to you. If you have management ability, you could seek a leadership position in law enforcement and the protective services. Work in the military gives you a chance to use technical and leadership skills while serving your country.

❋ **Manufacturing:** *Work that processes materials into intermediate or final products or that maintains and repairs products by using machines or hand tools.* In this cluster, you can work in one of many industries that mass-produce goods or work for a utility that distributes electrical power or other resources. You might enjoy manual work, using your hands or hand tools in highly skilled jobs such as assembling engines or electronic equipment. If you enjoy making machines run efficiently or fixing them when they break down, you could seek a job installing or repairing devices such as copiers, aircraft engines, cars, or watches. Perhaps you prefer to set up or operate machines that are used to manufacture products made of food, glass, or paper. You could enjoy cutting and grinding metal and plastic parts to desired shapes and measurements. Or you may want to operate equipment in systems that provide water and process wastewater. You may like inspecting, sorting, counting, or weighing products. Another option is to work with your hands and machinery to move boxes and freight in a warehouse. If leadership appeals to you, you could manage people engaged in production and repair.

❋ **Marketing, Sales, and Service:** *Work that anticipates the needs of people and organizations and communicates the benefits of products and services.* The jobs in this cluster involve understanding customer demand and using persuasion and selling. If you like using knowledge of science, you may enjoy selling pharmaceutical, medical, or electronic products or services. Real estate offers several kinds of sales jobs as well. If you like speaking on the phone, you could work as a telemarketer. Or you may enjoy selling apparel and other merchandise in a retail setting. If you prefer to help people, you may want a job in customer service.

❋ **Science, Technology, Engineering, and Mathematics:** *Work that discovers, collects, and analyzes information about the natural world; applies scientific research findings to problems in medicine, the life sciences, human behavior, and the natural sciences; imagines and manipulates quantitative data; and applies technology to manufacturing,* *transportation, and other economic activities.* In this cluster, you can work with the knowledge and processes of the sciences. You may enjoy researching and developing new knowledge in mathematics, or perhaps solving problems in the physical, life, or social sciences would appeal to you. You may want to study engineering and help create new machines, processes, and structures. If you want to work with scientific equipment and procedures, you could seek a job in a research or testing laboratory.

* **Transportation, Distribution, and Logistics:** *Work in operations that move people or materials.* In this cluster, you can manage a transportation service, help vehicles stay on their assigned schedules and routes, or drive or pilot a vehicle. If you enjoy taking responsibility, perhaps managing a rail line would appeal to you. If you work well with details and can take pressure on the job, you might consider being an air traffic controller. Or would you rather get out on the highway, on the water, or up in the air? If so, you could drive a truck from state to state, be employed on a ship, or fly a crop duster over a cornfield. If you prefer to stay closer to home, you could drive a delivery van, taxi, or school bus. You can use your physical strength to load freight and arrange it so that it gets to its destination in one piece.

Some sectors of our economy, such as agriculture, construction, finance, and tourism, are highly sensitive to the ups and downs of the business cycle. Jobs in these clusters may be highly rewarding in many ways, but they lack job security, and therefore the majors linked to them are not included in this book. That explains why some of the career clusters in the following lists are represented by very few high-security majors and why several clusters are linked to *no* majors.

Best High-Security Majors in the Agriculture, Food, and Natural Resources Cluster

Major	Annual Earnings	Percent Growth	Annual Openings
1. Graduate Study for College Teaching	$59,040	22.9%	237,478
2. Environmental Science	$58,380	25.1%	6,961

Best High-Security Majors in the Architecture and Construction Cluster

Major	Annual Earnings	Percent Growth	Annual Openings
1. Graduate Study for College Teaching	$59,040	22.9%	237,478

Best High-Security Majors in the Arts, Audio/Video Technology, and Communications Cluster

Major	Annual Earnings	Percent Growth	Annual Openings
1. Graduate Study for College Teaching	$59,040	22.9%	237,478
2. Public Relations	$49,800	17.6%	51,216
3. Family and Consumer Sciences	$49,307	12.5%	35,705
4. Communications Studies/Speech	$48,678	16.8%	26,284
5. Art History	$41,185	18.3%	1,184
6. English	$48,320	2.3%	20,193
7. Journalism and Mass Communications	$48,320	2.3%	20,193

Best High-Security Majors in the Business, Management, and Administration Cluster

Major	Annual Earnings	Percent Growth	Annual Openings
1. Graduate Study for College Teaching	$59,040	22.9%	237,478
2. Communications Studies/Speech	$49,800	17.6%	51,216
3. Public Relations	$49,800	17.6%	51,216
4. Mathematics	$69,900	8.5%	3,433
5. Statistics	$69,900	8.5%	3,433
6. Family and Consumer Sciences	$49,307	12.5%	35,705
7. English	$48,320	2.3%	20,193
8. Journalism and Mass Communications	$48,320	2.3%	20,193

Best High-Security Majors in the Education and Training Cluster

Major	Annual Earnings	Percent Growth	Annual Openings
1. Graduate Study for College Teaching	$58,930	22.9%	226,634
2. Chinese	$37,490	23.6%	6,630
3. Classics	$37,490	23.6%	6,630
4. French	$37,490	23.6%	6,630

Best High-Security Majors in the Education and Training Cluster

Major	Annual Earnings	Percent Growth	Annual Openings
5. German	$37,490	23.6%	6,630
6. Japanese	$37,490	23.6%	6,630
7. Modern Foreign Language	$37,490	23.6%	6,630
8. Russian	$37,490	23.6%	6,630
9. Spanish	$37,490	23.6%	6,630
10. Business Education	$49,420	5.6%	93,166
11. Secondary Education	$49,420	5.6%	93,166
12. Family and Consumer Sciences	$48,830	7.8%	84,218
13. Physical Education	$46,451	8.6%	73,179
14. Special Education	$49,342	11.6%	9,724
15. Library Science	$50,970	3.6%	18,945
16. Early Childhood Education	$29,294	23.5%	52,888

Best High-Security Majors in the Finance Cluster

Major	Annual Earnings	Percent Growth	Annual Openings
1. Actuarial Science	$85,690	23.7%	3,245
2. Graduate Study for College Teaching	$59,040	22.9%	237,478

Best High-Security Majors in the Government and Public Administration Cluster

Major	Annual Earnings	Percent Growth	Annual Openings
1. Graduate Study for College Teaching	$59,040	22.9%	237,478
2. Communications Studies/Speech	$49,800	17.6%	51,216
3. Family and Consumer Sciences	$49,800	17.6%	51,216
4. Public Relations	$49,800	17.6%	51,216
5. Political Science	$91,580	5.3%	318

Best High-Security Majors in the Health Science Cluster

Major	Annual Earnings	Percent Growth	Annual Openings
1. Medicine	$145,600+	14.2%	38,027
2. Nursing (R.N. Training)	$60,010	23.5%	233,499
3. Pharmacy	$100,480	21.7%	16,358
4. Graduate Study for College Teaching	$59,040	22.9%	237,478
5. Health Information Systems Administration	$76,990	16.4%	31,877
6. Hospital/Health Facilities Administration	$76,990	16.4%	31,877
7. Physical Therapy	$69,760	27.1%	12,072
8. Physician Assisting	$78,450	27.0%	7,147
9. Veterinary Medicine	$75,230	35.0%	5,301
10. Communications Studies/Speech	$49,800	17.6%	51,216
11. Public Relations	$49,800	17.6%	51,216
12. Occupational Therapy	$63,790	23.1%	8,338
13. Family and Consumer Sciences	$49,307	12.5%	35,705
14. Psychology	$62,269	15.8%	6,671
15. Optometry	$93,800	11.3%	1,789
16. Chiropractic	$65,890	14.4%	3,179
17. Podiatry	$110,510	9.5%	648
18. Medical Technology	$51,720	12.4%	11,457
19. Speech-Language Pathology and Audiology	$60,564	10.5%	6,070
20. English	$48,320	2.3%	20,193
21. Journalism and Mass Communications	$48,320	2.3%	20,193

Best High-Security Majors in the Human Services Cluster

Major	Annual Earnings	Percent Growth	Annual Openings
1. Graduate Study for College Teaching	$59,040	22.9%	237,478
2. Communications Studies/Speech	$49,800	17.6%	51,216
3. Public Relations	$49,800	17.6%	51,216
4. Early Childhood Education	$23,130	26.3%	78,172
5. Chinese	$37,490	23.6%	6,630
6. Classics	$37,490	23.6%	6,630
7. French	$37,490	23.6%	6,630

Best High-Security Majors in the Human Services Cluster

Major	Annual Earnings	Percent Growth	Annual Openings
8. German	$37,490	23.6%	6,630
9. Japanese	$37,490	23.6%	6,630
10. Modern Foreign Language	$37,490	23.6%	6,630
11. Philosophy	$40,460	18.9%	35,092
12. Religion/Religious Studies	$40,460	18.9%	35,092
13. Russian	$37,490	23.6%	6,630
14. Spanish	$37,490	23.6%	6,630
15. Family and Consumer Sciences	$49,307	12.5%	35,705
16. Psychology	$62,210	15.8%	8,309
17. Social Work	$40,312	17.8%	19,897
18. English	$48,320	2.3%	20,193
19. Journalism and Mass Communications	$48,320	2.3%	20,193
20. Mathematics	$90,870	10.2%	473
21. Statistics	$90,870	10.2%	473
22. Political Science	$91,580	5.3%	318

Best High-Security Majors in the Information Technology Cluster

Major	Annual Earnings	Percent Growth	Annual Openings
1. Graduate Study for College Teaching	$59,040	22.9%	237,478

Best High-Security Majors in the Law, Public Safety, Corrections, and Security Cluster

Major	Annual Earnings	Percent Growth	Annual Openings
1. Graduate Study for College Teaching	$59,040	22.9%	237,478
2. Communications Studies/Speech	$45,330	24.5%	2,620
3. Journalism and Mass Communications	$45,330	24.5%	2,620
4. Criminal Justice/Law Enforcement	$51,444	12.3%	19,681
5. Social Work	$38,620	19.1%	35,402

Best High-Security Majors in the Marketing, Sales, and Service Cluster

Major	Annual Earnings	Percent Growth	Annual Openings
1. Graduate Study for College Teaching	$59,040	22.9%	237,478

Best High-Security Majors in the Science, Technology, Engineering, and Mathematics Cluster

Major	Annual Earnings	Percent Growth	Annual Openings
1. Geophysics	$75,800	21.9%	2,471
2. Graduate Study for College Teaching	$59,040	22.9%	237,478
3. Medicine	$145,600+	14.2%	38,027
4. Geology	$74,183	22.4%	1,579
5. Oceanography	$74,183	22.4%	1,579
6. Mathematics	$72,399	8.7%	1,953
7. Statistics	$72,399	8.7%	1,953
8. Anthropology	$53,080	15.0%	446
9. Archeology	$53,080	15.0%	446
10. Art History	$41,185	18.3%	1,184
11. Political Science	$91,580	5.3%	318

Best High-Security Jobs Sorted by Personality Types

These lists organize the 50 best high-security majors into groups matching six personality types: Realistic, Investigative, Artistic, Social, Enterprising, and Conventional. This system was developed by John L. Holland and is used in the *Self-Directed Search (SDS)* and other career assessment inventories and information systems.

If you have used one of these career inventories or systems, the lists will help you identify majors that most closely match these personality types. Even if you haven't used one of these systems, the concept of personality types and the majors related to them can help you identify high-security majors (and the jobs related to them) that suit the type of person you are.

As we did for the career clusters, we have created only one list for each personality type. We've ranked the majors within each personality type based on their total combined scores for earnings, growth, and annual job openings of related jobs with high security. If a major is linked to only one secure O*NET job, the major is listed for the one personality type that the related job most closely matches. If a major is linked to two or more secure O*NET jobs representing different personality types, the major appears in two or more lists. Consider reviewing the majors for more than one personality type so that you don't overlook possible majors that would interest you.

Note that the economic facts for the majors in each list are based on the related secure jobs *of that personality type*. That's why, to cite just one example, the figures given for Graduate Study for College Teaching in the Social list are different from the figures in the Artistic list.

When we compiled these lists, we found that *none* of the high-security college majors is linked to a job for which Realistic is the *primary* personality type. In fact, a bachelor's degree is usually not an appropriate preparation route for Realistic jobs; instead, an apprenticeship or technical school program is generally more suitable. However, 18 of the 50 high-security college majors have Realistic as their *secondary* personality type, and those majors appear in the Realistic list in this section—and also in the list that covers their primary type.

Descriptions of the Six Personality Types

Following are brief descriptions for each of the six personality types used in the lists, worded in terms of jobs rather than in terms of what happens in the classroom of a related major. Select the two or three descriptions that most closely describe your preferences and then use the lists to identify majors that best fit these personality types.

- ❋ **Realistic:** These occupations frequently involve work activities that include practical, hands-on problems and solutions. They often deal with plants; animals; and real-world materials such as wood, tools, and machinery. Many of the occupations require working outside and don't involve a lot of paperwork or working closely with others.

- ❋ **Investigative:** These occupations frequently involve working with ideas and require an extensive amount of thinking. These occupations can involve searching for facts and figuring out problems mentally.

- ❋ **Artistic:** These occupations frequently involve working with forms, designs, and patterns. They often require self-expression, and the work can be done without following a clear set of rules.

⊛ **Social:** These occupations frequently involve working with, communicating with, and teaching people. These occupations often involve helping or providing service to others.

⊛ **Enterprising:** These occupations frequently involve starting up and carrying out projects. These occupations can involve leading people and making many decisions. They sometimes require risk taking and often deal with business.

⊛ **Conventional:** These occupations frequently involve following set procedures and routines. These occupations can include working with data and details more than with ideas. Usually there is a clear line of authority to follow.

Best High-Security Majors for People with a Realistic Personality Type

Major	Annual Earnings	Percent Growth	Annual Openings
1. Physical Therapy	$69,760	27.1%	12,072
2. Veterinary Medicine	$75,230	35.0%	5,301
3. Graduate Study for College Teaching	$59,040	22.9%	237,478
4. Medicine	$145,600+	14.2%	38,027
5. Occupational Therapy	$63,790	23.1%	8,338
6. Environmental Science	$58,380	25.1%	6,961
7. Geophysics	$75,800	21.9%	2,471
8. Geology	$74,183	22.4%	1,579
9. Oceanography	$74,183	22.4%	1,579
10. Chiropractic	$65,890	14.4%	3,179
11. Optometry	$93,800	11.3%	1,789
12. Physical Education	$27,840	14.6%	51,100
13. Criminal Justice/Law Enforcement	$51,081	11.7%	26,294
14. Medical Technology	$51,720	12.4%	11,457
15. Anthropology	$53,080	15.0%	446
16. Archeology	$53,080	15.0%	446
17. Art History	$35,350	15.9%	1,341

Best High-Security Majors for People with an Investigative Personality Type

Major	Annual Earnings	Percent Growth	Annual Openings
1. Physician Assisting	$78,450	27.0%	7,147
2. Pharmacy	$100,480	21.7%	16,358
3. Veterinary Medicine	$75,230	35.0%	5,301
4. Medicine	$145,600+	14.2%	38,027
5. Graduate Study for College Teaching	$59,040	22.9%	237,478
6. Geophysics	$75,800	21.9%	2,471
7. Environmental Science	$58,380	25.1%	6,961
8. Geology	$74,183	22.4%	1,579
9. Oceanography	$74,183	22.4%	1,579
10. Psychology	$62,328	15.8%	5,579
11. Optometry	$93,800	11.3%	1,789
12. Chiropractic	$65,890	14.4%	3,179
13. Medical Technology	$51,720	12.4%	11,457
14. Mathematics	$72,399	8.7%	1,953
15. Statistics	$72,399	8.7%	1,953
16. Political Science	$91,580	5.3%	318
17. Anthropology	$53,080	15.0%	446
18. Archeology	$53,080	15.0%	446
19. Art History	$43,110	14.4%	795

Best High-Security Majors for People with an Artistic Personality Type

Major	Annual Earnings	Percent Growth	Annual Openings
1. Graduate Study for College Teaching	$59,040	22.9%	237,478
2. Chinese	$37,490	23.6%	6,630
3. Classics	$37,490	23.6%	6,630
4. French	$37,490	23.6%	6,630
5. German	$37,490	23.6%	6,630
6. Japanese	$37,490	23.6%	6,630

(continued)

(continued)

Best High-Security Majors for People with an Artistic Personality Type

Major	Annual Earnings	Percent Growth	Annual Openings
7. Modern Foreign Language	$37,490	23.6%	6,630
8. Russian	$37,490	23.6%	6,630
9. Spanish	$37,490	23.6%	6,630
10. English	$48,320	2.3%	20,193
11. Family and Consumer Sciences	$48,320	2.3%	20,193
12. Library Science	$50,970	3.6%	18,945
13. Communications Studies/Speech	$45,330	24.5%	2,620
14. Journalism and Mass Communications	$47,914	5.3%	11,407
15. Art History	$40,596	19.5%	1,379

Best High-Security Majors for People with a Social Personality Type

Major	Annual Earnings	Percent Growth	Annual Openings
1. Nursing (R.N. Training)	$60,010	23.5%	233,499
2. Graduate Study for College Teaching	$58,832	22.9%	217,762
3. Physical Therapy	$69,760	27.1%	12,072
4. Occupational Therapy	$63,790	23.1%	8,338
5. Early Childhood Education	$29,294	23.5%	52,888
6. Business Education	$49,420	5.6%	93,166
7. Philosophy	$40,460	18.9%	35,092
8. Psychology	$62,210	15.8%	8,309
9. Religion/Religious Studies	$40,460	18.9%	35,092
10. Secondary Education	$49,420	5.6%	93,166
11. Criminal Justice/Law Enforcement	$49,450	10.8%	25,969
12. Family and Consumer Sciences	$48,830	7.8%	84,218
13. Physical Education	$48,830	7.8%	84,218
14. Podiatry	$110,510	9.5%	648
15. Speech-Language Pathology and Audiology	$60,564	10.5%	6,070
16. Social Work	$40,096	17.0%	26,869
17. Special Education	$49,342	11.6%	9,724
18. Communications Studies/Speech	$25,860	−0.2%	1,351

Best High-Security Majors for People with an Enterprising Personality Type

Major	Annual Earnings	Percent Growth	Annual Openings
1. Communications Studies/Speech	$49,800	17.6%	51,216
2. Family and Consumer Sciences	$49,800	17.6%	51,216
3. Public Relations	$49,800	17.6%	51,216
4. Health Information Systems Administration	$76,990	16.4%	31,877
5. Hospital/Health Facilities Administration	$76,990	16.4%	31,877
6. Criminal Justice/Law Enforcement	$55,571	17.5%	12,274
7. Physical Education	$27,840	14.6%	51,100

Best High-Security Majors for People with a Conventional Personality Type

Major	Annual Earnings	Percent Growth	Annual Openings
1. Actuarial Science	$85,690	23.7%	3,245
2. Criminal Justice/Law Enforcement	$59,930	17.3%	14,746

Best High-Security Majors by Level of Verbal and Math Skills

If you have ever applied for admission to a college, you are probably very aware of the verbal and math abilities you demonstrated on a standardized test. But have you thought about the relationship between verbal and math abilities and the different majors that are available in college?

One way to look at that relationship is to compare people's *intended* majors with their verbal and math scores on standardized tests. According to the College Board, in 2004–2005, the people with the highest verbal SAT scores intended to enroll in language and literature majors, library and archival sciences majors, and foreign/classical language majors. Those with the highest math SAT scores intended to enroll in mathematics majors, physical sciences majors, and engineering majors. These findings are not at all surprising, because people tend to plan enrollment in majors that seem consistent with their standardized test scores.

Another way to look at these abilities is to consider the verbal and math skills that are required for academic *success* when you're in the major. We don't have access to good data on this for a variety of majors, but you can make some inferences by looking at the Typical Sequence of College Courses listed for each major in Part III. Note whether there are several courses related to writing, literature, or public speaking (verbal subjects) or whether the curriculum is rich in math and science courses. If you look carefully, you may find some surprises; for example, the Psychology major requires a lot more math than you might expect.

A third way to consider the relationship of these skills to college majors is to look at the *jobs* that people are preparing for by enrolling in the majors. We have good information about the skill requirements of jobs (in the O*NET database), and therefore for each major described in Part III you can turn to the related jobs in Part IV to see whether verbal or math skills rank high among the skill requirements.

We used this job-related skill information to compile the sets of lists that follow, showing high-security majors linked to jobs that require a high and low level of verbal and math skills. For each set of lists, first we list the high-skill majors ordered by level of skill (but remember, it's the level required by the linked secure *jobs,* not by the major itself). Then we list the high-skill majors ordered by the standard economic criteria of related secure jobs: earnings, job growth, and job openings. Finally, we list the high-security majors linked to secure jobs that require the *lowest* level of skills, ordered first by skill level and then by the three economic criteria.

Understand that the relationship between skills required *in the major* and skills required *on the job* is not exact. Students sometimes complain that they are required to study math at a level that they're never going to use on the job or that they're required to read literary classics that have little relevance to their intended careers. Conversely, employers sometimes complain that graduates with excellent academic records are deficient in verbal or math skills they need at work. Nevertheless, the job-related skills are useful to know because one of the chief reasons you enroll in a major is to prepare for a job.

Best High-Security Majors Related to Jobs that Require a High Level of Verbal Skills

To rank the majors by their verbal skills, we looked at the ratings that O*NET gives to related secure jobs on two specific skills: Reading Comprehension and Writing. We took the average of these two ratings, represented it as a figure on a scale ranging from 0 to 100, and eliminated all majors linked to secure jobs scoring lower than 70.

High-Security Majors Related to Jobs that Require the Highest Level of Verbal Skills

Major	Level of Verbal Skills (Out of 100) of Related Jobs
1. Political Science	91.3
2. Archeology	87.4
3. Anthropology	87.4
4. Graduate Study for College Teaching	83.8
5. Podiatry	81.8
6. Medicine	79.8
7. Veterinary Medicine	79.6
8. English	78.2
9. Mathematics	77.8
10. Statistics	77.8
11. Journalism and Mass Communications	77.0
12. Religion/Religious Studies	75.9
13. Philosophy	75.9
14. Speech-Language Pathology and Audiology	75.7
15. Public Relations	74.8
16. Psychology	74.5
17. Library Science	73.8
18. Communications Studies/Speech	73.2
19. Business Education	73.2
20. Secondary Education	73.2
21. Family and Consumer Sciences	73.2
22. Pharmacy	72.1
23. Physical Education	71.5
24. Actuarial Science	71.5

The following list shows the 20 high-security majors from the previous list with the best combination of potential economic rewards.

Best High-Security Majors Related to Jobs that Require a High Level of Verbal Skills

Major	Level of Verbal Skills of Related Jobs	Annual Earnings of Related Jobs	Percent Growth of Related Jobs	Annual Openings of Related Jobs
1. Graduate Study for College Teaching	83.8	$56,567	22.9%	129,040
2. Medicine	79.8	$145,600+	14.2%	38,027
3. Pharmacy	72.1	$100,480	21.7%	16,358
4. Veterinary Medicine	79.6	$75,230	35.0%	5,301
5. Actuarial Science	71.5	$85,690	23.7%	3,245
6. Public Relations	74.8	$49,800	17.6%	51,216
7. Psychology	74.5	$62,449	15.9%	4,214
8. Religion/Religious Studies	75.9	$40,460	18.9%	35,092
9. Podiatry	81.8	$110,510	9.5%	648
10. Communications Studies/Speech	73.2	$48,648	17.3%	18,396
11. Philosophy	75.9	$38,821	18.9%	21,508
12. Speech-Language Pathology and Audiology	75.7	$60,567	10.5%	6,070
13. Business Education	73.2	$49,420	5.6%	93,166
14. Family and Consumer Sciences	73.2	$48,920	8.6%	59,961
15. Mathematics	77.8	$72,728	8.7%	1,953
16. Statistics	77.8	$72,728	8.7%	1,953
17. Physical Education	71.5	$46,990	8.6%	73,179
18. Secondary Education	73.2	$42,745	6.9%	127,178
19. Anthropology	87.4	$53,080	15.0%	446
20. Archeology	87.4	$53,080	15.0%	446

Best High-Security Majors Related to Jobs that Require a Lower Level of Verbal Skills

Maybe verbal ability is not one of your strengths, and you're looking for a high-security major that requires a relatively *low* level of verbal skills. To create the following list, we took the majors that did not exceed the cutoff score for the lists of highly verbal majors (a score of 70) and ranked them by their economic potential. Note that the major with the lowest verbal ability, Nursing (R.N. Training), still has a score of 51.0, which is not extremely low. College-level secure jobs tend to be highly skilled, so don't expect to qualify for one if your verbal skills are truly low.

Best High-Security Majors Related to Jobs that Require a Lower Level of Verbal Skills

Major	Level of Verbal Skills of Related Jobs	Annual Earnings of Related Jobs	Percent Growth of Related Jobs	Annual Openings of Related Jobs
1. Physician Assisting	59.8	$78,450	27.0%	7,147
2. Physical Therapy	57.2	$69,760	27.1%	12,072
3. Nursing (R.N. Training)	51.0	$60,010	23.5%	233,499
4. Health Information Systems Administration	65.3	$76,990	16.4%	31,877
5. Hospital/Health Facilities Administration	65.3	$76,990	16.4%	31,877
6. Environmental Science	65.3	$58,380	25.1%	6,961
7. Occupational Therapy	56.3	$63,790	23.1%	8,338
8. Chinese	61.8	$37,490	23.6%	6,630
9. Classics	61.8	$37,490	23.6%	6,630
10. French	61.8	$37,490	23.6%	6,630
11. German	61.8	$37,490	23.6%	6,630
12. Japanese	61.8	$37,490	23.6%	6,630
13. Modern Foreign Language	61.8	$37,490	23.6%	6,630
14. Russian	61.8	$37,490	23.6%	6,630
15. Spanish	61.8	$37,490	23.6%	6,630
16. Social Work	67.4	$40,373	17.8%	19,897
17. Geophysics	61.7	$75,800	21.9%	2,471
18. Criminal Justice/Law Enforcement	60.5	$50,109	12.1%	15,535
19. Geology	65.4	$74,296	22.4%	1,579
20. Medical Technology	54.4	$51,720	12.4%	11,457
21. Oceanography	65.4	$74,296	22.4%	1,579
22. Early Childhood Education	61.3	$29,980	15.4%	88,989
23. Special Education	69.7	$49,350	11.6%	9,724
24. Optometry	58.9	$93,800	11.3%	1,789
25. Chiropractic	59.9	$65,890	14.4%	3,179
26. Art History	69.5	$41,228	18.3%	1,184

Best High-Security Majors Related to Jobs that Require a High Level of Math Skills

All jobs in the O*NET database are rated on math skills, so we were able to use these ratings to assign math skill levels to each of the best high-security majors. We eliminated majors that scored less than 60 on a scale from 0 to 100. This was a lower cutoff level than we used for verbal skills, but we needed to go lower to retain a reasonable number of majors on the list.

High-Security Majors Related to Jobs that Require the Highest Level of Math Skills	
Major	Level of Math Skills (Out of 100) of Related Jobs
1. Actuarial Science	89.0
2. Statistics	82.5
3. Mathematics	82.5
4. Veterinary Medicine	70.3
5. Archeology	65.9
6. Anthropology	65.9
7. Geology	62.3
8. Oceanography	62.3
9. Pharmacy	62.1
10. Graduate Study for College Teaching	61.9
11. Podiatry	61.3

The following list shows the high-security majors from the previous list with the best combination of potential economic rewards.

Best High-Security Majors Related to Jobs that Require a High Level of Math Skills				
Major	Level of Math Skills of Related Jobs	Annual Earnings of Related Jobs	Percent Growth of Related Jobs	Annual Openings of Related Jobs
1. Veterinary Medicine	70.3	$75,230	35.0%	5,301
2. Actuarial Science	89.0	$85,690	23.7%	3,245
3. Pharmacy	62.1	$100,480	21.7%	16,358

Best High-Security Majors Related to Jobs that Require a High Level of Math Skills

Major	Level of Math Skills of Related Jobs	Annual Earnings of Related Jobs	Percent Growth of Related Jobs	Annual Openings of Related Jobs
4. Graduate Study for College Teaching	61.9	$56,567	22.9%	129,040
5. Geology	62.3	$74,296	22.4%	1,579
6. Oceanography	62.3	$74,296	22.4%	1,579
7. Podiatry	61.3	$110,510	9.5%	648
8. Mathematics	82.5	$72,728	8.7%	1,953
9. Statistics	82.5	$72,728	8.7%	1,953
10. Anthropology	65.9	$53,080	15.0%	446
11. Archeology	65.9	$53,080	15.0%	446

Best High-Security Majors Related to Jobs with a Lower Level of Math Skills

If you find math uninteresting or too challenging, the following list may suggest high-security majors that can suit this preference. The secure jobs related to these majors had an average math skill rating of less than 40, which is considerably lower than the cutoff score (60) used to create the previous lists of highly mathematical majors. These majors are ranked according to the usual economic criteria.

Don't assume from this list that you can enter these majors without a good background in math or complete them by taking only low-level math courses. Some of these majors may include courses in statistics or even calculus! However, the *jobs* that these majors usually lead to generally do not require workers to use a high level of math skill.

Why is there sometimes such a disconnect between course requirements and work tasks? The curriculum developers who design the majors want you to be able to understand the people you'll work with. In many jobs, you do not use a lot of math but work with people who do, so with a background in mathematical concepts, you can understand how these other workers produce their results and can tell the difference between meaningful and misleading results. You can challenge the output of those workers and ask them intelligent questions. For example, public relations specialists need to understand the procedures of survey researchers, and social workers need to understand how social science research works, even if they are not engaged in it. A background in math also makes it possible for you to specialize in research—although, if you are looking at this list, you probably are not interested in such math-intense pursuits.

Best High-Security Majors Related to Jobs that Require a Lower Level of Math Skills

Major	Level of Math Skills of Related Jobs	Annual Earnings of Related Jobs	Percent Growth of Related Jobs	Annual Openings of Related Jobs
1. Physician Assisting	37.4	$78,450	27.0%	7,147
2. Nursing (R.N. Training)	35.7	$60,010	23.5%	233,499
3. Chinese	32.7	$37,490	23.6%	6,630
4. Classics	32.7	$37,490	23.6%	6,630
5. French	32.7	$37,490	23.6%	6,630
6. German	32.7	$37,490	23.6%	6,630
7. Japanese	32.7	$37,490	23.6%	6,630
8. Modern Foreign Language	32.7	$37,490	23.6%	6,630
9. Occupational Therapy	37.4	$63,790	23.1%	8,338
10. Russian	32.7	$37,490	23.6%	6,630
11. Spanish	32.7	$37,490	23.6%	6,630
12. Public Relations	29.1	$49,800	17.6%	51,216
13. Social Work	38.4	$40,373	17.8%	19,897
14. Communications Studies/Speech	30.0	$48,648	17.3%	18,396
15. Medical Technology	30.3	$51,720	12.4%	11,457
16. Criminal Justice/Law Enforcement	38.7	$50,109	12.1%	15,535
17. Early Childhood Education	36.0	$29,980	15.4%	88,989
18. Chiropractic	26.9	$65,890	14.4%	3,179
19. Optometry	39.3	$93,800	11.3%	1,789

Bonus List: The Most Important Courses for a Secure Future

A major is only a collection of courses. The courses are supposed to add up to a complete curriculum, and it is probably true that the whole of the major is greater than the sum of its parts. That is, by completing the particular mix of courses that make up your major, you probably will come away with a greater understanding of a subject than you would if you took a random selection of courses.

Nevertheless, we think that certain courses are likely to be more frequent among the high-security majors. Wouldn't it be interesting to know which courses those are? You might want to take some of these courses as electives—that is, optional courses that are not required for your major—because they may contribute in some way to knowledge that will be particularly useful in jobs that are relatively secure during economic downturns.

To identify these courses, we performed some calculations based on our database of the typical course requirements of college majors. First, for each course, we calculated how often it is required among the 121 majors for which we have information. Next, we calculated how often it is required among the 50 high-security majors included in this book. Finally, we calculated the *ratio* between the course's inclusion among high-security majors and among all majors, and we sorted the courses by this ratio.

The following list shows the top 15 courses that appeared much more often among high-security majors than among all majors for which we had information.

The Most Important Courses for a Secure Future

1. Statistics for Business and Social Sciences
2. Calculus
3. Organic Chemistry
4. General Chemistry
5. Introduction to Computer Science
6. English Composition
7. Statistics
8. Seminar (reporting on research)
9. Foreign Language
10. General Biology
11. Introduction to Biochemistry
12. Introduction to Psychology
13. College Algebra
14. Oral Communication
15. General Microbiology

PART III

Descriptions of the Best High-Security Majors

This part provides descriptions for all the majors included in one or more of the lists in Part II and identifies the jobs related to these majors. The Introduction gives more details on how to use and interpret the descriptions of majors, but here is some additional information:

- The majors are arranged in alphabetical order by name. This approach allows you to find a description quickly if you know the major's correct title from one of the lists in Part II.

- Five additional majors are described here: African-American Studies, American Studies, Area Studies, Humanities, and Women's Studies. These majors are related to Graduate Study for College Teaching, but unlike that generic pseudo-major, they are specific majors linked to specific college teaching jobs. Some graduates of these programs go into fields other than college teaching, sometimes by earning a postgraduate degree in a different field.

- Consider the descriptions of majors in this section as a first step in exploring educational options. When you find a major that interests you, turn to the appendix for suggestions about resources for further exploration.

- For every major, you'll find at least one related secure job and its definition. Turn to Part IV for a more detailed description of each job. One or more recession-sensitive jobs may also be identified, but these are not defined or described in this book.

- If you are using this section to browse for interesting options, we suggest you begin with the Table of Contents. Part II features many interesting lists that will help you identify titles of majors to explore in more detail. If you have not browsed the lists in Part II, consider spending some time there. The lists are interesting and will help you identify majors you can find described in the material that follows. The titles of majors in Part II are also listed in the Table of Contents.

Actuarial Science

Useful Facts About the Major

Focuses on the mathematical and statistical analysis of risk and their applications to insurance and other business management problems.

Related CIP Program: 52.1304 Actuarial Science.

Specializations in the Major: Insurance; investment.

Typical Sequence of College Courses: Calculus, linear algebra, advanced calculus, introduction to computer science, introduction to probability, introduction to actuarial mathematics, mathematical statistics, applied regression, actuarial models, introduction to accounting, principles of microeconomics, principles of macroeconomics, financial management, programming in C, investment analysis, price theory, income and employment theory.

Typical Sequence of High School Courses: English, algebra, geometry, trigonometry, science, pre-calculus, calculus, computer science.

Career Snapshot

Actuarial science is the analysis of mathematical data to predict the likelihood of certain events, such as death, accident, or disability. Insurance companies are the main employers of actuaries; actuaries determine how much the insurers charge for policies. The usual entry route is a bachelor's degree, but actuaries continue to study and sit for exams to upgrade their professional standing over the course of 5 to 10 years. The occupation is expected to grow at a good pace, and there will probably be many openings for those who are able to pass the series of exams.

Other Programs Related to the Same Jobs

Business Statistics.

Related Secure Job

(See Part IV for the full job description.)

Actuaries. Analyze statistical data, such as mortality, accident, sickness, disability, and retirement rates, and construct probability tables to forecast risk and liability for payment of future benefits. May ascertain premium rates required and cash reserves necessary to ensure payment of future benefits.

Related Recession-Sensitive Job

None met the criteria.

African-American Studies

Useful Facts About the Major

Focuses on the history, sociology, politics, culture, and economics of the North American peoples descended from the African diaspora, focusing on the United States, Canada, and the Caribbean, but also including reference to Latin American elements of the diaspora.

Related CIP Program: 05.0201 African-American/Black Studies.

Specializations in the Major: Behavioral and social inquiry; history and culture; literature, language, and the arts.

Typical Sequence of College Courses: English composition, foreign language, American history, introduction to African-American studies, African-American literature, African-American history, African diaspora studies, research methods in African-American studies, seminar (reporting on research).

Typical Sequence of High School Courses: English, algebra, foreign language, history, literature, public speaking, social science.

Career Snapshot

African-American studies draws on a number of disciplines, including history, sociology, literature, linguistics, and political science. Usually you can shape the program to emphasize whichever appeals most to you. Graduates frequently pursue higher degrees as a means of establishing a career in a field such as college teaching or the law.

Other Programs Related to the Same Jobs

African Languages, Literatures, and Linguistics; African Studies; Agricultural Teacher Education; Albanian Language and Literature; American History; American Indian/Native American Studies; American Literature; American Studies; Ancient Near Eastern and Biblical Languages, Literatures, and Linguistics; Ancient/Classical Greek Language and Literature; Anthropology; Arabic Language and Literature; Archeology; Area Studies; Art History, Criticism, and Conservation; Art/Art Studies, General; Arts Management; Asian History; Asian Studies/Civilization; Asian-American Studies; Australian/Oceanic/Pacific Languages, Literatures, and Linguistics; Bahasa Indonesian/Bahasa Malay Languages and Literatures; Balkans Studies; Baltic Languages, Literatures, and Linguistics; Baltic Studies; Bengali Language and Literature; Bible/Biblical Studies; Biology Teacher Education; Broadcast Journalism; Buddhist Studies; Bulgarian Language and Literature; Burmese Language and Literature; Business Teacher Education; Business/Managerial Economics; Canadian History; Canadian Studies; Caribbean Studies; Catalan Language and Literature; Celtic Languages, Literatures, and Linguistics; Central/Middle and Eastern European Studies; Ceramic Arts and Ceramics; Chemistry Teacher Education; Chinese Language and Literature; Chinese Studies; Christian Studies; Cinematography and Film/Video Production; Classics and Classical Languages, Literatures, and Linguistics, General; Clinical Psychology; Cognitive Psychology and Psycholinguistics; Commercial Photography; Commonwealth Studies; Communications Studies/Speech Communication and Rhetoric; Communications, Journalism, and Related Fields, Other; Community Psychology; Comparative Literature; Comparative Psychology; Computer Teacher Education; Conducting; Counseling Psychology; Crafts/Craft Design, Folk Art, and Artisanry; Creative Writing; Czech Language and Literature; Dance, General; Danish Language and Literature; Design and Applied Arts, Other; Design and Visual Communications, General; others.

Related Secure Job

(See Part IV for the full job description.)

Area, Ethnic, and Cultural Studies Teachers, Postsecondary. Teach courses pertaining to the culture and development of an area (e.g., Latin America), an ethnic group, or any other group (e.g., women's studies, urban affairs).

Related Recession-Sensitive Job

None met the criteria.

American Studies

Useful Facts About the Major

Focuses on the history, society, politics, culture, and economics of the United States and its Pre-Columbian and colonial predecessors, including the flow of immigrants from other societies.

Related CIP Program: 05.0102 American/United States Studies/Civilization.

Specializations in the Major: History and political science; literature, language, and the arts; popular culture.

Typical Sequence of College Courses: English composition, American history, American government, American literature, American popular culture, seminar (reporting on research).

Typical Sequence of High School Courses: English, algebra, foreign language, history, literature, public speaking, social science.

Career Snapshot

American studies is an interdisciplinary major that allows you to concentrate on the aspect of American culture that is of greatest interest to you—for example, history, the arts, or social and ethnic groups. Many, perhaps most, graduates use this major as a springboard to postgraduate or professional training that prepares them for a career in college teaching, business, law, the arts, politics, or some other field.

Other Programs Related to the Same Jobs

African Languages, Literatures, and Linguistics; African Studies; African-American/Black Studies; Agricultural Teacher Education; Albanian Language and Literature; American History; American Indian/Native American Studies; American Literature; Ancient Near Eastern and Biblical Languages, Literatures, and Linguistics; Ancient/Classical Greek Language and Literature; Anthropology; Arabic Language and Literature; Archeology; Area Studies; Art History, Criticism, and Conservation; Art/Art Studies, General; Arts Management; Asian History; Asian Studies/Civilization; Asian-American Studies; Australian/Oceanic/Pacific Languages, Literatures, and Linguistics; Bahasa Indonesian/Bahasa Malay Languages and Literatures; Balkans Studies; Baltic Languages, Literatures, and Linguistics; Baltic Studies; Bengali Language and Literature; Bible/Biblical Studies; Biology Teacher Education; Broadcast Journalism; Buddhist Studies; Bulgarian Language and Literature; Burmese Language and Literature; Business Teacher Education; Business/Managerial Economics; Canadian History; Canadian Studies; Caribbean Studies; Catalan Language and Literature; Celtic Languages, Literatures, and Linguistics; Central/Middle and Eastern European Studies; Ceramic Arts and Ceramics; Chemistry Teacher Education; Chinese Language and Literature; Chinese Studies; Christian Studies; Cinematography and Film/Video Production; Classics and Classical Languages, Literatures, and Linguistics, General; Clinical Psychology; Cognitive Psychology and Psycholinguistics; Commercial Photography; Commonwealth Studies; Communications Studies/Speech Communication and Rhetoric; Communications, Journalism, and Related Fields, Other; Community Psychology; Comparative Literature;

Comparative Psychology; Computer Teacher Education; Conducting; Counseling Psychology; Crafts/Craft Design, Folk Art, and Artisanry; Creative Writing; Czech Language and Literature; Dance, General; Danish Language and Literature; Design and Applied Arts, Other; Design and Visual Communications, General; others.

Related Secure Job

(See Part IV for the full job description.)

Area, Ethnic, and Cultural Studies Teachers, Postsecondary. Teach courses pertaining to the culture and development of an area (e.g., Latin America), an ethnic group, or any other group (e.g., women's studies, urban affairs).

Related Recession-Sensitive Job

None met the criteria.

Anthropology

Useful Facts About the Major

Focuses on the systematic study of human beings, their antecedents and related primates, and their cultural behavior and institutions in comparative perspective.

Related CIP Program: 45.0201 Anthropology.

Specializations in the Major: Archaeology; biological/forensic; cultural.

Typical Sequence of College Courses: English composition, general biology, statistics for business and social sciences, human growth and

development, introduction to sociology, foreign language, cultural anthropology, physical anthropology, introduction to archeology, language and culture, history of anthropological theory, research methods in anthropology, current issues in anthropology.

Typical Sequence of High School Courses: Algebra, English, foreign language, social science, history, biology, public speaking, chemistry.

Career Snapshot

Some anthropologists study the social and cultural behavior of people. They investigate communities throughout the world, focusing on their arts, religions, and economic and social institutions. A graduate degree is usually needed to do research or college teaching in this field, but some graduates with bachelor's degrees find their skills useful in business, such as in marketing research, or in historic preservation. Other anthropologists specialize in human physical characteristics and may study human remains to understand history or evolution or to provide evidence in criminal investigations. A graduate degree is usually required for this specialization.

Other Programs Related to the Same Jobs

Archeology; Humanities/Humanistic Studies; Physical Anthropology; Social Science Teacher Education.

Related Secure Jobs

(See Part IV for the full job descriptions.)

1. Anthropologists. Research, evaluate, and establish public policy concerning the origins of humans; their physical, social, linguistic, and cultural development; and their behavior, as well as the cultures, organizations, and institutions they have created.

2. Archeologists. Conduct research to reconstruct record of past human life and culture from human remains, artifacts, architectural features, and structures recovered through excavation, underwater recovery, or other means of discovery.

Related Recession-Sensitive Job

None met the criteria.

Archeology

Useful Facts About the Major

Focuses on the systematic study of extinct societies and the past of living societies via the excavation, analysis, and interpretation of their artifactual, human, and associated remains.

Related CIP Program: 45.0301 Archeology.

Specializations in the Major: Ancient civilizations; field work; prehistoric archeology; preservation.

Typical Sequence of College Courses: English composition, statistics for business and social sciences, foreign language, introduction to archeology, world prehistory, ancient literate civilizations, field methods in archeology, new world archeology, seminar (reporting on research).

Typical Sequence of High School Courses: Algebra, English, foreign language, social science, history, biology, public speaking.

Career Snapshot

Archeology (also spelled archaeology) is the study of prehistoric and historic cultures through the discovery, preservation, and interpretation of their material remains. As a major, it is sometimes offered as a specialization within anthropology or classics. Students work with languages as well as physical objects, so they develop a number of skills that are appreciated in the business world. They may also get higher degrees in archeology in order to do museum work, field work, or college teaching.

Other Programs Related to the Same Jobs

Anthropology; Classics and Classical Languages, Literatures, and Linguistics, General; Humanities/Humanistic Studies; Physical Anthropology; Social Science Teacher Education.

Related Secure Jobs

(See Part IV for the full job descriptions.)

1. Anthropologists. Research, evaluate, and establish public policy concerning the origins of humans; their physical, social, linguistic, and cultural development; and their behavior, as well as the cultures, organizations, and institutions they have created.

2. Archeologists. Conduct research to reconstruct record of past human life and culture from human remains, artifacts, architectural features, and structures recovered through excavation, underwater recovery, or other means of discovery.

Related Recession-Sensitive Job

None met the criteria.

Area Studies

Useful Facts About the Major

Focuses on the history, society, politics, culture, and economics of one or more of the peoples of a geographical region, such as Africa, the United States, Asia, the Caribbean, Latin America, the Middle East, and so forth.

Related CIP Programs: 05.0101 African Studies; 05.0102 American/United States Studies/Civilization; 05.0103 Asian Studies/Civilization; 05.0116 Balkans Studies; 05.0117 Baltic Studies; 05.0115 Canadian Studies; 05.0119 Caribbean Studies; 05.0105 Central/Middle and Eastern European Studies; 05.0123 Chinese Studies; 05.0121 Commonwealth Studies; 05.0104 East Asian Studies; 05.0106 European Studies/Civilization; 05.0124 French Studies; 05.0125 German Studies; 05.0126 Italian Studies; 05.0127 Japanese Studies; 05.0128 Korean Studies; 05.0107 Latin American Studies; 05.0108 Near and Middle Eastern Studies; 05.0109 Pacific Area/Pacific Rim Studies; 05.0129 Polish Studies; 05.0122 Regional Studies (U.S., Canadian, Foreign); 05.0110 Russian Studies; 05.0111 Scandinavian Studies; 05.0118 Slavic Studies; 05.0112 South Asian Studies; 05.0113 Southeast Asian Studies; 05.0130 Spanish and Iberian Studies; 05.0131 Tibetan Studies; 05.0132 Ukraine Studies; 05.0120 Ural-Altaic and Central Asian Studies; 05.0114 Western European Studies.

Specializations in the Major: Economics and trade; history and culture; language and literature; political science.

Typical Sequence of College Courses: English composition, foreign language, foreign literature and culture, comparative governments, introduction to economics, international economics, seminar (reporting on research).

Typical Sequence of High School Courses: English, foreign language, history, literature, social science, algebra.

Career Snapshot

Certain very popular area studies—African-American studies, American studies, and women's studies—are described elsewhere in this book. But many colleges offer other area studies majors, usually defined in terms of a region of the world: East Asian studies, European studies, Latin American studies, and so on. These are interdisciplinary majors that may involve some combination of linguistics, literature, history, sociology, political science, economic development, or other disciplines. Usually you can emphasize whichever aspects interest you most. Graduates of area studies may go into a business or government career where knowledge of a foreign culture is an advantage. Many get higher degrees to prepare for a career in law or college teaching.

Other Programs Related to the Same Jobs

African Languages, Literatures, and Linguistics; African Studies; African-American/Black Studies; Agricultural Teacher Education; Albanian Language and Literature; American History; American Indian/Native American Studies; American Literature; American Studies; Ancient Near Eastern and Biblical Languages, Literatures, and Linguistics; Ancient/Classical Greek Language and Literature; Anthropology; Arabic

Language and Literature; Archeology; Art History, Criticism, and Conservation; Art/Art Studies, General; Arts Management; Asian History; Asian Studies/Civilization; Asian-American Studies; Australian/Oceanic/Pacific Languages, Literatures, and Linguistics; Bahasa Indonesian/Bahasa Malay Languages and Literatures; Balkans Studies; Baltic Languages, Literatures, and Linguistics; Baltic Studies; Bengali Language and Literature; Bible/Biblical Studies; Biology Teacher Education; Broadcast Journalism; Buddhist Studies; Bulgarian Language and Literature; Burmese Language and Literature; Business Teacher Education; Business/Managerial Economics; Canadian History; Canadian Studies; Caribbean Studies; Catalan Language and Literature; Celtic Languages, Literatures, and Linguistics; Central/Middle and Eastern European Studies; Ceramic Arts and Ceramics; Chemistry Teacher Education; Chinese Language and Literature; Chinese Studies; Christian Studies; Cinematography and Film/Video Production; Classics and Classical Languages, Literatures, and Linguistics, General; Clinical Psychology; Cognitive Psychology and Psycholinguistics; Commercial Photography; Commonwealth Studies; Communications Studies/Speech Communication and Rhetoric; Communications, Journalism, and Related Fields, Other; Community Psychology; Comparative Literature; Comparative Psychology; Computer Teacher Education; Conducting; Counseling Psychology; Crafts/Craft Design, Folk Art, and Artisanry; Creative Writing; Czech Language and Literature; Dance, General; Danish Language and Literature; Design and Applied Arts, Other; Design and Visual Communications, General; others.

Related Secure Job

(See Part IV for the full job description.)

Area, Ethnic, and Cultural Studies Teachers, Postsecondary. Teach courses pertaining to the culture and development of an area (e.g., Latin America), an ethnic group, or any other group (e.g., women's studies, urban affairs).

Related Recession-Sensitive Job

None met the criteria.

Art History

Useful Facts About the Major

Focuses on the study of the historical development of art as social and intellectual phenomenon, the analysis of works of art, and art conservation.

Related CIP Program: 50.0703 Art History, Criticism, and Conservation.

Specializations in the Major: A historical period; a particular artistic medium; a region of the world; criticism.

Typical Sequence of College Courses: English composition, foreign language, art and culture, studio art, world history to the early modern era, world history in the modern era, art history: prehistoric to Renaissance, art history: Renaissance to modern, non-Western art, critical study of visual art.

Typical Sequence of High School Courses: English, art, foreign language, history, literature, social science.

Career Snapshot

Art has been important to humans since people painted on cave walls, and art history majors learn how art forms, techniques, and traditions have developed since then within their historical and cultural contexts. Study abroad is often part of the curriculum. Graduates of art history programs with a bachelor's degree may work for museums, auction houses, or publishers. With additional education or training, they may work as college teachers or restorers.

Other Programs Related to the Same Jobs

Art/Art Studies, General; Fine/Studio Arts, General.

Related Secure Jobs

(See Part IV for the full job descriptions.)

1. Archivists. Appraise, edit, and direct safekeeping of permanent records and historically valuable documents. Participate in research activities based on archival materials.

2. Curators. Administer affairs of museum and conduct research programs. Direct instructional, research, and public service activities of institution.

3. Museum Technicians and Conservators. Prepare specimens, such as fossils, skeletal parts, lace, and textiles, for museum collection and exhibits. May restore documents or install, arrange, and exhibit materials.

Related Recession-Sensitive Job

None met the criteria.

Business Education

Useful Facts About the Major

Prepares individuals to teach vocational business programs at various educational levels.

Related CIP Program: 13.1303 Business Teacher Education.

Specializations in the Major: Distributive education; office skills.

Typical Sequence of College Courses: Introduction to psychology, English composition, oral communication, history and philosophy of education, human growth and development, introduction to accounting, legal environment of business, introduction to business management, business math, business information processing, keyboarding, statistics, business reports and communication, introduction to marketing, methods of teaching business subjects, student teaching.

Typical Sequence of High School Courses: English, algebra, geometry, trigonometry, science, foreign language, industrial arts, keyboarding, office computer applications, public speaking.

Career Snapshot

Business educators teach secondary school students skills and knowledge they will need to succeed in the business world. Therefore, they must know about one or more specific business fields—such as bookkeeping, retailing, or office computer applications—as well as about techniques for teaching and for managing the classroom. A bachelor's degree is often an entry route to the first teaching job, but job security and pay raises often require a master's degree.

Other Programs Related to the Same Jobs

None met the criteria.

Related Secure Job

(See Part IV for the full job description.)

Secondary School Teachers, Except Special and Vocational Education. Instruct students in secondary public or private schools in one or more subjects at the secondary level, such as English, mathematics, or social studies. May be designated according to subject matter specialty, such as typing instructors, commercial teachers, or English teachers.

Related Recession-Sensitive Job

None met the criteria.

Chinese

Useful Facts About the Major

Focuses on the Chinese language and its associated dialects and literature; includes the cultural and historical contexts and applications to business, science/technology, and other settings.

Related CIP Program: 16.0301 Chinese Language and Literature.

Specializations in the Major: History and culture; language education; literature; translation.

Typical Sequence of College Courses: Chinese language, conversation, composition, linguistics, Chinese literature, East Asian literature, East Asian studies, grammar, phonetics.

Typical Sequence of High School Courses: English, public speaking, foreign language, history, literature, social science.

Career Snapshot

Because Chinese is spoken by more people than any other language, and because U.S. trade with China expands each year, there is a growing need for Americans with knowledge of the Chinese language and culture. A bachelor's degree in Chinese, perhaps with additional education in business or law, may lead to an Asia-centered career in business or government. A graduate degree is good preparation for translation or college teaching.

Other Programs Related to the Same Jobs

African Languages, Literatures, and Linguistics; Albanian Language and Literature; American Indian/Native American Languages, Literatures, and Linguistics; American Sign Language (ASL); American Sign Language, Other; Ancient Near Eastern and Biblical Languages, Literatures, and Linguistics; Ancient/Classical Greek Language and Literature; Arabic Language and Literature; Australian/Oceanic/Pacific Languages, Literatures, and Linguistics; Bahasa Indonesian/Bahasa Malay Languages and Literatures; Baltic Languages, Literatures, and Linguistics; Bengali Language and Literature; Bulgarian Language and Literature; Burmese Language and Literature; Catalan Language and Literature; Celtic Languages, Literatures, and Linguistics; Classics and Classical Languages, Literatures, and Linguistics, General; Czech Language and Literature; Danish Language and Literature; Dutch/Flemish Language and Literature; East Asian Languages, Literatures, and Linguistics, General;

East Asian Languages, Literatures, and Linguistics, Other; Education/Teaching of Individuals with Hearing Impairments, Including Deafness; Filipino/Tagalog Language and Literature; Finnish and Related Languages, Literatures, and Linguistics; Foreign Languages, Literatures, and Linguistics, Other; Foreign Languages/Modern Languages, General; French Language and Literature; German Language and Literature; Germanic Languages, Literatures, and Linguistics, General; Germanic Languages, Literatures, and Linguistics, Other; Hebrew Language and Literature; Hindi Language and Literature; Humanities/Humanistic Studies; Hungarian/Magyar Language and Literature; Iranian/Persian Languages, Literatures, and Linguistics; Italian Language and Literature; Japanese Language and Literature; Khmer/Cambodian Language and Literature; Korean Language and Literature; Language Interpretation and Translation; Lao/Laotian Language and Literature; others.

Related Secure Job

(See Part IV for the full job description.)

Interpreters and Translators. Translate or interpret written, oral, or sign language text into another language for others.

Related Recession-Sensitive Job

None met the criteria.

Chiropractic

Useful Facts About the Major

Prepares individuals for the independent professional practice of chiropractic, a health-care and healing system based on the application of non-invasive treatments and spinal adjustments to alleviate health problems caused by vertebral misalignments affecting bodily function as derived from the philosophy of Daniel Palmer.

Related CIP Program: 51.0101 Chiropractic (DC).

Specializations in the Major: Diagnostic imaging; orthopedics; sports medicine.

Typical Sequence of College Courses: English composition, introduction to psychology, college algebra, calculus, introduction to sociology, oral communication, general chemistry, general biology, introduction to computer science, organic chemistry, human anatomy and physiology, general microbiology, genetics, introduction to biochemistry, veterinary gross anatomy, spinal anatomy, histology, biomechanics, physical diagnosis, neuroanatomy, neurophysiology, radiographic anatomy, emergency care, nutrition, neuromusculoskeletal diagnosis and treatment, chiropractic manipulative therapeutics, pathology, public health, patient examination and evaluation, pharmacology, minor surgery, clinical experience in obstetrics/gynecology, clinical experience in pediatrics, clinical experience in geriatrics, mental health, ethics in health care, professional practice management.

Typical Sequence of High School Courses: English, algebra, geometry, trigonometry, biology, computer science, public speaking, chemistry, foreign language, physics, pre-calculus.

Career Snapshot

Chiropractors are health practitioners who specialize in health problems associated with the muscular, nervous, and skeletal systems, especially the spine. They learn a variety of specialized diagnostic and treatment techniques but also tend to emphasize the patient's overall health and wellness, recommending changes in diet and lifestyle that can help the body's own healing powers. The educational program includes not only theory and laboratory work, but also a lot of supervised clinical work with patients. With the aging of the population and increased acceptance of chiropractic medicine, job opportunities for graduates are expected to be good.

Other Programs Related to the Same Jobs

None met the criteria.

Related Secure Job

(See Part IV for the full job description.)

Chiropractors. Adjust spinal column and other articulations of the body to correct abnormalities of the human body believed to be caused by interference with the nervous system. Examine patients to determine nature and extent of disorders. Manipulate spines or other involved areas. May utilize supplementary measures such as exercise, rest, water, light, heat, and nutritional therapy.

Related Recession-Sensitive Job

None met the criteria.

Classics

Useful Facts About the Major

Focuses on the Greek and Latin languages and their literatures during ancient times; includes the cultural and historical contexts; dialects; and applications to business, science/technology, and other settings.

Related CIP Programs: 16.1202 Ancient/Classical Greek Language and Literature; 16.1200 Classics and Classical Languages, Literatures, and Linguistics, General; 16.1203 Latin Language and Literature.

Specializations in the Major: Archeology; classical civilization; classical linguistics; classical literature/mythology; Greek; Latin.

Typical Sequence of College Courses: Latin, Greek, grammar, linguistics, literature of the Roman Empire, literature in ancient Greek, history of the ancient world.

Typical Sequence of High School Courses: English, public speaking, foreign language, history, literature, social science.

Career Snapshot

The classical languages—Latin and Greek—may be dead, but students who study them often end up in very lively careers. The mental discipline and critical-thinking skills learned in the classics can be first-rate preparation for law school and medical school, and business recruiters report that classics graduates have an exceptional breadth of view. The demand for Latin teachers in secondary schools is strong, but teaching requires coursework (and perhaps a master's) in teaching methods. A classics major is also a good first step to graduate training in archeology, history, or theology.

Other Programs Related to the Same Jobs

African Languages, Literatures, and Linguistics; Albanian Language and Literature; American Indian/Native American Languages, Literatures, and Linguistics; American Sign Language (ASL); American Sign Language, Other; Ancient Near Eastern and Biblical Languages, Literatures, and Linguistics; Arabic Language and Literature; Australian/Oceanic/Pacific Languages, Literatures, and Linguistics; Bahasa Indonesian/ Bahasa Malay Languages and Literatures; Baltic Languages, Literatures, and Linguistics; Bengali Language and Literature; Bulgarian Language and Literature; Burmese Language and Literature; Catalan Language and Literature; Celtic Languages, Literatures, and Linguistics; Chinese Language and Literature; Classics and Classical Languages, Literatures, and Linguistics, General; Czech Language and Literature; Danish Language and Literature; Dutch/Flemish Language and Literature; East Asian Languages, Literatures, and Linguistics, General; East Asian Languages, Literatures, and Linguistics, Other; Education/Teaching of Individuals with Hearing Impairments, Including Deafness; Filipino/Tagalog Language and Literature; Finnish and Related Languages, Literatures, and Linguistics; Foreign Languages, Literatures, and Linguistics, Other; Foreign Languages/Modern Languages, General; French Language and Literature; German Language and Literature; Germanic Languages, Literatures, and Linguistics, General; Germanic Languages, Literatures, and Linguistics, Other; Hebrew Language and Literature; Hindi Language and Literature; Humanities/Humanistic Studies; Hungarian/Magyar Language and Literature; Iranian/Persian Languages, Literatures, and Linguistics; Italian Language and Literature; Japanese Language and Literature; Khmer/Cambodian Language and Literature; Korean Language and Literature; Language Interpretation and Translation; Lao/ Laotian Language and Literature; others.

Related Secure Job

(See Part IV for the full job description.)

Interpreters and Translators. Translate or interpret written, oral, or sign language text into another language for others.

Related Recession-Sensitive Job

None met the criteria.

Communications Studies/ Speech

Useful Facts About the Major

Focuses on the scientific, humanistic, and critical study of human communication in a variety of formats, media, and contexts.

Related CIP Program: 09.0101 Communication Studies/Speech Communication and Rhetoric.

Specializations in the Major: Business communications; speech/rhetoric.

Typical Sequence of College Courses: Public speaking, introduction to psychology, English composition, communications theory, introduction to mass communication, argumentation and critical thinking, interpersonal communication, rhetorical tradition and techniques.

Typical Sequence of High School Courses: English, public speaking, foreign language, applied communications, social science.

Career Snapshot

This major is sometimes offered in the same department as mass communications or theater, but it is not designed to teach a technical skill such as television production or acting. Instead, it teaches how effective communication depends on a combination of verbal and nonverbal elements. Students work in various media and learn how to strike a balance between covering the subject matter, appealing to the listener or reader, and projecting the intended image of the speaker or writer. Graduates of communication and speech programs may go on to careers in sales, public relations, law, or teaching.

Other Programs Related to the Same Jobs

Advertising; Broadcast Journalism; Business/Corporate Communications; Communications, Journalism, and Related Fields, Other; Court Reporting/Court Reporter; Creative Writing; Digital Communications and Media/Multimedia; English Composition; Family and Consumer Sciences/Human Sciences Communications; Health Communications; Humanities/Humanistic Studies; Journalism; Journalism, Other; Mass Communications/Media Studies; Playwriting and Screenwriting; Political Communications; Public Relations/Image Management; Radio and Television; Technical and Business Writing.

Related Secure Jobs

(See Part IV for the full job descriptions.)

1. Court Reporters. Use verbatim methods and equipment to capture, store, retrieve, and transcribe pretrial and trial proceedings or other information. Includes stenocaptioners who operate computerized stenographic captioning equipment to provide captions of live or prerecorded broadcasts for hearing-impaired viewers.

2. Public Address System and Other Announcers. Make announcements over loudspeaker at sporting or other public events. May act as master of ceremonies or disc jockey at weddings, parties, clubs, or other gathering places.

3. Public Relations Specialists. Engage in promoting or creating good will for individuals, groups, or organizations by writing or selecting favorable publicity material and releasing it through various communications media. May prepare and arrange displays and make speeches.

Related Recession-Sensitive Jobs

Copy Writers; Poets, Lyricists, and Creative Writers; Technical Writers; Writers and Authors.

Criminal Justice/Law Enforcement

Useful Facts About the Major

Prepares individuals to perform the duties of police and public security officers, including patrol and investigative activities, traffic control, crowd control and public relations, witness interviewing, evidence collection and management, basic crime prevention methods, weapon and equipment operation and maintenance, report preparation, and other routine law enforcement responsibilities.

Related CIP Program: 43.0107 Criminal Justice/Police Science.

Specializations in the Major: Business security; homeland security; police administration; police work.

Typical Sequence of College Courses: Technical writing, introduction to criminal justice, introduction to psychology, American government, criminal law, criminal investigation, introduction to sociology, police organization and administration, criminal procedures, police-community relations, ethics, diversity and conflict, seminar (reporting on research).

Typical Sequence of High School Courses: Algebra, English, foreign language, social science, history, public speaking, computer science.

Career Snapshot

We live in a society that is governed by laws at the municipal, state, and federal levels. These laws are enforced by people who understand the laws themselves; the workings of the agencies that are empowered to enforce them; and the techniques for detecting violation of the laws, arresting violators, and processing them through the court system. Public concern about crime has created many job opportunities in this field, especially at the local level. Police officers need to be trained at a police academy; a degree in law enforcement can be good preparation and usually merits higher pay. Admission usually requires meeting physical and psychological requirements.

Other Programs Related to the Same Jobs

Corrections; Corrections Administration; Corrections and Criminal Justice, Other; Criminal Justice/Law Enforcement Administration; Criminal Justice/Safety Studies; Criminalistics and Criminal Science; Forensic Science and Technology; Juvenile Corrections; Security and Loss Prevention Services.

Related Secure Jobs

(See Part IV for the full job descriptions.)

1. Bailiffs. Maintain order in courts of law.

2. Criminal Investigators and Special Agents. Investigate alleged or suspected criminal violations of federal, state, or local laws to determine if evidence is sufficient to recommend prosecution.

3. Immigration and Customs Inspectors. Investigate and inspect persons, common carriers, goods, and merchandise arriving in or departing from the United States or moving between states to detect violations of immigration and customs laws and regulations.

4. Police Detectives. Conduct investigations to prevent crimes or solve criminal cases.

5. Police Identification and Records Officers. Collect evidence at crime scene, classify and identify fingerprints, and photograph evidence for use in criminal and civil cases.

6. Police Patrol Officers. Patrol assigned areas to enforce laws and ordinances, regulate traffic, control crowds, prevent crime, and arrest violators.

7. Private Detectives and Investigators. Detect occurrences of unlawful acts or infractions of rules in private establishment or seek, examine, and compile information for client.

8. Sheriffs and Deputy Sheriffs. Enforce law and order in rural or unincorporated districts or serve legal processes of courts. May patrol courthouse, guard court or grand jury, or escort defendants.

Related Recession-Sensitive Job

None met the criteria.

Early Childhood Education

Useful Facts About the Major

Prepares individuals to teach students in formal settings prior to beginning regular elementary school, usually ranging in age from three to six years (or grade one), depending on the school system or state regulations; includes preparation to teach all relevant subject matter.

Related CIP Programs: 13.1210 Early Childhood Education and Teaching; 13.1209 Kindergarten/Preschool Education and Teaching.

Specializations in the Major: Art education; bilingual education; music education; reading readiness.

Typical Sequence of College Courses: Introduction to psychology, English composition, oral communication, history and philosophy of education, human growth and development, teaching methods, educational alternatives for exceptional students, educational psychology, reading assessment and teaching, mathematics education, art education, music education, physical education,

health education, science education, children's literature, student teaching.

Typical Sequence of High School Courses: English, algebra, geometry, trigonometry, science, foreign language, public speaking.

Career Snapshot

Because very young children do not think exactly the same way as we do, an important part of an early childhood education major is learning effective educational techniques for this age group. As in any other teaching major, a bachelor's degree is the minimum requirement for employment, and a master's degree is often needed for job security and a pay raise. Although enrollments of very young students are expected to decline for some time, jobs will open to replace teachers who are retiring. Best opportunities are expected in high-growth regions of the country and in inner-city and rural schools.

Other Programs Related to the Same Jobs

Child Care and Support Services Management.

Related Secure Jobs

(See Part IV for the full job descriptions.)

1. Kindergarten Teachers, Except Special Education. Teach elemental natural and social science, personal hygiene, music, art, and literature to children from 4 to 6 years old. Promote physical, mental, and social development. May be required to hold state certification.

2. Preschool Teachers, Except Special Education. Instruct children (normally up to 5 years of age) in activities designed to promote social, physical, and intellectual growth needed for primary school in preschool, day care center, or other child development facility. May be required to hold state certification.

3. Teachers and Instructors, All Other. All teachers and instructors not listed separately.

Related Recession-Sensitive Job

None met the criteria.

English

Useful Facts About the Major

Focuses on the English language, including its history, structure, and related communications skills and the literature and culture of English-speaking peoples.

Related CIP Program: 23.0101 English Language and Literature, General.

Specializations in the Major: Creative writing; English education; language; literature.

Typical Sequence of College Courses: English composition, introduction to literary study, foreign language, survey of British literature, survey of American literature, a major writer (e.g., Shakespeare, Romantic poets), a genre (e.g., drama, short story, poetry), creative writing, history of the English language, comparative literature.

Typical Sequence of High School Courses: English, foreign language, literature, history, public speaking, social science.

Career Snapshot

English majors not only learn about a great literary tradition, but they also develop first-rate writing and critical-thinking skills that can be valuable in a variety of careers. Besides teaching, many of them go into business, law, and library science, usually with an appropriate master's or law degree. They are said to make excellent trainees in computer programming. In a wide range of careers, their humanistic skills often allow them to advance higher than those who prepare through more specifically career-oriented curricula.

Other Programs Related to the Same Jobs

American Literature (Canadian); American Literature (United States); Comparative Literature; Creative Writing; English Composition; English Language and Literature/Letters, Other; English Literature (British and Commonwealth); Humanities/Humanistic Studies; Technical and Business Writing.

Related Secure Job

(See Part IV for the full job description.)

Editors. Perform variety of editorial duties, such as laying out, indexing, and revising content of written materials, in preparation for final publication.

Related Recession-Sensitive Jobs

Copy Writers; Poets, Lyricists, and Creative Writers; Reporters and Correspondents; Writers and Authors.

Environmental Science

Useful Facts About the Major

Focuses on the application of biological, chemical, and physical principles to the study of the physical environment and the solution of environmental problems, including subjects such as abating or controlling environmental pollution and degradation, the interaction between human society and the natural environment, and natural resources management.

Related CIP Programs: 03.0104 Environmental Science; 03.0103 Environmental Studies.

Specializations in the Major: Environmental education; environmental policy; environmental technology; land resources; natural history.

Typical Sequence of College Courses: English composition, college algebra, general biology, general chemistry, organic chemistry, oral communication, statistics, introduction to computer science, introduction to geology, ecology, introduction to environmental science, natural resource management and water quality, microbiology, introduction to economics, introduction to ground water/hydrology, regional planning and environmental protection, environmental impact assessment, environmental economics, environmental law, environmental chemistry.

Typical Sequence of High School Courses: Biology, chemistry, algebra, geometry, trigonometry, computer science, English, public speaking, geography.

Career Snapshot

Environmental science (or studies) is a multidisciplinary subject that involves a number of sciences, such as biology, geology, and chemistry, as well as social sciences, such as economics and geography. It also touches on urban/regional planning and on law and public policy. With a bachelor's degree, you may work for an environmental consulting business or a government planning agency, or you may go on to get a graduate or professional degree in one of these related fields.

Other Programs Related to the Same Jobs

Environmental Studies; Environmental Science; Physical Science Technologies/Technicians, Other; Science Teacher Education/General Science Teacher Education; Science Technologies/Technicians, Other.

Related Secure Job

(See Part IV for the full job description.)

Environmental Scientists and Specialists, Including Health. Conduct research or perform investigation for the purpose of identifying, abating, or eliminating sources of pollutants or hazards that affect either the environment or the health of the population. Using knowledge of various scientific disciplines, may collect, synthesize, study, report, and take action based on data derived from measurements or observations of air, food, soil, water, and other sources.

Related Recession-Sensitive Job

Environmental Science and Protection Technicians, Including Health.

Family and Consumer Sciences

Useful Facts About the Major

Focuses on how individuals develop and function in family, work, and community settings and how they relate to their physical, social, emotional, and intellectual environments.

Related CIP Programs: 19.0201 Business Family and Consumer Sciences/Human Sciences; 19.0402 Consumer Economics; 19.0203 Consumer Merchandising/Retailing Management; 19.0403 Consumer Services and Advocacy; 13.1308 Family and Consumer Sciences/Home Economics Teacher Education; 19.0202 Family and Consumer Sciences/Human Sciences Communication; 19.0101 Family and Consumer Sciences/Human Sciences, General; 19.0401 Family Resource Management Studies, General.

Specializations in the Major: Child care and family life; clothing and textiles; consumer merchandising; consumer services and advocacy; family financial management; foods and nutrition; human sciences communication.

Typical Sequence of College Courses: Introduction to psychology, English composition, oral communication, history and philosophy of education, human growth and development, foods, textiles, introduction to nutrition, introduction to interior design, marriage and the family, consumer economics, housing, clothing and fashion, student teaching.

Typical Sequence of High School Courses: English, algebra, geometry, trigonometry, science, foreign language, home economics, public speaking.

Career Snapshot

Family and consumer sciences, which used to be called home economics, is a combination of several concerns related to families and their economic needs and behaviors. Some programs are designed to prepare home economics educators and therefore include courses on teaching strategies and classroom management, plus student teaching. Some graduates work in industries that market to families. Some become financial advisors. Others pursue a higher degree with the goal of working for the federal government as a cooperative extension agent.

Other Programs Related to the Same Jobs

Adult Development and Aging; Agricultural and Extension Education Services; Animal Nutrition; Animal/Livestock Husbandry and Production; Apparel and Textiles, General; Child Care and Support Services Management; Child Development; Consumer Economics; Consumer Merchandising/Retailing Management; Consumer Services and Advocacy; Crop Production; Family and Community Services; Family and Consumer Economics and Related Services, Other; Family and Consumer Sciences/Human Sciences, General; Family and Consumer Sciences/Human Sciences, Other; Family Resource Management Studies, General; Family Systems; Farm/Farm and Ranch Management; Foodservice Systems Administration/Management; Home Furnishings and Equipment Installers; Housing and Human Environments, General; Housing and Human Environments, Other; Human Development and Family Studies, General; Human Development, Family Studies, and Related Services, Other.

Related Secure Jobs

(See Part IV for the full job descriptions.)

1. Editors. Perform variety of editorial duties, such as laying out, indexing, and revising content of written materials, in preparation for final publication.

2. Middle School Teachers, Except Special and Vocational Education. Teach students in public or private schools in one or more subjects at the middle, intermediate, or junior high level, which falls between elementary and senior high school as defined by applicable state laws and regulations.

3. Public Relations Specialists. Engage in promoting or creating good will for individuals, groups, or organizations by writing or selecting favorable publicity material and releasing it through various communications media. May prepare and arrange displays and make speeches.

4. Secondary School Teachers, Except Special and Vocational Education. Instruct students in secondary public or private schools in one or more subjects at the secondary level, such as English, mathematics, or social studies. May be designated according to subject matter specialty, such as typing instructors, commercial teachers, or English teachers.

Related Recession-Sensitive Jobs

Copy Writers; Farm and Home Management Advisors; First-Line Supervisors/Managers of Retail Sales Workers; Marketing Managers; Poets, Lyricists, and Creative Writers; Sales Managers; Writers and Authors.

French

Useful Facts About the Major

Focuses on the French language and related dialects and creoles; includes the cultural and historical contexts and applications to business, science/technology, and other settings.

Related CIP Program: 16.0901 French Language and Literature.

Specializations in the Major: History and culture; language education; literature; translation.

Typical Sequence of College Courses: French language, conversation, composition, linguistics, French literature, French history and civilization, European history and civilization, grammar, phonetics.

Typical Sequence of High School Courses: English, public speaking, French, history, literature, social science.

Career Snapshot

French is a native tongue on several continents and in parts of the United States, and it has a rich cultural heritage associated with the arts and literature. French majors may go into careers in international business, travel, or teaching. Teaching at the secondary level requires education courses and, in many districts, a master's; college teaching requires a graduate degree.

Other Programs Related to the Same Jobs

African Languages, Literatures, and Linguistics; Albanian Language and Literature; American Indian/Native American Languages, Literatures, and Linguistics; American Sign Language (ASL); American Sign Language, Other; Ancient Near Eastern and Biblical Languages, Literatures, and Linguistics; Ancient/Classical Greek Language and Literature; Arabic Language and Literature; Australian/Oceanic/Pacific Languages, Literatures, and Linguistics; Bahasa Indonesian/Bahasa Malay Languages and Literatures; Baltic Languages, Literatures, and Linguistics; Bengali Language and Literature; Bulgarian Language and Literature; Burmese Language and Literature; Catalan Language and Literature; Celtic Languages, Literatures, and Linguistics; Chinese Language and Literature; Classics and Classical Languages, Literatures, and Linguistics, General; Czech Language and Literature; Danish Language and Literature; Dutch/Flemish Language and Literature; East Asian Languages, Literatures, and Linguistics, General; East Asian Languages, Literatures, and Linguistics, Other; Education/Teaching of Individuals with Hearing Impairments, Including Deafness; Filipino/Tagalog Language and Literature; Finnish and Related Languages, Literatures, and Linguistics; Foreign Languages, Literatures, and Linguistics, Other; Foreign Languages/Modern Languages, General; German Language and Literature; Germanic Languages, Literatures, and Linguistics, General; Germanic Languages, Literatures, and Linguistics, Other; Hebrew Language and Literature; Hindi Language and Literature; Humanities/Humanistic Studies; Hungarian/Magyar Language and Literature; Iranian/Persian Languages, Literatures, and Linguistics; Italian Language and Literature; Japanese Language and Literature; Khmer/Cambodian Language and Literature; Korean Language and Literature; Language Interpretation and Translation; Lao/Laotian Language and Literature; others.

Related Secure Job

(See Part IV for the full job description.)

Interpreters and Translators. Translate or interpret written, oral, or sign language text into another language for others.

Related Recession-Sensitive Job

None met the criteria.

Geology

Useful Facts About the Major

Focuses on the scientific study of the Earth; the forces acting upon it; and the behavior of the solids, liquids, and gases comprising it.

Related CIP Program: 40.0601 Geology/Earth Science, General.

Specializations in the Major: Engineering geology; geophysics; mineralogy; oceanography; paleontology; petroleum geology; stratigraphy; volcanology.

Typical Sequence of College Courses: English composition, calculus, introduction to computer science, general chemistry, general physics, introduction to geology, invertebrate paleontology, summer field geology, structural geology, mineralogy, optical mineralogy, igneous and metamorphic petrology, sedimentary petrology, stratigraphy.

Typical Sequence of High School Courses: English, algebra, geometry, trigonometry, chemistry, physics, pre-calculus, computer science, calculus.

Career Snapshot

Geology is the study of the physical makeup, processes, and history of the Earth. Geologists use knowledge of this field to locate water, mineral, and petroleum resources; to protect the environment; and to offer advice on construction and land-use projects. A bachelor's degree opens the door for many entry-level jobs, but a master's degree helps for advancement and is thought to be the degree that now leads to the best opportunities. Many research jobs in universities and the government require a Ph.D. Some field research requires going to remote places, but it is also possible to specialize in laboratory sciences.

Other Programs Related to the Same Jobs

Geochemistry; Geochemistry and Petrology; Geological and Earth Sciences/Geosciences, Other; Geophysics and Seismology; Oceanography; Oceanography, Chemical and Physical; Paleontology.

Related Secure Jobs

(See Part IV for the full job descriptions.)

1. Geoscientists, Except Hydrologists and Geographers. Study the composition, structure, and other physical aspects of the Earth. May use knowledge of geology, physics, and mathematics in exploration for oil, gas, minerals, or underground water or in waste disposal, land reclamation, or other environmental problems. May study the Earth's internal composition, atmospheres, and oceans and its magnetic, electrical, and gravitational forces. Includes mineralogists, crystallographers, paleontologists, stratigraphers, geodesists, and seismologists.

2. Hydrologists. Research the distribution, circulation, and physical properties of underground and surface waters; study the form and intensity of precipitation, its rate of infiltration into the soil, its movement through the earth, and its return to the ocean and atmosphere.

Related Recession-Sensitive Job

Natural Sciences Managers.

Geophysics

Useful Facts About the Major

Focuses on the scientific study of the physics of solids and its application to the study of the Earth and other planets.

Related CIP Program: 40.0603 Geophysics and Seismology.

Specializations in the Major: Atmospheric physics; environmental geophysics; geomagnetism; paleomagnetism; physical oceanography; remote sensing; seismology; volcanology.

Typical Sequence of College Courses: English composition, calculus, introduction to computer science, general chemistry, general physics, introduction to geology, summer field geology, structural geology, mineralogy, remote sensing, exploration geophysics, physical oceanography, stratigraphy, igneous and metamorphic petrology.

Typical Sequence of High School Courses: English, algebra, geometry, trigonometry, chemistry, physics, pre-calculus, computer science, calculus.

G

Career Snapshot

Geophysics uses physical measurements and mathematical models to describe the structure, composition, and processes of the Earth and planets. Geophysicists study seismic waves and variations in gravitation and terrestrial magnetism, thus learning where petroleum and minerals are deposited, where (and sometimes even when) earthquakes and volcanic eruptions are likely to strike, and how to solve environmental problems such as pollution. A bachelor's degree can lead to entry-level jobs, but a higher degree opens greater potential for advancement in research, as well as opportunities in college teaching.

Other Programs Related to the Same Jobs

Geochemistry; Geochemistry and Petrology; Geological and Earth Sciences/Geosciences, Other; Geology/Earth Science, General; Oceanography; Oceanography, Chemical and Physical; Paleontology.

Related Secure Job

(See Part IV for the full job description.)

Geoscientists, Except Hydrologists and Geographers. Study the composition, structure, and other physical aspects of the Earth. May use knowledge of geology, physics, and mathematics in exploration for oil, gas, minerals, or underground water or in waste disposal, land reclamation, or other environmental problems. May study the Earth's internal composition, atmospheres, and oceans and its magnetic, electrical, and gravitational forces. Includes mineralogists, crystallographers, paleontologists, stratigraphers, geodesists, and seismologists.

Related Recession-Sensitive Job

Natural Sciences Managers.

German

Useful Facts About the Major

Focuses on the German language and related dialects as used in Austria, Germany, Switzerland, neighboring European countries containing German-speaking minorities, and elsewhere; includes the cultural and historical contexts and applications to business, science/technology, and other settings.

Related CIP Program: 16.0501 German Language and Literature.

Specializations in the Major: History and culture; language education; literature; translation.

Typical Sequence of College Courses: German language, conversation, composition, linguistics, German literature, German history and civilization, European history and civilization, grammar, phonetics.

Typical Sequence of High School Courses: English, public speaking, German, history, literature, social science.

Career Snapshot

Since its reunification, Germany has become a major economic and cultural force in Europe and the world. A degree in German can open many doors in international business, travel, and law. Many employers are looking for graduates with an understanding of a second language and culture. Those with a graduate degree in German may go into translation or college teaching. With coursework in education, high school teaching is an option; many districts require a master's.

Other Programs Related to the Same Jobs

African Languages, Literatures, and Linguistics; Albanian Language and Literature; American Indian/Native American Languages, Literatures, and Linguistics; American Sign Language (ASL); American Sign Language, Other; Ancient Near Eastern and Biblical Languages, Literatures, and Linguistics; Ancient/Classical Greek Language and Literature; Arabic Language and Literature; Australian/Oceanic/Pacific Languages, Literatures, and Linguistics; Bahasa Indonesian/Bahasa Malay Languages and Literatures; Baltic Languages, Literatures, and Linguistics; Bengali Language and Literature; Bulgarian Language and Literature; Burmese Language and Literature; Catalan Language and Literature; Celtic Languages, Literatures, and Linguistics; Chinese Language and Literature; Classics and Classical Languages, Literatures, and Linguistics, General; Czech Language and Literature; Danish Language and Literature; Dutch/Flemish Language and Literature; East Asian Languages, Literatures, and Linguistics, General; East Asian Languages, Literatures, and Linguistics, Other; Education/Teaching of Individuals with Hearing Impairments, Including Deafness; Filipino/Tagalog Language and Literature; Finnish and Related Languages, Literatures, and Linguistics; Foreign Languages, Literatures, and Linguistics, Other; Foreign Languages/Modern Languages, General; French Language and Literature; Germanic Languages, Literatures, and Linguistics, General; Germanic Languages, Literatures, and Linguistics, Other; Hebrew Language and Literature; Hindi Language and Literature; Humanities/Humanistic Studies; Hungarian/Magyar Language and Literature; Iranian/Persian Languages, Literatures, and Linguistics; Italian Language and Literature; Japanese Language and Literature; Khmer/Cambodian Language and Literature; Korean Language and Literature; Language Interpretation and Translation; Lao/Laotian Language and Literature; others.

Related Secure Job

(See Part IV for the full job description.)

Interpreters and Translators. Translate or interpret written, oral, or sign language text into another language for others.

Related Recession-Sensitive Job

None met the criteria.

Graduate Study for College Teaching

Useful Facts About the Major

Focuses on an academic subject at an advanced level to prepare students to teach courses in a postsecondary institution such as a college, university, professional school, or adult school.

Related CIP Programs: No data available; a large number of CIP programs may be studied at the graduate level.

Specializations in the Major: Any of the subjects that are taught in postsecondary institutions: agricultural sciences; anthropology and

G

archeology; architecture; area, ethnic, and cultural studies; art, drama, and music; atmospheric, earth, marine, and space sciences; biological science; business; chemistry; communications; computer science; criminal justice and law enforcement; economics; education; engineering; English language and literature; environmental science; foreign language and literature; forestry and conservation science; geography; health specialties; history; home economics; law; library science; mathematical science; nursing; philosophy and religion; physics; political science; psychology; recreation and fitness studies; social sciences; social work; sociology; vocational education; others.

Typical Sequence of College Courses: Courses appropriate for a bachelor's program in an undergraduate major, followed by graduate courses in a related major, including seminars (where research is presented to the class) and research methods, concluding with an original research project and a dissertation describing it.

Typical Sequence of High School Courses: Biology, chemistry, algebra, geometry, trigonometry, computer science, English, public speaking. Also advanced courses in science, social science, or humanities.

Career Snapshot

Focuses on an academic subject at an advanced level to prepare students to teach courses in a postsecondary institution such as a college, university, professional school, or adult school.

Other Programs Related to the Same Jobs

None met the criteria.

Related Secure Jobs

(See Part IV for the full job descriptions.)

1. Agricultural Sciences Teachers, Postsecondary. Teach courses in the agricultural sciences, including agronomy, dairy sciences, fisheries management, horticultural sciences, poultry sciences, range management, and agricultural soil conservation.

2. Anthropology and Archeology Teachers, Postsecondary. Teach courses in anthropology or archeology.

3. Architecture Teachers, Postsecondary. Teach courses in architecture and architectural design, such as architectural environmental design, interior architecture/design, and landscape architecture.

4. Area, Ethnic, and Cultural Studies Teachers, Postsecondary. Teach courses pertaining to the culture and development of an area (e.g., Latin America), an ethnic group, or any other group (e.g., women's studies, urban affairs).

5. Art, Drama, and Music Teachers, Postsecondary. Teach courses in drama, music, and the arts, including fine and applied art, such as painting and sculpture or design and crafts.

6. Atmospheric, Earth, Marine, and Space Sciences Teachers, Postsecondary. Teach courses in the physical sciences, except chemistry and physics.

7. Biological Science Teachers, Postsecondary. Teach courses in biological sciences.

8. Business Teachers, Postsecondary. Teach courses in business administration and management, such as accounting, finance, human resources, labor relations, marketing, and operations research.

9. Chemistry Teachers, Postsecondary. Teach courses pertaining to the chemical and physical properties and compositional changes of substances. Work may include instruction in the methods of qualitative and quantitative chemical analysis. Includes both teachers primarily engaged in teaching and those who do a combination of both teaching and research.

10. Communications Teachers, Postsecondary. Teach courses in communications, such as organizational communications, public relations, radio/television broadcasting, and journalism.

11. Computer Science Teachers, Postsecondary. Teach courses in computer science. May specialize in a field of computer science, such as the design and function of computers or operations and research analysis.

12. Criminal Justice and Law Enforcement Teachers, Postsecondary. Teach courses in criminal justice, corrections, and law enforcement administration.

13. Economics Teachers, Postsecondary. Teach courses in economics.

14. Education Teachers, Postsecondary. Teach courses pertaining to education, such as counseling, curriculum, guidance, instruction, teacher education, and teaching English as a second language.

15. Engineering Teachers, Postsecondary. Teach courses pertaining to the application of physical laws and principles of engineering for the development of machines, materials, instruments, processes, and services. Includes teachers of subjects such as chemical, civil, electrical, industrial, mechanical, mineral, and petroleum engineering. Includes both teachers primarily engaged in teaching and those who do a combination of both teaching and research.

16. English Language and Literature Teachers, Postsecondary. Teach courses in English language and literature, including linguistics and comparative literature.

17. Environmental Science Teachers, Postsecondary. Teach courses in environmental science.

18. Foreign Language and Literature Teachers, Postsecondary. Teach courses in foreign (i.e., other than English) languages and literature.

19. Forestry and Conservation Science Teachers, Postsecondary. Teach courses in environmental and conservation science.

20. Geography Teachers, Postsecondary. Teach courses in geography.

21. Graduate Teaching Assistants. Assist department chairperson, faculty members, or other professional staff members in college or university by performing teaching or teaching-related duties, such as teaching lower-level courses, developing teaching materials, preparing and giving examinations, and grading examinations or papers. Graduate assistants must be enrolled in a graduate school program. Graduate assistants who primarily perform non-teaching duties, such as laboratory research, should be reported in the occupational category related to the work performed.

22. Health Specialties Teachers, Postsecondary. Teach courses in health specialties, such as veterinary medicine, dentistry, pharmacy, therapy, laboratory technology, and public health.

23. History Teachers, Postsecondary. Teach courses in human history and historiography.

24. Home Economics Teachers, Postsecondary. Teach courses in child care, family relations, finance, nutrition, and related subjects as pertaining to home management.

25. Law Teachers, Postsecondary. Teach courses in law.

26. Library Science Teachers, Postsecondary. Teach courses in library science.

27. Mathematical Science Teachers, Postsecondary. Teach courses pertaining to mathematical concepts, statistics, and actuarial science and to the application of original and standardized mathematical techniques in solving specific problems and situations.

28. Nursing Instructors and Teachers, Postsecondary. Demonstrate and teach patient care in classroom and clinical units to nursing students. Includes both teachers primarily engaged in teaching and those who do a combination of both teaching and research.

29. Philosophy and Religion Teachers, Postsecondary. Teach courses in philosophy, religion, and theology.

30. Physics Teachers, Postsecondary. Teach courses pertaining to the laws of matter and energy. Includes both teachers primarily engaged in teaching and those who do a combination of both teaching and research.

31. Political Science Teachers, Postsecondary. Teach courses in political science, international affairs, and international relations.

32. Psychology Teachers, Postsecondary. Teach courses in psychology, such as child, clinical, and developmental psychology and psychological counseling.

33. Recreation and Fitness Studies Teachers, Postsecondary. Teach courses pertaining to recreation, leisure, and fitness studies, including exercise physiology and facilities management.

34. Social Work Teachers, Postsecondary. Teach courses in social work.

35. Sociology Teachers, Postsecondary. Teach courses in sociology.

36. Vocational Education Teachers, Postsecondary. Teach or instruct vocational or occupational subjects at the postsecondary level (but at less than the baccalaureate) to students who have graduated or left high school. Includes correspondence school instructors; industrial, commercial, and government training instructors; and adult education teachers and instructors who prepare persons to operate industrial machinery and equipment and transportation and communications equipment. Teaching may take place in public or private schools whose primary business is education or in a school associated with an organization whose primary business is other than education.

37. Postsecondary Teachers, All Other. All postsecondary teachers not listed separately.

Related Recession-Sensitive Job

None met the criteria.

Health Information Systems Administration

Useful Facts About the Major

Prepares individuals to plan, design, and manage systems, processes, and facilities used to collect, store, secure, retrieve, analyze, and transmit medical records and other health information used by clinical professionals and health-care organizations.

Related CIP Program: 51.0706 Health Information/Medical Records Administration/Administrator.

Specializations in the Major: Information technology; management.

Typical Sequence of College Courses: English composition, introduction to computer science, college algebra, oral communication, introduction to psychology, accounting, introduction to business management, statistics for business and social sciences, epidemiology, introduction to medical terminology, financial management of health care, human resource management in health care facilities, legal aspects of health care, American health-care systems, introduction to health records, health data and analysis, clinical classification systems, fundamentals of medical science, health data research, seminar (reporting on research).

Typical Sequence of High School Courses: Algebra, English, geometry, trigonometry, pre-calculus, biology, chemistry, computer science, office computer applications, public speaking, foreign language, social science.

Career Snapshot

Health information systems are needed for much more than billing patients or their HMOs. Many medical discoveries have been made when researchers have examined large collections of health information. Therefore, health information systems administrators must know about the health-care system, about various kinds of diseases and vital statistics, about the latest database technologies, and about how researchers compile data to test hypotheses. Some people enter this field with a bachelor's degree, whereas others get a bachelor's degree in another field (perhaps related to health, information systems,

or management) and complete a post-graduate certification program.

Other Programs Related to the Same Jobs

Community Health and Preventive Medicine; Health and Medical Administrative Services, Other; Health Services Administration; Health Unit Manager/Ward Supervisor; Health/Health Care Administration/Management; Hospital and Health Care Facilities Administration/Management; Nursing Administration (MSN, MS, PhD); Public Health, General (MPH, DPH).

Related Secure Job

(See Part IV for the full job description.)

Medical and Health Services Managers. Plan, direct, or coordinate medicine and health services in hospitals, clinics, managed care organizations, public health agencies, or similar organizations.

Related Recession-Sensitive Job

None met the criteria.

Hospital/Health Facilities Administration

Useful Facts About the Major

Prepares individuals to apply managerial principles to the administration of hospitals, clinics, nursing homes, and other health-care facilities.

Related CIP Program: 51.0702 Hospital and Health-Care Facilities Administration/ Management.

Specializations in the Major: Health policy; hospital management; long-term care management.

Typical Sequence of College Courses: English composition, introduction to economics, college algebra, oral communication, introduction to psychology, accounting, introduction to business management, statistics for business and social sciences, American health-care systems, introduction to medical terminology, introduction to management information systems, financial management of health care, human resource management in health-care facilities, strategy and planning for health care, legal aspects of health care, health care and politics.

Typical Sequence of High School Courses: Algebra, English, geometry, trigonometry, pre-calculus, biology, chemistry, computer science, office computer applications, public speaking, social science, foreign language.

Career Snapshot

Hospital and health facilities administrators need to combine standard business management skills with an understanding of the American health-care system and its current issues and trends. They may be generalists who manage an entire facility, or they may specialize in running a department or some specific service of the facility. Generalists are usually expected to have a master's degree, especially in large facilities, whereas specialists or those seeking employment in small facilities may enter with a bachelor's degree. Best employment prospects are in home health agencies and practitioners' offices and clinics and for those who have experience in a specialized field, such as reimbursement.

Other Programs Related to the Same Jobs

Community Health and Preventive Medicine; Health and Medical Administrative Services, Other; Health Information/Medical Records Administration/Administrator; Health Services Administration; Health Unit Manager/ Ward Supervisor; Health/Health Care Administration/Management; Nursing Administration (MSN, MS, PhD); Public Health, General (MPH, DPH).

Related Secure Job

(See Part IV for the full job description.)

Medical and Health Services Managers. Plan, direct, or coordinate medicine and health services in hospitals, clinics, managed care organizations, public health agencies, or similar organizations.

Related Recession-Sensitive Job

None met the criteria.

Humanities

Useful Facts About the Major

Focuses on combined studies and research in the humanities subjects as distinguished from the social and physical sciences, emphasizing languages, literatures, art, music, philosophy, and religion.

Related CIP Program: 24.0103 Humanities/Humanistic Studies.

Specializations in the Major: History; language; literature; peace and justice studies; philosophy; religion; the arts.

Typical Sequence of College Courses: Foreign language, major thinkers and issues in philosophy, literature, art and culture, European history and civilization, writing, seminar (reporting on research).

Typical Sequence of High School Courses: English, algebra, foreign language, history, literature, public speaking, social science.

Career Snapshot

Humanities (sometimes called liberal arts) is an interdisciplinary major that covers a wide range of the arts and other non-scientific modes of thought, such as history, philosophy, religious studies, and language. Graduates of this major usually have strong skills for communicating and critical thinking, and they often advance further in the business world than those who hold more business-focused degrees. Some pursue careers in teaching, media, or the arts. Others get professional degrees in the law or medicine.

Other Programs Related to the Same Jobs

African Languages, Literatures, and Linguistics; African Studies; African-American/Black Studies; Agricultural Teacher Education; Albanian Language and Literature; American History; American Indian/Native American Studies; American Literature; American Studies; Ancient Near Eastern and Biblical Languages, Literatures, and Linguistics; Ancient/Classical Greek Language and Literature; Anthropology; Arabic Language and Literature; Archeology; Area Studies; Art History, Criticism, and Conservation; Art/Art Studies, General; Arts Management; Asian History; Asian Studies/Civilization; Asian-American Studies; Australian/Oceanic/Pacific Languages, Literatures, and Linguistics; Bahasa Indonesian/Bahasa Malay Languages and Literatures; Balkans Studies; Baltic Languages, Literatures, and Linguistics; Baltic Studies; Bengali Language and Literature; Bible/Biblical Studies; Biology Teacher Education; Broadcast Journalism; Buddhist Studies; Bulgarian Language and Literature; Burmese Language and Literature; Business Teacher Education; Business/Managerial Economics; Canadian History; Canadian Studies; Caribbean Studies; Catalan Language and Literature; Celtic Languages, Literatures, and Linguistics; Central/Middle and Eastern European Studies; Ceramic Arts and Ceramics; Chemistry Teacher Education; Chinese Language and Literature; Chinese Studies; Christian Studies; Cinematography and Film/Video Production; Classics and Classical Languages, Literatures, and Linguistics, General; Clinical Psychology; Cognitive Psychology and Psycholinguistics; Commercial Photography; Commonwealth Studies; Communications Studies/Speech Communication and Rhetoric; Communications, Journalism, and Related Fields, Other; Community Psychology; Comparative Literature; Comparative Psychology; Computer Teacher Education; Conducting; Counseling Psychology; Crafts/Craft Design, Folk Art, and Artisanry; Creative Writing; Czech Language and Literature; Dance, General; Danish Language and Literature; Design and Applied Arts, Other; Design and Visual Communications, General; others.

Related Secure Jobs

(See Part IV for the full job descriptions.)

1. Anthropology and Archeology Teachers, Postsecondary. Teach courses in anthropology or archeology.

2. Area, Ethnic, and Cultural Studies Teachers, Postsecondary. Teach courses pertaining to the culture and development of an area (e.g., Latin America), an ethnic group, or any other group (e.g., women's studies, urban affairs).

3. Art, Drama, and Music Teachers, Postsecondary. Teach courses in drama, music, and the arts, including fine and applied art, such as painting and sculpture or design and crafts.

4. Communications Teachers, Postsecondary. Teach courses in communications, such as organizational communications, public relations, radio/television broadcasting, and journalism.

5. Economics Teachers, Postsecondary. Teach courses in economics.

6. Education Teachers, Postsecondary. Teach courses pertaining to education, such as counseling, curriculum, guidance, instruction, teacher education, and teaching English as a second language.

7. English Language and Literature Teachers, Postsecondary. Teach courses in English language and literature, including linguistics and comparative literature.

8. Foreign Language and Literature Teachers, Postsecondary. Teach courses in foreign (i.e., other than English) languages and literature.

9. Geography Teachers, Postsecondary. Teach courses in geography.

10. History Teachers, Postsecondary. Teach courses in human history and historiography.

11. Philosophy and Religion Teachers, Postsecondary. Teach courses in philosophy, religion, and theology.

12. Postsecondary Teachers, All Other. All postsecondary teachers not listed separately.

Related Recession-Sensitive Job

None met the criteria.

Japanese

Useful Facts About the Major

Focuses on the Japanese language. Includes the cultural and historical contexts; dialects; and applications to business, science/technology, and other settings.

Related CIP Program: 16.0302 Japanese Language and Literature.

Specializations in the Major: History and culture; language education; literature; translation.

Typical Sequence of College Courses: Japanese language, conversation, composition, linguistics, Japanese literature, East Asian literature, East Asian studies, grammar, phonetics.

Typical Sequence of High School Courses: English, public speaking, foreign language, history, literature, social science.

Career Snapshot

Japan is a major trading partner of the United States, but comparatively few English speakers have mastered the Japanese language. This means that a major in Japanese can be a valuable entry route to careers in international business, travel, and law. A graduate degree in Japanese is good preparation for college teaching or translation.

Other Programs Related to the Same Jobs

African Languages, Literatures, and Linguistics; Albanian Language and Literature; American Indian/Native American Languages, Literatures, and Linguistics; American Sign Language (ASL); American Sign Language, Other; Ancient Near Eastern and Biblical Languages, Literatures, and Linguistics; Ancient/Classical Greek Language and Literature; Arabic Language and Literature; Australian/Oceanic/Pacific Languages, Literatures, and Linguistics; Bahasa Indonesian/Bahasa Malay Languages and Literatures; Baltic Languages, Literatures, and Linguistics; Bengali Language and Literature; Bulgarian Language and Literature; Burmese Language and Literature; Catalan Language and Literature; Celtic Languages, Literatures, and Linguistics; Chinese Language and Literature; Classics and Classical Languages, Literatures, and Linguistics, General; Czech Language and Literature; Danish Language and Literature; Dutch/Flemish Language and Literature; East Asian Languages, Literatures, and Linguistics, General; East Asian Languages, Literatures, and Linguistics, Other; Education/Teaching of Individuals with Hearing Impairments, Including Deafness; Filipino/Tagalog Language and Literature; Finnish and Related Languages, Literatures, and Linguistics; Foreign Languages, Literatures, and Linguistics, Other; Foreign Languages/Modern Languages, General; French Language and Literature; German Language and Literature; Germanic Languages, Literatures, and Linguistics, General; Germanic Languages, Literatures, and Linguistics, Other; Hebrew Language and Literature; Hindi Language and Literature; Humanities/Humanistic Studies; Hungarian/Magyar Language and Literature; Iranian/Persian Languages, Literatures, and Linguistics; Italian Language and Literature; Khmer/Cambodian Language and Literature; Korean Language and Literature; Language Interpretation and Translation; Lao/Laotian Language and Literature; others.

Related Secure Job

(See Part IV for the full job description.)

Interpreters and Translators. Translate or interpret written, oral, or sign language text into another language for others.

Related Recession-Sensitive Job

None met the criteria.

Journalism and Mass Communications

Useful Facts About the Major

Focuses on the theory and practice of gathering, processing, and delivering news and prepares individuals to be professional print journalists, news editors, and news managers.

Related CIP Program: 09.0401 Journalism.

Specializations in the Major: Media management; news editing and editorializing; news reporting; photojournalism; radio and television news.

Typical Sequence of College Courses: English composition, oral communication, American government, introduction to economics, foreign language, introduction to psychology, introduction to mass communication, writing for mass media, news writing and reporting, copy editing, mass communication law, communication ethics, feature writing, photojournalism, media management, visual design for media.

Typical Sequence of High School Courses: English, algebra, foreign language, art, literature, public speaking, social science.

Career Snapshot

Journalism is a good preparation not only for news reporting and writing, but also for advertising and (with specialized coursework) news media production. Competition for entry-level journalism jobs can be keen, especially for prestigious newspapers and media outlets. Expect to start in a smaller operation and move around to increasingly bigger employers as you build your career. Although some workers are losing jobs as media outlets merge, new media technologies (such as Web-based magazines) have created some new job openings.

Other Programs Related to the Same Jobs

Advertising; Agricultural Communications/ Journalism; Broadcast Journalism; Business/ Corporate Communications; Communications Studies/Speech Communication and Rhetoric; Communications, Journalism, and Related Fields, Other; Court Reporting/Court Reporter; Creative Writing; Digital Communications and Media/Multimedia; English Composition; Family and Consumer Sciences/Human Sciences Communications; Health Communications; Humanities/Humanistic Studies; Journalism, Other; Mass Communications/Media Studies; Photojournalism; Playwriting and Screenwriting; Political Communications; Public Relations/Image Management; Publishing; Radio and Television; Technical and Business Writing.

Related Secure Jobs

(See Part IV for the full job descriptions.)

1. Court Reporters. Use verbatim methods and equipment to capture, store, retrieve, and transcribe pretrial and trial proceedings or other information. Includes stenocaptioners who operate computerized stenographic captioning equipment to provide captions of live or prerecorded broadcasts for hearing-impaired viewers.

2. Editors. Perform variety of editorial duties, such as laying out, indexing, and revising content of written materials, in preparation for final publication.

Related Recession-Sensitive Jobs

Broadcast News Analysts; Copy Writers; Poets, Lyricists, and Creative Writers; Reporters and Correspondents; Writers and Authors.

Library Science

Useful Facts About the Major

Focuses on the knowledge and skills required to develop, organize, store, retrieve, administer, and facilitate the use of local, remote, and networked collections of information in print, audiovisual, and electronic formats and that prepare individuals for professional service as librarians and information consultants.

Related CIP Program: 25.0101 Library Science/ Librarianship.

Specializations in the Major: Archives; cataloguing; children's libraries; instructional libraries; map libraries; music libraries; online information retrieval; special interest libraries.

Typical Sequence of College Courses: English composition, oral communication, introduction to computer science, foreign language, introduction to library and information science, reference services and resources, management of libraries and information services, bibliographic control of library materials, library research and evaluation.

Typical Sequence of High School Courses: English, foreign language, computer science, algebra, public speaking, office computer applications, keyboarding, social science.

Career Snapshot

This major is sometimes called library and information science because increasingly the information that is needed by businesses, governments, and individuals is not available in books. Library science programs teach not only how to serve library users and manage library collections, but also how to retrieve and compile information from online databases. The master's degree is the entry-level credential in this field; a special librarian often needs an additional graduate or professional degree. Master's degree programs prefer applicants who have a bachelor's in a different field. The best employment opportunities will probably be in online information retrieval and in nontraditional settings.

Other Programs Related to the Same Jobs

Humanities/Humanistic Studies; Library Science, Other; School Librarian/School Library Media Specialist; Teacher Education and Professional Development, Specific Subject Areas, Other.

Related Secure Job

(See Part IV for the full job description.)

Librarians. Administer libraries and perform related library services. Work in a variety of settings, including public libraries, schools, colleges and universities, museums, corporations, government agencies, law firms, non-profit organizations, and health-care providers. Tasks may include selecting, acquiring, cataloguing, classifying, circulating, and maintaining library materials and furnishing reference, bibliographical, and readers' advisory services. May perform in-depth, strategic research and synthesize, analyze, edit, and filter information. May set up or work with databases and information systems to catalogue and access information.

Related Recession-Sensitive Job

None met the criteria.

Mathematics

Useful Facts About the Major

Focuses on the analysis of quantities, magnitudes, forms, and their relationships, using symbolic logic and language.

Related CIP Program: 27.0101 Mathematics, General.

Specializations in the Major: Applied mathematics; mathematical statistics; mathematics education; theoretical mathematics.

Typical Sequence of College Courses: Calculus, differential equations, introduction to computer science, programming in a language (e.g.,

M

C, Pascal, Java), statistics, linear algebra, introduction to abstract mathematics.

Typical Sequence of High School Courses: Algebra, geometry, trigonometry, pre-calculus, calculus, computer science, physics.

Career Snapshot

Mathematics is a science in its own right in which researchers with graduate degrees continue to discover new laws. It is also a tool for understanding and organizing many aspects of our world. Many mathematics majors apply their knowledge by getting additional education or training in a math-intense field, either in a master's program or on the job. For example, an insurance company might train them in actuarial science; a computer consulting company might train them in computer security; a bank might train them in financial modeling; they might get a graduate degree in economics, engineering, or accounting. Employment opportunities are very good for people who apply mathematical knowledge to other fields.

Other Programs Related to the Same Jobs

Algebra and Number Theory; Analysis and Functional Analysis; Applied Mathematics; Applied Mathematics, Other; Computational Mathematics; Geometry/Geometric Analysis; Mathematical Statistics and Probability; Mathematics and Statistics, Other; Mathematics, Other; Topology and Foundations.

Related Secure Jobs

(See Part IV for the full job descriptions.)

1. Mathematicians. Conduct research in fundamental mathematics or in application of mathematical techniques to science, management, and other fields. Solve or direct solutions to problems in various fields by mathematical methods.

2. Statisticians. Engage in the development of mathematical theory or apply statistical theory and methods to collect, organize, interpret, and summarize numerical data to provide usable information. May specialize in fields such as biostatistics, agricultural statistics, business statistics, economic statistics, or other fields.

Related Recession-Sensitive Job

Natural Sciences Managers.

Medical Technology

Useful Facts About the Major

Prepares individuals to conduct and supervise complex medical tests, clinical trials, and research experiments; manage clinical laboratories; and consult with physicians and clinical researchers on diagnoses, disease causation and spread, and research outcomes.

Related CIP Program: 51.1005 Clinical Laboratory Science/Medical Technology/Technologist.

Specializations in the Major: Blood banking; body fluid analysis; clinical chemistry; clinical microbiology; hematology; immunology.

Typical Sequence of College Courses: English composition, general biology, general chemistry, organic chemistry, human anatomy and physiology, general microbiology, introduction to biochemistry, college algebra, introduction to computer science, statistics, body fluid analysis, parasitology, clinical chemistry, hematology and coagulation, clinical microbiology, immunohematology, clinical immunology and serology, medical technology education, medical technology management and supervision.

Typical Sequence of High School Courses: Algebra, biology, chemistry, computer science, English, physics, geometry, trigonometry.

Career Snapshot

The detection, diagnosis, and prevention of disease depend heavily on various kinds of medical tests—of blood, urine, tissue samples, and so on. Medical technologists, also called clinical laboratory scientists, are trained to perform these tests after studying the principles of chemistry, microbiology, and other basic sciences, plus laboratory techniques that sometimes involve complex and sophisticated equipment. A bachelor's degree is the usual preparation. Job outlook is generally good.

Other Programs Related to the Same Jobs

Blood Bank Technology Specialist; Clinical/Medical Laboratory Science and Allied Professions, Other; Clinical/Medical Laboratory Technician; Clinical/Medical Laboratory Technician/Assistant (Certificate); Cytogenetics/Genetics/Clinical Genetics Technology/Technologist; Cytotechnology/Cytotechnologist; Hematology Technology/Technician; Histologic Technician; Histologic Technology/Histotechnologist; Renal/Dialysis Technologist/Technician.

Related Secure Job

(See Part IV for the full job description.)

Medical and Clinical Laboratory Technologists. Perform complex medical laboratory tests for diagnosis, treatment, and prevention of disease. May train or supervise staff.

Related Recession-Sensitive Job

None met the criteria.

Medicine

Useful Facts About the Major

Prepares individuals for the independent professional practice of medicine, involving the prevention, diagnosis, and treatment of illnesses, injuries, and other disorders of the human body.

Related CIP Programs: 51.1201 Medicine (MD); 51.1901 Osteopathic Medicine/Osteopathy (DO).

Specializations in the Major: Emergency medicine; family medicine; internal medicine; obstetrics/gynecology; pediatrics; psychiatry; radiology; surgery.

Typical Sequence of College Courses: English composition, introduction to psychology, college algebra, calculus, introduction to sociology, oral communication, general chemistry, general biology, introduction to computer science, organic chemistry, human anatomy and physiology, general microbiology, genetics, introduction to biochemistry, pathology, pharmacology, abnormal psychology, medical interviewing techniques, patient examination and evaluation, clinical laboratory procedures, ethics in health care, clinical experience in internal medicine, clinical experience in emergency medicine, clinical experience in obstetrics/gynecology, clinical experience in family medicine, clinical experience in psychiatry, clinical experience in surgery, clinical experience in pediatrics, clinical experience in geriatrics.

Typical Sequence of High School Courses: English, algebra, geometry, trigonometry, precalculus, biology, computer science, public speaking, chemistry, foreign language, physics.

Career Snapshot

Medicine requires long years of education—four years of college, four years of medical school, and three to eight years of internship and residency, depending on the specialty. Once you enter medical school, a hands-on learning style becomes as important as theoretical learning. Entrance to medical school is highly competitive. Although "pre-med" is often referred to as a major, many students meet the entry requirements for medical school while majoring in a nonscientific subject. This may be helpful to demonstrate that you are a well-rounded person and to prepare you for another career in case you are not admitted to medical school. Today, physicians are more likely than in the past to work as salaried employees of group practices or HMOs. Best opportunities are expected in rural and low-income areas.

Other Programs Related to the Same Jobs

None met the criteria.

Related Secure Jobs

(See Part IV for the full job descriptions.)

1. Anesthesiologists. Administer anesthetics during surgery or other medical procedures.

2. Family and General Practitioners. Diagnose, treat, and help prevent diseases and injuries that commonly occur in the general population.

3. Internists, General. Diagnose and provide non-surgical treatment of diseases and injuries of internal organ systems. Provide care mainly for adults who have a wide range of problems associated with the internal organs.

4. Obstetricians and Gynecologists. Diagnose, treat, and help prevent diseases of women, especially those affecting the reproductive system and the process of childbirth.

5. Physicians and Surgeons, All Other. All physicians and surgeons not listed separately.

6. Psychiatrists. Diagnose, treat, and help prevent disorders of the mind.

7. Pediatricians, General. Diagnose, treat, and help prevent children's diseases and injuries.

8. Surgeons. Treat diseases, injuries, and deformities by invasive methods, such as manual manipulation, or by using instruments and appliances.

Related Recession-Sensitive Job

None met the criteria.

Modern Foreign Language

Useful Facts About the Major

Focuses on a language being used in the modern world and includes related dialects; the cultural and historical contexts; and applications to business, science/technology, and other settings.

Related CIP Programs: 16.0201 African Languages, Literatures, and Linguistics; 16.0404 Albanian Language and Literature; 16.1001 American Indian/Native American Languages, Literatures, and Linguistics; 16.1101 Arabic Language and Literature; 16.1401 Australian/Oceanic/Pacific Languages, Literatures, and Linguistics; 16.1402 Bahasa Indonesian/Bahasa Malay Languages and Literatures; 16.0401 Baltic Languages, Literatures, and Linguistics; 16.0704 Bengali Language and Literature; 16.0405 Bulgarian Language and Literature; 16.1403 Burmese Language and Literature; 16.0907 Catalan Language and Literature; 16.1301 Celtic Languages, Literatures, and Linguistics; 16.0301 Chinese Language and Literature; 16.0406 Czech Language and Literature; 16.0503 Danish Language and Literature; 16.0504 Dutch/Flemish Language and Literature; 16.0300 East Asian Languages, Literatures, and Linguistics, General; 16.1404 Filipino/Tagalog Language and Literature; 16.1502 Finnish and Related Languages, Literatures, and Linguistics; 16.0901 French Language and Literature; 16.0501 German Language and Literature; others.

Specializations in the Major: History and culture; language education; literature; regional studies; translation.

Typical Sequence of College Courses: Foreign language, conversation, composition, linguistics, foreign literature and culture, grammar, phonetics, history of a world region.

Typical Sequence of High School Courses: English, public speaking, foreign language, history, social science.

Career Snapshot

The most popular foreign language majors—Chinese, French, German, Japanese, Russian, and Spanish—are described elsewhere in this book. But many colleges offer majors in other modern languages, such as Arabic, Hebrew, Hindi, Portuguese, Swahili, Swedish, or Turkish, to name just a few. As global trade continues to increase, a degree in a foreign language can lead to many job opportunities in international business, travel, and law. Many employers are looking for graduates with an understanding of a second language and culture. Translation or college teaching are options for those with a graduate degree in a foreign language.

Other Programs Related to the Same Jobs

African Languages, Literatures, and Linguistics; American Indian/Native American Languages, Literatures, and Linguistics; American Sign Language (ASL); American Sign Language, Other; Ancient Near Eastern and Biblical Languages, Literatures, and Linguistics; Ancient/Classical Greek Language and Literature; Arabic Language and Literature; Australian/Oceanic/Pacific Languages, Literatures, and Linguistics; Bahasa Indonesian/Bahasa Malay Languages and Literatures; Baltic Languages, Literatures, and Linguistics; Bengali Language and Literature; Bulgarian Language and Literature; Burmese Language and Literature; Catalan

M

Language and Literature; Celtic Languages, Literatures, and Linguistics; Chinese Language and Literature; Classics and Classical Languages, Literatures, and Linguistics, General; Czech Language and Literature; Danish Language and Literature; Dutch/Flemish Language and Literature; East Asian Languages, Literatures, and Linguistics, General; East Asian Languages, Literatures, and Linguistics, Other; Education/Teaching of Individuals with Hearing Impairments, Including Deafness; Filipino/Tagalog Language and Literature; Finnish and Related Languages, Literatures, and Linguistics; Foreign Languages, Literatures, and Linguistics, Other; Foreign Languages/Modern Languages, General; French Language and Literature; German Language and Literature; Germanic Languages, Literatures, and Linguistics, General; Germanic Languages, Literatures, and Linguistics, Other; Hebrew Language and Literature; Hindi Language and Literature; Humanities/Humanistic Studies; Hungarian/Magyar Language and Literature; Iranian/Persian Languages, Literatures, and Linguistics; Italian Language and Literature; Japanese Language and Literature; Khmer/Cambodian Language and Literature; Korean Language and Literature; Language Interpretation and Translation; Lao/Laotian Language and Literature; others.

Related Secure Job

(See Part IV for the full job description.)

Interpreters and Translators. Translate or interpret written, oral, or sign language text into another language for others.

Related Recession-Sensitive Job

None met the criteria.

Nursing (R.N. Training)

Useful Facts About the Major

Prepares individuals in the knowledge, techniques and procedures for promoting health and providing care for sick, disabled, informed, or other individuals or groups.

Related CIP Program: 51.1601 Nursing/Registered Nurse (RN, ASN, BSN, MSN).

Specializations in the Major: Community health nursing; mental health nursing; nursing administration; pediatric nursing.

Typical Sequence of College Courses: English composition, introduction to psychology, college algebra, introduction to sociology, oral communication, general chemistry, general biology, human anatomy and physiology, general microbiology, ethics in health care, patient examination and evaluation, pharmacology, reproductive health nursing, pediatric nursing, adult health nursing, mental health nursing, nursing leadership and management, community health nursing, clinical nursing experience.

Typical Sequence of High School Courses: English, algebra, geometry, trigonometry, biology, computer science, public speaking, chemistry, foreign language.

Career Snapshot

The study of nursing includes a combination of classroom and clinical work. Students learn what science tells us about the origins and treatment of disease, how to care effectively for the physical and emotional needs of sick and injured people, and how to teach people to maintain health. Nurses work in a variety of health-care settings, including physicians' offices, patients' homes, schools, and companies, and in desk jobs for HMOs. The employment outlook is excellent in all specialties.

Other Programs Related to the Same Jobs

Adult Health Nurse/Nursing; Family Practice Nurse/Nurse Practitioner; Maternal/Child Health Nurse/Nursing; Nurse Anesthetist; Nurse Midwife/Nursing Midwifery; Nursing Clinical Specialist; Nursing Science (MS, PhD); Pediatric Nurse/Nursing; Perioperative/Operating and Surgical Nurse/Nursing; Psychiatric/Mental Health Nurse/Nursing; Public Health/Community Nurse/Nursing.

Related Secure Job

(See Part IV for the full job description.)

Registered Nurses. Assess patient health problems and needs, develop and implement nursing care plans, and maintain medical records. Administer nursing care to ill, injured, convalescent, or disabled patients. May advise patients on health maintenance and disease prevention or provide case management. Licensing or registration required. Includes advance practice nurses such as nurse practitioners, clinical nurse specialists, certified nurse midwives, and certified registered nurse anesthetists. Advanced practice nursing is practiced by RNs who have specialized formal, post-basic education and who function in highly autonomous and specialized roles.

Related Recession-Sensitive Job

None met the criteria.

Occupational Therapy

Useful Facts About the Major

Prepares individuals to assist patients limited by physical, cognitive, psychosocial, mental, developmental, and learning disabilities, as well as adverse environmental conditions, to maximize their independence and maintain optimum health through a planned mix of acquired skills, performance motivation, environmental adaptations, assistive technologies, and physical agents.

Related CIP Program: 51.2306 Occupational Therapy/Therapist.

Specializations in the Major: Geriatric OT; pediatric OT; prosthetics.

Typical Sequence of College Courses: English composition, statistics for business and social sciences, general chemistry, general biology, human anatomy and physiology, introduction to psychology, human growth and development, introduction to computer science, abnormal psychology, fundamentals of medical science, neuroscience for therapy, occupational therapy for developmental problems, occupational therapy for physiological diagnoses, occupational therapy for psychosocial diagnoses, administration of occupational therapy services, research methods in occupational therapy, methods of facilitating therapeutic adaptation, occupational therapy fieldwork experience, seminar (reporting on research).

Typical Sequence of High School Courses: English, algebra, geometry, trigonometry, chemistry, physics, biology, foreign language, computer science.

Career Snapshot

Occupational therapists help people cope with disabilities and lead more productive and enjoyable lives. Some therapists enter the field with a bachelor's degree in occupational therapy; others get a master's after a bachelor's in another field. They learn about the nature of various kinds of disabilities—developmental, emotional, and so on—and how to help people overcome them or compensate for them in their daily lives. The long-range outlook for jobs is considered quite good, although in the short run it may be affected by cutbacks in Medicare coverage of therapies.

Other Programs Related to the Same Jobs

None met the criteria.

Related Secure Job

(See Part IV for the full job description.)

Occupational Therapists. Assess, plan, organize, and participate in rehabilitative programs that help restore vocational, homemaking, and daily living skills, as well as general independence, to disabled persons.

Related Recession-Sensitive Job

None met the criteria.

Oceanography

Useful Facts About the Major

Focuses on the scientific study of the ecology and behavior of microbes, plants, and animals inhabiting oceans, coastal waters, and saltwater wetlands and the chemical components, mechanisms, structure, and movement of ocean waters and their interaction with terrestrial and atmospheric phenomena.

Related CIP Programs: 26.1302 Marine Biology and Biological Oceanography; 40.0607 Oceanography, Chemical and Physical.

Specializations in the Major: Ocean biology; ocean chemistry; ocean geology; ocean meteorology.

Typical Sequence of College Courses: English composition, introduction to computer science, calculus, differential equations, general chemistry, general physics, agricultural power and machines, physical oceanography, chemical oceanography, geological oceanography, biological oceanography, seminar (reporting on research).

Typical Sequence of High School Courses: English, algebra, geometry, trigonometry, chemistry, pre-calculus, physics, computer science, biology, calculus.

Career Snapshot

Oceans cover more of the Earth than does dry land, yet many of the physical and biological characteristics of the oceans are poorly understood. Oceanographers use techniques of physical sciences to study the properties of ocean waters and how these affect coastal areas, climate, and weather. Those who specialize in ocean life work to improve the fishing industry, to protect the environment, and to understand the relationship between oceanic and terrestrial life forms. It is possible to get started in this field with a bachelor's degree; for advancement and many research jobs, however, a master's degree or Ph.D. is helpful or required.

Other Programs Related to the Same Jobs

Geological and Earth Sciences/Geosciences, Other; Oceanography, Chemical and Physical.

Related Secure Jobs

(See Part IV for the full job descriptions.)

1. Geoscientists, Except Hydrologists and Geographers. Study the composition, structure, and other physical aspects of the Earth. May use knowledge of geology, physics, and mathematics in exploration for oil, gas, minerals, or underground water or in waste disposal, land reclamation, or other environmental problems. May study the Earth's internal composition, atmospheres, and oceans and its magnetic, electrical, and gravitational forces. Includes mineralogists, crystallographers, paleontologists, stratigraphers, geodesists, and seismologists.

2. Hydrologists. Research the distribution, circulation, and physical properties of underground and surface waters; study the form and intensity of precipitation, its rate of infiltration into the soil, its movement through the earth, and its return to the ocean and atmosphere.

Related Recession-Sensitive Job

Natural Sciences Managers.

Optometry

Useful Facts About the Major

Focuses on the principles and techniques for examining, diagnosing, and treating conditions of the visual system.

Related CIP Program: 51.1701 Optometry (OD).

Specializations in the Major: Contact lenses; low vision.

Typical Sequence of College Courses: English composition, introduction to psychology, calculus, introduction to sociology, oral communication, general chemistry, general biology, organic chemistry, general microbiology, introduction to biochemistry, microbiology for optometry, geometric, physical and visual optics, ocular health assessment, neuroanatomy, ocular anatomy and physiology, pathology, theory and methods of refraction, general and ocular pharmacology, optical and motor aspects of vision, ophthalmic optics, environmental and occupational vision, assessment of oculomotor system, strabismus and vision therapy, visual information processing and perception, ocular disease, contact lenses, pediatric and developmental vision, ethics in health care, professional practice management, low vision and geriatric vision, clinical experience in optometry.

Typical Sequence of High School Courses: English, algebra, geometry, trigonometry, precalculus, biology, computer science, public speaking, chemistry, calculus, physics, foreign language.

Career Snapshot

Optometrists measure patients' visual ability and prescribe visual aids such as glasses and contact lenses. They may evaluate patients' suitability for laser surgery and/or provide post-operative care, but they do not perform surgery. The usual educational preparation is at least three years of college, followed by a four-year program of optometry school. The job outlook is good because the aging population will need increased attention to vision. The best opportunities probably will be at retail vision centers and outpatient clinics.

Other Programs Related to the Same Jobs

None met the criteria.

Related Secure Job

(See Part IV for the full job description.)

Optometrists. Diagnose, manage, and treat conditions and diseases of the human eye and visual system. Examine eyes and visual systems, diagnose problems or impairments, prescribe corrective lenses, and provide treatment. May prescribe therapeutic drugs to treat specific eye conditions.

Related Recession-Sensitive Job

None met the criteria.

Pharmacy

Useful Facts About the Major

Prepares individuals for the independent or employed practice of preparing and dispensing drugs and medications in consultation with prescribing physicians and other health-care professionals and for managing pharmacy practices and counseling patients.

Related CIP Program: 51.2001 Pharmacy (PharmD [USA], PharmD or BS/BPharm [Canada]).

Specializations in the Major: Pharmaceutical chemistry; pharmacology; pharmacy administration.

Typical Sequence of College Courses: English composition, introduction to psychology, calculus, introduction to sociology, oral communication, general chemistry, general biology, organic chemistry, introduction to biochemistry, human anatomy and physiology, pharmaceutical calculations, pharmacology, pharmaceutics, microbiology and immunology, patient assessment and education, medicinal chemistry, therapeutics, pharmacy law and ethics, pharmacokinetics, electrical inspection.

Typical Sequence of High School Courses: English, algebra, geometry, trigonometry, biology, computer science, public speaking, chemistry, calculus, physics, foreign language.

Career Snapshot

Pharmacists dispense medications as prescribed by physicians and other health practitioners and give advice to patients about how to use medications. Pharmacists must be knowledgeable about the chemical and physical properties of drugs, how they behave in the body, and how they may interact with other drugs and substances. Schools of pharmacy take about four years to complete and usually require at least one or two years of prior college work. Some pharmacists go on to additional graduate training to prepare for research, administration, or college teaching. Some find work in sales for pharmaceutical companies or in marketing research for managed-care organizations. The job outlook for pharmacists is expected to be good, thanks to the aging of the population combined with the shift of medical care from the scalpel to the pill.

Other Programs Related to the Same Jobs

Clinical and Industrial Drug Development (MS, PhD); Clinical, Hospital, and Managed Care Pharmacy (MS, PhD); Industrial and Physical Pharmacy and Cosmetic Sciences (MS, PhD); Medicinal and Pharmaceutical Chemistry (MS, PhD); Natural Products Chemistry and Pharmacognosy (MS, PhD); Pharmaceutics and Drug Design (MS, PhD); Pharmacoeconomics/Pharmaceutical Economics (MS, PhD); Pharmacy Administration and Pharmacy Policy and Regulatory Affairs (MS, PhD).

Related Secure Job

(See Part IV for the full job description.)

Pharmacists. Compound and dispense medications, following prescriptions issued by physicians, dentists, or other authorized medical practitioners.

Related Recession-Sensitive Job

None met the criteria.

Philosophy

Useful Facts About the Major

Focuses on ideas and their logical structure, including arguments and investigations about abstract and real phenomena.

Related CIP Program: 38.0101 Philosophy.

Specializations in the Major: Esthetics; ethics; history of philosophy; logic.

Typical Sequence of College Courses: English composition, foreign language, introduction to logic, major thinkers and issues in philosophy, ethical/moral theory, classical philosophy, modern philosophy, contemporary philosophy, esthetics.

Typical Sequence of High School Courses: Algebra, English, foreign language, social science, history, geometry.

Career Snapshot

Philosophy is concerned with the most basic questions about the human experience, such as what reality is, what the ultimate values are, and how we know what we know. Philosophy majors are trained to think independently and critically and to write clearly and persuasively. They may go to work in a number of business careers where these skills are appreciated—perhaps most of all in the long run as these former philosophy majors advance to positions of leadership. Some find that a philosophy major combines well with further training in law, computer science, or religious studies. Those with a graduate degree in philosophy may teach in college.

Other Programs Related to the Same Jobs

Ethics; Humanities/Humanistic Studies; Philosophy and Religion, Other; Philosophy, Other.

Related Secure Jobs

(See Part IV for the full job descriptions.)

1. Clergy. Conduct religious worship and perform other spiritual functions associated with beliefs and practices of religious faith or denomination. Provide spiritual and moral guidance and assistance to members.

2. Religious Workers, All Other. All religious workers not listed separately.

Related Recession-Sensitive Job

Directors, Religious Activities and Education.

Physical Education

Useful Facts About the Major

Prepares individuals to teach physical education programs and/or to coach sports at various educational levels.

Related CIP Program: 13.1314 Physical Education Teaching and Coaching.

Specializations in the Major: Coaching; health education; recreation; sports activities.

Typical Sequence of College Courses: Introduction to psychology, English composition, oral communication, history and philosophy of education, human growth and development, introduction to special education, history and philosophy of physical education, first aid and CPR, methods of teaching physical education, human anatomy and physiology, kinesiology, special needs in physical education, psychomotor development, organization and administration of physical education, evaluation in physical education, methods of teaching dance, methods of teaching sports activities, methods of teaching aerobics and weight training, swimming and water safety, student teaching.

Typical Sequence of High School Courses: English, algebra, geometry, trigonometry, science, foreign language, public speaking.

Career Snapshot

This major covers not only educational techniques, but also the workings of the human body. Thanks to a national concern for fitness and health, physical education graduates are finding employment not only as teachers, but also as instructors and athletic directors in health and sports clubs. Most jobs are still to be found in elementary and secondary schools, where a bachelor's degree is often sufficient for entry, but a master's may be required for advancement to a more secure and better-paid position. Some graduates may go on to get a master's in athletic training and work for a college or professional sports team.

Other Programs Related to the Same Jobs

Parks, Recreation, and Leisure Studies; Sport and Fitness Administration/Management.

Related Secure Jobs

(See Part IV for the full job descriptions.)

1. Coaches and Scouts. Instruct or coach groups or individuals in the fundamentals of sports. Demonstrate techniques and methods of participation. May evaluate athletes' strengths and weaknesses as possible recruits or to improve the athletes' technique to prepare them for competition.

2. Middle School Teachers, Except Special and Vocational Education. Teach students in public or private schools in one or more subjects at the middle, intermediate, or junior high level, which falls between elementary and senior high school as defined by applicable state laws and regulations.

3. Secondary School Teachers, Except Special and Vocational Education. Instruct students in secondary public or private schools in one or more subjects at the secondary level, such as English, mathematics, or social studies. May be designated according to subject matter specialty, such as typing instructors, commercial teachers, or English teachers.

Related Recession-Sensitive Job

Fitness Trainers and Aerobics Instructors.

Physical Therapy

Useful Facts About the Major

Prepares individuals to alleviate physical and functional impairments and limitations caused by injury or disease through the design and implementation of therapeutic interventions to promote fitness and health.

Related CIP Program: 51.2308 Physical Therapy/Therapist.

Specializations in the Major: Geriatric physical therapy; neurological physical therapy; orthopedics; physical therapy education; sports medicine.

Typical Sequence of College Courses: English composition, statistics for business and social sciences, general chemistry, general biology, human anatomy and physiology, introduction to psychology, human growth and development, introduction to computer science, abnormal psychology, fundamentals of medical science, neuroanatomy, neuroscience for therapy, cardiopulmonary system, musculoskeletal system, clinical orthopedics, clinical applications of neurophysiology, therapeutic exercise techniques, physical and electrical agents in physical therapy, medical considerations in physical therapy, psychomotor development throughout the life span, psychosocial aspects of physical disability, research in physical therapy practice, research in physical therapy practice.

Typical Sequence of High School Courses: English, algebra, geometry, trigonometry, chemistry, physics, biology, foreign language, computer science.

Career Snapshot

Physical therapists help people overcome pain and limited movement caused by disease or injury and help them avoid further disabilities. They review patients' medical records and the prescriptions of physicians, evaluate patients' mobility, and then guide patients through appropriate exercise routines and apply therapeutic agents such as heat and electrical stimulation. They need to

P

be knowledgeable about many disabling conditions and therapeutic techniques. The master's program is currently the standard requirement for entry into this field, but it will be replaced by the doctorate by 2020. Entry to master's programs is extremely competitive. The short-term job outlook has been hurt by cutbacks in Medicare coverage of therapy; however, the long-term outlook is expected to be good because of the aging of the population.

Other Programs Related to the Same Jobs

Kinesiotherapy/Kinesiotherapist.

Related Secure Job

(See Part IV for the full job description.)

Physical Therapists. Assess, plan, organize, and participate in rehabilitative programs that improve mobility, relieve pain, increase strength, and decrease or prevent deformity of patients suffering from disease or injury.

Related Recession-Sensitive Job

None met the criteria.

Physician Assisting

Useful Facts About the Major

Prepares individuals to practice medicine, including diagnoses and treatment therapies, under the supervision of a physician.

Related CIP Program: 51.0912 Physician Assistant.

Specializations in the Major: Emergency medicine; family medicine; internal medicine; pediatrics.

Typical Sequence of College Courses: English composition, college algebra, general chemistry, general biology, introduction to psychology, human growth and development, general microbiology, human physiology, human anatomy, pharmacology, medical interviewing techniques, patient examination and evaluation, clinical laboratory procedures, ethics in health care, clinical experience in internal medicine, clinical experience in emergency medicine, clinical experience in obstetrics/gynecology, clinical experience in family medicine, clinical experience in psychiatry, clinical experience in surgery, clinical experience in pediatrics, clinical experience in geriatrics.

Typical Sequence of High School Courses: English, algebra, geometry, trigonometry, precalculus, biology, computer science, public speaking, chemistry, foreign language.

Career Snapshot

Physician assistants work under the supervision of physicians, but in some cases they provide care in settings where a physician may be present only a couple of days per week. They perform many of the diagnostic, therapeutic, and preventative functions that we are used to associating with physicians. The typical educational program results in a bachelor's degree. It often takes only two years to complete, but entrants usually must have at least two years of prior college and often must have work experience in the field of health care. Employment opportunities are expected to be good.

Other Programs Related to the Same Jobs

None met the criteria.

Related Secure Job

(See Part IV for the full job description.)

Physician Assistants. Under the supervision of physicians, provide health-care services typically performed by a physician. Conduct complete physicals, provide treatment, and counsel patients. May, in some cases, prescribe medication. Must graduate from an accredited educational program for physician assistants.

Related Recession-Sensitive Job

None met the criteria.

Podiatry

Useful Facts About the Major

Prepares individuals for the independent professional practice of podiatric medicine, involving the prevention, diagnosis, and treatment of diseases, disorders, and injuries to the foot and lower extremities.

Related CIP Program: 51.2101 Podiatric Medicine/Podiatry (DPM).

Specializations in the Major: Orthopedics; sports medicine; surgery.

Typical Sequence of College Courses: English composition, introduction to psychology, college algebra, calculus, introduction to sociology, oral communication, general chemistry, general biology, introduction to computer science, organic chemistry, human anatomy and physiology, general microbiology, genetics, introduction to biochemistry, gross anatomy, histology, patient examination and evaluation, lower extremity anatomy, neuroanatomy, human physiology, microbiology and immunology, pathology, biomechanics, radiology, podiatric surgery, dermatology, general medicine, traumatology, professional practice management, clinical experience in podiatric medicine.

Typical Sequence of High School Courses: English, algebra, geometry, trigonometry, biology, computer science, public speaking, chemistry, foreign language, physics, pre-calculus.

Career Snapshot

Podiatrists are health-care practitioners who specialize in the feet and lower extremities. The educational process is much like that for medical doctors—for almost all students, first a bachelor's degree, then four years of study and clinical practice in a school of podiatric medicine, followed by one to three years of a hospital residency program. The bachelor's degree can be in any subject as long as it includes certain coursework in science and math. Job opportunities will probably be better in group medical practices, clinics, and health networks than in traditional solo practices.

Other Programs Related to the Same Jobs

None met the criteria.

Related Secure Job

(See Part IV for the full job description.)

P

Podiatrists. Diagnose and treat diseases and deformities of the human foot.

Related Recession-Sensitive Job

None met the criteria.

Political Science

Useful Facts About the Major

Focuses on the systematic study of political institutions and behavior.

Related CIP Program: 45.1001 Political Science and Government, General.

Specializations in the Major: Comparative politics; international relations; political theory; public administration; public opinion; public policy.

Typical Sequence of College Courses: English composition, introduction to psychology, introduction to sociology, American government, foreign language, statistics, introduction to economics, statistics for business and social sciences, state and local government, comparative governments, introduction to international relations, political theory, political science research methods, public policy analysis, seminar (reporting on research).

Typical Sequence of High School Courses: Algebra, English, foreign language, social science, trigonometry, history.

Career Snapshot

Political science is the study of how political systems and public policy are created and evolve. It is concerned with many levels of political activity, from the campaigns of candidates for representation of a city precinct to the maneuvers of nations trying to resolve regional conflicts. Most political scientists with graduate degrees work as researchers and teachers in universities; some work for nonprofits, political lobbyists, and social organizations. Many holders of the bachelor's degree use it as an entry route to law school or public administration.

Other Programs Related to the Same Jobs

American Government and Politics (United States); Canadian Government and Politics; Humanities/Humanistic Studies; International Relations and Affairs; International/Global Studies; Political Science and Government, Other; Social Science Teacher Education.

Related Secure Job

(See Part IV for the full job description.)

Political Scientists. Study the origin, development, and operation of political systems. Research a wide range of subjects, such as relations between the United States and foreign countries, the beliefs and institutions of foreign nations, or the politics of small towns or a major metropolis. May study topics such as public opinion, political decision making, and ideology. May analyze the structure and operation of governments, as well as various political entities. May conduct public opinion surveys, analyze election results, or analyze public documents.

Related Recession-Sensitive Job

None met the criteria.

Psychology

Useful Facts About the Major

Focuses on the scientific study of individual and collective behavior, the physical and environmental bases of behavior, and the analysis and treatment of behavior problems and disorders.

Related CIP Program: 42.0101 Psychology, General.

Specializations in the Major: Clinical/counseling psychology; educational psychology; industrial psychology; research clinical psychology.

Typical Sequence of College Courses: Introduction to psychology, English composition, statistics, research methods in speech pathology and audiology, experimental psychology, psychology of learning, abnormal psychology, social psychology, developmental psychology, sensation and perception, cognitive psychology, biopsychology, psychology of personality, quantitative analysis in psychology, psychological testing and measurements.

Typical Sequence of High School Courses: Algebra, biology, English, foreign language, social science, trigonometry.

Career Snapshot

Psychology is the study of human behavior. It may take place in a clinical, educational, industrial, or experimental setting. Those with a bachelor's degree usually must find employment in another field, such as marketing research. A bachelor's degree can also be a good first step toward graduate education in education, law, social work, or another field. To be licensed as a clinical or counseling psychologist, you usually need a Ph.D.; industrial-organizational psychologists need a master's. School psychologists need an educational specialist degree and may enjoy the best job opportunities in this field. Competition for graduate school is expected to be keen. More than one-third of psychologists are self-employed. Because psychology is about behavior, many people don't realize that it uses scientific methods and that students are expected to become competent in statistics.

Other Programs Related to the Same Jobs

Clinical Child Psychology; Clinical Psychology; Cognitive Psychology and Psycholinguistics; Community Psychology; Comparative Psychology; Counseling Psychology; Developmental and Child Psychology; Educational Psychology; Experimental Psychology; Humanities/Humanistic Studies; Industrial and Organizational Psychology; Marriage and Family Therapy/ Counseling; Personality Psychology; Physiological Psychology/Psychobiology; Psychoanalysis and Psychotherapy; Psychology Teacher Education; Psychology, Other; Psychometrics and Quantitative Psychology; School Psychology; Social Psychology; Social Science Teacher Education.

Related Secure Jobs

(See Part IV for the full job descriptions.)

1. Clinical Psychologists. Diagnose or evaluate mental and emotional disorders of individuals through observation, interview, and psychological tests and formulate and administer programs of treatment.

2. Counseling Psychologists. Assess and evaluate individuals' problems through the use of case history, interview, and observation and provide individual or group counseling services to assist individuals in achieving more effective personal, social, educational, and vocational development and adjustment.

3. Industrial-Organizational Psychologists. Apply principles of psychology to personnel, administration, management, sales, and marketing problems. Activities may include policy planning; employee screening, training, and development; and organizational development and analysis. May work with management to reorganize the work setting to improve worker productivity.

4. School Psychologists. Investigate processes of learning and teaching and develop psychological principles and techniques applicable to educational problems.

Related Recession-Sensitive Job

None met the criteria.

Public Relations

Useful Facts About the Major

Focuses on the theories and methods for managing the media image of a business, organization, or individual and the communication process with stakeholders, constituencies, audiences, and the general public. Prepares individuals to function as public relations assistants, technicians, and managers.

Related CIP Program: 09.0902 Public Relations/Image Management.

Specializations in the Major: Creative process; management; new media.

Typical Sequence of College Courses: English composition, oral communication, introduction to marketing, introduction to economics, principles of public relations, communications theory, public relations message strategy, communication ethics, public relations media, public relations writing, public relations techniques and campaigns, organizational communications, mass communication law, introduction to communication research, visual design for media.

Typical Sequence of High School Courses: English, algebra, foreign language, art, literature, public speaking, social science.

Career Snapshot

Public relations specialists work for business, government, and nonprofit organizations and encourage public support for the employer's policies and practices. Often several "publics" with differing interests and needs have to be targeted with different messages. The work requires an understanding of psychology, the business and social environments, effective writing, and techniques used in various media for persuasive communications. A bachelor's degree is good preparation for an entry-level job in this competitive field, and an internship or work experience is an important advantage. On-the-job experience may lead to a job managing public relations campaigns; a master's degree can speed up the process of advancement.

Other Programs Related to the Same Jobs

Advertising; Broadcast Journalism; Communications Studies/Speech Communication and

Rhetoric; Communications, Journalism, and Related Fields, Other; Digital Communications and Media/Multimedia; Health Communications; Humanities/Humanistic Studies; Journalism; Journalism, Other; Marketing/Marketing Management, General; Mass Communications/Media Studies; Political Communications; Radio and Television.

Related Secure Job

(See Part IV for the full job description.)

Public Relations Specialists. Engage in promoting or creating good will for individuals, groups, or organizations by writing or selecting favorable publicity material and releasing it through various communications media. May prepare and arrange displays and make speeches.

Related Recession-Sensitive Jobs

Advertising and Promotions Managers; Public Relations Managers.

Religion/Religious Studies

Useful Facts About the Major

Prepares individuals for ordination as ministers or priests in any of the Christian religious traditions. Focuses on the nature of religious belief and specific religious and quasi-religious systems.

Related CIP Programs: 39.0602 Divinity/Ministry (BD, MDiv.); 38.0201 Religion/Religious Studies.

Specializations in the Major: Ecumenical studies; missionary work; pastoral counseling; pastoral studies; scriptural texts/language.

Typical Sequence of College Courses: English composition, foreign language, introduction to religious studies, introduction to philosophy, ethical/moral theory, Hebrew Bible, New Testament, non-Western religions, philosophy of religion, history of religion in the West, contemporary theologies, religious ethics.

Typical Sequence of High School Courses: Algebra, English, foreign language, social science, history, geometry, public speaking.

Career Snapshot

Interest in religion continues to grow in America, and many colleges were founded by churches, so the religious studies major continues to attract students, some of whom do not feel the call to become professional clergy. A graduate of a religious studies major has skills in language, literature, critical thinking, and writing that are valuable in many careers in the secular world. The amount of education required to be ordained in the clergy depends on the person's religious denomination. For some, there may be no formal requirement; most require several years of seminary training, often following four years of college. Clergy find work in churches, synagogues, and religious schools; as chaplains for hospitals, prisons, and the military; and as missionaries.

Other Programs Related to the Same Jobs

Bible/Biblical Studies; Buddhist Studies; Christian Studies; Clinical Pastoral Counseling/Patient Counseling; Divinity/Ministry (BD,

MDiv.); Ethics; Hindu Studies; Humanities/ Humanistic Studies; Missions/Missionary Studies and Missiology; Pastoral Counseling and Specialized Ministries, Other; Pastoral Studies/Counseling; Philosophy; Philosophy and Religion, Other; Philosophy, Other; Pre-Theology/Pre-Ministerial Studies; Rabbinical Studies (M.H.L./Rav); Religious Education; Religious/ Sacred Music; Talmudic Studies; Theological and Ministerial Studies, Other; Theological Studies and Religious Vocations, Other; Theology/Theological Studies; Youth Ministry.

Related Secure Job

(See Part IV for the full job description.)

Clergy. Conduct religious worship and perform other spiritual functions associated with beliefs and practices of religious faith or denomination. Provide spiritual and moral guidance and assistance to members.

Related Recession-Sensitive Job

None met the criteria.

Russian

Useful Facts About the Major

Focuses on the Russian language. Includes the cultural and historical contexts; dialects; and applications to business, science/technology, and other settings.

Related CIP Program: 16.0402 Russian Language and Literature.

Specializations in the Major: History and culture; language education; literature; translation.

Typical Sequence of College Courses: Russian language, conversation, composition, linguistics, Russian literature, Russian history and civilization, European history and civilization, grammar, phonetics.

Typical Sequence of High School Courses: English, public speaking, foreign language, history, literature, social science.

Career Snapshot

Despite the breakup of the Soviet Union, Russian is still an important world language that not many Americans know. As business and governmental ties with Russia continue to increase as it opens to free trade, a degree in Russian can lead to careers in international business, travel, and law. College teaching and translation are options for those with a graduate degree in Russian.

Other Programs Related to the Same Jobs

African Languages, Literatures, and Linguistics; Albanian Language and Literature; American Indian/Native American Languages, Literatures, and Linguistics; American Sign Language (ASL); American Sign Language, Other; Ancient Near Eastern and Biblical Languages, Literatures, and Linguistics; Ancient/Classical Greek Language and Literature; Arabic Language and Literature; Australian/Oceanic/Pacific Languages, Literatures, and Linguistics; Bahasa Indonesian/ Bahasa Malay Languages and Literatures; Baltic Languages, Literatures, and Linguistics; Bengali Language and Literature; Bulgarian Language and Literature; Burmese Language and Literature; Catalan Language and Literature; Celtic

Languages, Literatures, and Linguistics; Chinese Language and Literature; Classics and Classical Languages, Literatures, and Linguistics, General; Czech Language and Literature; Danish Language and Literature; Dutch/Flemish Language and Literature; East Asian Languages, Literatures, and Linguistics, General; East Asian Languages, Literatures, and Linguistics, Other; Education/Teaching of Individuals with Hearing Impairments, Including Deafness; Filipino/Tagalog Language and Literature; Finnish and Related Languages, Literatures, and Linguistics; Foreign Languages, Literatures, and Linguistics, Other; Foreign Languages/Modern Languages, General; French Language and Literature; German Language and Literature; Germanic Languages, Literatures, and Linguistics, General; Germanic Languages, Literatures, and Linguistics, Other; Hebrew Language and Literature; Hindi Language and Literature; Humanities/Humanistic Studies; Hungarian/Magyar Language and Literature; Iranian/Persian Languages, Literatures, and Linguistics; Italian Language and Literature; Japanese Language and Literature; Khmer/Cambodian Language and Literature; Korean Language and Literature; Language Interpretation and Translation; others.

Related Secure Job

(See Part IV for the full job description.)

Interpreters and Translators. Translate or interpret written, oral, or sign language text into another language for others.

Related Recession-Sensitive Job

None met the criteria.

Secondary Education

Useful Facts About the Major

Prepares individuals to teach students in the secondary grades, which may include grades seven through twelve, depending on the school system or state regulations. May include preparation to teach a comprehensive curriculum or specific subject matter.

Related CIP Program: 13.1205 Secondary Education and Teaching.

Specializations in the Major: Art education; bilingual education; language education; mathematics education; music education; remedial and developmental reading; science education; social studies education.

Typical Sequence of College Courses: Introduction to psychology, English composition, oral communication, history and philosophy of education, human growth and development, teaching methods, educational alternatives for exceptional students, educational psychology, courses in subject to be taught, student teaching.

Typical Sequence of High School Courses: English, algebra, geometry, trigonometry, science, foreign language, public speaking.

Career Snapshot

A bachelor's is the minimum for starting a secondary teaching career, and a master's may be required or encouraged for job security and a pay raise. A teacher-education program covers not only the subjects you will teach, but also basic principles of educational psychology and classroom management. Demand for secondary school teachers is expected to be better than that for lower grades, but it will vary according to subject field and geographic area. Job opportunities will be best in inner-city and rural locations.

Other Programs Related to the Same Jobs

Agricultural Teacher Education; Art Teacher Education; Biology Teacher Education; Business Teacher Education; Chemistry Teacher Education; Computer Teacher Education; Drama and Dance Teacher Education; Driver and Safety Teacher Education; English/Language Arts Teacher Education; Family and Consumer Sciences/Home Economics Teacher Education; Foreign Language Teacher Education; French Language Teacher Education; Geography Teacher Education; German Language Teacher Education; Health Occupations Teacher Education; Health Teacher Education; History Teacher Education; Junior High/Intermediate/Middle School Education and Teaching; Latin Teacher Education; Mathematics Teacher Education; Music Teacher Education; Physical Education Teaching and Coaching; Physics Teacher Education; Reading Teacher Education; Sales and Marketing Operations/Marketing and Distribution Teacher Education; Science Teacher Education/General Science Teacher Education; Social Science Teacher Education; Social Studies Teacher Education; Spanish Language Teacher Education; Speech Teacher Education; Teacher Education and Professional Development, Specific Subject Areas, Other; Teacher Education, Multiple Levels; Technology Teacher Education/Industrial Arts Teacher Education.

Related Secure Jobs

(See Part IV for the full job descriptions.)

1. Secondary School Teachers, Except Special and Vocational Education. Instruct students in secondary public or private schools in one or more subjects at the secondary level, such as English, mathematics, or social studies. May be designated according to subject matter specialty, such as typing instructors, commercial teachers, or English teachers.

2. Teachers and Instructors, All Other. All teachers and instructors not listed separately.

Related Recession-Sensitive Job

None met the criteria.

Social Work

Useful Facts About the Major

Prepares individuals for the professional practice of social welfare administration and counseling. Focuses on the study of organized means of providing basic support services for vulnerable individuals and groups.

Related CIP Program: 44.0701 Social Work.

Specializations in the Major: Advocacy; child welfare; domestic violence; health care; mental health; mental retardation; school; substance abuse.

Typical Sequence of College Courses: English composition, human growth and development, American government, introduction to psychology, introduction to sociology, introduction to philosophy, statistics for business and social sciences, cultural diversity, human anatomy and physiology, development of social welfare, human behavior and the social environment, social work methods, social welfare policy and issues, field experience/internship, social work research methods, foreign language, seminar (reporting on research).

Typical Sequence of High School Courses: Algebra, biology, English, foreign language, social science, trigonometry.

Career Snapshot

Social workers improve people's lives by helping them cope with problems of bad health, substance abuse, disability, old age, family conflicts, mental illness, or poverty. A large number of them work for public agencies and health-care institutions. A master's degree is becoming standard preparation for this field. Job opportunities are expected to be best in rural areas and in the specializations of substance abuse and gerontology.

Other Programs Related to the Same Jobs

Clinical Pastoral Counseling/Patient Counseling; Clinical/Medical Social Work; Juvenile Corrections; Marriage and Family Therapy/Counseling; Teacher Education and Professional Development, Specific Subject Areas, Other; Youth Services/Administration.

Related Secure Jobs

(See Part IV for the full job descriptions.)

1. Child, Family, and School Social Workers. Provide social services and assistance to improve the social and psychological functioning of children and their families and to maximize the family well-being and the academic functioning of children. May assist single parents, arrange adoptions, and find foster homes for abandoned or abused children. In schools, they address such problems as teenage pregnancy, misbehavior, and truancy. May also advise teachers on how to deal with problem children.

2. Marriage and Family Therapists. Diagnose and treat mental and emotional disorders, whether cognitive, affective, or behavioral, within the context of marriage and family systems. Apply psychotherapeutic and family systems theories and techniques in the delivery of professional services to individuals, couples, and families for the purpose of treating such diagnosed nervous and mental disorders.

3. Probation Officers and Correctional Treatment Specialists. Provide social services to assist in rehabilitation of law offenders in custody or on probation or parole. Make recommendations for actions involving formulation of rehabilitation plan and treatment of offender, including conditional release and education and employment stipulations.

Related Recession-Sensitive Job

None met the criteria.

Spanish

Useful Facts About the Major

Focuses on the Spanish language and related dialects; includes the cultural and historical contexts and applications to business, science/technology, and other settings.

Related CIP Program: 16.0905 Spanish Language and Literature.

Specializations in the Major: History and culture; language education; literature; translation.

Typical Sequence of College Courses: Spanish language, conversation, composition, linguistics, Spanish literature, Spanish-American literature, Spanish history and civilization, European history and civilization, grammar, phonetics.

Typical Sequence of High School Courses: English, public speaking, Spanish, history, literature, social science.

Career Snapshot

Spanish has become the second language in the United States, as well as maintaining its importance as a world language, especially in the Western Hemisphere. A degree in Spanish can be useful preparation (perhaps with an additional degree) for many careers in business, travel, and public service, and not just with an international orientation. High school teaching usually requires a master's degree for security and advancement.

Other Programs Related to the Same Jobs

African Languages, Literatures, and Linguistics; Albanian Language and Literature; American Indian/Native American Languages, Literatures, and Linguistics; American Sign Language (ASL); American Sign Language, Other; Ancient Near Eastern and Biblical Languages, Literatures, and Linguistics; Ancient/Classical Greek Language and Literature; Arabic Language and Literature; Australian/Oceanic/Pacific Languages, Literatures, and Linguistics; Bahasa Indonesian/Bahasa Malay Languages and Literatures; Baltic Languages, Literatures, and Linguistics; Bengali Language and Literature; Bulgarian Language and Literature; Burmese Language

and Literature; Catalan Language and Literature; Celtic Languages, Literatures, and Linguistics; Chinese Language and Literature; Classics and Classical Languages, Literatures, and Linguistics, General; Czech Language and Literature; Danish Language and Literature; Dutch/Flemish Language and Literature; East Asian Languages, Literatures, and Linguistics, General; East Asian Languages, Literatures, and Linguistics, Other; Education/Teaching of Individuals with Hearing Impairments, Including Deafness; Filipino/Tagalog Language and Literature; Finnish and Related Languages, Literatures, and Linguistics; Foreign Languages, Literatures, and Linguistics, Other; Foreign Languages/Modern Languages, General; French Language and Literature; German Language and Literature; Germanic Languages, Literatures, and Linguistics, General; Germanic Languages, Literatures, and Linguistics, Other; Hebrew Language and Literature; Hindi Language and Literature; Humanities/Humanistic Studies; Hungarian/Magyar Language and Literature; Iranian/Persian Languages, Literatures, and Linguistics; Italian Language and Literature; Japanese Language and Literature; Khmer/Cambodian Language and Literature; Korean Language and Literature; Language Interpretation and Translation; others.

Related Secure Job

(See Part IV for the full job description.)

Interpreters and Translators. Translate or interpret written, oral, or sign language text into another language for others.

Related Recession-Sensitive Job

None met the criteria.

Special Education

Useful Facts About the Major

Focuses on the design and provision of teaching and other educational services to children or adults with special learning needs or disabilities. May prepare individuals to function as special education teachers.

Related CIP Program: 13.1001 Special Education and Teaching, General.

Specializations in the Major: Autism; multiple disabilities; specific learning disabilities; speech-language impairments; traumatic brain injury; visual impairments.

Typical Sequence of College Courses: Introduction to psychology, English composition, oral communication, history and philosophy of education, human growth and development, introduction to special education, curriculum and methods for special education, educational psychology, psychology of the exceptional child, assessment in special education, classroom/laboratory management, behavior modification techniques in education, education for moderate and severe disabilities, reading assessment and teaching, mathematics education, student teaching.

Typical Sequence of High School Courses: English, algebra, geometry, trigonometry, science, foreign language, public speaking.

Career Snapshot

Special education covers a wide variety of learning and developmental disabilities and other conditions that require nonstandard educational techniques. Many states require a master's degree for licensure, but some states are offering alternative entry routes. Job opportunity in this field is excellent, especially in rural areas and inner cities and for specializations such as multiple disabilities, autism, and bilingual special education.

Other Programs Related to the Same Jobs

Education/Teaching of Individuals with Autism; Education/Teaching of Individuals with Emotional Disturbances; Education/Teaching of Individuals with Hearing Impairments, Including Deafness; Education/Teaching of Individuals with Mental Retardation; Education/Teaching of Individuals with Multiple Disabilities; Education/Teaching of Individuals with Orthopedic and Other Physical Health Impairments; Education/Teaching of Individuals with Specific Learning Disabilities; Education/Teaching of Individuals with Speech or Language Impairments; Education/Teaching of Individuals with Traumatic Brain Injuries; Education/Teaching of Individuals with Vision Impairments, Including Blindness; Special Education and Teaching, Other.

Related Secure Jobs

(See Part IV for the full job descriptions.)

1. Special Education Teachers, Middle School. Teach middle school subjects to educationally and physically handicapped students. Includes teachers who specialize and work with audibly and visually handicapped students and those who teach basic academic and life processes skills to the mentally impaired.

2. Special Education Teachers, Secondary School. Teach secondary school subjects to educationally and physically handicapped students.

Includes teachers who specialize and work with audibly and visually handicapped students and those who teach basic academic and life processes skills to the mentally impaired.

Related Recession-Sensitive Job

Special Education Teachers, Preschool, Kindergarten, and Elementary School.

Speech-Language Pathology and Audiology

Useful Facts About the Major

Integrates or coordinates several subjects to prepare individuals as audiologists and speech-language pathologists.

Related CIP Program: 51.0204 Audiology/Audiologist and Speech-Language Pathology/Pathologist.

Specializations in the Major: Audiology; speech-language pathology.

Typical Sequence of College Courses: General biology, English composition, general physics, introduction to psychology, human growth and development, statistics, introduction to sociology, introduction to speech, language and hearing, phonetics, anatomy of the speech and hearing mechanism, linguistics, psychoacoustics, neuroscience, auditory anatomy and physiology, stuttering and other fluency disorders, voice disorders, hearing problems, psycholinguistics and speech perception, diagnostic procedures in audiology, aural rehabilitation, research methods in speech pathology and audiology, student teaching.

Typical Sequence of High School Courses: English, algebra, geometry, trigonometry, biology, chemistry, physics, computer science, public speaking, social science, pre-calculus.

Career Snapshot

Speech-language pathologists and audiologists help people with a variety of communication disorders. About half of speech-language pathologists work in schools, most of the rest for health-care facilities. Among audiologists, about half work in health-care settings, with a smaller number in schools. A master's degree is the standard entry route for speech-language pathologists. For audiologists, a master's still suffices in many states, but a doctoral degree is becoming the standard. It is possible to complete the requirements for entering both kinds of graduate program within a variety of undergraduate majors. Because of the aging of the population and an emphasis on early diagnosis, job opportunities are expected to be excellent for speech-language pathologists, though less certain for audiologists. Knowledge of a second language is an advantage.

Other Programs Related to the Same Jobs

Audiology/Audiologist and Hearing Sciences; Communication Disorders, General; Speech-Language Pathology/Pathologist.

Related Secure Jobs

(See Part IV for the full job descriptions.)

1. Audiologists. Assess and treat persons with hearing and related disorders. May fit hearing aids and provide auditory training. May perform research related to hearing problems.

2. Speech-Language Pathologists. Assess and treat persons with speech, language, voice, and fluency disorders. May select alternative communication systems and teach their use. May perform research related to speech and language problems.

Related Recession-Sensitive Job

None met the criteria.

Statistics

Useful Facts About the Major

Focuses on the relationships between groups of measurements, and similarities and differences, using probability theory and techniques derived from it.

Related CIP Programs: 27.0502 Mathematical Statistics and Probability; 27.0501 Statistics, General.

Specializations in the Major: Computer applications; experimental design; mathematical statistics; probability; psychometrics.

Typical Sequence of College Courses: Calculus, introduction to computer science, programming in a language (e.g., C, Pascal, Java), statistics, linear algebra, experimental design and analysis, mathematical statistics, seminar (reporting on research).

Typical Sequence of High School Courses: Algebra, geometry, trigonometry, pre-calculus, calculus, computer science, physics.

Career Snapshot

Statistical analysis is a valuable tool that is used by every discipline that deals in quantitative information—social sciences, laboratory sciences, and business studies. Statisticians find meaningful patterns in data sets that are harvested from experiments, surveys, and other procedures such as bookkeeping. Graduates of statistics programs are in demand in many parts of the economy, from basic research to business management, from government to academia. Some get advanced degrees to specialize in research or college teaching or get a degree in a second field, such as psychology, computer science, or business.

Other Programs Related to the Same Jobs

Algebra and Number Theory; Analysis and Functional Analysis; Applied Mathematics; Applied Mathematics, Other; Biostatistics; Business Statistics; Computational Mathematics; Geometry/Geometric Analysis; Logic; Mathematical Statistics and Probability; Mathematics and Statistics, Other; Mathematics, General; Mathematics, Other; Statistics, General; Statistics, Other; Topology and Foundations.

Related Secure Jobs

(See Part IV for the full job descriptions.)

1. Mathematicians. Conduct research in fundamental mathematics or in application of mathematical techniques to science, management, and other fields. Solve or direct solutions to problems in various fields by mathematical methods.

2. Statisticians. Engage in the development of mathematical theory or apply statistical theory and methods to collect, organize, interpret, and summarize numerical data to provide usable information. May specialize in fields such as biostatistics, agricultural statistics, business statistics, economic statistics, or other fields.

Related Recession-Sensitive Job

Natural Sciences Managers.

Veterinary Medicine

Useful Facts About the Major

Prepares individuals for the independent professional practice of veterinary medicine, involving the diagnosis, treatment, and health-care management of animals and animal populations and the prevention and management of diseases that may be transmitted to humans.

Related CIP Program: 51.2401 Veterinary Medicine (DVM).

Specializations in the Major: Companion animals; large animals (horses; cattle); public health; research.

Typical Sequence of College Courses: English composition, introduction to psychology, college algebra, calculus, introduction to sociology, oral communication, general chemistry, general biology, introduction to computer science, organic chemistry, human anatomy and physiology, general microbiology, genetics, introduction to biochemistry, veterinary gross anatomy, neuroanatomy, veterinary histology and cell biology, veterinary radiology, animal nutrition and nutritional diseases, neuroanatomy, pathology, veterinary microbiology, pharmacology, veterinary

ophthalmology, public health, veterinary surgery, reproduction, veterinary toxicology, clinical veterinary experience.

Typical Sequence of High School Courses: English, algebra, geometry, trigonometry, biology, computer science, public speaking, chemistry, foreign language, physics, pre-calculus.

Career Snapshot

Veterinarians care for the health of animals (from dogs and cats to horses and cattle to exotic zoo animals), protect humans from diseases carried by animals, and conduct basic research on animal health. Most of them work in private practices. Some inspect animals or animal products for government agencies. Most students who enter the four-year veterinary school program have already completed a bachelor's degree that includes math and science coursework. Competition for entry to veterinary school is keen, but the job outlook is expected to be good.

Other Programs Related to the Same Jobs

Veterinary Anatomy (Cert, MS, PhD); Veterinary Anesthesiology; Veterinary Biomedical and Clinical Sciences, Other (Cert, MS. PhD); Veterinary Dentistry; Veterinary Dermatology; Veterinary Emergency and Critical Care Medicine; Veterinary Infectious Diseases (Cert, MS, PhD); Veterinary Internal Medicine; Veterinary Microbiology; Veterinary Microbiology and Immunobiology (Cert, MS, PhD); Veterinary Nutrition; Veterinary Ophthalmology; Veterinary Pathology; Veterinary Pathology and Pathobiology (Cert, MS, PhD); Veterinary Physiology (Cert, MS, PhD); Veterinary Practice; Veterinary Preventive Medicine; Veterinary Preventive

Medicine, Epidemiology, and Public Health (Cert, MS, PhD); Veterinary Radiology; Veterinary Residency Programs, Other; Veterinary Sciences/Veterinary Clinical Sciences, General (Cert, MS, PhD); Veterinary Surgery; Veterinary Toxicology; Veterinary Toxicology and Pharmacology (Cert, MS, PhD); Veterinary/Animal Health Technology/Technician and Veterinary Assistant; Zoological Medicine.

Related Secure Job

(See Part IV for the full job description.)

Veterinarians. Diagnose and treat diseases and dysfunctions of animals. May engage in a particular function, such as research and development, consultation, administration, technical writing, sale or production of commercial products, or rendering of technical services to commercial firms or other organizations. Includes veterinarians who inspect livestock.

Related Recession-Sensitive Job

None met the criteria.

Women's Studies

Useful Facts About the Major

Focuses on the history, sociology, politics, culture, and economics of women and the development of modern feminism in relation to the roles played by women in different periods and locations in North America and the world.

Related CIP Program: 05.0207 Women's Studies.

Specializations in the Major: Feminist theory; history of feminism; women's issues in art and culture; women's political issues.

Typical Sequence of College Courses: English composition, foreign language, American history, introduction to women's studies, women of color, theories of feminism, historical and philosophical origins of feminism, feminism from a global perspective, seminar (reporting on research).

Typical Sequence of High School Courses: English, algebra, foreign language, history, literature, public speaking, social science.

Career Snapshot

Women's studies is an interdisciplinary major that looks at the experience of women from the perspectives of history, literature, psychology, and sociology, among others. Graduates of this major may go into business fields where understanding of women's issues can be helpful—for example, advertising or human resources management. With further education, they may also find careers in fields where they can affect the lives of women, such as social work, law, public health, or public administration.

Other Programs Related to the Same Jobs

African Languages, Literatures, and Linguistics; African Studies; African-American/Black Studies; Agricultural Teacher Education; Albanian Language and Literature; American History; American Indian/Native American Studies; American Literature; American Studies; Ancient Near Eastern and Biblical Languages, Literatures, and Linguistics; Ancient/Classical Greek Language and Literature; Anthropology; Arabic

Language and Literature; Archeology; Area Studies; Art History, Criticism, and Conservation; Art/Art Studies, General; Arts Management; Asian History; Asian Studies/Civilization; Asian-American Studies; Australian/Oceanic/Pacific Languages, Literatures, and Linguistics; Bahasa Indonesian/Bahasa Malay Languages and Literatures; Balkans Studies; Baltic Languages, Literatures, and Linguistics; Baltic Studies; Bengali Language and Literature; Bible/Biblical Studies; Biology Teacher Education; Broadcast Journalism; Buddhist Studies; Bulgarian Language and Literature; Burmese Language and Literature; Business Teacher Education; Business/Managerial Economics; Canadian History; Canadian Studies; Caribbean Studies; Catalan Language and Literature; Celtic Languages, Literatures, and Linguistics; Central/Middle and Eastern European Studies; Ceramic Arts and Ceramics; Chemistry Teacher Education; Chinese Language and Literature; Chinese Studies; Christian Studies; Cinematography and Film/Video Production; Classics and Classical Languages, Literatures, and Linguistics, General; Clinical Psychology; Cognitive Psychology and Psycholinguistics; Commercial Photography; Commonwealth Studies; Communications Studies/Speech Communication and Rhetoric; Communications, Journalism, and Related Fields, Other; Community Psychology; Comparative Literature; Comparative Psychology; Computer Teacher Education; Conducting; Counseling Psychology; Crafts/Craft Design, Folk Art, and Artisanry; Creative Writing; Czech Language and Literature; Dance, General; Danish Language and Literature; Design and Applied Arts, Other; Design and Visual Communications, General; others.

Related Secure Job

(See Part IV for the full job description.)

Area, Ethnic, and Cultural Studies Teachers, Postsecondary. Teach courses pertaining to the culture and development of an area (e.g., Latin America), an ethnic group, or any other group (e.g., women's studies, urban affairs).

Related Recession-Sensitive Job

None met the criteria.

PART IV

Descriptions of Related Secure Jobs

This part provides descriptions for all the secure jobs referred to in Part III. The introduction gives more details on how to use and interpret the job descriptions, but here is some additional information:

- Job descriptions are arranged in alphabetical order by job title. This approach allows you to find a description quickly if you know its correct title from one of the descriptions of majors in Part III.

- Consider the job descriptions in this section as a first step in career exploration. When you find a job that interests you, turn to the appendix for suggestions about resources for further exploration.

- If you are using this section to browse for interesting options, we suggest you begin with the Table of Contents. You may also use this section to identify interesting majors and then read about them in Part III, where they are ordered alphabetically.

Actuaries

Related Major: Actuarial Science

* Education/Training Required: Work experience plus degree
* Annual Earnings: $85,690
* Beginning Wage: $48,750
* Earnings Growth Potential: High (43.1%)
* Growth: 23.7%
* Annual Job Openings: 3,245
* Self-Employed: 0.0%
* Part-Time: 5.9%

Industries with Greatest Employment: Insurance Carriers and Related Activities (59.9%); Professional, Scientific, and Technical Services (21.1%); Management of Companies and Enterprises (8.5%).

Highest-Growth Industries (Projected Growth for This Job): Professional, Scientific, and Technical Services (75.7%); Securities, Commodity Contracts, and Other Financial Investments and Related Activities (44.1%); Management of Companies and Enterprises (38.3%); Administrative and Support Services (26.5%); Funds, Trusts, and Other Financial Vehicles (23.3%).

Lowest-Growth Industries (Projected Growth for This Job): Federal Government (–5.5%); State Government (–1.9%); Insurance Carriers and Related Activities (5.4%); Credit Intermediation and Related Activities (10.8%); Local Government (12.0%).

Fastest-Growing Metropolitan Areas (Recent Growth for This Job): Columbus, OH (176.5%); Providence–Fall River–Warwick, RI-MA (100.0%); Buffalo–Niagara Falls, NY (50.0%); San Diego–Carlsbad–San Marcos, CA (50.0%); Phoenix-Mesa-Scottsdale, AZ (44.4%).

Other Considerations for Job Security: Opportunities for actuaries should be good, particularly for those who have passed at least one or two of the initial exams. Candidates with additional knowledge or experience, such as computer programming skills, will be particularly attractive to employers. Most jobs in this occupation are located in urban areas, but opportunities vary by geographic location. Steady demand by the insurance industry should ensure that actuarial jobs in this key industry will remain stable through 2016.

Analyze statistical data, such as mortality, accident, sickness, disability, and retirement rates, and construct probability tables to forecast risk and liability for payment of future benefits. May ascertain premium rates required and cash reserves necessary to ensure payment of future benefits. Ascertain premium rates required and cash reserves and liabilities necessary to ensure payment of future benefits. Analyze statistical information to estimate mortality, accident, sickness, disability, and retirement rates. Design, review, and help administer insurance, annuity, and pension plans, determining financial soundness and calculating premiums. Collaborate with programmers, underwriters, accountants, claims experts, and senior management to help companies develop plans for new lines of business or for improving existing business. Determine or help determine company policy and explain complex technical matters to company executives, government officials, shareholders, policyholders, or the public. Testify before public agencies on proposed legislation affecting businesses. Provide advice to clients on a contract basis, working as a consultant. Testify in court as expert witness or to provide legal evidence on matters such as the value of potential lifetime earnings of a person who is disabled or killed in an accident. Construct probability tables for events such as fires, natural disasters, and unemployment, based on analysis of statistical data and other pertinent information. Determine policy contract provisions for each type of insurance. Manage credit and help price corporate security offerings. Provide expertise to help financial institutions manage risks and maximize returns associated with investment products or credit offerings. Determine equitable basis for distributing surplus earnings under participating insurance and annuity contracts in mutual companies. Explain changes in contract provisions to customers.

Personality Type: Conventional-Investigative. Conventional occupations frequently involve following set procedures and routines. These occupations can include working with data and details more than with ideas. Usually there is a clear line of authority to follow.

Career Cluster: 06 Finance. **Career Pathway:** 06.4 Insurance Services.

Skills—Programming: Writing computer programs for various purposes. **Mathematics:** Using mathematics to solve problems. **Operations Analysis:** Analyzing needs and product requirements to create a design. **Complex Problem Solving:** Identifying complex problems and reviewing related information to develop and evaluate options and implement solutions. **Active Learning:** Understanding the implications of new information for both current and future problem-solving and decision making. **Quality Control Analysis:** Conducting tests and inspections of products, services, or processes to evaluate quality or performance.

Related Knowledge/Courses—Mathematics: Numbers and their operations and interrelationships, including arithmetic, algebra, geometry, calculus, and statistics and their applications.

Economics and Accounting: Economic and accounting principles and practices, the financial markets, banking, and the analysis and reporting of financial data. **Sales and Marketing:** Principles and methods involved in showing, promoting, and selling products or services. This includes marketing strategies and tactics, product demonstration and sales techniques, and sales control systems. **Computers and Electronics:** Electric circuit boards, processors, chips, and computer hardware and software, including applications and programming. **Personnel and Human Resources:** Principles and procedures for personnel recruitment; selection; training; compensation and benefits; labor relations and negotiation; and personnel information systems. **Law and Government:** Laws, legal codes, court procedures, precedents, government regulations, executive orders, agency rules, and the democratic political process.

Work Environment: Indoors; sitting; using hands on objects, tools, or controls; repetitive motions.

Agricultural Sciences Teachers, Postsecondary

Related Major: Graduate Study for College Teaching

- ❋ Education/Training Required: Master's degree
- ❋ Annual Earnings: $78,460
- ❋ Beginning Wage: $43,050
- ❋ Earnings Growth Potential: High (45.1%)
- ❋ Growth: 22.9%
- ❋ Annual Job Openings: 1,840
- ❋ Self-Employed: 0.4%
- ❋ Part-Time: 27.8%

Industries with Greatest Employment: Educational Services, Public and Private (97.3%).

Highest-Growth Industries (Projected Growth for This Job): Administrative and Support Services (48.3%); Amusement, Gambling, and Recreation Industries (45.2%); Social Assistance (38.6%); Support Activities for Transportation (32.8%); Religious, Grantmaking, Civic, Professional, and Similar Organizations (29.9%); Professional, Scientific, and Technical Services (28.8%); Management of Companies and Enterprises (26.8%); Local Government (23.5%); Educational Services, Public and Private (22.8%); Hospitals, Public and Private (21.4%).

Lowest-Growth Industries (Projected Growth for This Job): Other Information Services (7.4%); State Government (7.9%); Sporting Goods, Hobby, Book, and Music Stores (13.3%); Performing Arts, Spectator Sports, and Related Industries (13.4%); Insurance Carriers and Related Activities (13.8%).

Fastest-Growing Metropolitan Areas (Recent Growth for This Job): Lakeland, FL (22.2%).

Other Considerations for Job Security: Retirements of current postsecondary teachers should create numerous openings for all types of postsecondary teachers, so job opportunities are generally expected to be very good. One of the main reasons why students attend postsecondary institutions is to prepare themselves for careers, so the best job prospects for postsecondary teachers are likely to be in rapidly growing fields, such as agricultural sciences, that offer many nonacademic career options. Community colleges and other institutions offering career and technical education have been among the most rapidly growing, and these institutions are expected to offer some of the best opportunities for postsecondary teachers.

Teach courses in the agricultural sciences, including agronomy, dairy sciences, fisheries management, horticultural sciences, poultry sciences, range management, and agricultural soil conservation. Prepare course materials such as syllabi, homework assignments, and handouts. Evaluate and grade students' classwork, laboratory work, assignments, and papers. Keep abreast of developments in agriculture by reading current literature, talking with colleagues, and participating in professional conferences. Prepare and deliver lectures to undergraduate and/or graduate students on topics such as crop production, plant genetics, and soil chemistry. Initiate, facilitate, and moderate classroom discussions. Conduct research in a particular field of knowledge and publish findings in professional journals, books, and/or electronic media. Supervise laboratory sessions and fieldwork and coordinate laboratory operations. Supervise undergraduate and/or graduate teaching, internship, and research work. Compile, administer, and grade examinations or assign this work to others. Advise students on academic and vocational curricula and on career issues. Plan, evaluate, and revise curricula, course content, and course materials and methods of instruction. Maintain student attendance records, grades, and other required records. Write grant proposals to procure external research funding. Collaborate with colleagues to address teaching and research issues. Maintain regularly scheduled office hours in order to advise and assist students. Participate in student recruitment, registration, and placement activities. Select and obtain materials and supplies such as textbooks and laboratory equipment. Act as advisers to student organizations. Participate in campus and community events. Serve on academic or administrative committees that deal with institutional policies, departmental matters, and academic issues. Provide professional consulting services to government and/or industry. Perform administrative duties such as serving as department head. Compile bibliographies of specialized materials for outside reading assignments.

Personality Type: Investigative-Social. Investigative occupations frequently involve working with ideas and require an extensive amount of thinking. These occupations can involve searching for facts and figuring out problems mentally.

Career Clusters: 01 Agriculture, Food, and Natural Resources; 05 Education and Training. **Career Pathways:** 01.1 Food Products and Processing Systems; 01.2 Plant Systems; 01.3 Animal Systems; 01.4 Power Structure and Technical Systems; 01.7 Agribusiness Systems; 05.3 Teaching/Training.

Skills—Science: Using scientific rules and methods to solve problems. **Management of Financial Resources:** Determining how money will be spent to get the work done and accounting for these expenditures. **Writing:** Communicating effectively in writing as appropriate for the needs of the audience. **Reading Comprehension:** Understanding written sentences and paragraphs in work-related documents. **Instructing:** Teaching others how to do something. **Complex Problem Solving:** Identifying complex problems and reviewing related information to develop and evaluate options and implement solutions.

Related Knowledge/Courses—Biology: Plant and animal living tissue, cells, organisms, and entities, including their functions, interdependencies, and interactions with each other and the environment. **Food Production:** Techniques and equipment for planting, growing, and harvesting of food for consumption, including crop-

rotation methods, animal husbandry, and food storage/handling techniques. **Education and Training:** Instructional methods and training techniques, including curriculum design principles, learning theory, group and individual teaching techniques, design of individual development plans, and test design principles. **Geography:** Various methods for describing the location and distribution of land, sea, and air masses, including their physical locations, relationships, and characteristics. **Chemistry:** The composition, structure, and properties of substances and of the chemical processes and transformations that they undergo. This includes uses of chemicals and their interactions, danger signs, production techniques, and disposal methods. **Communications and Media:** Media production, communication, and dissemination techniques and methods, including alternative ways to inform and entertain via written, oral, and visual media.

Work Environment: Indoors; sitting.

Anesthesiologists

Related Major: Medicine

- ✸ Education/Training Required: First professional degree
- ✸ Annual Earnings: More than $145,600
- ✸ Beginning Wage: $118,320
- ✸ Earnings Growth Potential: Cannot be calculated
- ✸ Growth: 14.2%
- ✸ Annual Job Openings: 38,027
- ✸ Self-Employed: 14.7%
- ✸ Part-Time: 8.1%

Industries with Greatest Employment: Ambulatory Health Care Services (55.9%); Hospitals, Public and Private (17.8%).

Highest-Growth Industries (Projected Growth for This Job): Social Assistance (58.6%); Administrative and Support Services (26.8%); Professional, Scientific, and Technical Services (22.6%); Nursing and Residential Care Facilities (21.0%); Ambulatory Health Care Services (19.4%); Religious, Grantmaking, Civic, Professional, and Similar Organizations (16.7%); Management of Companies and Enterprises (15.3%).

Lowest-Growth Industries (Projected Growth for This Job): Federal Government (–5.5%); State Government (–1.9%); Insurance Carriers and Related Activities (4.6%); Health and Personal Care Stores (5.3%); Hospitals, Public and Private (9.9%); Educational Services, Public and Private (11.8%); Local Government (12.3%).

Fastest-Growing Metropolitan Areas (Recent Growth for This Job): Mayaguez, PR (66.7%); Mobile, AL (66.7%); Austin–Round Rock, TX (55.0%); Memphis, TN-MS-AR (54.5%); Columbus, OH (52.6%).

Other Considerations for Job Security: Opportunities for individuals interested in becoming physicians and surgeons are expected to be very good. Unlike their predecessors, new physicians are much less likely to enter solo practice and more likely to take salaried jobs in group medical practices, clinics, and health networks. Reports of shortages in some specialties, such as general or family practice, internal medicine, and OB/GYN, or in rural or low-income areas should attract new entrants, encouraging schools to expand programs and hospitals to increase available residency slots. However, because physician training is so lengthy, employment change happens gradually. Opportunities should be particularly good in rural and low-income areas, as some physicians find these areas unattractive because of less control over work hours, isolation from medical colleagues, or other reasons.

Administer anesthetics during surgery or other medical procedures. Administer anesthetic or sedation during medical procedures, using local, intravenous, spinal, or caudal methods. Monitor patient before, during, and after anesthesia and counteract adverse reactions or complications. Provide and maintain life support and airway management and help prepare patients for emergency surgery. Record type and amount of anesthesia and patient condition throughout procedure. Examine patient; obtain medical history; and use diagnostic tests to determine risk during surgical, obstetrical, and other medical procedures. Position patient on operating table to maximize patient comfort and surgical accessibility. Decide when patients have recovered or stabilized enough to be sent to another room or ward or to be sent home following outpatient surgery. Coordinate administration of anesthetics with surgeons during operation. Confer with other medical professionals to determine type and method of anesthetic or sedation to render patient insensible to pain. Coordinate and direct work of nurses, medical technicians, and other health-care providers. Order laboratory tests, X rays, and other diagnostic procedures. Diagnose illnesses, using examinations, tests, and reports. Manage anesthesiological services, coordinating them with other medical activities and formulating plans and procedures. Provide medical care and consultation in many settings, prescribing medication and treatment and referring patients for surgery. Inform students and staff of types and methods of anesthesia administration, signs of complications, and emergency methods to counteract reactions. Schedule and maintain use of surgical suite, including operating, wash-up, and waiting rooms and anesthetic and sterilizing equipment. Instruct individuals and groups on ways to preserve health and prevent disease. Conduct medical research to aid in controlling and curing disease, to investigate new medications, and to develop and test new medical techniques.

Personality Type: Investigative-Realistic. Investigative occupations frequently involve working with ideas and require an extensive amount of thinking. These occupations can involve searching for facts and figuring out problems mentally.

Career Cluster: 08 Health Science. **Career Pathway:** 08.1 Therapeutic Services.

Skills—Operation Monitoring: Watching gauges, dials, or other indicators to make sure a machine is working properly. **Science:** Using scientific rules and methods to solve problems. **Operation and Control:** Controlling operations of equipment or systems. **Judgment and Decision Making:** Considering the relative costs and benefits of potential actions to choose the most appropriate one. **Equipment Selection:** Determining the kind of tools and equipment needed to do a job. **Monitoring:** Monitoring/assessing your performance or that of other individuals or organizations to make improvements or take corrective action.

Related Knowledge/Courses—Medicine and Dentistry: The information and techniques needed to diagnose and treat injuries, diseases, and deformities. This includes symptoms, treatment alternatives, drug properties and interactions, and preventive health-care measures. **Biology:** Plant and animal living tissue, cells, organisms, and entities, including their functions, interdependencies, and interactions with each other and the environment. **Chemistry:** The composition, structure, and properties of substances and of the chemical processes and transformations that they undergo. This includes uses of chemicals and their interactions, danger

signs, production techniques, and disposal methods. **Psychology:** Human behavior and performance, mental processes, psychological research methods, and the assessment and treatment of behavioral and affective disorders. **Physics:** Physical principles, laws, and applications, including air, water, material dynamics, light, atomic principles, heat, electric theory, earth formations, and meteorological and related natural phenomena. **Therapy and Counseling:** Information and techniques needed to rehabilitate physical and mental ailments and to provide career guidance, including alternative treatments, rehabilitation equipment and its proper use, and methods to evaluate treatment effects.

Work Environment: Indoors; contaminants; radiation; disease or infections; standing; using hands on objects, tools, or controls.

Anthropologists

Related Majors: Anthropology; Archeology
  - ⊛ Education/Training Required: Master's degree
  - ⊛ Annual Earnings: $53,080
  - ⊛ Beginning Wage: $31,130
  - ⊛ Earnings Growth Potential: High (41.4%)
  - ⊛ Growth: 15.0%
  - ⊛ Annual Job Openings: 446
  - ⊛ Self-Employed: 6.1%
  - ⊛ Part-Time: 20.1%

Industries with Greatest Employment: Professional, Scientific, and Technical Services (50.7%); Federal Government (25.2%); State Government (6.8%).

Highest-Growth Industries (Projected Growth for This Job): Museums, Historical

Sites, and Similar Institutions (36.2%); Professional, Scientific, and Technical Services (27.8%).

Lowest-Growth Industries (Projected Growth for This Job): Federal Government (–5.4%); State Government (–1.9%); Educational Services, Public and Private (11.8%); Local Government (12.5%).

Fastest-Growing Metropolitan Areas (Recent Growth for This Job): New York–Northern New Jersey–Long Island, NY-NJ-PA (73.3%); Portland-Vancouver-Beaverton, OR-WA (71.4%); Farmington, NM (40.0%).

Other Considerations for Job Security: Job seekers may face competition, and those with higher educational attainment will have the best prospects. Anthropologists will experience the majority of their job growth in the management, scientific, and technical consulting services industry. Anthropologists who work as consultants apply anthropological knowledge and methods to problems ranging from economic development issues to forensics. There will be keen competition for tenured positions as university faculty.

Research, evaluate, and establish public policy concerning the origins of humans; their physical, social, linguistic, and cultural development; and their behavior, as well as the cultures, organizations, and institutions they have created. Collect information and make judgments through observation, interviews, and the review of documents. Plan and direct research to characterize and compare the economic, demographic, health-care, social, political, linguistic, and religious institutions of distinct cultural groups, communities, and organizations. Write about and present research findings for a variety of specialized and general

audiences. Advise government agencies, private organizations, and communities regarding proposed programs, plans, and policies and their potential impacts on cultural institutions, organizations, and communities. Identify culturally specific beliefs and practices affecting health status and access to services for distinct populations and communities in collaboration with medical and public health officials. Build and use text-based database management systems to support the analysis of detailed firsthand observational records, or "field notes." Develop intervention procedures, utilizing techniques such as individual and focus group interviews, consultations, and participant observation of social interaction. Construct and test data collection methods. Explain the origins and physical, social, or cultural development of humans, including physical attributes, cultural traditions, beliefs, languages, resource management practices, and settlement patterns. Conduct participatory action research in communities and organizations to assess how work is done and to design work systems, technologies, and environments. Train others in the application of ethnographic research methods to solve problems in organizational effectiveness, communications, technology development, policy making, and program planning. Formulate general rules that describe and predict the development and behavior of cultures and social institutions. Collaborate with economic development planners to decide on the implementation of proposed development policies, plans, and programs based on culturally institutionalized barriers and facilitating circumstances. Create data records for use in describing and analyzing social patterns and processes, using photography, videography, and audio recordings.

Personality Type: Investigative-Social-Artistic. Investigative occupations frequently involve working with ideas and require an extensive amount of thinking. These occupations can involve searching for facts and figuring out problems mentally.

Career Cluster: 15 Science, Technology, Engineering, and Mathematics. **Career Pathway:** 15.3 Science and Mathematics.

Skills—Writing: Communicating effectively in writing as appropriate for the needs of the audience. **Science:** Using scientific rules and methods to solve problems. **Social Perceptiveness:** Being aware of others' reactions and understanding why they react as they do. **Complex Problem Solving:** Identifying complex problems and reviewing related information to develop and evaluate options and implement solutions. **Systems Evaluation:** Identifying measures or indicators of system performance and the actions needed to improve or correct performance relative to the goals of the system. **Reading Comprehension:** Understanding written sentences and paragraphs in work-related documents.

Related Knowledge/Courses—Sociology and Anthropology: Group behavior and dynamics; societal trends and influences; and cultures and their history, migrations, ethnicity, and origins. **History and Archeology:** Historical events and their causes, indicators, and impact on particular civilizations and cultures. **Foreign Language:** The structure and content of a foreign (non-English) language, including the meaning and spelling of words, rules of composition and grammar, and pronunciation. **Philosophy and Theology:** Different philosophical systems and religions, including their basic principles, values, ethics, ways of thinking, customs, and practices and their impact on human culture. **Geography:** Various methods for describing the location and distribution of land, sea, and air masses, including their physical locations, relationships, and

characteristics. **Biology:** Plant and animal living tissue, cells, organisms, and entities, including their functions, interdependencies, and interactions with each other and the environment.

Work Environment: Indoors; sitting.

Anthropology and Archeology Teachers, Postsecondary

Related Major: Graduate Study for College Teaching

- ❋ Education/Training Required: Master's degree
- ❋ Annual Earnings: $64,530
- ❋ Beginning Wage: $38,840
- ❋ Earnings Growth Potential: Medium (39.8%)
- ❋ Growth: 22.9%
- ❋ Annual Job Openings: 910
- ❋ Self-Employed: 0.4%
- ❋ Part-Time: 27.8%

Industries with Greatest Employment: Educational Services, Public and Private (97.3%).

Highest-Growth Industries (Projected Growth for This Job): Administrative and Support Services (48.3%); Amusement, Gambling, and Recreation Industries (45.2%); Social Assistance (38.6%); Support Activities for Transportation (32.8%); Religious, Grantmaking, Civic, Professional, and Similar Organizations (29.9%); Professional, Scientific, and Technical Services (28.8%); Management of Companies and Enterprises (26.8%); Local Government (23.5%); Educational Services, Public and Private (22.8%); Hospitals, Public and Private (21.4%).

Lowest-Growth Industries (Projected Growth for This Job): Other Information Services

(7.4%); State Government (7.9%); Sporting Goods, Hobby, Book, and Music Stores (13.3%); Performing Arts, Spectator Sports, and Related Industries (13.4%); Insurance Carriers and Related Activities (13.8%).

Fastest-Growing Metropolitan Areas (Recent Growth for This Job): Los Angeles–Long Beach–Santa Ana, CA (80.0%); Riverside–San Bernardino–Ontario, CA (33.3%); Boston-Cambridge-Quincy, MA-NH (18.2%); Washington-Arlington-Alexandria, DC-VA-MD-WV (16.7%); Atlanta–Sandy Springs–Marietta, GA (14.3%).

Other Considerations for Job Security: Retirements of current postsecondary teachers should create numerous openings for all types of postsecondary teachers, so job opportunities are generally expected to be very good. However, one of the main reasons why students attend postsecondary institutions is to prepare themselves for careers, so the best job prospects for postsecondary teachers are likely to be in rapidly growing fields that offer many nonacademic career options—unlike anthropology and archeology. Community colleges and other institutions offering career and technical education have been among the most rapidly growing, and these institutions are expected to offer some of the best opportunities for postsecondary teachers.

Teach courses in anthropology or archeology. Conduct research in a particular field of knowledge and publish findings in professional journals, books, and electronic media. Keep abreast of developments in their field by reading current literature, talking with colleagues, and participating in professional conferences. Prepare and deliver lectures to undergraduate and graduate students on topics such as research methods, urban anthropology, and language and culture. Evaluate and grade students' classwork, assignments, and papers. Initiate, facilitate, and moderate classroom discussions. Write grant proposals to procure external research funding. Supervise undergraduate and/or graduate teaching, internship, and research work. Prepare course materials such as syllabi, homework assignments, and handouts. Compile, administer, and grade examinations or assign this work to others. Supervise students' laboratory work or fieldwork. Plan, evaluate, and revise curricula, course content, and course materials and methods of instruction. Advise students on academic and vocational curricula, career issues, and laboratory and field research. Maintain student attendance records, grades, and other required records. Maintain regularly scheduled office hours in order to advise and assist students. Collaborate with colleagues to address teaching and research issues. Compile bibliographies of specialized materials for outside reading assignments. Perform administrative duties such as serving as department head. Select and obtain materials and supplies such as textbooks and laboratory equipment. Serve on academic or administrative committees that deal with institutional policies, departmental matters, and academic issues. Participate in student recruitment, registration, and placement activities. Participate in campus and community events. Provide professional consulting services to government and industry. Act as advisers to student organizations.

Personality Type: Social-Investigative-Artistic. Social occupations frequently involve working with, communicating with, and teaching people. These occupations often involve helping or providing service to others.

Career Clusters: 12 Law, Public Safety, Corrections, and Security; 15 Science, Technology, Engineering, and Mathematics. **Career Pathways:** 12.4 Law Enforcement Services; 15.3 Science and Mathematics.

Skills—Science: Using scientific rules and methods to solve problems. **Writing:** Communicating effectively in writing as appropriate for the needs of the audience. **Critical Thinking:** Using logic and reasoning to identify the strengths and weaknesses of alternative solutions, conclusions, or approaches to problems. **Reading Comprehension:** Understanding written sentences and paragraphs in work-related documents. **Active Learning:** Understanding the implications of new information for both current and future problem-solving and decision-making. **Instructing:** Teaching others how to do something.

Related Knowledge/Courses—Sociology and Anthropology: Group behavior and dynamics; societal trends and influences; and cultures and their history, migrations, ethnicity, and origins. **History and Archeology:** Historical events and their causes, indicators, and impact on particular civilizations and cultures. **Geography:** Various methods for describing the location and distribution of land, sea, and air masses, including their physical locations, relationships, and characteristics. **Foreign Language:** The structure and content of a foreign (non-English) language, including the meaning and spelling of words, rules of composition and grammar, and pronunciation. **Philosophy and Theology:** Different philosophical systems and religions, including their basic principles, values, ethics, ways of thinking, customs, and practices and their impact on human culture. **English Language:** The structure and content of the English language, including the meaning and spelling of words, rules of composition, and grammar.

Work Environment: Indoors; sitting.

Archeologists

Related Majors: Anthropology; Archeology

- Education/Training Required: Master's degree
- Annual Earnings: $53,080
- Beginning Wage: $31,130
- Earnings Growth Potential: High (41.4%)
- Growth: 15.0%
- Annual Job Openings: 446
- Self-Employed: 6.1%
- Part-Time: 20.1%

Industries with Greatest Employment: Professional, Scientific, and Technical Services (50.7%); Federal Government (25.2%); State Government (6.8%).

Highest-Growth Industries (Projected Growth for This Job): Museums, Historical Sites, and Similar Institutions (36.2%); Professional, Scientific, and Technical Services (27.8%).

Lowest-Growth Industries (Projected Growth for This Job): Federal Government (–5.4%); State Government (–1.9%); Educational Services, Public and Private (11.8%); Local Government (12.5%).

Fastest-Growing Metropolitan Areas (Recent Growth for This Job): New York–Northern New Jersey–Long Island, NY-NJ-PA (73.3%); Portland-Vancouver-Beaverton, OR-WA (71.4%); Farmington, NM (40.0%).

Other Considerations for Job Security: Job seekers may face competition, and those with higher educational attainment will have the best prospects. As construction projects increase, more archaeologists will be needed to monitor the work, ensuring that historical sites and artifacts are preserved. Some people with social science degrees will find opportunities as university faculty rather than as applied social scientists. Although there will be keen competition for tenured positions, the number of faculty expected to retire over the decade and the increasing number of part-time or short-term faculty positions will lead to better opportunities in colleges and universities than in the past.

Conduct research to reconstruct record of past human life and culture from human remains, artifacts, architectural features, and structures recovered through excavation, underwater recovery, or other means of discovery. Write, present, and publish reports that record site history, methodology, and artifact analysis results, along with recommendations for conserving and interpreting findings. Compare findings from one site with archeological data from other sites to find similarities or differences. Research, survey, or assess sites of past societies and cultures in search of answers to specific research questions. Study objects and structures recovered by excavation to identify, date, and authenticate them and to interpret their significance. Develop and test theories concerning the origin and development of past cultures. Consult site reports, existing artifacts, and topographic maps to identify archeological sites. Create a grid of each site and draw and update maps of unit profiles, stratum surfaces, features, and findings. Record the exact locations and conditions of artifacts uncovered in diggings or surveys, using drawings and photographs as necessary. Assess archeological sites for resource management, development, or conservation purposes and recommend methods for site protection. Describe artifacts' physical properties or attributes, such as the materials from which artifacts are made and their size, shape, function, and decoration. Teach archeology at colleges and universities.

Collect artifacts made of stone, bone, metal, and other materials, placing them in bags and marking them to show where they were found. Create artifact typologies to organize and make sense of past material cultures. Lead field training sites and train field staff, students, and volunteers in excavation methods. Clean, restore, and preserve artifacts.

Personality Type: Investigative-Realistic. Investigative occupations frequently involve working with ideas and require an extensive amount of thinking. These occupations can involve searching for facts and figuring out problems mentally.

Career Cluster: 15 Science, Technology, Engineering, and Mathematics. **Career Pathway:** 15.3 Science and Mathematics.

Skills—Science: Using scientific rules and methods to solve problems. **Management of Financial Resources:** Determining how money will be spent to get the work done and accounting for these expenditures. **Writing:** Communicating effectively in writing as appropriate for the needs of the audience. **Management of Personnel Resources:** Motivating, developing, and directing people as they work, identifying the best people for the job. **Reading Comprehension:** Understanding written sentences and paragraphs in work-related documents. **Active Learning:** Understanding the implications of new information for both current and future problem-solving and decision-making.

Related Knowledge/Courses—History and Archeology: Historical events and their causes, indicators, and impact on particular civilizations and cultures. **Sociology and Anthropology:** Group behavior and dynamics; societal trends and influences; and cultures and their history, migrations, ethnicity, and origins. **Geography:**

Various methods for describing the location and distribution of land, sea, and air masses, including their physical locations, relationships, and characteristics. **Philosophy and Theology:** Different philosophical systems and religions, including their basic principles, values, ethics, ways of thinking, customs, and practices and their impact on human culture. **Foreign Language:** The structure and content of a foreign (non-English) language, including the meaning and spelling of words, rules of composition and grammar, and pronunciation. **Biology:** Plant and animal living tissue, cells, organisms, and entities, including their functions, interdependencies, and interactions with each other and the environment.

Work Environment: More often indoors than outdoors; sitting; using hands on objects, tools, or controls.

Architecture Teachers, Postsecondary

Related Major: Graduate Study for College Teaching

- ❋ Education/Training Required: Master's degree
- ❋ Annual Earnings: $68,540
- ❋ Beginning Wage: $41,080
- ❋ Earnings Growth Potential: High (40.1%)
- ❋ Growth: 22.9%
- ❋ Annual Job Openings: 1,044
- ❋ Self-Employed: 0.4%
- ❋ Part-Time: 27.8%

Industries with Greatest Employment: Educational Services, Public and Private (97.3%).

Highest-Growth Industries (Projected Growth for This Job): Administrative and Support Services (48.3%); Amusement, Gambling, and Recreation Industries (45.2%); Social Assistance (38.6%); Support Activities for Transportation (32.8%); Religious, Grantmaking, Civic, Professional, and Similar Organizations (29.9%); Professional, Scientific, and Technical Services (28.8%); Management of Companies and Enterprises (26.8%); Local Government (23.5%); Educational Services, Public and Private (22.8%); Hospitals, Public and Private (21.4%).

Lowest-Growth Industries (Projected Growth for This Job): Other Information Services (7.4%); State Government (7.9%); Sporting Goods, Hobby, Book, and Music Stores (13.3%); Performing Arts, Spectator Sports, and Related Industries (13.4%); Insurance Carriers and Related Activities (13.8%).

Fastest-Growing Metropolitan Areas (Recent Growth for This Job): New York–Northern New Jersey–Long Island, NY-NJ-PA (85.0%); Milwaukee–Waukesha–West Allis, WI (16.7%).

Other Considerations for Job Security: Retirements of current postsecondary teachers should create numerous openings for all types of postsecondary teachers, so job opportunities are generally expected to be very good. One of the main reasons why students attend postsecondary institutions is to prepare themselves for careers, so the best job prospects for postsecondary teachers are likely to be in rapidly growing fields that offer many nonacademic career options. Community colleges and other institutions offering career and technical education have been among the most rapidly growing, and these institutions are expected to offer some of the best opportunities for postsecondary teachers.

Teach courses in architecture and architectural design, such as architectural environmental design, interior architecture/design, and landscape architecture. Evaluate and grade students' work, including work performed in design studios. Prepare and deliver lectures to undergraduate and/or graduate students on topics such as architectural design methods, aesthetics and design, and structures and materials. Prepare course materials such as syllabi, homework assignments, and handouts. Initiate, facilitate, and moderate classroom discussions. Plan, evaluate, and revise curricula, course content, and course materials and methods of instruction. Keep abreast of developments in their field by reading current literature, talking with colleagues, and participating in professional conferences. Maintain student attendance records, grades, and other required records. Maintain regularly scheduled office hours to advise and assist students. Compile, administer, and grade examinations or assign this work to others. Conduct research in a particular field of knowledge and publish findings in professional journals, books, and/or electronic media. Supervise undergraduate and/or graduate teaching, internship, and research work. Advise students on academic and vocational curricula and on career issues. Collaborate with colleagues to address teaching and research issues. Compile bibliographies of specialized materials for outside reading assignments. Serve on academic or administrative committees that deal with institutional policies, departmental matters, and academic issues. Participate in student recruitment, registration, and placement activities. Select and obtain materials and supplies such as textbooks and laboratory equipment. Write grant proposals to procure external research funding. Provide professional consulting services to government and/or industry. Perform administrative duties such as serving as department head. Act as advisers to student organizations. Participate in campus and community events.

Personality Type: No data available.

Career Clusters: 02 Architecture and Construction; 05 Education and Training; 07 Government and Public Administration; 15 Science, Technology, Engineering, and Mathematics. **Career Pathways:** 02.1 Design/Pre-Construction; 05.3 Teaching/Training; 07.4 Planning; 15.1 Engineering and Technology.

Skills—Technology Design: Generating or adapting equipment and technology to serve user needs. **Operations Analysis:** Analyzing needs and product requirements to create a design. **Instructing:** Teaching others how to do something. **Writing:** Communicating effectively in writing as appropriate for the needs of the audience. **Science:** Using scientific rules and methods to solve problems. **Complex Problem Solving:** Identifying complex problems and reviewing related information to develop and evaluate options and implement solutions.

Related Knowledge/Courses—Fine Arts: Theory and techniques required to produce, compose, and perform works of music, dance, visual arts, drama, and sculpture. **Design:** Design techniques, principles, tools, and instruments involved in the production and use of precision technical plans, blueprints, drawings, and models. **Building and Construction:** Materials, methods, and the appropriate tools to construct objects, structures, and buildings. **History and Archeology:** Historical events and their causes, indicators, and impact on particular civilizations and cultures. **Philosophy and Theology:** Different philosophical systems and religions, including their basic principles, values, ethics, ways of thinking, customs, and practices and their impact on human culture. **Geography:** Various methods for describing the location and distribution of land, sea, and air masses, including their physical locations, relationships, and characteristics.

Work Environment: Indoors; sitting.

Archivists

Related Major: Art History

- ❋ Education/Training Required: Master's degree
- ❋ Annual Earnings: $43,110
- ❋ Beginning Wage: $26,330
- ❋ Earnings Growth Potential: Medium (38.9%)
- ❋ Growth: 14.4%
- ❋ Annual Job Openings: 795
- ❋ Self-Employed: 1.3%
- ❋ Part-Time: 18.4%

Industries with Greatest Employment: Educational Services, Public and Private (25.5%); Museums, Historical Sites, and Similar Institutions (19.7%); State Government (11.0%); Federal Government (6.6%).

Highest-Growth Industries (Projected Growth for This Job): Museums, Historical Sites, and Similar Institutions (36.2%); Administrative and Support Services (31.8%); Performing Arts, Spectator Sports, and Related Industries (28.8%).

Lowest-Growth Industries (Projected Growth for This Job): Publishing Industries (Except Internet) (−8.6%); Federal Government (−5.4%); State Government (−1.8%); Professional, Scientific, and Technical Services (11.0%); Educational Services, Public and Private (11.9%); Local Government (12.5%); Management of Companies and Enterprises (14.7%).

Fastest-Growing Metropolitan Areas (Recent Growth for This Job): Dallas–Fort Worth–Arlington, TX (166.7%); Los Angeles–Long Beach–Santa Ana, CA (57.9%); Rochester, NY (33.3%); St. Louis, MO-IL (33.3%); Atlanta–Sandy Springs–Marietta, GA (20.0%).

Other Considerations for Job Security: Keen competition is expected because qualified applicants generally outnumber job openings. Demand for archivists who specialize in electronic records and records management will grow more rapidly than the demand for archivists who specialize in older media formats. Graduates with highly specialized training, such as master's degrees in both library science and history with a concentration in archives or records management and extensive computer skills, should have the best opportunities for jobs as archivists.

Appraise, edit, and direct safekeeping of permanent records and historically valuable documents. Participate in research activities based on archival materials. Create and maintain accessible, retrievable computer archives and databases, incorporating current advances in electric information storage technology. Organize archival records and develop classification systems to facilitate access to archival materials. Authenticate and appraise historical documents and archival materials. Provide reference services and assistance for users needing archival materials. Direct activities of workers who assist in arranging, cataloguing, exhibiting, and maintaining collections of valuable materials. Prepare archival records, such as document descriptions, to allow easy access to information. Preserve records, documents, and objects, copying records to film, videotape, audiotape, disk, or computer formats as necessary. Establish and administer policy guidelines concerning public access and use of materials. Locate new materials and direct their acquisition and display. Research and record the origins and historical significance of archival materials. Specialize in an area of history or technology, researching topics or items relevant to collections to determine what should be retained or acquired. Coordinate educational and public outreach programs such as tours, workshops, lectures, and classes. Select and edit documents for publication and display, applying knowledge of subject, literary expression, and presentation techniques.

Personality Type: Investigative-Conventional. Investigative occupations frequently involve working with ideas and require an extensive amount of thinking. These occupations can involve searching for facts and figuring out problems mentally.

Career Clusters: 03 Arts, Audio/Video Technology, and Communications; 15 Science, Technology, Engineering, and Mathematics. **Career Pathways:** 03.1 Audio and Video Technology and Film; 15.3 Science and Mathematics.

Skills—No data available.

Related Knowledge/Courses—Clerical Practices: Administrative and clerical procedures and systems such as word-processing systems, filing and records management systems, stenography and transcription, forms, design principles, and other office procedures and terminology. **History and Archeology:** Historical events and their causes, indicators, and impact on particular civilizations and cultures. **Computers and Electronics:** Electric circuit boards; processors; chips; and computer hardware and software, including applications and programming. **English Language:** The structure and content

of the English language, including the meaning and spelling of words, rules of composition, and grammar. **Administration and Management:** Principles and processes involved in business and organizational planning, coordination, and execution. This includes strategic planning, resource allocation, manpower modeling, leadership techniques, and production methods. **Customer and Personal Service:** Principles and processes for providing customer and personal services, including needs assessment techniques, quality service standards, alternative delivery systems, and customer satisfaction evaluation techniques.

Work Environment: Indoors; sitting.

Area, Ethnic, and Cultural Studies Teachers, Postsecondary

Related Major: Graduate Study for College Teaching

- ✳ Education/Training Required: Master's degree
- ✳ Annual Earnings: $59,150
- ✳ Beginning Wage: $32,940
- ✳ Earnings Growth Potential: High (44.3%)
- ✳ Growth: 22.9%
- ✳ Annual Job Openings: 1,252
- ✳ Self-Employed: 0.4%
- ✳ Part-Time: 27.8%

Industries with Greatest Employment: Educational Services, Public and Private (97.3%).

Highest-Growth Industries (Projected Growth for This Job): Administrative and Support Services (48.3%); Amusement, Gambling, and Recreation Industries (45.2%); Social

Assistance (38.6%); Support Activities for Transportation (32.8%); Religious, Grantmaking, Civic, Professional, and Similar Organizations (29.9%); Professional, Scientific, and Technical Services (28.8%); Management of Companies and Enterprises (26.8%); Local Government (23.5%); Educational Services, Public and Private (22.8%); Hospitals, Public and Private (21.4%).

Lowest-Growth Industries (Projected Growth for This Job): Other Information Services (7.4%); State Government (7.9%); Sporting Goods, Hobby, Book, and Music Stores (13.3%); Performing Arts, Spectator Sports, and Related Industries (13.4%); Insurance Carriers and Related Activities (13.8%).

Fastest-Growing Metropolitan Areas (Recent Growth for This Job): Columbus, OH (50.0%); Washington-Arlington-Alexandria, DC-VA-MD-WV (38.5%); Phoenix-Mesa-Scottsdale, AZ (25.0%).

Other Considerations for Job Security: Retirements of current postsecondary teachers should create numerous openings for all types of postsecondary teachers, so job opportunities are generally expected to be very good. However, one of the main reasons why students attend postsecondary institutions is to prepare themselves for careers, so the best job prospects for postsecondary teachers are likely to be in rapidly growing fields that offer many nonacademic career options—unlike area, ethnic, and cultural studies. Community colleges and other institutions offering career and technical education have been among the most rapidly growing, and these institutions are expected to offer some of the best opportunities for postsecondary teachers.

Teach courses pertaining to the culture and development of an area (e.g., Latin America), an ethnic group, or any other group (e.g., **women's studies, urban affairs).** Keep abreast of developments in their field by reading current literature, talking with colleagues, and participating in professional conferences. Conduct research in a particular field of knowledge and publish findings in professional journals, books, and/or electronic media. Evaluate and grade students' classwork, assignments, and papers. Prepare course materials such as syllabi, homework assignments, and handouts. Prepare and deliver lectures to undergraduate and/or graduate students on topics such as race and ethnic relations, gender studies, and cross-cultural perspectives. Initiate, facilitate, and moderate classroom discussions. Compile, administer, and grade examinations or assign this work to others. Maintain regularly scheduled office hours in order to advise and assist students. Plan, evaluate, and revise curricula, course content, and course materials and methods of instruction. Maintain student attendance records, grades, and other required records. Advise students on academic and vocational curricula and on career issues. Supervise undergraduate and/or graduate teaching, internship, and research work. Select and obtain materials and supplies such as textbooks. Collaborate with colleagues to address teaching and research issues. Serve on academic or administrative committees that deal with institutional policies, departmental matters, and academic issues. Compile bibliographies of specialized materials for outside reading assignments. Write grant proposals to procure external research funding. Participate in campus and community events. Participate in student recruitment, registration, and placement activities. Act as advisers to student organizations. Incorporate experiential/site visit components into courses. Perform administrative duties such as serving as department head. Provide professional consulting services to government and/or industry.

Personality Type: Social-Investigative-Artistic. Social occupations frequently involve working with, communicating with, and teaching people. These occupations often involve helping or providing service to others.

Career Clusters: 10 Human Services; 15 Science, Technology, Engineering, and Mathematics. **Career Pathways:** 10.2 Counseling and Mental Health Services; 15.3 Science and Mathematics.

Skills—Writing: Communicating effectively in writing as appropriate for the needs of the audience. **Critical Thinking:** Using logic and reasoning to identify the strengths and weaknesses of alternative solutions, conclusions, or approaches to problems. **Instructing:** Teaching others how to do something. **Persuasion:** Persuading others to change their minds or behavior. **Active Learning:** Understanding the implications of new information for both current and future problem-solving and decision-making. **Learning Strategies:** Selecting and using training/instructional methods and procedures appropriate for the situation when learning or teaching new things.

Related Knowledge/Courses—History and Archeology: Historical events and their causes, indicators, and impact on particular civilizations and cultures. **Sociology and Anthropology:** Group behavior and dynamics; societal trends and influences; and cultures and their history, migrations, ethnicity, and origins. **Foreign Language:** The structure and content of a foreign (non-English) language, including the meaning and spelling of words, rules of composition and grammar, and pronunciation. **Philosophy and Theology:** Different philosophical systems and religions, including their basic principles, values, ethics, ways of thinking, customs, and practices and their impact on human culture. **Geography:**

Various methods for describing the location and distribution of land, sea, and air masses, including their physical locations, relationships, and characteristics. **Education and Training:** Instructional methods and training techniques, including curriculum design principles, learning theory, group and individual teaching techniques, design of individual development plans, and test design principles.

Work Environment: Indoors; sitting.

Art, Drama, and Music Teachers, Postsecondary

Related Major: Graduate Study for College Teaching

- ✳ Education/Training Required: Master's degree
- ✳ Annual Earnings: $55,190
- ✳ Beginning Wage: $30,340
- ✳ Earnings Growth Potential: High (45.0%)
- ✳ Growth: 22.9%
- ✳ Annual Job Openings: 12,707
- ✳ Self-Employed: 0.4%
- ✳ Part-Time: 27.8%

Industries with Greatest Employment: Educational Services, Public and Private (97.3%).

Highest-Growth Industries (Projected Growth for This Job): Administrative and Support Services (48.3%); Amusement, Gambling, and Recreation Industries (45.2%); Social Assistance (38.6%); Support Activities for Transportation (32.8%); Religious, Grantmaking, Civic, Professional, and Similar Organizations (29.9%); Professional, Scientific, and Technical Services (28.8%); Management of Companies and Enterprises (26.8%); Local Government

(23.5%); Educational Services, Public and Private (22.8%); Hospitals, Public and Private (21.4%).

Lowest-Growth Industries (Projected Growth for This Job): Other Information Services (7.4%); State Government (7.9%); Sporting Goods, Hobby, Book, and Music Stores (13.3%); Performing Arts, Spectator Sports, and Related Industries (13.4%); Insurance Carriers and Related Activities (13.8%).

Fastest-Growing Metropolitan Areas (Recent Growth for This Job): Phoenix-Mesa-Scottsdale, AZ (237.5%); Orlando-Kissimmee, FL (151.6%); Spokane, WA (78.9%); Cedar Rapids, IA (75.0%); Eugene-Springfield, OR (75.0%).

Other Considerations for Job Security: Retirements of current postsecondary teachers should create numerous openings for all types of postsecondary teachers, so job opportunities are generally expected to be very good. However, one of the main reasons why students attend postsecondary institutions is to prepare themselves for careers, so the best job prospects for postsecondary teachers are likely to be in rapidly growing fields that offer many nonacademic career options. Community colleges and other institutions offering career and technical education have been among the most rapidly growing, and these institutions are expected to offer some of the best opportunities for postsecondary teachers.

Teach courses in drama; music; and the arts, including fine and applied art, such as painting and sculpture, or design and crafts. Evaluate and grade students' classwork, performances, projects, assignments, and papers. Explain and demonstrate artistic techniques. Prepare students for performances, exams, or assessments. Prepare and deliver lectures to undergraduate or graduate students on topics such as acting techniques, fundamentals of music, and art history. Organize performance groups and direct their rehearsals. Prepare course materials such as syllabi, homework assignments, and handouts. Initiate, facilitate, and moderate classroom discussions. Keep abreast of developments in their field by reading current literature, talking with colleagues, and participating in professional conferences. Advise students on academic and vocational curricula and on career issues. Maintain student attendance records, grades, and other required records. Conduct research in a particular field of knowledge and publish findings in professional journals, books, or electronic media. Supervise undergraduate and/or graduate teaching, internship, and research work. Plan, evaluate, and revise curricula, course content, and course materials and methods of instruction. Maintain regularly scheduled office hours to advise and assist students. Compile, administer, and grade examinations or assign this work to others. Participate in student recruitment, registration, and placement activities. Select and obtain materials and supplies such as textbooks and performance pieces. Collaborate with colleagues to address teaching and research issues. Serve on academic or administrative committees that deal with institutional policies, departmental matters, and academic issues. Participate in campus and community events. Keep students informed of community events such as plays and concerts. Compile bibliographies of specialized materials for outside reading assignments. Display students' work in schools, galleries, and exhibitions. Perform administrative duties such as serving as department head. Act as advisers to student organizations. Write grant proposals to procure external research funding. Provide professional consulting services to government or industry.

Personality Type: Artistic-Social-Investigative. Artistic occupations frequently involve working with forms, designs, and patterns. They often require self-expression, and the work can be done without following a clear set of rules.

Career Clusters: 03 Arts, Audio/Video Technology, and Communications; 08 Health Science. **Career Pathways:** 03.1 Audio and Video Technology and Film; 03.2 Printing Technology; 03.3 Visual Arts; 03.4 Performing Arts; 08.1 Therapeutic Services.

Skills—Instructing: Teaching others how to do something. **Social Perceptiveness:** Being aware of others' reactions and understanding why they react as they do. **Speaking:** Talking to others to convey information effectively. **Active Listening:** Giving full attention to what other people are saying, taking time to understand the points being made, asking questions as appropriate, and not interrupting at inappropriate times. **Persuasion:** Persuading others to change their minds or behavior. **Learning Strategies:** Selecting and using training/instructional methods and procedures appropriate for the situation when learning or teaching new things.

Related Knowledge/Courses—Fine Arts: Theory and techniques required to produce, compose, and perform works of music, dance, visual arts, drama, and sculpture. **History and Archeology:** Historical events and their causes, indicators, and impact on particular civilizations and cultures. **Philosophy and Theology:** Different philosophical systems and religions, including their basic principles, values, ethics, ways of thinking, customs, and practices and their impact on human culture. **Education and Training:** Instructional methods and training techniques, including curriculum design principles, learning theory, group and individual teaching techniques, design of individual development plans, and test design principles. **Communications and Media:** Media production, communication, and dissemination techniques and methods, including alternative ways to inform and entertain via written, oral, and visual media. **Sociology and Anthropology:** Group behavior and dynamics; societal trends and influences; and cultures and their history, migrations, ethnicity, and origins.

Work Environment: Indoors; noisy; sitting.

Atmospheric, Earth, Marine, and Space Sciences Teachers, Postsecondary

Related Major: Graduate Study for College Teaching

- ⊛ Education/Training Required: Master's degree
- ⊛ Annual Earnings: $73,280
- ⊛ Beginning Wage: $39,840
- ⊛ Earnings Growth Potential: High (45.6%)
- ⊛ Growth: 22.9%
- ⊛ Annual Job Openings: 1,553
- ⊛ Self-Employed: 0.4%
- ⊛ Part-Time: 27.8%

Industries with Greatest Employment: Educational Services, Public and Private (97.3%).

Highest-Growth Industries (Projected Growth for This Job): Administrative and Support Services (48.3%); Amusement, Gambling, and Recreation Industries (45.2%); Social Assistance (38.6%); Support Activities for Transportation (32.8%); Religious, Grantmaking, Civic, Professional, and Similar Organizations (29.9%); Professional, Scientific, and Technical Services (28.8%); Management of Companies and Enterprises (26.8%); Local Government (23.5%); Educational Services, Public and Private (22.8%); Hospitals, Public and Private (21.4%).

Lowest-Growth Industries (Projected Growth for This Job): Other Information Services (7.4%); State Government (7.9%); Sporting Goods, Hobby, Book, and Music Stores (13.3%); Performing Arts, Spectator Sports, and Related Industries (13.4%); Insurance Carriers and Related Activities (13.8%).

Fastest-Growing Metropolitan Areas (Recent Growth for This Job): Phoenix-Mesa-Scottsdale, AZ (66.7%); Riverside–San Bernardino–Ontario, CA (50.0%); Dayton, OH (33.3%); Cincinnati-Middletown, OH-KY-IN (25.0%); Washington-Arlington-Alexandria, DC-VA-MD-WV (13.3%).

Other Considerations for Job Security: Retirements of current postsecondary teachers should create numerous openings for all types of postsecondary teachers, so job opportunities are generally expected to be very good. One of the main reasons why students attend postsecondary institutions is to prepare themselves for careers, so the best job prospects for postsecondary teachers are likely to be in rapidly growing fields that offer many nonacademic career options. Community colleges and other institutions offering career and technical education have been among the most rapidly growing, and these institutions are expected to offer some of the best opportunities for postsecondary teachers.

Teach courses in the physical sciences, except chemistry and physics. Conduct research in a particular field of knowledge and publish findings in professional journals, books, and/or electronic media. Write grant proposals to procure external research funding. Keep abreast of developments in their field by reading current literature, talking with colleagues, and participating in professional conferences. Supervise undergraduate and/or graduate teaching, internships, and research work. Prepare and deliver lectures to undergraduate and/or graduate students on topics such as structural geology, micrometeorology, and atmospheric thermodynamics. Supervise laboratory work and fieldwork. Evaluate and grade students' classwork, assignments, and papers. Prepare course materials such as syllabi, homework assignments, and handouts. Collaborate with colleagues to address teaching and research issues. Compile, administer, and grade examinations or assign this work to others. Plan, evaluate, and revise curricula, course content, course materials, and methods of instruction. Initiate, facilitate, and moderate classroom discussions. Maintain regularly scheduled office hours to advise and assist students. Advise students on academic and vocational curricula and on career issues. Maintain student attendance records, grades, and other required records. Participate in student recruitment, registration, and placement activities. Perform administrative duties such as serving as department head. Select and obtain materials and supplies such as textbooks and laboratory equipment. Serve on academic or administrative committees that deal with institutional policies, departmental matters, and academic issues. Compile bibliographies of specialized materials for outside reading assignments. Provide professional consulting services to government and/or industry. Act as adviser to student organizations. Participate in campus and community events.

Personality Type: No data available.

Career Clusters: 05 Education and Training; 15 Science, Technology, Engineering, and Mathematics. **Career Pathways:** 05.3 Teaching/Training; 15.3 Science and Mathematics.

Skills—Science: Using scientific rules and methods to solve problems. **Programming:** Writing computer programs for various purposes. **Mathematics:** Using mathematics to solve problems. **Management of Financial Resources:** Determining how money will be spent to get the work done and accounting for these expenditures. **Complex Problem Solving:** Identifying complex problems and reviewing related information to develop and evaluate options and implement solutions. **Writing:** Communicating effectively in writing as appropriate for the needs of the audience.

Related Knowledge/Courses—Physics: Physical principles, laws, and applications, including air, water, material dynamics, light, atomic principles, heat, electric theory, earth formations, and meteorological and related natural phenomena. **Geography:** Various methods for describing the location and distribution of land, sea, and air masses, including their physical locations, relationships, and characteristics. **Chemistry:** The composition, structure, and properties of substances and of the chemical processes and transformations that they undergo. This includes uses of chemicals and their interactions, danger signs, production techniques, and disposal methods. **Biology:** Plant and animal living tissue, cells, organisms, and entities, including their functions, interdependencies, and interactions with each other and the environment. **Mathematics:** Numbers and their operations and interrelationships, including arithmetic, algebra, geometry, calculus, and statistics and their applications. **Education and Training:** Instructional methods and training techniques, including curriculum design principles, learning theory, group and individual teaching techniques, design of individual development plans, and test design principles.

Work Environment: Indoors; sitting.

Audiologists

Related Major: Speech-Language Pathology and Audiology

* Education/Training Required: First professional degree
* Annual Earnings: $59,440
* Beginning Wage: $38,390
* Earnings Growth Potential: Medium (35.4%)
* Growth: 9.8%
* Annual Job Openings: 980
* Self-Employed: 10.2%
* Part-Time: 28.3%

Industries with Greatest Employment: Ambulatory Health Care Services (42.9%); Health and Personal Care Stores (16.0%); Educational Services, Public and Private (13.0%); Hospitals, Public and Private (12.0%).

Highest-Growth Industries (Projected Growth for This Job): Professional, Scientific, and Technical Services (21.1%); Nursing and Residential Care Facilities (18.2%); Local Government (17.2%).

Lowest-Growth Industries (Projected Growth for This Job): Health and Personal Care Stores (–3.3%); Computer and Electronic Product Manufacturing (0.0%); State Government (2.6%); Educational Services, Public and Private (4.0%); Hospitals, Public and Private (9.5%); Ambulatory Health Care Services (14.6%).

Fastest-Growing Metropolitan Areas (Recent Growth for This Job): Pittsburgh, PA (80.0%); Houston–Sugar Land–Baytown, TX (77.8%); Birmingham-Hoover, AL (75.0%); Seattle-

Tacoma-Bellevue, WA (69.2%); Salt Lake City, UT (66.7%).

Other Considerations for Job Security: Employment in educational services will increase along with growth in elementary and secondary school enrollments, including enrollment of special education students. Growth in employment of audiologists will be moderated by limitations on reimbursements made by third-party payers for the tests and services they provide. Job prospects will be favorable for those possessing the Au.D. degree. Only a few job openings for audiologists will arise from the need to replace those who leave the occupation, because the occupation is relatively small and workers tend to stay in this occupation until they retire.

Assess and treat persons with hearing and related disorders. May fit hearing aids and provide auditory training. May perform research related to hearing problems. Evaluate hearing and speech/language disorders to determine diagnoses and courses of treatment. Administer hearing or speech/language evaluations, tests, or examinations to patients to collect information on type and degree of impairment, using specialized instruments and electronic equipment. Fit and dispense assistive devices, such as hearing aids. Maintain client records at all stages, including initial evaluation and discharge. Refer clients to additional medical or educational services if needed. Counsel and instruct clients in techniques to improve hearing or speech impairment, including sign language or lipreading. Monitor clients' progress and discharge them from treatment when goals are attained. Plan and conduct treatment programs for clients' hearing or speech problems, consulting with physicians, nurses, psychologists, and other health-care personnel as necessary. Recommend assistive devices according to clients' needs or nature of impairments. Participate in conferences or training to update or share knowledge of new hearing or speech disorder treatment methods or technologies. Instruct clients, parents, teachers, or employers in how to avoid behavior patterns that lead to miscommunication. Examine and clean patients' ear canals. Advise educators or other medical staff on speech or hearing topics. Educate and supervise audiology students and health-care personnel. Fit and tune cochlear implants, providing rehabilitation for adjustment to listening with implant amplification systems. Work with multidisciplinary teams to assess and rehabilitate recipients of implanted hearing devices. Develop and supervise hearing screening programs. Conduct or direct research on hearing or speech topics and report findings to help in the development of procedures, technology, or treatments. Measure noise levels in workplaces and conduct hearing protection programs in industry, schools, and communities.

Personality Type: Social-Investigative. Social occupations frequently involve working with, communicating with, and teaching people. These occupations often involve helping or providing service to others.

Career Cluster: 08 Health Science. **Career Pathway:** 08.1 Therapeutic Services.

Skills—Science: Using scientific rules and methods to solve problems. **Social Perceptiveness:** Being aware of others' reactions and understanding why they react as they do. **Service Orientation:** Actively looking for ways to help people. **Equipment Selection:** Determining the kind of tools and equipment needed to do a job. **Persuasion:** Persuading others to change their minds or behavior. **Reading Comprehension:** Understanding written sentences and paragraphs in work-related documents.

Related Knowledge/Courses—Therapy and Counseling: Information and techniques needed to rehabilitate physical and mental ailments and to provide career guidance, including alternative treatments, rehabilitation equipment and its proper use, and methods to evaluate treatment effects. **Medicine and Dentistry:** The information and techniques needed to diagnose and treat injuries, diseases, and deformities. This includes symptoms, treatment alternatives, drug properties and interactions, and preventive health-care measures. **Psychology:** Human behavior and performance, mental processes, psychological research methods, and the assessment and treatment of behavioral and affective disorders. **Sales and Marketing:** Principles and methods involved in showing, promoting, and selling products or services. This includes marketing strategies and tactics, product demonstration and sales techniques, and sales control systems. **Customer and Personal Service:** Principles and processes for providing customer and personal services, including needs assessment techniques, quality service standards, alternative delivery systems, and customer satisfaction evaluation techniques. **Sociology and Anthropology:** Group behavior and dynamics; societal trends and influences; and cultures and their history, migrations, ethnicity, and origins.

Work Environment: Indoors; disease or infections; sitting; using hands on objects, tools, or controls.

Bailiffs

Related Major: Criminal Justice/Law Enforcement

- Education/Training Required: Moderate-term on-the-job training
- Annual Earnings: $36,900
- Beginning Wage: $19,130
- Earnings Growth Potential: High (48.2%)
- Growth: 11.2%
- Annual Job Openings: 2,223
- Self-Employed: 0.0%
- Part-Time: 1.8%

Industries with Greatest Employment: Local Government (73.4%); State Government (26.6%).

Highest-Growth Industries (Projected Growth for This Job): None met the criteria.

Lowest-Growth Industries (Projected Growth for This Job): State Government (8.0%); Local Government (12.3%).

Fastest-Growing Metropolitan Areas (Recent Growth for This Job): Orlando-Kissimmee, FL (163.6%); Canton-Massillon, OH (33.3%); New Orleans–Metairie–Kenner, LA (25.0%); Boston-Cambridge-Quincy, MA-NH (23.8%); Albany-Schenectady-Troy, NY (18.2%).

Other Considerations for Job Security: Outlook information for bailiffs is subsumed under the information for correctional officers. Job opportunities for correctional officers are expected to be excellent. The need to replace correctional officers who transfer to other occupations, retire, or leave the labor force, coupled with rising employment demand, will generate thousands of job openings each year. This situation is expected to continue. Layoffs of correctional officers are rare because of increasing offender populations.

Maintain order in courts of law. Collect and retain unauthorized firearms from persons entering courtroom. Maintain order in courtroom during trial and guard jury from outside contact. Guard lodging of sequestered jury. Provide jury escort to restaurant and other areas outside of courtroom to prevent jury contact with public. Enforce courtroom rules of behavior and warn persons not to smoke or disturb court procedure. Report need for police or medical assistance to sheriff's office. Check courtroom for security and cleanliness and assure availability of sundry supplies for use of judge. Announce entrance of judge. Stop people from entering courtroom while judge charges jury.

Personality Type: Social-Enterprising-Conventional. Social occupations frequently involve working with, communicating with, and teaching people. These occupations often involve helping or providing service to others.

Career Cluster: 12 Law, Public Safety, Corrections, and Security. **Career Pathway:** 12.4 Law Enforcement Services.

Skills—No data available.

Related Knowledge/Courses—Public Safety and Security: Weaponry; public safety; security operations, rules, regulations, precautions, and prevention; and the protection of people, data, and property. **Law and Government:** Laws, legal codes, court procedures, precedents, government regulations, executive orders, agency rules, and the democratic political process. **Philosophy and Theology:** Different philosophical systems and religions, including their basic principles, values, ethics, ways of thinking, customs, and practices and their impact on human culture. **Customer and Personal Service:** Principles and processes for providing customer and personal services, including needs assessment techniques, quality service standards, alternative delivery systems, and customer satisfaction evaluation techniques. **Psychology:** Human behavior and performance, mental processes, psychological research methods, and the assessment and treatment of behavioral and affective disorders. **Sociology and Anthropology:** Group behavior and dynamics; societal trends and influences; and cultures and their history, migrations, ethnicity, and origins.

Work Environment: Indoors; contaminants; disease or infections; sitting.

Biological Science Teachers, Postsecondary

Related Major: Graduate Study for College Teaching

- ❋ Education/Training Required: Master's degree
- ❋ Annual Earnings: $71,780
- ❋ Beginning Wage: $39,100
- ❋ Earnings Growth Potential: High (45.5%)
- ❋ Growth: 22.9%
- ❋ Annual Job Openings: 9,039
- ❋ Self-Employed: 0.4%
- ❋ Part-Time: 27.8%

Industries with Greatest Employment: Educational Services, Public and Private (97.3%).

Highest-Growth Industries (Projected Growth for This Job): Administrative and Support Services (48.3%); Amusement, Gambling, and Recreation Industries (45.2%); Social Assistance (38.6%); Support Activities for Transportation (32.8%); Religious, Grantmaking, Civic,

Professional, and Similar Organizations (29.9%); Professional, Scientific, and Technical Services (28.8%); Management of Companies and Enterprises (26.8%); Local Government (23.5%); Educational Services, Public and Private (22.8%); Hospitals, Public and Private (21.4%).

Lowest-Growth Industries (Projected Growth for This Job): Other Information Services (7.4%); State Government (7.9%); Sporting Goods, Hobby, Book, and Music Stores (13.3%); Performing Arts, Spectator Sports, and Related Industries (13.4%); Insurance Carriers and Related Activities (13.8%).

Fastest-Growing Metropolitan Areas (Recent Growth for This Job): Des Moines–West Des Moines, IA (100.0%); Springfield, MO (85.7%); Chattanooga, TN-GA (75.0%); Harrisburg-Carlisle, PA (45.5%); Indianapolis-Carmel, IN (42.9%).

Other Considerations for Job Security: Retirements of current postsecondary teachers should create numerous openings for all types of postsecondary teachers, so job opportunities are generally expected to be very good. One of the main reasons why students attend postsecondary institutions is to prepare themselves for careers, so the best job prospects for postsecondary teachers are likely to be in rapidly growing fields that offer many nonacademic career options. These will include the biological sciences. Community colleges and other institutions offering career and technical education have been among the most rapidly growing, and these institutions are expected to offer some of the best opportunities for postsecondary teachers.

Teach courses in biological sciences. Prepare and deliver lectures to undergraduate and/or graduate students on topics such as molecular biology, marine biology, and botany. Evaluate and grade students' classwork, laboratory work, assignments, and papers. Prepare course materials such as syllabi, homework assignments, and handouts. Compile, administer, and grade examinations or assign this work to others. Supervise students' laboratory work. Keep abreast of developments in their field by reading current literature, talking with colleagues, and participating in professional conferences. Maintain student attendance records, grades, and other required records. Initiate, facilitate, and moderate classroom discussions. Plan, evaluate, and revise curricula, course content, course materials, and methods of instruction. Advise students on academic and vocational curricula and on career issues. Maintain regularly scheduled office hours to advise and assist students. Supervise undergraduate and/or graduate teaching, internships, and research work. Select and obtain materials and supplies such as textbooks and laboratory equipment. Collaborate with colleagues to address teaching and research issues. Conduct research in a particular field of knowledge and publish findings in professional journals, books, and/or electronic media. Serve on academic or administrative committees that deal with institutional policies, departmental matters, and academic issues. Participate in student recruitment, registration, and placement activities. Write grant proposals to procure external research funding. Perform administrative duties such as serving as department head. Act as advisers to student organizations. Compile bibliographies of specialized materials for outside reading assignments. Participate in campus and community events. Provide professional consulting services to government and/or industry.

Personality Type: Investigative-Social. Investigative occupations frequently involve working with ideas and require an extensive amount of thinking. These occupations can involve searching for facts and figuring out problems mentally.

Career Clusters: 01 Agriculture, Food, and Natural Resources; 15 Science, Technology, Engineering, and Mathematics. **Career Pathways:** 01.5 Natural Resources Systems; 15.3 Science and Mathematics.

Skills—Science: Using scientific rules and methods to solve problems. **Instructing:** Teaching others how to do something. **Writing:** Communicating effectively in writing as appropriate for the needs of the audience. **Reading Comprehension:** Understanding written sentences and paragraphs in work-related documents. **Learning Strategies:** Selecting and using training/instructional methods and procedures appropriate for the situation when learning or teaching new things. **Speaking:** Talking to others to convey information effectively.

Related Knowledge/Courses—Biology: Plant and animal living tissue, cells, organisms, and entities, including their functions, interdependencies, and interactions with each other and the environment. **Chemistry:** The composition, structure, and properties of substances and of the chemical processes and transformations that they undergo. This includes uses of chemicals and their interactions, danger signs, production techniques, and disposal methods. **Education and Training:** Instructional methods and training techniques, including curriculum design principles, learning theory, group and individual teaching techniques, design of individual development plans, and test design principles. **Medicine and Dentistry:** The information and techniques needed to diagnose and treat injuries, diseases, and deformities. This includes symptoms, treatment alternatives, drug properties and interactions, and preventive health-care measures. **Physics:** Physical principles, laws,

and applications, including air, water, material dynamics, light, atomic principles, heat, electric theory, earth formations, and meteorological and related natural phenomena. **Geography:** Various methods for describing the location and distribution of land, sea, and air masses, including their physical locations, relationships, and characteristics.

Work Environment: Indoors; more often sitting than standing.

Business Teachers, Postsecondary

Related Major: Graduate Study for College Teaching

- ❋ Education/Training Required: Master's degree
- ❋ Annual Earnings: $64,900
- ❋ Beginning Wage: $32,770
- ❋ Earnings Growth Potential: High (49.5%)
- ❋ Growth: 22.9%
- ❋ Annual Job Openings: 11,643
- ❋ Self-Employed: 0.4%
- ❋ Part-Time: 27.8%

Industries with Greatest Employment: Educational Services, Public and Private (97.3%).

Highest-Growth Industries (Projected Growth for This Job): Administrative and Support Services (48.3%); Amusement, Gambling, and Recreation Industries (45.2%); Social Assistance (38.6%); Support Activities for Transportation (32.8%); Religious, Grantmaking, Civic, Professional, and Similar Organizations (29.9%); Professional, Scientific, and Technical Services (28.8%); Management of Companies and Enterprises (26.8%); Local Government

(23.5%); Educational Services, Public and Private (22.8%); Hospitals, Public and Private (21.4%).

Lowest-Growth Industries (Projected Growth for This Job): Other Information Services (7.4%); State Government (7.9%); Sporting Goods, Hobby, Book, and Music Stores (13.3%); Performing Arts, Spectator Sports, and Related Industries (13.4%); Insurance Carriers and Related Activities (13.8%).

Fastest-Growing Metropolitan Areas (Recent Growth for This Job): Syracuse, NY (225.0%); Des Moines–West Des Moines, IA (169.2%); Rome, GA (120.0%); Worcester, MA-CT (93.8%); Lubbock, TX (50.0%).

Other Considerations for Job Security: Retirements of current postsecondary teachers should create numerous openings for all types of postsecondary teachers, so job opportunities are generally expected to be very good. One of the main reasons why students attend postsecondary institutions is to prepare themselves for careers, so the best job prospects for postsecondary teachers are likely to be in rapidly growing fields that offer many nonacademic career options. Business is one of the most rapidly growing of these fields. Community colleges and other institutions offering career and technical education have been among the most rapidly growing, and these institutions are expected to offer some of the best opportunities for postsecondary teachers.

Teach courses in business administration and management, such as accounting, finance, human resources, labor relations, marketing, and operations research. Prepare and deliver lectures to undergraduate and/or graduate students on topics such as financial accounting, principles of marketing, and operations management. Evaluate and grade students' classwork, assignments, and papers. Compile, administer, and grade examinations or assign this work to others. Prepare course materials such as syllabi, homework assignments, and handouts. Maintain student attendance records, grades, and other required records. Initiate, facilitate, and moderate classroom discussions. Plan, evaluate, and revise curricula, course content, and course materials and methods of instruction. Keep abreast of developments in their field by reading current literature, talking with colleagues, and participating in professional organizations and conferences. Maintain regularly scheduled office hours to advise and assist students. Advise students on academic and vocational curricula and on career issues. Select and obtain materials and supplies such as textbooks. Collaborate with colleagues to address teaching and research issues. Collaborate with members of the business community to improve programs, to develop new programs, and to provide student access to learning opportunities such as internships. Participate in student recruitment, registration, and placement activities. Serve on academic or administrative committees that deal with institutional policies, departmental matters, and academic issues. Participate in campus and community events. Compile bibliographies of specialized materials for outside reading assignments. Perform administrative duties such as serving as department head. Supervise undergraduate and/or graduate teaching, internship, and research work. Conduct research in a particular field of knowledge and publish findings in professional journals, books, and/or electronic media. Act as advisers to student organizations. Provide professional consulting services to government and/or industry. Write grant proposals to procure external research funding.

Personality Type: No data available.

Career Clusters: 04 Business, Management, and Administration; 05 Education and Training; 06 Finance; 14 Marketing, Sales, and Service. **Career Pathways:** 04.1 Management; 04.2 Business Financial Management and Accounting; 04.3 Human Resources; 04.5 Marketing; 05.3 Teaching/Training; 06.1 Financial and Investment Planning; 06.4 Insurance Services; 14.1 Management and Entrepreneurship; 14.5 Marketing Information Management and Research.

Skills—Instructing: Teaching others how to do something. **Learning Strategies:** Selecting and using training/instructional methods and procedures appropriate for the situation when learning or teaching new things. **Writing:** Communicating effectively in writing as appropriate for the needs of the audience. **Monitoring:** Monitoring/assessing your performance or that of other individuals or organizations to make improvements or take corrective action. **Speaking:** Talking to others to convey information effectively. **Active Learning:** Understanding the implications of new information for both current and future problem-solving and decision-making.

Related Knowledge/Courses—Economics and Accounting: Economic and accounting principles and practices, the financial markets, banking, and the analysis and reporting of financial data. **Education and Training:** Instructional methods and training techniques, including curriculum design principles, learning theory, group and individual teaching techniques, design of individual development plans, and test design principles. **Sociology and Anthropology:** Group behavior and dynamics; societal trends and influences; and cultures and their history, migrations, ethnicity, and origins. **Sales and Marketing:** Principles and methods involved in showing, promoting, and selling products or services. This includes marketing strategies and tactics, product demonstration and sales techniques, and sales control systems. **Philosophy and Theology:** Different philosophical systems and religions, including their basic principles, values, ethics, ways of thinking, customs, and practices and their impact on human culture. **English Language:** The structure and content of the English language, including the meaning and spelling of words, rules of composition, and grammar.

Work Environment: Indoors; sitting.

Chemistry Teachers, Postsecondary

Related Major: Graduate Study for College Teaching

- ❋ Education/Training Required: Master's degree
- ❋ Annual Earnings: $63,870
- ❋ Beginning Wage: $37,810
- ❋ Earnings Growth Potential: High (40.8%)
- ❋ Growth: 22.9%
- ❋ Annual Job Openings: 3,405
- ❋ Self-Employed: 0.4%
- ❋ Part-Time: 27.8%

Industries with Greatest Employment: Educational Services, Public and Private (97.3%).

Highest-Growth Industries (Projected Growth for This Job): Administrative and Support Services (48.3%); Amusement, Gambling, and Recreation Industries (45.2%); Social Assistance (38.6%); Support Activities for Transportation (32.8%); Religious, Grantmaking, Civic, Professional, and Similar Organizations (29.9%); Professional, Scientific, and Technical Services (28.8%); Management of Companies and Enterprises (26.8%); Local Government (23.5%); Educational Services, Public and Private (22.8%); Hospitals, Public and Private (21.4%).

Lowest-Growth Industries (Projected Growth for This Job): Other Information Services (7.4%); State Government (7.9%); Sporting Goods, Hobby, Book, and Music Stores (13.3%); Performing Arts, Spectator Sports, and Related Industries (13.4%); Insurance Carriers and Related Activities (13.8%).

Fastest-Growing Metropolitan Areas (Recent Growth for This Job): Duluth, MN-WI (66.7%); Indianapolis-Carmel, IN (50.0%); Asheville, NC (33.3%); New York–Northern New Jersey–Long Island, NY-NJ-PA (27.4%); Columbus, OH (25.0%).

Other Considerations for Job Security: Retirements of current postsecondary teachers should create numerous openings for all types of postsecondary teachers, so job opportunities are generally expected to be very good. One of the main reasons why students attend postsecondary institutions is to prepare themselves for careers, so the best job prospects for postsecondary teachers are likely to be in rapidly growing fields that offer many nonacademic career options. Chemistry is a key part of the curriculum for healthcare majors. Community colleges and other institutions offering career and technical education have been among the most rapidly growing, and these institutions are expected to offer some of the best opportunities for postsecondary teachers.

Teach courses pertaining to the chemical and physical properties and compositional changes of substances. Work may include instruction in the methods of qualitative and quantitative chemical analysis. Includes both teachers primarily engaged in teaching and

those who do a combination of both teaching and research. Prepare and deliver lectures to undergraduate and/or graduate students on topics such as organic chemistry, analytical chemistry, and chemical separation. Supervise students' laboratory work. Evaluate and grade students' classwork, laboratory performance, assignments, and papers. Compile, administer, and grade examinations or assign this work to others. Maintain student attendance records, grades, and other required records. Prepare course materials such as syllabi, homework assignments, and handouts. Maintain regularly scheduled office hours to advise and assist students. Plan, evaluate, and revise curricula, course content, course materials, and methods of instruction. Supervise undergraduate and/or graduate teaching, internships, and research work. Keep abreast of developments in the field by reading current literature, talking with colleagues, and participating in professional conferences. Initiate, facilitate, and moderate classroom discussions. Select and obtain materials and supplies such as textbooks and laboratory equipment. Conduct research in a particular field of knowledge and publish findings in professional journals, books, and/or electronic media. Advise students on academic and vocational curricula and on career issues. Collaborate with colleagues to address teaching and research issues. Serve on academic or administrative committees that deal with institutional policies, departmental matters, and academic issues. Write grant proposals to procure external research funding. Participate in student recruitment, registration, and placement activities. Prepare and submit required reports related to instruction. Perform administrative duties such as serving as a department head. Act as advisers to student organizations. Compile bibliographies of specialized materials for outside reading assignments. Participate in campus and community events. Provide professional consulting services to government and/or industry.

Personality Type: Investigative-Social-Realistic. Investigative occupations frequently involve working with ideas and require an extensive amount of thinking. These occupations can involve searching for facts and figuring out problems mentally.

Career Cluster: 15 Science, Technology, Engineering, and Mathematics. **Career Pathway:** 15.3 Science and Mathematics.

Skills—Science: Using scientific rules and methods to solve problems. **Mathematics:** Using mathematics to solve problems. **Instructing:** Teaching others how to do something. **Writing:** Communicating effectively in writing as appropriate for the needs of the audience. **Reading Comprehension:** Understanding written sentences and paragraphs in work-related documents. **Active Learning:** Understanding the implications of new information for both current and future problem-solving and decision-making.

Related Knowledge/Courses—Chemistry: The composition, structure, and properties of substances and of the chemical processes and transformations that they undergo. This includes uses of chemicals and their interactions, danger signs, production techniques, and disposal methods. **Biology:** Plant and animal living tissue, cells, organisms, and entities, including their functions, interdependencies, and interactions with each other and the environment. **Physics:** Physical principles, laws, and applications, including air, water, material dynamics, light, atomic principles, heat, electric theory, earth formations, and meteorological and related natural phenomena. **Education and Training:** Instructional methods and training techniques,

including curriculum design principles, learning theory, group and individual teaching techniques, design of individual development plans, and test design principles. **Mathematics:** Numbers and their operations and interrelationships, including arithmetic, algebra, geometry, calculus, and statistics and their applications. **English Language:** The structure and content of the English language, including the meaning and spelling of words, rules of composition, and grammar.

Work Environment: Indoors; contaminants; hazardous conditions; sitting.

Child, Family, and School Social Workers

Related Major: Social Work

- ❋ Education/Training Required: Bachelor's degree
- ❋ Annual Earnings: $38,620
- ❋ Beginning Wage: $25,160
- ❋ Earnings Growth Potential: Low (34.9%)
- ❋ Growth: 19.1%
- ❋ Annual Job Openings: 35,402
- ❋ Self-Employed: 2.8%
- ❋ Part-Time: 9.4%

Industries with Greatest Employment: Social Assistance (24.4%); State Government (24.1%); Local Government (17.5%); Educational Services, Public and Private (14.0%); Nursing and Residential Care Facilities (5.4%); Religious, Grantmaking, Civic, Professional, and Similar Organizations (5.0%).

Highest-Growth Industries (Projected Growth for This Job): Social Assistance (54.0%); Administrative and Support Services

(28.0%); Ambulatory Health Care Services (22.6%); Nursing and Residential Care Facilities (21.3%); Management of Companies and Enterprises (15.3%); Religious, Grantmaking, Civic, Professional, and Similar Organizations (15.2%).

Lowest-Growth Industries (Projected Growth for This Job): State Government (–1.9%); Hospitals, Public and Private (1.5%); Educational Services, Public and Private (7.4%); Local Government (12.3%); Professional, Scientific, and Technical Services (13.4%).

Fastest-Growing Metropolitan Areas (Recent Growth for This Job): Spokane, WA (133.3%); Bay City, MI (100.0%); Johnstown, PA (92.3%); Yuma, AZ (83.3%); Seattle-Tacoma-Bellevue, WA (72.0%).

Other Considerations for Job Security: Job prospects are generally expected to be favorable. Social workers, particularly family social workers, will be needed to assist in finding the best care for the aging and to support their families. Furthermore, demand for school social workers will increase and lead to more jobs as efforts are expanded to respond to rising student enrollments as well as the continued emphasis on integrating disabled children into the general school population. There could be competition for school social work jobs in some areas because of the limited number of openings. The availability of federal, state, and local funding will be a major factor in determining the actual job growth in schools. The demand for child and family social workers may also be tied to the availability of government funding.

Provide social services and assistance to improve the social and psychological functioning of children and their families and to maximize the family well-being and the academic functioning of children. May assist single parents, arrange adoptions, and find foster homes for abandoned or abused children. In schools, they address such problems as teenage pregnancy, misbehavior, and truancy. May also advise teachers on how to deal with problem children. Interview clients individually, in families, or in groups, assessing their situations, capabilities, and problems, to determine what services are required to meet their needs. Counsel individuals, groups, families, or communities regarding issues including mental health, poverty, unemployment, substance abuse, physical abuse, rehabilitation, social adjustment, child care, or medical care. Maintain case history records and prepare reports. Counsel students whose behavior, school progress, or mental or physical impairment indicate a need for assistance, diagnosing students' problems and arranging for needed services. Consult with parents, teachers, and other school personnel to determine causes of problems such as truancy and misbehavior and to implement solutions. Counsel parents with child-rearing problems, interviewing the child and family to determine whether further action is required. Develop and review service plans in consultation with clients and perform follow-ups assessing the quantity and quality of services provided. Collect supplementary information needed to assist clients, such as employment records, medical records, or school reports. Address legal issues, such as child abuse and discipline, assisting with hearings and providing testimony to inform custody arrangements. Provide, find, or arrange for support services, such as child care, homemaker service, prenatal care, substance abuse treatment, job training, counseling, or parenting classes, to prevent more serious problems from developing. Refer clients to community resources for services such as job placement, debt counseling,

C

legal aid, housing, medical treatment, or financial assistance and provide concrete information, such as where to go and how to apply. Arrange for medical, psychiatric, and other tests that may disclose causes of difficulties and indicate remedial measures. Work in child and adolescent residential institutions. Administer welfare programs. Evaluate personal characteristics and home conditions of foster home or adoption applicants. Serve as liaisons between students, homes, schools, family services, child guidance clinics, courts, protective services, doctors, and other contacts to help children who face problems such as disabilities, abuse, or poverty.

Personality Type: Social. Social occupations frequently involve working with, communicating with, and teaching people. These occupations often involve helping or providing service to others.

Career Clusters: 10 Human Services; 12 Law, Public Safety, Corrections, and Security. **Career Pathways:** 10.3 Family and Community Services; 12.1 Correction Services.

Skills—Social Perceptiveness: Being aware of others' reactions and understanding why they react as they do. **Service Orientation:** Actively looking for ways to help people. **Speaking:** Talking to others to convey information effectively. **Monitoring:** Monitoring/assessing your performance or that of other individuals or organizations to make improvements or take corrective action. **Writing:** Communicating effectively in writing as appropriate for the needs of the audience. **Learning Strategies:** Selecting and using training/instructional methods and procedures appropriate for the situation when learning or teaching new things.

Related Knowledge/Courses—Therapy and Counseling: Information and techniques needed to rehabilitate physical and mental ailments and to provide career guidance, including alternative treatments, rehabilitation equipment and its proper use, and methods to evaluate treatment effects. **Psychology:** Human behavior and performance, mental processes, psychological research methods, and the assessment and treatment of behavioral and affective disorders. **Sociology and Anthropology:** Group behavior and dynamics; societal trends and influences; and cultures and their history, migrations, ethnicity, and origins. **Philosophy and Theology:** Different philosophical systems and religions, including their basic principles, values, ethics, ways of thinking, customs, and practices and their impact on human culture. **Customer and Personal Service:** Principles and processes for providing customer and personal services, including needs assessment techniques, quality service standards, alternative delivery systems, and customer satisfaction evaluation techniques. **Law and Government:** Laws, legal codes, court procedures, precedents, government regulations, executive orders, agency rules, and the democratic political process.

Work Environment: Indoors; sitting.

Chiropractors

Related Major: Chiropractic

- ❀ Education/Training Required: First professional degree
- ❀ Annual Earnings: $65,890
- ❀ Beginning Wage: $32,530
- ❀ Earnings Growth Potential: Very high (50.6%)
- ❀ Growth: 14.4%
- ❀ Annual Job Openings: 3,179
- ❀ Self-Employed: 51.7%
- ❀ Part-Time: 23.6%

Industries with Greatest Employment: Ambulatory Health Care Services (46.9%).

Highest-Growth Industries (Projected Growth for This Job): Ambulatory Health Care Services (23.4%).

Lowest-Growth Industries (Projected Growth for This Job): Hospitals, Public and Private (12.2%).

Fastest-Growing Metropolitan Areas (Recent Growth for This Job): Deltona–Daytona Beach–Ormond Beach, FL (100.0%); Oklahoma City, OK (77.8%); Canton-Massillon, OH (50.0%); Phoenix-Mesa-Scottsdale, AZ (40.0%); Tulsa, OK (40.0%).

Other Considerations for Job Security: Job prospects for new chiropractors are expected to be good. In this occupation, replacement needs arise almost entirely from retirements. Chiropractors usually remain in the occupation until they retire; few transfer to other occupations. Establishing a new practice will be easiest in areas with a low concentration of chiropractors. Employment is expected to grow faster than average because of increasing consumer demand for alternative health care. Demand for chiropractic treatment, however, is related to the ability of patients to pay, either directly or through health insurance. Although more insurance plans now cover chiropractic services, the extent of such coverage varies among plans.

Adjust spinal column and other articulations of the body to correct abnormalities of the human body believed to be caused by interference with the nervous system. Examine patients to determine nature and extent of disorders. Manipulate spines or other involved areas. May utilize supplementary measures such as exercise, rest, water, light, heat, and nutritional therapy. Diagnose health problems by reviewing patients' health and medical histories; questioning, observing, and examining patients; and interpreting X rays. Maintain accurate case histories of patients. Evaluate the functioning of the neuromuscularskeletal system and the spine, using systems of chiropractic diagnosis. Perform a series of manual adjustments to spines, or other articulations of the body, to correct musculoskeletal systems. Obtain and record patients' medical histories. Advise patients about recommended courses of treatment. Consult with and refer patients to appropriate health practitioners when necessary. Analyze X rays to locate the sources of patients' difficulties and to rule out fractures or diseases as sources of problems. Counsel patients about nutrition, exercise, sleeping habits, stress management, and other matters. Arrange for diagnostic X rays to be taken. Suggest and apply the use of supports such as straps, tapes, bandages, and braces if necessary.

Personality Type: Investigative-Realistic-Social. Investigative occupations frequently involve working with ideas and require an extensive amount of thinking. These occupations can involve searching for facts and figuring out problems mentally.

Career Cluster: 08 Health Science. **Career Pathway:** 08.1 Therapeutic Services.

Skills—No data available.

Related Knowledge/Courses—Medicine and Dentistry: The information and techniques needed to diagnose and treat injuries, diseases, and deformities. This includes symptoms, treatment alternatives, drug properties and interactions, and preventive health-care measures. **Therapy and Counseling:** Information and techniques needed to rehabilitate physical and mental ailments and to provide career guidance, including alternative treatments, rehabilitation equipment and its proper use, and methods to evaluate treatment effects. **Biology:** Plant and animal living tissue, cells, organisms, and entities, including their functions, interdependencies, and interactions with each other and the environment. **Psychology:** Human behavior and performance, mental processes, psychological research methods, and the assessment and treatment of behavioral and affective disorders. **Personnel and Human Resources:** Principles and procedures for personnel recruitment; selection; training; compensation and benefits; labor relations and negotiation; and personnel information systems. **Sales and Marketing:** Principles and methods involved in showing, promoting, and selling products or services. This includes marketing strategies and tactics, product demonstration and sales techniques, and sales control systems.

Work Environment: Indoors; disease or infections; standing; using hands on objects, tools, or controls; bending or twisting the body; repetitive motions.

Clergy

Related Majors: Philosophy; Religion/Religious Studies

- ❊ Education/Training Required: Master's degree
- ❊ Annual Earnings: $40,460
- ❊ Beginning Wage: $20,240
- ❊ Earnings Growth Potential: High (50.0%)
- ❊ Growth: 18.9%
- ❊ Annual Job Openings: 35,092
- ❊ Self-Employed: 0.1%
- ❊ Part-Time: 10.0%

Industries with Greatest Employment: Religious, Grantmaking, Civic, Professional, and Similar Organizations (95.5%).

Highest-Growth Industries (Projected Growth for This Job): Professional, Scientific, and Technical Services (55.1%); Ambulatory Health Care Services (53.2%); Social Assistance (36.6%); Administrative and Support Services (33.0%); Personal and Laundry Services (30.5%); Real Estate (22.1%); Nursing and Residential Care Facilities (21.4%); Religious, Grantmaking, Civic, Professional, and Similar Organizations (18.9%); Management of Companies and Enterprises (15.3%).

Lowest-Growth Industries (Projected Growth for This Job): Federal Government (–5.5%); State Government (–1.9%); Educational Services, Public and Private (9.2%); Hospitals, Public and Private (10.0%); Local Government (12.2%).

Fastest-Growing Metropolitan Areas (Recent Growth for This Job): New Orleans–Metairie–Kenner, LA (175.0%); Sarasota-Bradenton-Venice, FL (175.0%); Vallejo-Fairfield, CA (133.3%);

Lansing–East Lansing, MI (100.0%); Tucson, AZ (100.0%).

Other Considerations for Job Security: No data available.

Conduct religious worship and perform other spiritual functions associated with beliefs and practices of religious faith or denomination. Provide spiritual and moral guidance and assistance to members. Pray and promote spirituality. Read from sacred texts such as the Bible, Torah, or Koran. Prepare and deliver sermons and other talks. Organize and lead regular religious services. Share information about religious issues by writing articles, giving speeches, or teaching. Instruct people who seek conversion to a particular faith. Visit people in homes, hospitals, and prisons to provide them with comfort and support. Counsel individuals and groups concerning their spiritual, emotional, and personal needs. Train leaders of church, community, and youth groups. Administer religious rites or ordinances. Study and interpret religious laws, doctrines, or traditions. Conduct special ceremonies such as weddings, funerals, and confirmations. Plan and lead religious education programs for congregation. Respond to requests for assistance during emergencies or crises. Devise ways in which congregation membership can be expanded. Collaborate with committees and individuals to address financial and administrative issues pertaining to congregation. Prepare people for participation in religious ceremonies. Perform administrative duties such as overseeing building management, ordering supplies, contracting for services and repairs, and supervising the work of staff members and volunteers. Refer people to community support services, psychologists, and doctors as necessary. Participate in fundraising activities to support congregation activities and facilities. Organize and engage in interfaith, community, civic, educational, and recreational activities sponsored by or related to their religion.

Personality Type: Social-Artistic-Enterprising. Social occupations frequently involve working with, communicating with, and teaching people. These occupations often involve helping or providing service to others.

Career Cluster: 10 Human Services. **Career Pathway:** 10.2 Counseling and Mental Health Services.

Skills—Management of Personnel Resources: Motivating, developing, and directing people as they work, identifying the best people for the job. **Management of Financial Resources:** Determining how money will be spent to get the work done and accounting for these expenditures. **Service Orientation:** Actively looking for ways to help people. **Negotiation:** Bringing others together and trying to reconcile differences. **Judgment and Decision Making:** Considering the relative costs and benefits of potential actions to choose the most appropriate one. **Persuasion:** Persuading others to change their minds or behavior.

Related Knowledge/Courses—Philosophy and Theology: Different philosophical systems and religions, including their basic principles, values, ethics, ways of thinking, customs, and practices and their impact on human culture. **Therapy and Counseling:** Information and techniques needed to rehabilitate physical and mental ailments and to provide career guidance, including alternative treatments, rehabilitation equipment and its proper use, and methods to evaluate treatment effects. **Sociology and Anthropology:** Group behavior and dynamics; societal trends and influences; and cultures and their history, migrations, ethnicity, and origins.

Psychology: Human behavior and performance, mental processes, psychological research methods, and the assessment and treatment of behavioral and affective disorders. **Public Safety and Security:** Weaponry; public safety; security operations, rules, regulations, precautions, and prevention; and the protection of people, data, and property. **Customer and Personal Service:** Principles and processes for providing customer and personal services, including needs assessment techniques, quality service standards, alternative delivery systems, and customer satisfaction evaluation techniques.

Work Environment: Indoors; sitting.

Clinical Psychologists

Related Major: Psychology

- ✳ Education/Training Required: Doctoral degree
- ✳ Annual Earnings: $62,210
- ✳ Beginning Wage: $37,300
- ✳ Earnings Growth Potential: High (40.0%)
- ✳ Growth: 15.8%
- ✳ Annual Job Openings: 8,309
- ✳ Self-Employed: 34.2%
- ✳ Part-Time: 24.0%

Industries with Greatest Employment: Educational Services, Public and Private (30.4%); Ambulatory Health Care Services (13.2%); Hospitals, Public and Private (6.0%); Social Assistance (5.9%).

Highest-Growth Industries (Projected Growth for This Job): Social Assistance (56.2%); Professional, Scientific, and Technical Services (34.6%); Ambulatory Health Care Services (26.8%); Nursing and Residential Care

Facilities (24.8%); Funds, Trusts, and Other Financial Vehicles (23.3%); Religious, Grant-making, Civic, Professional, and Similar Organizations (19.4%); Management of Companies and Enterprises (15.2%).

Lowest-Growth Industries (Projected Growth for This Job): Hospitals, Public and Private (–3.5%); State Government (–1.9%); Educational Services, Public and Private (6.9%); Local Government (12.3%).

Fastest-Growing Metropolitan Areas (Recent Growth for This Job): Hattiesburg, MS (300.0%); Albuquerque, NM (171.4%); Little Rock–North Little Rock, AR (82.4%); Fayetteville-Springdale-Rogers, AR-MO (75.0%); Boise City–Nampa, ID (70.6%).

Other Considerations for Job Security: Job prospects should be the best for people who have a doctoral degree from a leading university. Master's degree holders will face keen competition for jobs. The rise in health-care costs associated with unhealthy lifestyles, such as smoking, alcoholism, and obesity, has made prevention and treatment more critical. An increase in the number of employee assistance programs, which help workers deal with personal problems, also should lead to employment growth for clinical and counseling specialties. Clinical and counseling psychologists also will be needed to help people deal with depression and other mental disorders, marriage and family problems, job stress, and addiction. The growing number of elderly will increase the demand for psychologists trained in geropsychology to help people deal with the mental and physical changes that occur as individuals grow older. There also will be increased need for psychologists to work with returning veterans.

Diagnose or evaluate mental and emotional disorders of individuals through observation,

interview, and psychological tests and formulate and administer programs of treatment. Identify psychological, emotional, or behavioral issues and diagnose disorders, using information obtained from interviews, tests, records, and reference materials. Develop and implement individual treatment plans, specifying type, frequency, intensity, and duration of therapy. Interact with clients to assist them in gaining insight, defining goals, and planning action to achieve effective personal, social, educational, and vocational development and adjustment. Discuss the treatment of problems with clients. Utilize a variety of treatment methods such as psychotherapy, hypnosis, behavior modification, stress reduction therapy, psychodrama, and play therapy. Counsel individuals and groups regarding problems such as stress, substance abuse, and family situations to modify behavior or to improve personal, social, and vocational adjustment. Write reports on clients and maintain required paperwork. Evaluate the effectiveness of counseling or treatments and the accuracy and completeness of diagnoses; then modify plans and diagnoses as necessary. Obtain and study medical, psychological, social, and family histories by interviewing individuals, couples, or families and by reviewing records. Consult reference material such as textbooks, manuals, and journals to identify symptoms, make diagnoses, and develop approaches to treatment. Maintain current knowledge of relevant research. Observe individuals at play, in group interactions, or in other contexts to detect indications of mental deficiency, abnormal behavior, or maladjustment. Select, administer, score, and interpret psychological tests to obtain information on individuals' intelligence, achievements, interests, and personalities. Refer clients to other specialists, institutions, or support services as necessary. Develop, direct, and participate in training programs for staff and students. Provide psychological or administrative services and advice to private firms and community agencies regarding mental health programs or individual cases. Provide occupational, educational, and other information to individuals so that they can make educational and vocational plans.

Personality Type: Investigative-Artistic-Social. Investigative occupations frequently involve working with ideas and require an extensive amount of thinking. These occupations can involve searching for facts and figuring out problems mentally.

Career Clusters: 08 Health Science; 10 Human Services. **Career Pathways:** 08.1 Therapeutic Services; 08.3 Health Informatics; 10.2 Counseling and Mental Health Services.

Skills—Social Perceptiveness: Being aware of others' reactions and understanding why they react as they do. **Service Orientation:** Actively looking for ways to help people. **Complex Problem Solving:** Identifying complex problems and reviewing related information to develop and evaluate options and implement solutions. **Learning Strategies:** Selecting and using training/instructional methods and procedures appropriate for the situation when learning or teaching new things. **Active Listening:** Giving full attention to what other people are saying, taking time to understand the points being made, asking questions as appropriate, and not interrupting at inappropriate times. **Negotiation:** Bringing others together and trying to reconcile differences.

Related Knowledge/Courses—Therapy and Counseling: Information and techniques needed to rehabilitate physical and mental ailments and to provide career guidance, including alternative treatments, rehabilitation equipment and its proper use, and methods to evaluate treatment effects. **Psychology:** Human behavior and performance, mental processes, psychological research methods, and the assessment and treatment of behavioral and affective disorders. **Sociology and Anthropology:** Group behavior and dynamics; societal trends and influences; and cultures and their history, migrations, ethnicity, and origins. **Philosophy and Theology:** Different philosophical systems and religions, including their basic principles, values, ethics, ways of thinking, customs, and practices and their impact on human culture. **Customer and Personal Service:** Principles and processes for providing customer and personal services, including needs assessment techniques, quality service standards, alternative delivery systems, and customer satisfaction evaluation techniques. **Medicine and Dentistry:** The information and techniques needed to diagnose and treat injuries, diseases, and deformities. This includes symptoms, treatment alternatives, drug properties and interactions, and preventive health-care measures.

Work Environment: Indoors; sitting.

Coaches and Scouts

Related Major: Physical Education

- ⊛ Education/Training Required: Long-term on-the-job training
- ⊛ Annual Earnings: $27,840
- ⊛ Beginning Wage: $14,860
- ⊛ Earnings Growth Potential: High (46.6%)
- ⊛ Growth: 14.6%
- ⊛ Annual Job Openings: 51,100
- ⊛ Self-Employed: 22.7%
- ⊛ Part-Time: 39.1%

Industries with Greatest Employment: Educational Services, Public and Private (54.0%); Amusement, Gambling, and Recreation Industries (12.3%).

Highest-Growth Industries (Projected Growth for This Job): Social Assistance (40.5%); Amusement, Gambling, and Recreation Industries (31.1%); Administrative and Support Services (28.6%); Performing Arts, Spectator Sports, and Related Industries (25.2%); Accommodation, Including Hotels and Motels (15.6%); Educational Services, Public and Private (15.0%).

Lowest-Growth Industries (Projected Growth for This Job): Animal Production (–10.9%); Federal Government (–5.4%); Sporting Goods, Hobby, Book, and Music Stores (6.6%); Support Activities for Agriculture and Forestry (7.7%); Local Government (12.3%); Religious, Grantmaking, Civic, Professional, and Similar Organizations (13.1%).

Fastest-Growing Metropolitan Areas (Recent Growth for This Job): Lebanon, PA (200.0%); Niles–Benton Harbor, MI (150.0%); Kokomo, IN (128.6%); Salt Lake City, UT (113.4%); Asheville, NC (100.0%).

Other Considerations for Job Security: Persons who are state-certified to teach academic subjects in addition to physical education are likely to have the best prospects for obtaining coaching and instructor jobs. The need to replace the many high school coaches who change occupations or leave the labor force entirely also will provide some coaching opportunities. Competition should be keen for jobs as scouts, particularly for professional teams, because the number of available positions is limited.

Instruct or coach groups or individuals in the fundamentals of sports. Demonstrate

techniques and methods of participation. May evaluate athletes' strengths and weaknesses as possible recruits or to improve the athletes' technique to prepare them for competition. Plan, organize, and conduct practice sessions. Provide training direction, encouragement, and motivation to prepare athletes for games, competitive events, or tours. Identify and recruit potential athletes, arranging and offering incentives such as athletic scholarships. Plan strategies and choose team members for individual games or sports seasons. Plan and direct physical conditioning programs that will enable athletes to achieve maximum performance. Adjust coaching techniques based on the strengths and weaknesses of athletes. File scouting reports that detail player assessments, provide recommendations on athlete recruitment, and identify locations and individuals to be targeted for future recruitment efforts. Keep records of athlete, team, and opposing team performance. Instruct individuals or groups in sports rules, game strategies, and performance principles such as specific ways of moving the body, hands, and feet in order to achieve desired results. Analyze the strengths and weaknesses of opposing teams to develop game strategies. Evaluate athletes' skills and review performance records to determine their fitness and potential in a particular area of athletics. Keep abreast of changing rules, techniques, technologies, and philosophies relevant to their sport. Monitor athletes' use of equipment to ensure safe and proper use. Explain and enforce safety rules and regulations. Develop and arrange competition schedules and programs. Serve as organizer, leader, instructor, or referee for outdoor and indoor games such as volleyball, football, and soccer. Explain and demonstrate the use of sports and training equipment, such as trampolines or weights. Perform activities that support a team or a specific sport, such as

meeting with media representatives and appearing at fundraising events. Arrange and conduct sports-related activities such as training camps, skill-improvement courses, clinics, or pre-season try-outs. Select, acquire, store, and issue equipment and other materials as necessary. Negotiate with professional athletes or their representatives to obtain services and arrange contracts.

Personality Type: Enterprising-Realistic-Social. Enterprising occupations frequently involve starting up and carrying out projects. These occupations can involve leading people and making many decisions. They sometimes require risk taking and often deal with business.

Career Cluster: 05 Education and Training. **Career Pathways:** 05.1 Administration and Administrative Support; 05.3 Teaching/Training.

Skills—Social Perceptiveness: Being aware of others' reactions and understanding why they react as they do. **Management of Personnel Resources:** Motivating, developing, and directing people as they work, identifying the best people for the job. **Management of Financial Resources:** Determining how money will be spent to get the work done and accounting for these expenditures. **Persuasion:** Persuading others to change their minds or behavior. **Negotiation:** Bringing others together and trying to reconcile differences. **Instructing:** Teaching others how to do something.

Related Knowledge/Courses—Psychology: Human behavior and performance, mental processes, psychological research methods, and the assessment and treatment of behavioral and affective disorders. **Therapy and Counseling:** Information and techniques needed to rehabilitate physical and mental ailments and to provide career guidance, including alternative treatments, rehabilitation equipment and its proper use, and methods to evaluate treatment effects. **Education and Training:** Instructional methods and training techniques, including curriculum design principles, learning theory, group and individual teaching techniques, design of individual development plans, and test design principles. **Sales and Marketing:** Principles and methods involved in showing, promoting, and selling products or services. This includes marketing strategies and tactics, product demonstration and sales techniques, and sales control systems. **Personnel and Human Resources:** Principles and procedures for personnel recruitment; selection; training; compensation and benefits; labor relations and negotiation; and personnel information systems. **Sociology and Anthropology:** Group behavior and dynamics; societal trends and influences; and cultures and their history, migrations, ethnicity, and origins.

Work Environment: More often indoors than outdoors; noisy; standing; walking and running.

Communications Teachers, Postsecondary

Related Major: Graduate Study for College Teaching

- ❋ Education/Training Required: Master's degree
- ❋ Annual Earnings: $54,720
- ❋ Beginning Wage: $29,700
- ❋ Earnings Growth Potential: High (45.7%)
- ❋ Growth: 22.9%
- ❋ Annual Job Openings: 4,074
- ❋ Self-Employed: 0.4%
- ❋ Part-Time: 27.8%

Industries with Greatest Employment: Educational Services, Public and Private (97.3%).

Highest-Growth Industries (Projected Growth for This Job): Administrative and Support Services (48.3%); Amusement, Gambling, and Recreation Industries (45.2%); Social Assistance (38.6%); Support Activities for Transportation (32.8%); Religious, Grantmaking, Civic, Professional, and Similar Organizations (29.9%); Professional, Scientific, and Technical Services (28.8%); Management of Companies and Enterprises (26.8%); Local Government (23.5%); Educational Services, Public and Private (22.8%); Hospitals, Public and Private (21.4%).

Lowest-Growth Industries (Projected Growth for This Job): Other Information Services (7.4%); State Government (7.9%); Sporting Goods, Hobby, Book, and Music Stores (13.3%); Performing Arts, Spectator Sports, and Related Industries (13.4%); Insurance Carriers and Related Activities (13.8%).

Fastest-Growing Metropolitan Areas (Recent Growth for This Job): El Paso, TX (87.5%); Harrisburg-Carlisle, PA (83.3%); Phoenix-Mesa-Scottsdale, AZ (52.9%); Virginia Beach–Norfolk–Newport News, VA-NC (50.0%); Charlotte-Gastonia-Concord, NC-SC (33.3%).

Other Considerations for Job Security: Retirements of current postsecondary teachers should create numerous openings for all types of postsecondary teachers, so job opportunities are generally expected to be very good. One of the main reasons why students attend postsecondary institutions is to prepare themselves for careers, so the best job prospects for postsecondary teachers are likely to be in rapidly growing fields that offer many nonacademic career options. Community colleges and other institutions offering career and technical education have been among the most rapidly growing, and these institutions are expected to offer some of the best opportunities for postsecondary teachers.

Teach courses in communications, such as organizational communications, public relations, radio/television broadcasting, and journalism. Evaluate and grade students' classwork, assignments, and papers. Prepare course materials such as syllabi, homework assignments, and handouts. Initiate, facilitate, and moderate classroom discussions. Prepare and deliver lectures to undergraduate or graduate students on topics such as public speaking, media criticism, and oral traditions. Compile, administer, and grade examinations or assign this work to others. Maintain student attendance records, grades, and other required records. Plan, evaluate, and revise curricula, course content, and course materials and methods of instruction. Maintain regularly scheduled office hours to advise and assist students. Keep abreast of developments in their field by reading current literature, talking with colleagues, and participating in professional conferences. Advise students on academic and vocational curricula and on career issues. Supervise undergraduate or graduate teaching, internship, and research work. Select and obtain materials and supplies such as textbooks. Collaborate with colleagues to address teaching and research issues. Conduct research in a particular field of knowledge and publish findings in professional journals, books, or electronic media. Participate in student recruitment, registration, and placement activities. Serve on academic or administrative committees that deal with institutional policies, departmental matters, and academic issues. Compile bibliographies of specialized materials for outside reading assignments. Act as advisers to student organizations. Participate in campus and community events. Perform administrative duties such as serving as department head. Write grant proposals to procure external research funding. Provide professional consulting services to government or industry.

Personality Type: No data available.

Career Clusters: 03 Arts, Audio/Video Technology, and Communications; 04 Business, Management, and Administration; 07 Government and Public Administration; 08 Health Science. **Career Pathways:** 03.5 Journalism and Broadcasting; 04.1 Management; 04.5 Marketing; 07.1 Governance; 08.3 Health Informatics.

Skills—Instructing: Teaching others how to do something. **Writing:** Communicating effectively in writing as appropriate for the needs of the audience. **Persuasion:** Persuading others to change their minds or behavior. **Learning Strategies:** Selecting and using training/instructional methods and procedures appropriate for the situation when learning or teaching new things. **Monitoring:** Monitoring/assessing your performance or that of other individuals or organizations to make improvements or take corrective action. **Speaking:** Talking to others to convey information effectively.

Related Knowledge/Courses—Communications and Media: Media production, communication, and dissemination techniques and methods, including alternative ways to inform and entertain via written, oral, and visual media. **Education and Training:** Instructional methods and training techniques, including curriculum design principles, learning theory, group and individual teaching techniques, design of individual development plans, and test design principles. **Philosophy and Theology:** Different philosophical systems and religions, including their basic principles, values, ethics, ways of thinking, customs, and practices and their impact on human culture. **Sociology and**

Anthropology: Group behavior and dynamics; societal trends and influences; and cultures and their history, migrations, ethnicity, and origins. **English Language:** The structure and content of the English language, including the meaning and spelling of words, rules of composition, and grammar. **History and Archeology:** Historical events and their causes, indicators, and impact on particular civilizations and cultures.

Work Environment: Indoors; sitting.

Computer Science Teachers, Postsecondary

Related Major: Graduate Study for College Teaching

- ❀ Education/Training Required: Master's degree
- ❀ Annual Earnings: $62,020
- ❀ Beginning Wage: $33,720
- ❀ Earnings Growth Potential: High (45.6%)
- ❀ Growth: 22.9%
- ❀ Annual Job Openings: 5,820
- ❀ Self-Employed: 0.4%
- ❀ Part-Time: 27.8%

Industries with Greatest Employment: Educational Services, Public and Private (97.3%).

Highest-Growth Industries (Projected Growth for This Job): Administrative and Support Services (48.3%); Amusement, Gambling, and Recreation Industries (45.2%); Social Assistance (38.6%); Support Activities for Transportation (32.8%); Religious, Grantmaking, Civic, Professional, and Similar Organizations (29.9%); Professional, Scientific, and Technical Services (28.8%); Management of Companies and Enterprises (26.8%); Local Government

(23.5%); Educational Services, Public and Private (22.8%); Hospitals, Public and Private (21.4%).

Lowest-Growth Industries (Projected Growth for This Job): Other Information Services (7.4%); State Government (7.9%); Sporting Goods, Hobby, Book, and Music Stores (13.3%); Performing Arts, Spectator Sports, and Related Industries (13.4%); Insurance Carriers and Related Activities (13.8%).

Fastest-Growing Metropolitan Areas (Recent Growth for This Job): Memphis, TN-MS-AR (125.0%); San Jose–Sunnyvale–Santa Clara, CA (77.8%); Buffalo–Niagara Falls, NY (75.0%); New Orleans–Metairie–Kenner, LA (66.7%); South Bend–Mishawaka, IN-MI (66.7%).

Other Considerations for Job Security: Retirements of current postsecondary teachers should create numerous openings for all types of postsecondary teachers, so job opportunities are generally expected to be very good. However, one of the main reasons why students attend postsecondary institutions is to prepare themselves for careers, so the best job prospects for postsecondary teachers are likely to be in rapidly growing fields that offer many nonacademic career options. Computer science courses are commonly required as part of many business, science, and technology majors. Community colleges and other institutions offering career and technical education have been among the most rapidly growing, and these institutions are expected to offer some of the best opportunities for postsecondary teachers.

Teach courses in computer science. May specialize in a field of computer science, such as the design and function of computers or operations and research analysis. Evaluate and grade students' classwork, laboratory work, assignments, and papers. Maintain student attendance records, grades, and other required records. Prepare and deliver lectures to undergraduate and/or graduate students on topics such as programming, data structures, and software design. Prepare course materials such as syllabi, homework assignments, and handouts. Compile, administer, and grade examinations or assign this work to others. Keep abreast of developments in their field by reading current literature, talking with colleagues, and participating in professional conferences. Initiate, facilitate, and moderate classroom discussions. Plan, evaluate, and revise curricula, course content, and course materials and methods of instruction. Supervise students' laboratory work. Maintain regularly scheduled office hours to advise and assist students. Select and obtain materials and supplies such as textbooks and laboratory equipment. Advise students on academic and vocational curricula and on career issues. Participate in student recruitment, registration, and placement activities. Collaborate with colleagues to address teaching and research issues. Serve on academic or administrative committees that deal with institutional policies, departmental matters, and academic issues. Act as advisers to student organizations. Supervise undergraduate and/or graduate teaching, internship, and research work. Perform administrative duties such as serving as department head. Conduct research in a particular field of knowledge and publish findings in professional journals, books, and/or electronic media. Direct research of other teachers or of graduate students working for advanced academic degrees. Provide professional consulting services to government and/or industry. Participate in campus and community events. Compile bibliographies of specialized materials for outside reading assignments. Write grant proposals to procure external research funding.

Personality Type: Investigative-Conventional. Investigative occupations frequently involve working with ideas and require an extensive amount of thinking. These occupations can involve searching for facts and figuring out problems mentally.

Career Cluster: 11 Information Technology. **Career Pathways:** 11.1 Network Systems; 11.2 Information Support Services; 11.4 Programming and Software Development.

Skills—Programming: Writing computer programs for various purposes. **Instructing:** Teaching others how to do something. **Operations Analysis:** Analyzing needs and product requirements to create a design. **Technology Design:** Generating or adapting equipment and technology to serve user needs. **Science:** Using scientific rules and methods to solve problems. **Mathematics:** Using mathematics to solve problems.

Related Knowledge/Courses—Computers and Electronics: Electric circuit boards, processors, chips, and computer hardware and software, including applications and programming. **Education and Training:** Instructional methods and training techniques, including curriculum design principles, learning theory, group and individual teaching techniques, design of individual development plans, and test design principles. **Telecommunications:** Transmission, broadcasting, switching, control, and operation of telecommunications systems. **Mathematics:** Numbers and their operations and interrelationships, including arithmetic, algebra, geometry, calculus, and statistics and their applications. **Engineering and Technology:** Equipment, tools, and mechanical devices and their uses to produce motion, light, power, technology, and other applications. **English Language:** The structure and content of the English language, including the meaning and spelling of words, rules of composition, and grammar.

Work Environment: Indoors; sitting.

Counseling Psychologists

Related Major: Psychology

- ❋ Education/Training Required: Doctoral degree
- ❋ Annual Earnings: $62,210
- ❋ Beginning Wage: $37,300
- ❋ Earnings Growth Potential: High (40.0%)
- ❋ Growth: 15.8%
- ❋ Annual Job Openings: 8,309
- ❋ Self-Employed: 34.2%
- ❋ Part-Time: 24.0%

Industries with Greatest Employment: Educational Services, Public and Private (30.4%); Ambulatory Health Care Services (13.2%); Hospitals, Public and Private (6.0%); Social Assistance (5.9%).

Highest-Growth Industries (Projected Growth for This Job): Social Assistance (56.2%); Professional, Scientific, and Technical Services (34.6%); Ambulatory Health Care Services (26.8%); Nursing and Residential Care Facilities (24.8%); Funds, Trusts, and Other Financial Vehicles (23.3%); Religious, Grant-making, Civic, Professional, and Similar Organizations (19.4%); Management of Companies and Enterprises (15.2%).

Lowest-Growth Industries (Projected Growth for This Job): Hospitals, Public and Private (–3.5%); State Government (–1.9%); Educational Services, Public and Private (6.9%); Local Government (12.3%).

Fastest-Growing Metropolitan Areas (Recent Growth for This Job): Hattiesburg, MS (300.0%); Albuquerque, NM (171.4%); Little Rock–North Little Rock, AR (82.4%); Fayette-ville-Springdale-Rogers, AR-MO (75.0%); Boise City–Nampa, ID (70.6%).

Other Considerations for Job Security: Job prospects should be the best for people who have a doctoral degree from a leading university. Master's degree holders will face keen competition for jobs. The rise in health-care costs associated with unhealthy lifestyles, such as smoking, alcoholism, and obesity, has made prevention and treatment more critical. An increase in the number of employee assistance programs, which help workers deal with personal problems, also should lead to employment growth for clinical and counseling specialties. Clinical and counseling psychologists also will be needed to help people deal with depression and other mental disorders, marriage and family problems, job stress, and addiction. The growing number of elderly will increase the demand for psychologists trained in geropsychology to help people deal with the mental and physical changes that occur as individuals grow older. There also will be increased need for psychologists to work with returning veterans.

Assess and evaluate individuals' problems through the use of case history, interview, and observation and provide individual or group counseling services to assist individuals in achieving more effective personal, social, educational, and vocational development and adjustment. Collect information about individuals or clients, using interviews, case histories, observational techniques, and other assessment methods. Counsel individuals, groups, or families to help them understand problems, define goals, and develop realistic action plans. Develop therapeutic and treatment plans based on clients' interests, abilities, and needs. Consult with other professionals to discuss therapies, treatments, counseling resources, or techniques and to share occupational information. Analyze data such as interview notes, test results, and reference manuals in order to identify symptoms and to diagnose the nature of clients' problems. Advise clients on how they could be helped by counseling. Evaluate the results of counseling methods to determine the reliability and validity of treatments. Provide consulting services to schools, social service agencies, and businesses. Refer clients to specialists or to other institutions for non-counseling treatment of problems. Select, administer, and interpret psychological tests to assess intelligence, aptitudes, abilities, or interests. Conduct research to develop or improve diagnostic or therapeutic counseling techniques.

Personality Type: Social-Investigative-Artistic. Social occupations frequently involve working with, communicating with, and teaching people. These occupations often involve helping or providing service to others.

Career Clusters: 08 Health Science; 10 Human Services. **Career Pathways:** 08.1 Therapeutic Services; 10.2 Counseling and Mental Health Services.

Skills—Social Perceptiveness: Being aware of others' reactions and understanding why they react as they do. **Active Listening:** Giving full attention to what other people are saying, taking time to understand the points being made, asking questions as appropriate, and not interrupting at inappropriate times. **Persuasion:** Persuading others to change their minds or behavior. **Service Orientation:** Actively looking for ways to help people. **Coordination:** Adjusting actions in relation to others' actions. **Monitoring:** Monitoring/assessing your performance

or that of other individuals or organizations to make improvements or take corrective action.

Related Knowledge/Courses—Therapy and Counseling: Information and techniques needed to rehabilitate physical and mental ailments and to provide career guidance, including alternative treatments, rehabilitation equipment and its proper use, and methods to evaluate treatment effects. **Philosophy and Theology:** Different philosophical systems and religions, including their basic principles, values, ethics, ways of thinking, customs, and practices and their impact on human culture. **Sociology and Anthropology:** Group behavior and dynamics; societal trends and influences; and cultures and their history, migrations, ethnicity, and origins. **Psychology:** Human behavior and performance, mental processes, psychological research methods, and the assessment and treatment of behavioral and affective disorders. **English Language:** The structure and content of the English language, including the meaning and spelling of words, rules of composition, and grammar. **Customer and Personal Service:** Principles and processes for providing customer and personal services, including needs assessment techniques, quality service standards, alternative delivery systems, and customer satisfaction evaluation techniques.

Work Environment: Indoors; sitting.

Court Reporters

Related Majors: Communications Studies/Speech; Journalism and Mass Communications

- ❋ Education/Training Required: Postsecondary vocational training
- ❋ Annual Earnings: $45,330
- ❋ Beginning Wage: $23,810
- ❋ Earnings Growth Potential: High (47.5%)
- ❋ Growth: 24.5%
- ❋ Annual Job Openings: 2,620
- ❋ Self-Employed: 7.9%
- ❋ Part-Time: 13.6%

Industries with Greatest Employment: Administrative and Support Services (35.9%); Local Government (32.9%); State Government (21.1%).

Highest-Growth Industries (Projected Growth for This Job): Administrative and Support Services (56.3%).

Lowest-Growth Industries (Projected Growth for This Job): Federal Government (–5.4%); State Government (–1.9%); Local Government (12.3%).

Fastest-Growing Metropolitan Areas (Recent Growth for This Job): Indianapolis-Carmel, IN (87.5%); Oklahoma City, OK (64.3%); Washington-Arlington-Alexandria, DC-VA-MD-WV (63.3%); Beaumont–Port Arthur, TX (33.3%); Toledo, OH (33.3%).

Other Considerations for Job Security: Job opportunities should be excellent, especially for those with certification. Demand for court reporter services will be spurred by the continuing need for accurate transcription of proceedings in courts and in pretrial depositions, by the growing need to create captions for live television, and by the need to provide other real-time broadcast captioning and translating services for the deaf and hard-of-hearing.

Use verbatim methods and equipment to capture, store, retrieve, and transcribe pretrial and trial proceedings or other information. Includes stenocaptioners who operate computerized stenographic captioning equipment to provide captions of live or prerecorded broadcasts for hearing-impaired viewers. Take notes in shorthand or use a stenotype or shorthand machine that prints letters on a paper tape. Provide transcripts of proceedings upon request of judges, lawyers, or the public. Record verbatim proceedings of courts, legislative assemblies, committee meetings, and other proceedings, using computerized recording equipment, electronic stenograph machines, or stenomasks. Transcribe recorded proceedings in accordance with established formats. Ask speakers to clarify inaudible statements. File a legible transcript of records of a court case with the court clerk's office. File and store shorthand notes of court session. Respond to requests during court sessions to read portions of the proceedings already recorded. Record depositions and other proceedings for attorneys. Verify accuracy of transcripts by checking copies against original records of proceedings and accuracy of rulings by checking with judges. Record symbols on computer disks or CD-ROM; then translate and display them as text in computer-aided transcription process.

Personality Type: Artistic-Social-Conventional. Artistic occupations frequently involve working with forms, designs, and patterns. They often require self-expression, and the work can be done without following a clear set of rules.

Career Cluster: 12 Law, Public Safety, Corrections, and Security. **Career Pathway:** 12.5 Legal Services.

Skills—Reading Comprehension: Understanding written sentences and paragraphs in work-related documents. **Active Listening:** Giving full attention to what other people are saying, taking time to understand the points being made, asking questions as appropriate, and not interrupting at inappropriate times. **Equipment Selection:** Determining the kind of tools and equipment needed to do a job. **Operation and Control:** Controlling operations of equipment or systems. **Equipment Maintenance:** Performing routine maintenance on equipment and determining when and what kind of maintenance is needed. **Operation Monitoring:** Watching gauges, dials, or other indicators to make sure a machine is working properly.

Related Knowledge/Courses—Clerical Practices: Administrative and clerical procedures and systems such as word-processing systems, filing and records management systems, stenography and transcription, forms, design principles, and other office procedures and terminology. **English Language:** The structure and content of the English language, including the meaning and spelling of words, rules of composition, and grammar. **Law and Government:** Laws, legal codes, court procedures, precedents, government regulations, executive orders, agency rules, and the democratic political process. **Computers and Electronics:** Electric circuit boards, processors, chips, and computer hardware and software, including applications and programming. **Production and Processing:** Inputs, outputs, raw materials, waste, quality control, costs, and techniques for maximizing the manufacture and distribution of goods. **Customer and Personal Service:** Principles and processes for providing customer and personal services, including needs assessment techniques, quality service standards, alternative delivery systems, and customer satisfaction evaluation techniques.

Work Environment: Indoors; noisy; sitting; using hands on objects, tools, or controls; repetitive motions.

Criminal Investigators and Special Agents

Related Major: Criminal Justice/Law Enforcement

* Education/Training Required: Work experience in a related occupation
* Annual Earnings: $59,930
* Beginning Wage: $35,600
* Earnings Growth Potential: High (40.6%)
* Growth: 17.3%
* Annual Job Openings: 14,746
* Self-Employed: 0.3%
* Part-Time: 2.2%

Industries with Greatest Employment: Local Government (47.3%); Federal Government (37.2%); State Government (14.9%).

Highest-Growth Industries (Projected Growth for This Job): Local Government (23.6%).

Lowest-Growth Industries (Projected Growth for This Job): State Government (7.9%); Educational Services, Public and Private (11.9%); Federal Government (13.3%).

Fastest-Growing Metropolitan Areas (Recent Growth for This Job): Davenport–Moline–Rock Island, IA-IL (100.0%); Harrisburg-Carlisle, PA (69.2%); Anniston-Oxford, AL (66.7%);

C

Springfield, IL (66.7%); Springfield, MA-CT (50.0%).

Other Considerations for Job Security: Overall opportunities in local police departments will be excellent for individuals who meet the psychological, personal, and physical qualifications. There will be more competition for jobs in federal and state law enforcement agencies than for jobs in local agencies. Less competition for jobs will occur in departments that offer relatively low salaries or those in urban communities where the crime rate is relatively high. Applicants with military experience or college training in police science will have the best opportunities in local and state departments. Applicants with a bachelor's degree and several years of law enforcement or military experience, especially investigative experience, will have the best opportunities in federal agencies. The level of government spending determines the level of employment for police and detectives, but layoffs are rare because retirements enable most staffing cuts to be handled through attrition.

Investigate alleged or suspected criminal violations of federal, state, or local laws to determine if evidence is sufficient to recommend prosecution. Record evidence and documents, using equipment such as cameras and photocopy machines. Obtain and verify evidence by interviewing and observing suspects and witnesses or by analyzing records. Examine records to locate links in chains of evidence or information. Prepare reports that detail investigation findings. Determine scope, timing, and direction of investigations. Collaborate with other offices and agencies to exchange information and coordinate activities. Testify before grand juries concerning criminal activity investigations. Analyze evidence in laboratories or in the field. Investigate organized crime, public corruption, financial crime, copyright infringement, civil rights violations, bank robbery, extortion, kidnapping, and other violations of federal or state statutes. Identify case issues and evidence needed, based on analysis of charges, complaints, or allegations of law violations. Obtain and use search and arrest warrants. Serve subpoenas or other official papers. Collaborate with other authorities on activities such as surveillance, transcription, and research. Develop relationships with informants to obtain information related to cases. Search for and collect evidence, such as fingerprints, using investigative equipment. Collect and record physical information about arrested suspects, including fingerprints, height and weight measurements, and photographs. Compare crime scene fingerprints with those from suspects or fingerprint files to identify perpetrators, using computers. Administer counter-terrorism and counter-narcotics reward programs. Provide protection for individuals such as government leaders, political candidates, and visiting foreign dignitaries. Perform undercover assignments and maintain surveillance, including monitoring authorized wiretaps. Manage security programs designed to protect personnel, facilities, and information. Issue security clearances.

Personality Type: Enterprising-Investigative. Enterprising occupations frequently involve starting up and carrying out projects. These occupations can involve leading people and making many decisions. They sometimes require risk taking and often deal with business.

Career Cluster: 12 Law, Public Safety, Corrections, and Security. **Career Pathway:** 12.4 Law Enforcement Services.

Skills—Negotiation: Bringing others together and trying to reconcile differences. **Operations Analysis:** Analyzing needs and product requirements to create a design. **Programming:** Writing computer programs for various purposes. **Judgment and Decision Making:** Considering the relative costs and benefits of potential actions to choose the most appropriate one. **Service Orientation:** Actively looking for ways to help people. **Complex Problem Solving:** Identifying complex problems and reviewing related information to develop and evaluate options and implement solutions.

Related Knowledge/Courses—Law and Government: Laws, legal codes, court procedures, precedents, government regulations, executive orders, agency rules, and the democratic political process. **Psychology:** Human behavior and performance, mental processes, psychological research methods, and the assessment and treatment of behavioral and affective disorders. **Geography:** Various methods for describing the location and distribution of land, sea, and air masses, including their physical locations, relationships, and characteristics. **Public Safety and Security:** Weaponry; public safety; security operations, rules, regulations, precautions, and prevention; and the protection of people, data, and property. **Clerical Practices:** Administrative and clerical procedures and systems such as word-processing systems, filing and records management systems, stenography and transcription, forms, design principles, and other office procedures and terminology. **Telecommunications:** Transmission, broadcasting, switching, control, and operation of telecommunications systems.

Work Environment: More often outdoors than indoors; noisy; very hot or cold; standing.

Criminal Justice and Law Enforcement Teachers, Postsecondary

Related Major: Graduate Study for College Teaching

* Education/Training Required: Master's degree
* Annual Earnings: $51,060
* Beginning Wage: $30,420
* Earnings Growth Potential: High (40.4%)
* Growth: 22.9%
* Annual Job Openings: 1,911
* Self-Employed: 0.4%
* Part-Time: 27.8%

Industries with Greatest Employment: Educational Services, Public and Private (97.3%).

Highest-Growth Industries (Projected Growth for This Job): Administrative and Support Services (48.3%); Amusement, Gambling, and Recreation Industries (45.2%); Social Assistance (38.6%); Support Activities for Transportation (32.8%); Religious, Grantmaking, Civic, Professional, and Similar Organizations (29.9%); Professional, Scientific, and Technical Services (28.8%); Management of Companies and Enterprises (26.8%); Local Government (23.5%); Educational Services, Public and Private (22.8%); Hospitals, Public and Private (21.4%).

Lowest-Growth Industries (Projected Growth for This Job): Other Information Services (7.4%); State Government (7.9%); Sporting Goods, Hobby, Book, and Music Stores (13.3%); Performing Arts, Spectator Sports, and Related Industries (13.4%); Insurance Carriers and Related Activities (13.8%).

Fastest-Growing Metropolitan Areas (Recent Growth for This Job): Des Moines–West Des Moines, IA (66.7%); Kansas City, MO-KS (66.7%); St. Louis, MO-IL (50.0%); Phoenix-Mesa-Scottsdale, AZ (40.0%); Greensboro–High Point, NC (33.3%).

Other Considerations for Job Security: Retirements of current postsecondary teachers should create numerous openings for all types of postsecondary teachers. However, one of the main reasons why students attend postsecondary institutions is to prepare themselves for careers, so the best job prospects for postsecondary teachers are likely to be in rapidly growing fields that offer many nonacademic career options, such as criminal justice and law enforcement. Community colleges and other institutions offering career and technical education have been among the most rapidly growing, and these institutions are expected to offer some of the best opportunities for postsecondary teachers.

Teach courses in criminal justice, corrections, and law enforcement administration. Initiate, facilitate, and moderate classroom discussions. Keep abreast of developments in their field by reading current literature, talking with colleagues, and participating in professional conferences. Evaluate and grade students' classwork, assignments, and papers. Compile, administer, and grade examinations or assign this work to others. Prepare and deliver lectures to undergraduate or graduate students on topics such as criminal law, defensive policing, and investigation techniques. Prepare course materials such as syllabi, homework assignments, and handouts. Conduct research in a particular field of knowledge and publish findings in professional journals, books, and/or electronic media. Plan, evaluate, and revise curricula, course content, and course materials and methods of instruction.

Supervise undergraduate and/or graduate teaching, internship, and research work. Maintain student attendance records, grades, and other required records. Select and obtain materials and supplies such as textbooks. Advise students on academic and vocational curricula and on career issues. Maintain regularly scheduled office hours to advise and assist students. Collaborate with colleagues to address teaching and research issues. Write grant proposals to procure external research funding. Serve on academic or administrative committees that deal with institutional policies, departmental matters, and academic issues. Compile bibliographies of specialized materials for outside reading assignments. Participate in student recruitment, registration, and placement activities. Provide professional consulting services to government and/or industry. Perform administrative duties such as serving as department head. Participate in campus and community events. Act as advisers to student organizations.

Personality Type: No data available.

Career Clusters: 05 Education and Training; 12 Law, Public Safety, Corrections, and Security. **Career Pathways:** 05.3 Teaching/Training; 12.1 Correction Services; 12.3 Security and Protective Services; 12.4 Law Enforcement Services.

Skills—Writing: Communicating effectively in writing as appropriate for the needs of the audience. **Critical Thinking:** Using logic and reasoning to identify the strengths and weaknesses of alternative solutions, conclusions, or approaches to problems. **Instructing:** Teaching others how to do something. **Active Learning:** Understanding the implications of new information for both current and future problem-solving and decision-making. **Reading Comprehension:** Understanding written sentences and paragraphs in work-related documents. **Persuasion:** Persuading others to change their minds or behavior.

Related Knowledge/Courses—Sociology and Anthropology: Group behavior and dynamics; societal trends and influences; and cultures and their history, migrations, ethnicity, and origins. **Philosophy and Theology:** Different philosophical systems and religions, including their basic principles, values, ethics, ways of thinking, customs, and practices and their impact on human culture. **History and Archeology:** Historical events and their causes, indicators, and impact on particular civilizations and cultures. **Law and Government:** Laws, legal codes, court procedures, precedents, government regulations, executive orders, agency rules, and the democratic political process. **English Language:** The structure and content of the English language, including the meaning and spelling of words, rules of composition, and grammar. **Education and Training:** Instructional methods and training techniques, including curriculum design principles, learning theory, group and individual teaching techniques, design of individual development plans, and test design principles.

Work Environment: Indoors; sitting.

Curators

Related Major: Art History

- ❋ Education/Training Required: Master's degree
- ❋ Annual Earnings: $46,000
- ❋ Beginning Wage: $26,100
- ❋ Earnings Growth Potential: High (43.3%)
- ❋ Growth: 23.3%
- ❋ Annual Job Openings: 1,416
- ❋ Self-Employed: 1.3%
- ❋ Part-Time: 18.4%

Industries with Greatest Employment: Museums, Historical Sites, and Similar Institutions (50.5%); Educational Services, Public and Private (18.8%); Local Government (11.8%); State Government (5.5%).

Highest-Growth Industries (Projected Growth for This Job): Museums, Historical Sites, and Similar Institutions (36.2%); Amusement, Gambling, and Recreation Industries (32.0%); Performing Arts, Spectator Sports, and Related Industries (22.4%).

Lowest-Growth Industries (Projected Growth for This Job): Federal Government (–5.4%); Other Information Services (–2.3%); State Government (–1.9%); Educational Services, Public and Private (12.0%); Local Government (12.3%); Religious, Grantmaking, Civic, Professional, and Similar Organizations (13.3%).

Fastest-Growing Metropolitan Areas (Recent Growth for This Job): New Orleans–Metairie–Kenner, LA (125.0%); St. Louis, MO-IL (120.0%); Kansas City, MO-KS (100.0%); Cleveland-Elyria-Mentor, OH (75.0%); Portland-Vancouver-Beaverton, OR-WA (66.7%).

Other Considerations for Job Security: Keen competition is expected because qualified applicants generally outnumber job openings. Curator jobs, in particular, are attractive to many people, and many applicants have the necessary training and knowledge of the subject. But because there are relatively few openings, candidates may have to work part time, as an intern, or even as a volunteer assistant curator or research associate after completing their formal education. Substantial work experience in collection management, research, exhibit design, or restoration, as well as database management skills, will be necessary for permanent status.

Administer affairs of museum and conduct research programs. Direct instructional, research, and public service activities of institution. Plan and organize the acquisition, storage, and exhibition of collections and related materials, including the selection of exhibition themes and designs. Develop and maintain an institution's registration, cataloguing, and basic record-keeping systems, using computer databases. Provide information from the institution's holdings to other curators and to the public. Inspect premises to assess the need for repairs and to ensure that climate and pest-control issues are addressed. Train and supervise curatorial, fiscal, technical, research, and clerical staff, as well as volunteers or interns. Negotiate and authorize purchase, sale, exchange, or loan of collections. Plan and conduct special research projects in area of interest or expertise. Conduct or organize tours, workshops, and instructional sessions to acquaint individuals with an institution's facilities and materials. Confer with the board of directors to formulate and interpret policies, to determine budget requirements, and to plan overall operations. Attend meetings, conventions, and civic events to promote use of institution's services, to seek financing, and to maintain community alliances. Schedule events and organize details, including refreshments, entertainment, decorations, and the collection of any fees. Write and review grant proposals, journal articles, institutional reports, and publicity materials. Study, examine, and test acquisitions to authenticate their origin, composition, and history and to assess their current value. Arrange insurance coverage for objects on loan or for special exhibits and recommend changes in coverage for the entire collection. Establish specifications for reproductions and oversee their manufacture or select items from commercially available replica sources.

Personality Type: Artistic-Investigative. Artistic occupations frequently involve working with forms, designs, and patterns. They often require self-expression, and the work can be done without following a clear set of rules.

Career Clusters: 03 Arts, Audio/Video Technology, and Communications; 15 Science, Technology, Engineering, and Mathematics. **Career Pathways:** 03.1 Audio and Video Technology and Film; 15.3 Science and Mathematics.

Skills—Management of Financial Resources: Determining how money will be spent to get the work done and accounting for these expenditures. **Management of Personnel Resources:** Motivating, developing, and directing people as they work, identifying the best people for the job. **Writing:** Communicating effectively in writing as appropriate for the needs of the audience. **Time Management:** Managing one's own time and the time of others. **Speaking:** Talking to others to convey information effectively. **Persuasion:** Persuading others to change their minds or behavior.

Related Knowledge/Courses—Fine Arts: Theory and techniques required to produce, compose, and perform works of music, dance, visual arts, drama, and sculpture. **History and Archeology:** Historical events and their causes, indicators, and impact on particular civilizations and cultures. **Clerical Practices:** Administrative and clerical procedures and systems such as word-processing systems, filing and records management systems, stenography and transcription, forms, design principles, and other office procedures and terminology. **Philosophy and Theology:** Different philosophical systems and religions, including their basic principles, values, ethics, ways of thinking, customs, and practices and their impact on human culture. **Sociology and Anthropology:** Group behavior and dynamics; societal trends and influences; and cultures and their history, migrations, ethnicity, and origins. **Geography:** Various methods for describing the location and distribution of land, sea, and air masses, including their physical locations, relationships, and characteristics.

Work Environment: Indoors; sitting.

Economics Teachers, Postsecondary

Related Major: Graduate Study for College Teaching

- ✸ Education/Training Required: Master's degree
- ✸ Annual Earnings: $75,300
- ✸ Beginning Wage: $41,650
- ✸ Earnings Growth Potential: High (44.7%)
- ✸ Growth: 22.9%
- ✸ Annual Job Openings: 2,208
- ✸ Self-Employed: 0.4%
- ✸ Part-Time: 27.8%

Industries with Greatest Employment: Educational Services, Public and Private (97.3%).

Highest-Growth Industries (Projected Growth for This Job): Administrative and Support Services (48.3%); Amusement, Gambling, and Recreation Industries (45.2%); Social Assistance (38.6%); Support Activities for Transportation (32.8%); Religious, Grantmaking, Civic, Professional, and Similar Organizations (29.9%); Professional, Scientific, and Technical Services (28.8%); Management of Companies and Enterprises (26.8%); Local Government (23.5%); Educational Services, Public and Private (22.8%); Hospitals, Public and Private (21.4%).

Lowest-Growth Industries (Projected Growth for This Job): Other Information Services (7.4%); State Government (7.9%); Sporting Goods, Hobby, Book, and Music Stores (13.3%); Performing Arts, Spectator Sports, and Related Industries (13.4%); Insurance Carriers and Related Activities (13.8%).

Fastest-Growing Metropolitan Areas (Recent Growth for This Job): Los Angeles–Long Beach–Santa Ana, CA (76.9%); New Haven, CT (50.0%); Washington-Arlington-Alexandria, DC-VA-MD-WV (26.2%); Atlanta–Sandy Springs–Marietta, GA (25.0%); Scranton–Wilkes-Barre, PA (25.0%).

Other Considerations for Job Security: Retirements of current postsecondary teachers should create numerous openings for all types of postsecondary teachers, so job opportunities are generally expected to be very good. However, one of the main reasons why students attend postsecondary institutions is to prepare themselves for careers, so the best job prospects for postsecondary teachers are likely to be in rapidly growing fields that offer many nonacademic career options. Economics courses are commonly required as part of business majors. Community colleges and other institutions offering career and technical education have been among the most rapidly growing, and these institutions are expected to offer some of the best opportunities for postsecondary teachers.

Teach courses in economics. Prepare and deliver lectures to undergraduate and/or graduate students on topics such as econometrics, price theory, and macroeconomics. Prepare course materials such as syllabi, homework assignments, and handouts. Evaluate and grade students' classwork, assignments, and papers. Compile, administer, and grade examinations or assign this work to others. Keep abreast of developments in their field by reading current literature, talking with colleagues, and participating in professional conferences. Maintain student attendance records, grades, and other required records. Initiate, facilitate, and moderate classroom discussions. Maintain regularly scheduled office hours in order to advise and assist students. Select and obtain materials and supplies such as textbooks. Plan, evaluate, and revise curricula, course content, and course materials and methods of instruction. Conduct research in a particular field of knowledge and publish findings in professional journals, books, and/or electronic media. Supervise undergraduate and/or graduate teaching, internship, and research work. Advise students on academic and vocational curricula and on career issues. Serve on academic or administrative committees that deal with institutional policies, departmental matters, and academic issues. Collaborate with colleagues to address teaching and research issues. Compile bibliographies of specialized materials for outside reading assignments. Participate in student recruitment, registration, and placement activities. Perform administrative duties such as serving as department head. Write grant proposals to procure external research funding. Participate in campus and community events. Provide professional consulting services to government and/or industry. Act as advisers to student organizations.

Personality Type: Social-Investigative-Artistic. Social occupations frequently involve working with, communicating with, and teaching people. These occupations often involve helping or providing service to others.

Career Clusters: 04 Business, Management, and Administration; 15 Science, Technology, Engineering, and Mathematics. **Career Pathways:** 04.1 Management; 15.3 Science and Mathematics.

Skills—Mathematics: Using mathematics to solve problems. **Writing:** Communicating effectively in writing as appropriate for the needs of the audience. **Instructing:** Teaching others how to do something. **Speaking:** Talking to others to convey information effectively. **Reading Comprehension:** Understanding written sentences and paragraphs in work-related documents. **Critical Thinking:** Using logic and reasoning to identify the strengths and weaknesses of alternative solutions, conclusions, or approaches to problems.

Related Knowledge/Courses—Economics and Accounting: Economic and accounting principles and practices, the financial markets, banking, and the analysis and reporting of financial data. **History and Archeology:** Historical events and their causes, indicators, and impact on particular civilizations and cultures. **Mathematics:** Numbers and their operations and interrelationships, including arithmetic, algebra, geometry, calculus, and statistics and their applications. **Philosophy and Theology:** Different philosophical systems and religions, including their basic principles, values, ethics, ways of thinking, customs, and practices and their impact on human culture. **Education and Training:** Instructional methods and training techniques, including curriculum design principles, learning theory, group and individual teaching techniques, design of individual development plans, and test design principles. **English Language:** The structure and content of the English language, including the meaning and spelling of words, rules of composition, and grammar.

Work Environment: Indoors; sitting.

Editors

Related Majors: English; Family and Consumer Sciences; Journalism and Mass Communications

- ❋ Education/Training Required: Bachelor's degree
- ❋ Annual Earnings: $48,320
- ❋ Beginning Wage: $27,360
- ❋ Earnings Growth Potential: High (43.4%)
- ❋ Growth: 2.3%
- ❋ Annual Job Openings: 20,193
- ❋ Self-Employed: 13.4%
- ❋ Part-Time: 14.6%

Industries with Greatest Employment: Publishing Industries (Except Internet) (49.5%); Religious, Grantmaking, Civic, Professional, and Similar Organizations (8.2%); Professional, Scientific, and Technical Services (5.2%).

Highest-Growth Industries (Projected Growth for This Job): Securities, Commodity Contracts, and Other Financial Investments and Related Activities (45.7%); Social Assistance

(43.9%); Internet Publishing and Broadcasting (40.3%); Administrative and Support Services (36.6%); Museums, Historical Sites, and Similar Institutions (36.3%); Professional, Scientific, and Technical Services (29.0%); Nonstore Retailers (24.2%); Performing Arts, Spectator Sports, and Related Industries (21.2%); Motion Picture, Video, and Sound Recording Industries (16.2%); Management of Companies and Enterprises (15.3%).

Lowest-Growth Industries (Projected Growth for This Job): Printing and Related Support Activities (–20.7%); Sporting Goods, Hobby, Book, and Music Stores (–18.8%); Internet Service Providers, Web Search Portals, and Data Processing Services (–13.3%); Computer and Electronic Product Manufacturing (–11.8%); Publishing Industries (Except Internet) (–10.6%); Federal Government (–5.2%); Other Information Services (–2.1%); State Government (–1.9%); Transportation Equipment Manufacturing (1.4%); Educational Services, Public and Private (3.8%); others.

Fastest-Growing Metropolitan Areas (Recent Growth for This Job): Scranton–Wilkes-Barre, PA (316.7%); Dayton, OH (225.0%); Charlotte-Gastonia-Concord, NC-SC (92.7%); Medford, OR (80.0%); Dubuque, IA (77.8%).

Other Considerations for Job Security: Opportunities should be best for technical editors and those with training in a specialized field, such as law, medicine, or economics. Rapid growth and change in the high-technology and electronics industries result in a greater need for people to edit users' guides, instruction manuals, and training materials. In addition to job openings created by employment growth, some openings will arise as experienced workers retire, transfer to other occupations, or leave the labor force.

E

Perform variety of editorial duties, such as laying out, indexing, and revising content of written materials, in preparation for final publication. Prepare, rewrite, and edit copy to improve readability or supervise others who do this work. Read copy or proof to detect and correct errors in spelling, punctuation, and syntax. Allocate print space for story text, photos, and illustrations according to space parameters and copy significance, using knowledge of layout principles. Plan the contents of publications according to the publication's style, editorial policy, and publishing requirements. Verify facts, dates, and statistics, using standard reference sources. Review and approve proofs submitted by composing room prior to publication production. Develop story or content ideas, considering reader or audience appeal. Oversee publication production, including artwork, layout, computer typesetting, and printing, ensuring adherence to deadlines and budget requirements. Confer with management and editorial staff members regarding placement and emphasis of developing news stories. Assign topics, events, and stories to individual writers or reporters for coverage. Read, evaluate, and edit manuscripts or other materials submitted for publication and confer with authors regarding changes in content, style or organization, or publication. Monitor news-gathering operations to ensure utilization of all news sources, such as press releases, telephone contacts, radio, television, wire services, and other reporters. Meet frequently with artists, typesetters, layout personnel, marketing directors, and production managers to discuss projects and resolve problems. Supervise and coordinate work of reporters and other editors. Make manuscript acceptance or revision recommendations to the publisher. Select local, state, national, and international news items received from wire services based on assessment of items' significance and interest value. Interview and hire writers and reporters or negotiate contracts, royalties, and payments for authors or freelancers. Direct the policies and departments of newspapers, magazines, and other publishing establishments. Arrange for copyright permissions. Read material to determine index items and arrange them alphabetically or topically, indicating page or chapter location.

Personality Type: Artistic-Social-Enterprising. Artistic occupations frequently involve working with forms, designs, and patterns. They often require self-expression, and the work can be done without following a clear set of rules.

Career Clusters: 03 Arts, Audio/Video Technology, and Communications; 04 Business, Management, and Administration; 08 Health Science; 10 Human Services. **Career Pathways:** 03.5 Journalism and Broadcasting; 04.5 Marketing; 08.3 Health Informatics; 10.5 Consumer Services Career.

Skills—Writing: Communicating effectively in writing as appropriate for the needs of the audience. **Reading Comprehension:** Understanding written sentences and paragraphs in work-related documents. **Active Listening:** Giving full attention to what other people are saying, taking time to understand the points being made, asking questions as appropriate, and not interrupting at inappropriate times. **Judgment and Decision Making:** Considering the relative costs and benefits of potential actions to choose the most appropriate one. **Time Management:** Managing one's own time and the time of others. **Critical Thinking:** Using logic and reasoning to identify the strengths and weaknesses of alternative solutions, conclusions, or approaches to problems.

Related Knowledge/Courses—Communications and Media: Media production, communication, and dissemination techniques and methods, including alternative ways to inform and entertain via written, oral, and visual media. **History and Archeology:** Historical events and their causes, indicators, and impact on particular civilizations and cultures. **Geography:** Various methods for describing the location and distribution of land, sea, and air masses, including their physical locations, relationships, and characteristics. **English Language:** The structure and content of the English language, including the meaning and spelling of words, rules of composition, and grammar. **Sales and Marketing:** Principles and methods involved in showing, promoting, and selling products or services. This includes marketing strategies and tactics, product demonstration and sales techniques, and sales control systems. **Clerical Practices:** Administrative and clerical procedures and systems such as word-processing systems, filing and records management systems, stenography and transcription, forms, design principles, and other office procedures and terminology.

Work Environment: Indoors; sitting; using hands on objects, tools, or controls; repetitive motions.

Education Teachers, Postsecondary

Related Major: Graduate Study for College Teaching

⊛ Education/Training Required: Master's degree

⊛ Annual Earnings: $54,220

⊛ Beginning Wage: $29,060

⊛ Earnings Growth Potential: High (46.4%)

⊛ Growth: 22.9%

⊛ Annual Job Openings: 9,359

⊛ Self-Employed: 0.4%

⊛ Part-Time: 27.8%

Industries with Greatest Employment: Educational Services, Public and Private (97.3%).

Highest-Growth Industries (Projected Growth for This Job): Administrative and Support Services (48.3%); Amusement, Gambling, and Recreation Industries (45.2%); Social Assistance (38.6%); Support Activities for Transportation (32.8%); Religious, Grantmaking, Civic, Professional, and Similar Organizations (29.9%); Professional, Scientific, and Technical Services (28.8%); Management of Companies and Enterprises (26.8%); Local Government (23.5%); Educational Services, Public and Private (22.8%); Hospitals, Public and Private (21.4%).

Lowest-Growth Industries (Projected Growth for This Job): Other Information Services (7.4%); State Government (7.9%); Sporting Goods, Hobby, Book, and Music Stores (13.3%); Performing Arts, Spectator Sports, and Related Industries (13.4%); Insurance Carriers and Related Activities (13.8%).

Fastest-Growing Metropolitan Areas (Recent Growth for This Job): New Haven, CT (360.0%); Anchorage, AK (85.7%); Roanoke, VA (66.7%); Houston–Sugar Land–Baytown, TX (62.2%); Baltimore-Towson, MD (56.8%).

Other Considerations for Job Security: Retirements of current postsecondary teachers should create numerous openings for all types of postsecondary teachers, so job opportunities are generally expected to be very good. However, one of the main reasons why students attend postsecondary institutions is to prepare themselves for careers, and the education industry is growing rapidly, so many prospective teachers and teacher aides will come to colleges. Community colleges and other institutions offering career and technical education have been among the most rapidly growing, and these institutions are expected to offer some of the best opportunities for postsecondary teachers.

Teach courses pertaining to education, such as counseling, curriculum, guidance, instruction, teacher education, and teaching English as a second language. Prepare course materials such as syllabi, homework assignments, and handouts. Prepare and deliver lectures to undergraduate and/or graduate students on topics such as children's literature, learning and development, and reading instruction. Initiate, facilitate, and moderate classroom discussions. Evaluate and grade students' classwork, assignments, and papers. Plan, evaluate, and revise curricula, course content, and course materials and methods of instruction. Supervise students' fieldwork, internship, and research work. Keep abreast of developments in their field by reading current literature, talking with colleagues, and participating in professional conferences. Advise students on academic and vocational curricula and on career issues. Maintain regularly scheduled office hours to advise and assist students. Maintain student attendance records, grades, and other required records. Collaborate with colleagues to address teaching and research issues. Compile, administer, and grade examinations or assign this work to others. Conduct research in a particular field of knowledge and publish findings in professional journals, books, or electronic media. Select and obtain materials and supplies such as textbooks. Participate in student recruitment, registration, and placement activities. Advise and instruct teachers employed in school systems by providing activities such as in-service seminars. Serve on academic or administrative committees that deal with institutional policies, departmental matters, and academic issues. Compile bibliographies of specialized materials for outside reading assignments. Write grant proposals to procure external research funding. Participate in campus and community events. Perform administrative duties such as serving as department head. Act as advisers to student organizations. Provide professional consulting services to government and/or industry.

Personality Type: No data available.

Career Cluster: 05 Education and Training. **Career Pathway:** 05.3 Teaching/Training.

Skills—Learning Strategies: Selecting and using training/instructional methods and procedures appropriate for the situation when learning or teaching new things. **Instructing:** Teaching others how to do something. **Writing:** Communicating effectively in writing as appropriate for the needs of the audience. **Social Perceptiveness:** Being aware of others' reactions and understanding why they react as they do. **Speaking:** Talking to others to convey information effectively. **Persuasion:** Persuading others to change their minds or behavior.

Related Knowledge/Courses—Therapy and Counseling: Information and techniques needed to rehabilitate physical and mental ailments and to provide career guidance, including alternative treatments, rehabilitation equipment and its proper use, and methods to evaluate treatment effects. **Education and Training:** Instructional methods and training techniques, including curriculum design principles, learning theory, group and individual teaching techniques, design of individual development plans, and test design principles. **Sociology and Anthropology:** Group behavior and dynamics; societal trends and influences; and cultures and their history, migrations, ethnicity, and origins. **Philosophy and Theology:** Different philosophical systems and religions, including their basic principles, values, ethics, ways of thinking, customs, and practices and their impact on human culture. **Psychology:** Human behavior and performance, mental processes, psychological research methods, and the assessment and treatment of behavioral and affective disorders. **English Language:** The structure and content of the English language, including the meaning and spelling of words, rules of composition, and grammar.

Work Environment: Indoors; sitting.

Engineering Teachers, Postsecondary

Related Major: Graduate Study for College Teaching

- ⚘ Education/Training Required: Master's degree
- ⚘ Annual Earnings: $79,510
- ⚘ Beginning Wage: $43,090
- ⚘ Earnings Growth Potential: High (45.8%)
- ⚘ Growth: 22.9%
- ⚘ Annual Job Openings: 5,565
- ⚘ Self-Employed: 0.4%
- ⚘ Part-Time: 27.8%

Industries with Greatest Employment: Educational Services, Public and Private (97.3%).

Highest-Growth Industries (Projected Growth for This Job): Administrative and Support Services (48.3%); Amusement, Gambling, and Recreation Industries (45.2%); Social Assistance (38.6%); Support Activities for Transportation (32.8%); Religious, Grantmaking, Civic, Professional, and Similar Organizations (29.9%); Professional, Scientific, and Technical Services (28.8%); Management of Companies and Enterprises (26.8%); Local Government (23.5%); Educational Services, Public and Private (22.8%); Hospitals, Public and Private (21.4%).

Lowest-Growth Industries (Projected Growth for This Job): Other Information Services (7.4%); State Government (7.9%); Sporting Goods, Hobby, Book, and Music Stores (13.3%); Performing Arts, Spectator Sports, and Related Industries (13.4%); Insurance Carriers and Related Activities (13.8%).

E

Fastest-Growing Metropolitan Areas (Recent Growth for This Job): New Haven, CT (33.3%); New York–Northern New Jersey–Long Island, NY-NJ-PA (28.2%); Portland-Vancouver-Beaverton, OR-WA (16.7%).

Other Considerations for Job Security: Retirements of current postsecondary teachers should create numerous openings for all types of postsecondary teachers, so job opportunities are generally expected to be very good. However, one of the main reasons why students attend postsecondary institutions is to prepare themselves for careers, so the best job prospects for postsecondary teachers are likely to be in rapidly growing fields that offer many nonacademic career options. Community colleges and other institutions offering career and technical education have been among the most rapidly growing, and these institutions are expected to offer some of the best opportunities for postsecondary teachers.

Teach courses pertaining to the application of physical laws and principles of engineering for the development of machines, materials, instruments, processes, and services. Includes teachers of subjects such as chemical, civil, electrical, industrial, mechanical, mineral, and petroleum engineering. Includes both teachers primarily engaged in teaching and those who do a combination of both teaching and research. Prepare and deliver lectures to undergraduate and/or graduate students on topics such as mechanics, hydraulics, and robotics. Keep abreast of developments in their field by reading current literature, talking with colleagues, and participating in professional conferences. Supervise undergraduate and/or graduate teaching, internship, and research work. Evaluate and grade students' classwork, laboratory work, assignments, and papers. Conduct research in a particular field of knowledge and publish findings in professional journals, books, and/or electronic media. Prepare course materials such as syllabi, homework assignments, and handouts. Compile, administer, and grade examinations or assign this work to others. Write grant proposals to procure external research funding. Supervise students' laboratory work. Initiate, facilitate, and moderate class discussions. Maintain regularly scheduled office hours to advise and assist students. Plan, evaluate, and revise curricula, course content, and course materials and methods of instruction. Advise students on academic and vocational curricula and on career issues. Maintain student attendance records, grades, and other required records. Collaborate with colleagues to address teaching and research issues. Select and obtain materials and supplies such as textbooks and laboratory equipment. Participate in student recruitment, registration, and placement activities. Serve on academic or administrative committees that deal with institutional policies, departmental matters, and academic issues. Perform administrative duties such as serving as department head. Provide professional consulting services to government and/or industry. Compile bibliographies of specialized materials for outside reading assignments. Act as advisers to student organizations. Participate in campus and community events.

Personality Type: Investigative-Realistic-Social. Investigative occupations frequently involve working with ideas and require an extensive amount of thinking. These occupations can involve searching for facts and figuring out problems mentally.

Career Clusters: 02 Architecture and Construction; 04 Business, Management, and Administration; 05 Education and Training; 11 Information Technology; 15 Science, Technology, Engineering, and Mathematics. **Career**

Pathways: 02.1 Design/Pre-Construction; 04.4 Business Analysis; 05.3 Teaching/Training; 11.4 Programming and Software Development; 15.1 Engineering and Technology; 15.3 Science and Mathematics.

Skills—Science: Using scientific rules and methods to solve problems. **Programming:** Writing computer programs for various purposes. **Mathematics:** Using mathematics to solve problems. **Technology Design:** Generating or adapting equipment and technology to serve user needs. **Complex Problem Solving:** Identifying complex problems and reviewing related information to develop and evaluate options and implement solutions. **Management of Financial Resources:** Determining how money will be spent to get the work done and accounting for these expenditures.

Related Knowledge/Courses—Engineering and Technology: Equipment, tools, and mechanical devices and their uses to produce motion, light, power, technology, and other applications. **Physics:** Physical principles, laws, and applications, including air, water, material dynamics, light, atomic principles, heat, electric theory, earth formations, and meteorological and related natural phenomena. **Design:** Design techniques, principles, tools, and instruments involved in the production and use of precision technical plans, blueprints, drawings, and models. **Mathematics:** Numbers and their operations and interrelationships, including arithmetic, algebra, geometry, calculus, and statistics and their applications. **Education and Training:** Instructional methods and training techniques, including curriculum design principles, learning theory, group and individual teaching techniques, design of individual development plans, and test design principles. **Telecommunications:** Transmission, broadcasting, switching,

control, and operation of telecommunications systems.

Work Environment: Indoors; sitting.

English Language and Literature Teachers, Postsecondary

Related Major: Graduate Study for College Teaching

- Education/Training Required: Master's degree
- Annual Earnings: $54,000
- Beginning Wage: $30,680
- Earnings Growth Potential: High (43.2%)
- Growth: 22.9%
- Annual Job Openings: 10,475
- Self-Employed: 0.4%
- Part-Time: 27.8%

Industries with Greatest Employment: Educational Services, Public and Private (97.3%).

Highest-Growth Industries (Projected Growth for This Job): Administrative and Support Services (48.3%); Amusement, Gambling, and Recreation Industries (45.2%); Social Assistance (38.6%); Support Activities for Transportation (32.8%); Religious, Grantmaking, Civic, Professional, and Similar Organizations (29.9%); Professional, Scientific, and Technical Services (28.8%); Management of Companies and Enterprises (26.8%); Local Government (23.5%); Educational Services, Public and Private (22.8%); Hospitals, Public and Private (21.4%).

Lowest-Growth Industries (Projected Growth for This Job): Other Information Services (7.4%); State Government (7.9%); Sporting

Goods, Hobby, Book, and Music Stores (13.3%); Performing Arts, Spectator Sports, and Related Industries (13.4%); Insurance Carriers and Related Activities (13.8%).

Fastest-Growing Metropolitan Areas (Recent Growth for This Job): Syracuse, NY (214.3%); Manchester, NH (100.0%); New Haven, CT (87.5%); Cedar Rapids, IA (75.0%); Los Angeles–Long Beach–Santa Ana, CA (73.0%).

Other Considerations for Job Security: Retirements of current postsecondary teachers should create numerous openings for all types of postsecondary teachers, so job opportunities are generally expected to be very good. One of the main reasons why students attend postsecondary institutions is to prepare themselves for careers, so the best job prospects for postsecondary teachers are likely to be in rapidly growing fields that offer many nonacademic career options. English composition is a key part of the curriculum for most majors. Community colleges and other institutions offering career and technical education have been among the most rapidly growing, and these institutions are expected to offer some of the best opportunities for postsecondary teachers.

Teach courses in English language and literature, including linguistics and comparative literature. Initiate, facilitate, and moderate classroom discussions. Evaluate and grade students' classwork, assignments, and papers. Prepare course materials such as syllabi, homework assignments, and handouts. Prepare and deliver lectures to undergraduate and graduate students on topics such as poetry, novel structure, and translation and adaptation. Maintain student attendance records, grades, and other required records. Plan, evaluate, and revise curricula, course content, and course materials and methods of instruction. Compile, administer, and grade examinations or assign this work to others. Maintain regularly scheduled office hours in order to advise and assist students. Keep abreast of developments in their field by reading current literature, talking with colleagues, and participating in professional conferences. Select and obtain materials and supplies such as textbooks. Advise students on academic and vocational curricula and on career issues. Conduct research in a particular field of knowledge and publish findings in professional journals, books, or electronic media. Collaborate with colleagues to address teaching and research issues. Serve on academic or administrative committees that deal with institutional policies, departmental matters, and academic issues. Participate in campus and community events. Participate in student recruitment, registration, and placement activities. Compile bibliographies of specialized materials for outside reading assignments. Supervise undergraduate and/or graduate teaching, internship, and research work. Provide assistance to students in college writing centers. Perform administrative duties such as serving as department head. Recruit, train, and supervise student writing instructors. Act as advisers to student organizations. Write grant proposals to procure external research funding. Provide professional consulting services to government or industry.

Personality Type: Artistic-Social-Investigative. Artistic occupations frequently involve working with forms, designs, and patterns. They often require self-expression, and the work can be done without following a clear set of rules.

Career Clusters: 03 Arts, Audio/Video Technology, and Communications; 05 Education and Training. **Career Pathways:** 03.5 Journalism and Broadcasting; 05.3 Teaching/Training.

Skills—Instructing: Teaching others how to do something. **Writing:** Communicating effectively in writing as appropriate for the needs of the audience. **Learning Strategies:** Selecting and using training/instructional methods and procedures appropriate for the situation when learning or teaching new things. **Social Perceptiveness:** Being aware of others' reactions and understanding why they react as they do. **Reading Comprehension:** Understanding written sentences and paragraphs in work-related documents. **Persuasion:** Persuading others to change their minds or behavior.

Related Knowledge/Courses—Philosophy and Theology: Different philosophical systems and religions, including their basic principles, values, ethics, ways of thinking, customs, and practices and their impact on human culture. **English Language:** The structure and content of the English language, including the meaning and spelling of words, rules of composition, and grammar. **History and Archeology:** Historical events and their causes, indicators, and impact on particular civilizations and cultures. **Education and Training:** Instructional methods and training techniques, including curriculum design principles, learning theory, group and individual teaching techniques, design of individual development plans, and test design principles. **Fine Arts:** Theory and techniques required to produce, compose, and perform works of music, dance, visual arts, drama, and sculpture. **Sociology and Anthropology:** Group behavior and dynamics; societal trends and influences; and cultures and their history, migrations, ethnicity, and origins.

Work Environment: Indoors; sitting.

Environmental Science Teachers, Postsecondary

Related Major: Graduate Study for College Teaching

- ✸ Education/Training Required: Master's degree
- ✸ Annual Earnings: $64,850
- ✸ Beginning Wage: $35,120
- ✸ Earnings Growth Potential: High (45.8%)
- ✸ Growth: 22.9%
- ✸ Annual Job Openings: 769
- ✸ Self-Employed: 0.4%
- ✸ Part-Time: 27.8%

Industries with Greatest Employment: Educational Services, Public and Private (97.3%).

Highest-Growth Industries (Projected Growth for This Job): Administrative and Support Services (48.3%); Amusement, Gambling, and Recreation Industries (45.2%); Social Assistance (38.6%); Support Activities for Transportation (32.8%); Religious, Grantmaking, Civic, Professional, and Similar Organizations (29.9%); Professional, Scientific, and Technical Services (28.8%); Management of Companies and Enterprises (26.8%); Local Government (23.5%); Educational Services, Public and Private (22.8%); Hospitals, Public and Private (21.4%).

Lowest-Growth Industries (Projected Growth for This Job): Other Information Services (7.4%); State Government (7.9%); Sporting Goods, Hobby, Book, and Music Stores (13.3%); Performing Arts, Spectator Sports, and Related Industries (13.4%); Insurance Carriers and Related Activities (13.8%).

Fastest-Growing Metropolitan Areas (Recent Growth for This Job): Washington-Arlington-Alexandria, DC-VA-MD-WV (11.1%).

Other Considerations for Job Security: Retirements of current postsecondary teachers should create numerous openings for all types of postsecondary teachers, so job opportunities are generally expected to be very good. One of the main reasons why students attend postsecondary institutions is to prepare themselves for careers, so the best job prospects for postsecondary teachers are likely to be in rapidly growing fields that offer many nonacademic career options. Community colleges and other institutions offering career and technical education have been among the most rapidly growing, and these institutions are expected to offer some of the best opportunities for postsecondary teachers.

Teach courses in environmental science. Supervise undergraduate and/or graduate teaching, internship, and research work. Conduct research in a particular field of knowledge and publish findings in professional journals, books, and/or electronic media. Keep abreast of developments in their field by reading current literature, talking with colleagues, and participating in professional conferences. Evaluate and grade students' classwork, laboratory work, assignments, and papers. Write grant proposals to procure external research funding. Supervise students' laboratory work and fieldwork. Prepare course materials such as syllabi, homework assignments, and handouts. Plan, evaluate, and revise curricula, course content, and course materials and methods of instruction. Compile, administer, and grade examinations or assign this work to others. Initiate, facilitate, and moderate classroom discussions. Advise students on academic and vocational curricula and on career issues. Prepare and deliver lectures to undergraduate and/or graduate students on topics such as hazardous waste management, industrial safety, and environmental toxicology. Maintain student attendance records, grades, and other required records. Select and obtain materials and supplies such as textbooks and laboratory equipment. Maintain regularly scheduled office hours in order to advise and assist students. Collaborate with colleagues to address teaching and research issues. Perform administrative duties such as serving as department head. Participate in student recruitment, registration, and placement activities. Provide professional consulting services to government and/or industry. Serve on academic or administrative committees that deal with institutional policies, departmental matters, and academic issues. Compile bibliographies of specialized materials for outside reading assignments. Participate in campus and community events. Act as advisers to student organizations.

Personality Type: No data available.

Career Clusters: 01 Agriculture, Food, and Natural Resources; 05 Education and Training. **Career Pathways:** 01.5 Natural Resources Systems; 05.3 Teaching/Training.

Skills—Science: Using scientific rules and methods to solve problems. **Writing:** Communicating effectively in writing as appropriate for the needs of the audience. **Reading Comprehension:** Understanding written sentences and paragraphs in work-related documents. **Instructing:** Teaching others how to do something. **Mathematics:** Using mathematics to solve problems. **Management of Financial Resources:** Determining how money will be spent to get the work done and accounting for these expenditures.

Related Knowledge/Courses—Biology: Plant and animal living tissue, cells, organisms, and entities, including their functions, interdependencies, and interactions with each other and the environment. **Geography:** Various methods for describing the location and distribution of land, sea, and air masses, including their physical locations, relationships, and characteristics. **Chemistry:** The composition, structure, and properties of substances and of the chemical processes and transformations that they undergo. This includes uses of chemicals and their interactions, danger signs, production techniques, and disposal methods. **Education and Training:** Instructional methods and training techniques, including curriculum design principles, learning theory, group and individual teaching techniques, design of individual development plans, and test design principles. **Physics:** Physical principles, laws, and applications, including air, water, material dynamics, light, atomic principles, heat, electric theory, earth formations, and meteorological and related natural phenomena. **History and Archeology:** Historical events and their causes, indicators, and impact on particular civilizations and cultures.

Work Environment: Indoors; sitting.

Environmental Scientists and Specialists, Including Health

Related Major: Environmental Science
- ✸ Education/Training Required: Master's degree
- ✸ Annual Earnings: $58,380
- ✸ Beginning Wage: $35,630
- ✸ Earnings Growth Potential: Medium (39.0%)
- ✸ Growth: 25.1%
- ✸ Annual Job Openings: 6,961
- ✸ Self-Employed: 2.2%
- ✸ Part-Time: 5.3%

Industries with Greatest Employment: Professional, Scientific, and Technical Services (42.4%); State Government (23.7%); Local Government (11.6%); Federal Government (7.5%); Educational Services, Public and Private (5.5%).

Highest-Growth Industries (Projected Growth for This Job): Professional, Scientific, and Technical Services (54.3%); Administrative and Support Services (32.1%); Waste Management and Remediation Services (29.3%); Management of Companies and Enterprises (15.3%); Religious, Grantmaking, Civic, Professional, and Similar Organizations (15.2%).

Lowest-Growth Industries (Projected Growth for This Job): Paper Manufacturing (–29.1%); Chemical Manufacturing (–8.3%); Merchant Wholesalers, Nondurable Goods (–7.5%); Utilities (–6.9%); Federal Government (–5.5%); State Government (–1.9%); Oil and Gas Extraction (–1.7%); Transportation Equipment Manufacturing (2.6%); Mining (Except Oil and Gas) (5.1%); Hospitals, Public and Private (8.9%); others.

Fastest-Growing Metropolitan Areas (Recent Growth for This Job): Boulder, CO (407.7%); Grand Forks, ND-MN (333.3%); Sioux Falls, SD (225.0%); Santa Rosa–Petaluma, CA (200.0%); Charlottesville, VA (175.0%).

Other Considerations for Job Security: Job prospects for environmental scientists will be good. Funding for federal and state geological surveys depend largely on the political climate and the current budget. Thus, job security for environmental scientists may vary. During periods of economic recession, layoffs of environmental scientists may occur in consulting firms; layoffs are much less likely in government.

Conduct research or perform investigation for the purpose of identifying, abating,

E

or eliminating sources of pollutants or hazards that affect either the environment or the health of the population. Using knowledge of various scientific disciplines, may collect, synthesize, study, report, and take action based on data derived from measurements or observations of air, food, soil, water, and other sources. Collect, synthesize, analyze, manage, and report environmental data such as pollution emission measurements, atmospheric monitoring measurements, meteorological and mineralogical information, and soil or water samples. Analyze data to determine validity, quality, and scientific significance, and to interpret correlations between human activities and environmental effects. Communicate scientific and technical information to the public, organizations, or internal audiences through oral briefings, written documents, workshops, conferences, training sessions, or public hearings. Provide scientific and technical guidance, support, coordination, and oversight to governmental agencies, environmental programs, industry, or the public. Process and review environmental permits, licenses, and related materials. Review and implement environmental technical standards, guidelines, policies, and formal regulations that meet all appropriate requirements. Prepare charts or graphs from data samples, providing summary information on the environmental relevance of the data. Determine data collection methods to be employed in research projects and surveys. Investigate and report on accidents affecting the environment. Research sources of pollution to determine their effects on the environment and to develop theories or methods of pollution abatement or control. Provide advice on proper standards and regulations or the development of policies, strategies, and codes of practice for environmental management. Monitor effects of pollution and land degradation, and recommend means of prevention or control. Supervise or train students, environmental technologists, technicians, or other related staff. Evaluate violations or problems discovered during inspections to determine appropriate regulatory actions or to provide advice on the development and prosecution of regulatory cases. Conduct environmental audits and inspections, and investigations of violations. Plan and develop research models, using knowledge of mathematical and statistical concepts. Conduct applied research on environmental topics such as waste control and treatment and pollution abatement methods.

Personality Type: Investigative-Realistic. Investigative occupations frequently involve working with ideas and require an extensive amount of thinking. These occupations can involve searching for facts and figuring out problems mentally.

Career Cluster: 01 Agriculture, Food, and Natural Resources. **Career Pathway:** 01.5 Natural Resources Systems.

Skills—No data available.

Related Knowledge/Courses—Biology: Plant and animal living tissue, cells, organisms, and entities, including their functions, interdependencies, and interactions with each other and the environment. **Geography:** Various methods for describing the location and distribution of land, sea, and air masses, including their physical locations, relationships, and characteristics. **Chemistry:** The composition, structure, and properties of substances and of the chemical processes and transformations that they undergo. This includes uses of chemicals and their interactions, danger signs, production techniques, and disposal methods. **Physics:** Physical principles, laws, and applications, including air, water, material dynamics, light, atomic principles, heat, electric theory, earth formations, and meteorological and related natural phenomena. **Law and Government:** Laws, legal codes, court procedures, precedents, government regulations, executive orders, agency rules, and the democratic political process. **Engineering and Technology:** Equipment, tools, and mechanical devices and their uses to produce motion, light, power, technology, and other applications.

Work Environment: More often indoors than outdoors; noisy; sitting.

Family and General Practitioners

Related Major: Medicine

- ❋ Education/Training Required: First professional degree
- ❋ Annual Earnings: More than $145,600
- ❋ Beginning Wage: $67,400
- ❋ Earnings Growth Potential: Cannot be calculated
- ❋ Growth: 14.2%
- ❋ Annual Job Openings: 38,027
- ❋ Self-Employed: 14.7%
- ❋ Part-Time: 8.1%

Industries with Greatest Employment: Ambulatory Health Care Services (55.9%); Hospitals, Public and Private (17.8%).

Highest-Growth Industries (Projected Growth for This Job): Social Assistance (58.6%); Administrative and Support Services (26.8%); Professional, Scientific, and Technical Services (22.6%); Nursing and Residential Care Facilities (21.0%); Ambulatory Health Care Services (19.4%); Religious, Grantmaking, Civic, Professional, and Similar Organizations

(16.7%); Management of Companies and Enterprises (15.3%).

Lowest-Growth Industries (Projected Growth for This Job): Federal Government (−5.5%); State Government (−1.9%); Insurance Carriers and Related Activities (4.6%); Health and Personal Care Stores (5.3%); Hospitals, Public and Private (9.9%); Educational Services, Public and Private (11.8%); Local Government (12.3%).

Fastest-Growing Metropolitan Areas (Recent Growth for This Job): Bellingham, WA (200.0%); Anchorage, AK (160.0%); St. Louis, MO-IL (140.9%); Chattanooga, TN-GA (100.0%); Lakeland, FL (100.0%).

Other Considerations for Job Security: Opportunities for individuals interested in becoming physicians and surgeons are expected to be very good. Unlike their predecessors, new physicians are much less likely to enter solo practice and more likely to take salaried jobs in group medical practices, clinics, and health networks. Reports of shortages in some specialties, such as general or family practice, internal medicine, and OB/GYN, or in rural or low-income areas should attract new entrants, encouraging schools to expand programs and hospitals to increase available residency slots. However, because physician training is so lengthy, employment change happens gradually. Opportunities should be particularly good in rural and low-income areas, as some physicians find these areas unattractive because of less control over work hours, isolation from medical colleagues, or other reasons.

Diagnose, treat, and help prevent diseases and injuries that commonly occur in the general population. Prescribe or administer treatment, therapy, medication, vaccination, and other specialized medical care to treat or prevent illness, disease, or injury. Order, perform, and interpret tests and analyze records, reports, and examination information to diagnose patients' condition. Monitor the patients' conditions and progress and re-evaluate treatments as necessary. Explain procedures and discuss test results or prescribed treatments with patients. Collect, record, and maintain patient information, such as medical history, reports, and examination results. Advise patients and community members concerning diet, activity, hygiene, and disease prevention. Refer patients to medical specialists or other practitioners when necessary. Direct and coordinate activities of nurses, students, assistants, specialists, therapists, and other medical staff. Coordinate work with nurses, social workers, rehabilitation therapists, pharmacists, psychologists, and other health-care providers. Deliver babies. Operate on patients to remove, repair, or improve functioning of diseased or injured body parts and systems. Plan, implement, or administer health programs or standards in hospital, business, or community for information, prevention, or treatment of injury or illness. Prepare reports for government or management of birth, death, and disease statistics; workforce evaluations; or medical status of individuals. Conduct research to study anatomy and develop or test medications, treatments, or procedures to prevent or control disease or injury.

Personality Type: Investigative. Investigative occupations frequently involve working with ideas and require an extensive amount of thinking. These occupations can involve searching for facts and figuring out problems mentally.

Career Clusters: 08 Health Science; 15 Science, Technology, Engineering, and Mathematics. **Career Pathways:** 08.1 Therapeutic Services; 15.3 Science and Mathematics.

Skills—Science: Using scientific rules and methods to solve problems. **Social Perceptiveness:** Being aware of others' reactions and understanding why they react as they do. **Reading Comprehension:** Understanding written sentences and paragraphs in work-related documents. **Complex Problem Solving:** Identifying complex problems and reviewing related information to develop and evaluate options and implement solutions. **Persuasion:** Persuading others to change their minds or behavior. **Service Orientation:** Actively looking for ways to help people.

Related Knowledge/Courses—Medicine and Dentistry: The information and techniques needed to diagnose and treat injuries, diseases, and deformities. This includes symptoms, treatment alternatives, drug properties and interactions, and preventive health-care measures. **Biology:** Plant and animal living tissue, cells, organisms, and entities, including their functions, interdependencies, and interactions with each other and the environment. **Therapy and Counseling:** Information and techniques needed to rehabilitate physical and mental ailments and to provide career guidance, including alternative treatments, rehabilitation equipment and its proper use, and methods to evaluate treatment effects. **Psychology:** Human behavior and performance, mental processes, psychological research methods, and the assessment and treatment of behavioral and affective disorders. **Sociology and Anthropology:** Group behavior and dynamics; societal trends and influences; and cultures and their history, migrations, ethnicity, and origins. **Chemistry:** The composition, structure, and properties of substances and of the chemical processes and transformations that they undergo. This includes uses of chemicals and their interactions, danger signs, production techniques, and disposal methods.

Work Environment: Indoors; disease or infections; standing; using hands on objects, tools, or controls.

Foreign Language and Literature Teachers, Postsecondary

Related Major: Graduate Study for College Teaching

- ❋ Education/Training Required: Master's degree
- ❋ Annual Earnings: $53,610
- ❋ Beginning Wage: $30,590
- ❋ Earnings Growth Potential: High (42.9%)
- ❋ Growth: 22.9%
- ❋ Annual Job Openings: 4,317
- ❋ Self-Employed: 0.4%
- ❋ Part-Time: 27.8%

Industries with Greatest Employment: Educational Services, Public and Private (97.3%).

Highest-Growth Industries (Projected Growth for This Job): Administrative and Support Services (48.3%); Amusement, Gambling, and Recreation Industries (45.2%); Social Assistance (38.6%); Support Activities for Transportation (32.8%); Religious, Grantmaking, Civic, Professional, and Similar Organizations (29.9%); Professional, Scientific, and Technical Services (28.8%); Management of Companies and Enterprises (26.8%); Local Government (23.5%); Educational Services, Public and Private (22.8%); Hospitals, Public and Private (21.4%).

Lowest-Growth Industries (Projected Growth for This Job): Other Information Services (7.4%); State Government (7.9%); Sporting Goods, Hobby, Book, and Music Stores (13.3%); Performing Arts, Spectator Sports, and Related Industries (13.4%); Insurance Carriers and Related Activities (13.8%).

Fastest-Growing Metropolitan Areas (Recent Growth for This Job): Los Angeles–Long Beach–Santa Ana, CA (89.1%); Utica-Rome, NY (66.7%); Duluth, MN-WI (50.0%); Nashville–Davidson County–Murfreesboro, TN (40.0%); Portland-Vancouver-Beaverton, OR-WA (38.5%).

Other Considerations for Job Security: Retirements of current postsecondary teachers should create numerous openings for all types of postsecondary teachers, so job opportunities are generally expected to be very good. However, one of the main reasons why students attend postsecondary institutions is to prepare themselves for careers, so the best job prospects for postsecondary teachers are likely to be in rapidly growing fields that offer many nonacademic career options—unlike foreign language and literature. On the other hand, foreign language courses are required for many majors. Community colleges and other institutions offering career and technical education have been among the most rapidly growing, and these institutions are expected to offer some of the best opportunities for postsecondary teachers.

Teach courses in foreign (i.e., other than English) languages and literature. Evaluate and grade students' classwork, assignments, and papers. Prepare course materials such as syllabi, homework assignments, and handouts. Initiate, facilitate, and moderate classroom discussions. Maintain student attendance records, grades, and other required records. Compile, administer, and grade examinations or assign this work to others. Plan, evaluate, and revise curricula, course content, and course materials and methods of instruction. Prepare and deliver lectures to undergraduate and graduate students on topics such as how to speak and write a foreign language and the cultural aspects of areas where a particular language is used. Maintain regularly scheduled office hours to advise and assist students. Select and obtain materials and supplies such as textbooks. Keep abreast of developments in their field by reading current literature, talking with colleagues, and participating in professional organizations and activities. Advise students on academic and vocational curricula and on career issues. Conduct research in a particular field of knowledge and publish findings in scholarly journals, books, and/or electronic media. Collaborate with colleagues to address teaching and research issues. Serve on academic or administrative committees that deal with institutional policies, departmental matters, and academic issues. Participate in student recruitment, registration, and placement activities. Compile bibliographies of specialized materials for outside reading assignments. Participate in campus and community events. Act as advisers to student organizations. Perform administrative duties such as serving as department head. Supervise undergraduate and graduate teaching, internship, and research work. Write grant proposals to procure external research funding. Provide professional consulting services to government or industry.

Personality Type: Artistic-Social-Investigative. Artistic occupations frequently involve working with forms, designs, and patterns. They often require self-expression, and the work can be done without following a clear set of rules.

Career Cluster: 05 Education and Training. **Career Pathway:** 05.3 Teaching/Training.

Skills—Learning Strategies: Selecting and using training/instructional methods and procedures appropriate for the situation when learning or teaching new things. **Instructing:** Teaching others how to do something. **Writing:** Communicating effectively in writing as appropriate for the needs of the audience. **Reading Comprehension:** Understanding written sentences and paragraphs in work-related documents. **Speaking:** Talking to others to convey information effectively. **Persuasion:** Persuading others to change their minds or behavior.

Related Knowledge/Courses—Foreign Language: The structure and content of a foreign (non-English) language, including the meaning and spelling of words, rules of composition and grammar, and pronunciation. **Philosophy and Theology:** Different philosophical systems and religions, including their basic principles, values, ethics, ways of thinking, customs, and practices and their impact on human culture. **History and Archeology:** Historical events and their causes, indicators, and impact on particular civilizations and cultures. **Sociology and Anthropology:** Group behavior and dynamics; societal trends and influences; and cultures and their history, migrations, ethnicity, and origins. **Geography:** Various methods for describing the location and distribution of land, sea, and air masses, including their physical locations, relationships, and characteristics. **English Language:** The structure and content of the English language, including the meaning and spelling of words, rules of composition, and grammar.

Work Environment: Indoors; sitting.

Forestry and Conservation Science Teachers, Postsecondary

Related Major: Graduate Study for College Teaching

* Education/Training Required: Master's degree
* Annual Earnings: $63,790
* Beginning Wage: $36,270
* Earnings Growth Potential: High (43.1%)
* Growth: 22.9%
* Annual Job Openings: 454
* Self-Employed: 0.4%
* Part-Time: 27.8%

Industries with Greatest Employment: Educational Services, Public and Private (97.3%).

Highest-Growth Industries (Projected Growth for This Job): Administrative and Support Services (48.3%); Amusement, Gambling, and Recreation Industries (45.2%); Social Assistance (38.6%); Support Activities for Transportation (32.8%); Religious, Grantmaking, Civic, Professional, and Similar Organizations (29.9%); Professional, Scientific, and Technical Services (28.8%); Management of Companies and Enterprises (26.8%); Local Government (23.5%); Educational Services, Public and Private (22.8%); Hospitals, Public and Private (21.4%).

Lowest-Growth Industries (Projected Growth for This Job): Other Information Services (7.4%); State Government (7.9%); Sporting Goods, Hobby, Book, and Music Stores (13.3%); Performing Arts, Spectator Sports, and Related Industries (13.4%); Insurance Carriers and Related Activities (13.8%).

Fastest-Growing Metropolitan Areas (Recent Growth for This Job): None with fast growth.

Other Considerations for Job Security: Retirements of current postsecondary teachers should create numerous openings for all types of postsecondary teachers, so job opportunities are generally expected to be very good. One of the main reasons why students attend postsecondary institutions is to prepare themselves for careers, so the best job prospects for postsecondary teachers are likely to be in rapidly growing fields that offer many nonacademic career options. Community colleges and other institutions offering career and technical education have been among the most rapidly growing, and these institutions are expected to offer some of the best opportunities for postsecondary teachers.

Teach courses in environmental and conservation science. Conduct research in a particular field of knowledge and publish findings in books, professional journals, and/or electronic media. Keep abreast of developments in their field by reading current literature, talking with colleagues, and participating in professional conferences. Prepare and deliver lectures to undergraduate and/or graduate students on topics such as forest resource policy, forest pathology, and mapping. Evaluate and grade students' classwork, assignments, and papers. Write grant proposals to procure external research funding. Supervise undergraduate and/or graduate teaching, internship, and research work. Plan, evaluate, and revise curricula, course content, and course materials and methods of instruction. Prepare course materials such as syllabi, homework assignments, and handouts. Compile, administer, and grade examinations or assign this work to others. Advise students on academic and vocational curricula and on career issues. Initiate, facilitate, and moderate classroom discussions.

Supervise students' laboratory work and field-work. Maintain student attendance records, grades, and other required records. Collaborate with colleagues to address teaching and research issues. Maintain regularly scheduled office hours in order to advise and assist students. Select and obtain materials and supplies such as textbooks and laboratory equipment. Participate in student recruitment, registration, and placement activities. Serve on academic or administrative committees that deal with institutional policies, departmental matters, and academic issues. Provide professional consulting services to government and/or industry. Perform administrative duties such as serving as department head. Compile bibliographies of specialized materials for outside reading assignments. Act as advisers to student organizations. Participate in campus and community events.

Personality Type: Investigative-Social. Investigative occupations frequently involve working with ideas and require an extensive amount of thinking. These occupations can involve searching for facts and figuring out problems mentally.

Career Cluster: 05 Education and Training. **Career Pathway:** 05.3 Teaching/Training.

Skills—Science: Using scientific rules and methods to solve problems. **Management of Financial Resources:** Determining how money will be spent to get the work done and accounting for these expenditures. **Writing:** Communicating effectively in writing as appropriate for the needs of the audience. **Instructing:** Teaching others how to do something. **Mathematics:** Using mathematics to solve problems. **Management of Personnel Resources:** Motivating, developing, and directing people as they work, identifying the best people for the job.

Related Knowledge/Courses—Biology: Plant and animal living tissue, cells, organisms, and entities, including their functions, interdependencies, and interactions with each other and the environment. **Geography:** Various methods for describing the location and distribution of land, sea, and air masses, including their physical locations, relationships, and characteristics. **Education and Training:** Instructional methods and training techniques, including curriculum design principles, learning theory, group and individual teaching techniques, design of individual development plans, and test design principles. **Mathematics:** Numbers and their operations and interrelationships, including arithmetic, algebra, geometry, calculus, and statistics and their applications. **Chemistry:** The composition, structure, and properties of substances and of the chemical processes and transformations that they undergo. This includes uses of chemicals and their interactions, danger signs, production techniques, and disposal methods. **History and Archeology:** Historical events and their causes, indicators, and impact on particular civilizations and cultures.

Work Environment: Indoors; sitting.

Geography Teachers, Postsecondary

Related Major: Graduate Study for College Teaching

- Education/Training Required: Master's degree
- Annual Earnings: $61,310
- Beginning Wage: $36,070
- Earnings Growth Potential: High (41.2%)
- Growth: 22.9%
- Annual Job Openings: 697
- Self-Employed: 0.4%
- Part-Time: 27.8%

Industries with Greatest Employment: Educational Services, Public and Private (97.3%).

Highest-Growth Industries (Projected Growth for This Job): Administrative and Support Services (48.3%); Amusement, Gambling, and Recreation Industries (45.2%); Social Assistance (38.6%); Support Activities for Transportation (32.8%); Religious, Grantmaking, Civic, Professional, and Similar Organizations (29.9%); Professional, Scientific, and Technical Services (28.8%); Management of Companies and Enterprises (26.8%); Local Government (23.5%); Educational Services, Public and Private (22.8%); Hospitals, Public and Private (21.4%).

Lowest-Growth Industries (Projected Growth for This Job): Other Information Services (7.4%); State Government (7.9%); Sporting Goods, Hobby, Book, and Music Stores (13.3%); Performing Arts, Spectator Sports, and Related Industries (13.4%); Insurance Carriers and Related Activities (13.8%).

Fastest-Growing Metropolitan Areas (Recent Growth for This Job): Baltimore-Towson, MD (216.7%); San Antonio, TX (25.0%); St. Louis, MO-IL (25.0%).

Other Considerations for Job Security: Retirements of current postsecondary teachers should create numerous openings for all types of postsecondary teachers. However, one of the main reasons why students attend postsecondary institutions is to prepare themselves for careers, so the best job prospects for postsecondary teachers are likely to be in rapidly growing fields that offer many nonacademic career options. Community colleges and other institutions offering career and technical education have been among the most rapidly growing, and these institutions are expected to offer some of the best opportunities for postsecondary teachers.

Teach courses in geography. Prepare and deliver lectures to undergraduate and/or graduate students on topics such as urbanization, environmental systems, and cultural geography. Evaluate and grade students' classwork, assignments, and papers. Compile, administer, and grade examinations or assign this work to others. Initiate, facilitate, and moderate classroom discussions. Maintain student attendance records, grades, and other required records. Prepare course materials such as syllabi, homework assignments, and handouts. Keep abreast of developments in their field by reading current literature, talking with colleagues, and participating in professional conferences. Supervise undergraduate and/or graduate teaching, internship, and research work. Plan, evaluate, and revise curricula, course content, and course materials and methods of instruction. Maintain regularly scheduled office hours to advise and assist students. Supervise students' laboratory work and fieldwork. Conduct research in a particular field of knowledge and publish findings in professional journals, books, and electronic media. Collaborate with colleagues to address teaching and research issues. Select and obtain materials and supplies such as textbooks. Advise students on academic and vocational curricula and on career issues. Serve on academic or administrative committees that deal with institutional policies, departmental matters, and academic issues. Participate in student recruitment, registration, and placement activities. Participate in campus and community events. Compile bibliographies of specialized materials for outside reading assignments. Perform administrative duties such as serving as department head. Write grant proposals to procure external research funding. Maintain geographic information systems laboratories, performing duties such as updating software. Perform spatial analysis and modeling, using geographic information system techniques. Act as advisers to student organizations. Provide professional consulting services to government and industry.

Personality Type: No data available.

Career Clusters: 05 Education and Training; 15 Science, Technology, Engineering, and Mathematics. **Career Pathways:** 05.3 Teaching/Training; 15.3 Science and Mathematics.

Skills—Science: Using scientific rules and methods to solve problems. **Writing:** Communicating effectively in writing as appropriate for the needs of the audience. **Instructing:** Teaching others how to do something. **Learning Strategies:** Selecting and using training/instructional methods and procedures appropriate for the situation when learning or teaching new things. **Reading Comprehension:** Understanding written sentences and paragraphs in work-related documents. **Speaking:** Talking to others to convey information effectively.

Related Knowledge/Courses—Geography: Various methods for describing the location and distribution of land, sea, and air masses, including their physical locations, relationships, and characteristics. **Sociology and Anthropology:** Group behavior and dynamics; societal trends and influences; and cultures and their history, migrations, ethnicity, and origins. **History and Archeology:** Historical events and their causes, indicators, and impact on particular civilizations and cultures. **Philosophy and Theology:** Different philosophical systems and religions, including their basic principles, values, ethics, ways of thinking, customs, and practices and their impact on human culture. **Education and Training:** Instructional methods and training techniques, including curriculum design principles, learning theory, group and individual teaching techniques, design of individual development plans, and test design principles. **Communications and Media:** Media production, communication, and dissemination techniques and methods, including alternative ways to inform and entertain via written, oral, and visual media.

Work Environment: Indoors; sitting.

Geoscientists, Except Hydrologists and Geographers

Related Majors: Geology; Geophysics; Oceanography

* ⊛ Education/Training Required: Master's degree
* ⊛ Annual Earnings: $75,800
* ⊛ Beginning Wage: $41,020
* ⊛ Earnings Growth Potential: High (45.9%)
* ⊛ Growth: 21.9%
* ⊛ Annual Job Openings: 2,471
* ⊛ Self-Employed: 2.2%
* ⊛ Part-Time: 5.3%

Industries with Greatest Employment: Professional, Scientific, and Technical Services (43.7%); Oil and Gas Extraction (17.9%); State Government (9.4%); Federal Government (8.4%); Support Activities for Mining (6.5%).

Highest-Growth Industries (Projected Growth for This Job): Professional, Scientific, and Technical Services (45.2%); Securities, Commodity Contracts, and Other Financial Investments and Related Activities (40.7%); Waste Management and Remediation Services (32.1%); Administrative and Support Services (26.8%); Management of Companies and Enterprises (15.4%).

Lowest-Growth Industries (Projected Growth for This Job): Support Activities for Mining (–6.0%); Federal Government (–5.5%); State Government (–1.9%); Mining (Except Oil and Gas) (6.5%); Oil and Gas Extraction (8.2%); Educational Services, Public and Private (11.7%); Local Government (12.1%).

Fastest-Growing Metropolitan Areas (Recent Growth for This Job): Raleigh-Cary, NC (142.9%); Reno-Sparks, NV (80.0%); Tulsa, OK (77.8%); Portland–South Portland–Biddeford, ME (66.7%); Charlotte-Gastonia-Concord, NC-SC (60.0%).

Other Considerations for Job Security: Graduates with a master's degree can expect excellent job opportunities; very few geoscientist jobs are available to bachelor's degree holders. Ph.D.s should face competition for basic research and college teaching jobs. Historically, employment of petroleum geologists, geophysicists, and some other geoscientists has been cyclical and affected considerably by the price of oil and gas. When prices are low, oil and gas producers curtail exploration activities and lay off geologists. When prices were higher, companies had the funds and incentive to renew exploration efforts and to hire geoscientists in larger numbers. In recent years, however, a growing worldwide demand for oil and gas and for new exploration and recovery techniques has created some stability in the petroleum industry. Geoscientists who speak a foreign language and who are willing to work abroad should enjoy the best opportunities.

Study the composition, structure, and other physical aspects of the Earth. May use knowledge of geology, physics, and mathematics in exploration for oil, gas, minerals, or underground water or in waste disposal, land reclamation, or other environmental problems. May study the Earth's internal composition, atmospheres, and oceans and its magnetic, electrical, and gravitational forces. Includes mineralogists, crystallographers, paleontologists, stratigraphers, geodesists, and seismologists. Analyze and interpret geological, geochemical, and geophysical information from sources such as survey data, well logs, bore holes, and aerial photos. Locate and estimate probable natural gas, oil, and mineral ore deposits and underground water resources, using aerial photographs, charts, or research and survey results. Plan and conduct geological, geochemical, and geophysical field studies and surveys, sample collection, or drilling and testing programs used to collect data for research or application. Analyze and interpret geological data, using computer software. Search for and review research articles or environmental, historical, and technical reports. Assess ground and surface water movement to provide advice regarding issues such as waste management, route and site selection, and the restoration of contaminated sites. Prepare geological maps, cross-sectional diagrams, charts, and reports concerning mineral extraction, land use, and resource management, using results of field work and laboratory research. Investigate the composition, structure, and history of the Earth's crust through the collection, examination, measurement, and classification of soils, minerals, rocks, or fossil remains. Conduct geological and geophysical studies to provide information for use in regional development, site selection, and development of public works projects. Measure characteristics of the Earth, such as gravity and magnetic fields, using equipment such as seismographs, gravimeters, torsion balances, and magnetometers. Inspect construction projects to analyze engineering problems, applying geological knowledge and using test equipment and drilling machinery. Design geological mine maps, monitor mine structural integrity, or advise and monitor mining crews. Identify risks for natural disasters such as mudslides, earthquakes, and volcanic eruptions, providing advice on mitigation of potential damage. Advise construction firms and government agencies on dam and road construction, foundation design, or land use and resource management.

Test industrial diamonds and abrasives, soil, or rocks to determine their geological characteristics, using optical, X-ray, heat, acid, and precision instruments.

Personality Type: Investigative-Realistic. Investigative occupations frequently involve working with ideas and require an extensive amount of thinking. These occupations can involve searching for facts and figuring out problems mentally.

Career Cluster: 15 Science, Technology, Engineering, and Mathematics. **Career Pathway:** 15.3 Science and Mathematics.

Skills—No data available.

Related Knowledge/Courses—Geography: Various methods for describing the location and distribution of land, sea, and air masses, including their physical locations, relationships, and characteristics. **Engineering and Technology:** Equipment, tools, and mechanical devices and their uses to produce motion, light, power, technology, and other applications. **Physics:** Physical principles, laws, and applications, including air, water, material dynamics, light, atomic principles, heat, electric theory, earth formations, and meteorological and related natural phenomena. **Chemistry:** The composition, structure, and properties of substances and of the chemical processes and transformations that they undergo. This includes uses of chemicals and their interactions, danger signs, production techniques, and disposal methods. **Mathematics:** Numbers and their operations and interrelationships, including arithmetic, algebra, geometry, calculus, and statistics and their applications. **Design:** Design techniques, principles, tools, and instruments involved in the production and use of precision technical plans, blueprints, drawings, and models.

Work Environment: Indoors; sitting.

Graduate Teaching Assistants

Related Major: Graduate Study for College Teaching

- ⚛ Education/Training Required: Master's degree
- ⚛ Annual Earnings: $28,060
- ⚛ Beginning Wage: $15,660
- ⚛ Earnings Growth Potential: High (44.2%)
- ⚛ Growth: 22.9%
- ⚛ Annual Job Openings: 20,601
- ⚛ Self-Employed: 0.4%
- ⚛ Part-Time: 27.8%

Industries with Greatest Employment: Educational Services, Public and Private (97.3%).

Highest-Growth Industries (Projected Growth for This Job): Administrative and Support Services (48.3%); Amusement, Gambling, and Recreation Industries (45.2%); Social Assistance (38.6%); Support Activities for Transportation (32.8%); Religious, Grantmaking, Civic, Professional, and Similar Organizations (29.9%); Professional, Scientific, and Technical Services (28.8%); Management of Companies and Enterprises (26.8%); Local Government (23.5%); Educational Services, Public and Private (22.8%); Hospitals, Public and Private (21.4%).

Lowest-Growth Industries (Projected Growth for This Job): Other Information Services (7.4%); State Government (7.9%); Sporting Goods, Hobby, Book, and Music Stores (13.3%); Performing Arts, Spectator Sports, and Related Industries (13.4%); Insurance Carriers and Related Activities (13.8%).

Fastest-Growing Metropolitan Areas (Recent Growth for This Job): Philadelphia-Camden-Wilmington, PA-NJ-DE-MD (110.5%); Baltimore-Towson, MD (46.4%).

Other Considerations for Job Security: Retirements of current postsecondary teachers should create numerous openings for all types of postsecondary teachers, so job opportunities are generally expected to be very good. However, one of the main reasons why students attend postsecondary institutions is to prepare themselves for careers, so the best job prospects for postsecondary teachers are likely to be in rapidly growing fields that offer many nonacademic career options. Community colleges and other institutions offering career and technical education have been among the most rapidly growing, and these institutions are expected to offer some of the best opportunities for postsecondary teachers.

Assist department chairperson, faculty members, or other professional staff members in colleges or universities by performing teaching or teaching-related duties such as teaching lower-level courses, developing teaching materials, preparing and giving examinations, and grading examinations or papers. Graduate assistants must be enrolled in graduate school programs. Graduate assistants who primarily perform non-teaching duties such as laboratory research, should be reported in the occupational category related to the work performed. Lead discussion sections, tutorials, and laboratory sections. Evaluate and grade examinations, assignments, and papers, and record grades. Return assignments to students in accordance with established deadlines. Schedule and maintain regular office hours to meet with students. Inform students of the procedures for completing and submitting class work such as lab reports. Prepare and proctor examinations. Notify instructors of errors or problems with assignments. Meet with supervisors to discuss students' grades, and to complete required grade-related paperwork. Copy and distribute classroom materials. Demonstrate use of laboratory equipment, and enforce laboratory rules. Teach undergraduate level courses. Complete laboratory projects prior to assigning them to students so that any needed modifications can be made. Develop teaching materials such as syllabi, visual aids, answer keys, supplementary notes, and course websites. Provide assistance to faculty members or staff with laboratory or field research. Arrange for supervisors to conduct teaching observations; meet with supervisors to receive feedback about teaching performance. Attend lectures given by the instructors whom they are assisting. Order or obtain materials needed for classes. Provide instructors with assistance in the use of audiovisual equipment. Assist faculty members or staff with student conferences.

Personality Type: Social-Investigative-Conventional. Social occupations frequently involve working with, communicating with, and teaching people. These occupations often involve helping or providing service to others.

Career Cluster: 05 Education and Training. **Career Pathway:** 05.3 Teaching/Training.

Skills—Learning Strategies: Selecting and using training/instructional methods and procedures appropriate for the situation when learning or teaching new things. **Instructing:** Teaching others how to do something. **Social Perceptiveness:** Being aware of others' reactions and understanding why they react as they do. **Reading Comprehension:** Understanding written sentences and paragraphs in work-related documents. **Writing:** Communicating effectively in writing as appropriate for the needs of the audience. **Speaking:** Talking to others to convey information effectively.

Related Knowledge/Courses—Sociology and Anthropology: Group behavior and dynamics; societal trends and influences; and cultures and their history, migrations, ethnicity, and origins. **Education and Training:** Instructional methods and training techniques, including curriculum design principles, learning theory, group and individual teaching techniques, design of individual development plans, and test design principles. **English Language:** The structure and content of the English language, including the meaning and spelling of words, rules of composition, and grammar. **Philosophy and Theology:** Different philosophical systems and religions, including their basic principles, values, ethics, ways of thinking, customs, and practices and their impact on human culture. **Communications and Media:** Media production, communication, and dissemination techniques and methods, including alternative ways to inform and entertain via written, oral, and visual media. **Psychology:** Human behavior and performance, mental processes, psychological research methods, and the assessment and treatment of behavioral and affective disorders.

Work Environment: Indoors; sitting.

Health Specialties Teachers, Postsecondary

Related Major: Graduate Study for College Teaching

- ❀ Education/Training Required: Master's degree
- ❀ Annual Earnings: $80,700
- ❀ Beginning Wage: $37,890
- ❀ Earnings Growth Potential: Very high (53.0%)
- ❀ Growth: 22.9%
- ❀ Annual Job Openings: 19,617
- ❀ Self-Employed: 0.4%
- ❀ Part-Time: 27.8%

Industries with Greatest Employment: Educational Services, Public and Private (97.3%).

Highest-Growth Industries (Projected Growth for This Job): Administrative and Support Services (48.3%); Amusement, Gambling, and Recreation Industries (45.2%); Social Assistance (38.6%); Support Activities for Transportation (32.8%); Religious, Grantmaking, Civic, Professional, and Similar Organizations (29.9%); Professional, Scientific, and Technical Services (28.8%); Management of Companies and Enterprises (26.8%); Local Government (23.5%); Educational Services, Public and Private (22.8%); Hospitals, Public and Private (21.4%).

Lowest-Growth Industries (Projected Growth for This Job): Other Information Services (7.4%); State Government (7.9%); Sporting Goods, Hobby, Book, and Music Stores (13.3%); Performing Arts, Spectator Sports, and Related Industries (13.4%); Insurance Carriers and Related Activities (13.8%).

Fastest-Growing Metropolitan Areas (Recent Growth for This Job): Virginia Beach–Norfolk–Newport News, VA-NC (135.7%); Springfield, MO (87.5%); Buffalo–Niagara Falls, NY (86.7%); Raleigh-Cary, NC (60.0%); St. Louis, MO-IL (44.3%).

Other Considerations for Job Security: Retirements of current postsecondary teachers should create numerous openings for all types of postsecondary teachers, so job opportunities are generally expected to be very good. However, one of the main reasons why students attend postsecondary institutions is to prepare themselves for careers, so the best job prospects for postsecondary teachers are likely to be in rapidly growing fields that offer many nonacademic career options, such as the health sciences. Community colleges and other institutions offering career and technical education have been among the most rapidly growing, and these institutions are expected to offer some of the best opportunities for postsecondary teachers.

Teach courses in health specialties, such as veterinary medicine, dentistry, pharmacy, therapy, laboratory technology, and public health. Initiate, facilitate, and moderate classroom discussions. Keep abreast of developments in their field by reading current literature, talking with colleagues, and participating in professional conferences. Compile, administer, and grade examinations or assign this work to others. Evaluate and grade students' classwork, assignments, and papers. Prepare course materials such as syllabi, homework assignments, and handouts. Prepare and deliver lectures to undergraduate or graduate students on topics such as public health, stress management, and worksite health promotion. Plan, evaluate, and revise curricula, course content, and course materials and methods of instruction. Supervise undergraduate or graduate teaching, internship, and research work. Conduct research in a particular field of knowledge and publish findings in professional journals, books, or electronic media. Collaborate with colleagues to address teaching and research issues. Supervise laboratory sessions. Maintain student attendance records, grades, and other required records. Maintain regularly scheduled office hours in order to advise and assist students. Advise students on academic and vocational curricula and on career issues. Participate in student recruitment, registration, and placement activities. Write grant proposals to procure external research funding. Serve on academic or administrative committees that deal with institutional policies, departmental matters, and academic issues. Select and obtain materials and supplies such as textbooks and laboratory equipment. Act as advisers to student organizations. Perform administrative duties such as serving as department head. Compile bibliographies of specialized materials for outside reading assignments. Provide professional consulting services to government and industry. Participate in campus and community events.

Personality Type: Investigative-Social. Investigative occupations frequently involve working with ideas and require an extensive amount of thinking. These occupations can involve searching for facts and figuring out problems mentally.

Career Clusters: 05 Education and Training; 08 Health Science; 15 Science, Technology, Engineering, and Mathematics. **Career Pathways:** 05.3 Teaching/Training; 08.1 Therapeutic Services; 08.2 Diagnostics Services; 08.3 Health Informatics; 08.5 Biotechnology Research and Development; 15.3 Science and Mathematics.

Skills—Science: Using scientific rules and methods to solve problems. **Instructing:** Teaching others how to do something. **Writing:** Communicating effectively in writing as appropriate for the needs of the audience. **Reading Comprehension:** Understanding written sentences and paragraphs in work-related documents. **Learning Strategies:** Selecting and using training/instructional methods and procedures appropriate for the situation when learning or teaching new things. **Complex Problem Solving:** Identifying complex problems and reviewing related information to develop and evaluate options and implement solutions.

Related Knowledge/Courses—Biology: Plant and animal living tissue, cells, organisms, and entities, including their functions, interdependencies, and interactions with each other and the environment. **Medicine and Dentistry:** The information and techniques needed to diagnose and treat injuries, diseases, and deformities. This includes symptoms, treatment alternatives, drug properties and interactions, and preventive health-care measures. **Education and Training:** Instructional methods and training techniques, including curriculum design principles, learning theory, group and individual teaching techniques, design of individual development plans, and test design principles. **Therapy and Counseling:** Information and techniques needed to rehabilitate physical and mental ailments and to provide career guidance, including alternative treatments, rehabilitation equipment and its proper use, and methods to evaluate treatment effects. **Sociology and Anthropology:** Group behavior and dynamics; societal trends and influences; and cultures and their history, migrations, ethnicity, and origins. **Psychology:** Human behavior and performance, mental processes, psychological research methods, and the assessment and treatment of behavioral and affective disorders.

Work Environment: Indoors; sitting.

History Teachers, Postsecondary

Related Major: Graduate Study for College Teaching

- ✸ Education/Training Required: Master's degree
- ✸ Annual Earnings: $59,160
- ✸ Beginning Wage: $33,540
- ✸ Earnings Growth Potential: High (43.3%)
- ✸ Growth: 22.9%
- ✸ Annual Job Openings: 3,570
- ✸ Self-Employed: 0.4%
- ✸ Part-Time: 27.8%

Industries with Greatest Employment: Educational Services, Public and Private (97.3%).

Highest-Growth Industries (Projected Growth for This Job): Administrative and Support Services (48.3%); Amusement, Gambling, and Recreation Industries (45.2%); Social Assistance (38.6%); Support Activities for Transportation (32.8%); Religious, Grantmaking, Civic, Professional, and Similar Organizations (29.9%); Professional, Scientific, and Technical Services (28.8%); Management of Companies and Enterprises (26.8%); Local Government (23.5%); Educational Services, Public and Private (22.8%); Hospitals, Public and Private (21.4%).

Lowest-Growth Industries (Projected Growth for This Job): Other Information Services (7.4%); State Government (7.9%); Sporting Goods, Hobby, Book, and Music Stores (13.3%); Performing Arts, Spectator Sports, and Related Industries (13.4%); Insurance Carriers and Related Activities (13.8%).

Fastest-Growing Metropolitan Areas (Recent Growth for This Job): Knoxville, TN (83.3%); Los Angeles–Long Beach–Santa Ana, CA (37.1%); Fargo, ND-MN (33.3%); Huntsville, AL (33.3%); Phoenix-Mesa-Scottsdale, AZ (33.3%).

Other Considerations for Job Security: Retirements of current postsecondary teachers should create numerous openings for all types of postsecondary teachers, so job opportunities are generally expected to be very good. However, one of the main reasons why students attend postsecondary institutions is to prepare themselves for careers, so the best job prospects for postsecondary teachers are likely to be in rapidly growing fields that offer many nonacademic career options—unlike history. On the other hand, history courses are required for many majors. Community colleges and other institutions offering career and technical education have been among the most rapidly growing, and these institutions are expected to offer some of the best opportunities for postsecondary teachers.

Teach courses in human history and historiography. Prepare and deliver lectures to undergraduate and/or graduate students on topics such as ancient history, postwar civilizations, and the history of third-world countries. Evaluate and grade students' classwork, assignments, and papers. Prepare course materials such as syllabi, homework assignments, and handouts. Compile, administer, and grade examinations or assign this work to others. Initiate, facilitate, and moderate classroom discussions. Keep abreast of developments in their field by reading current literature, talking with colleagues, and participating in professional conferences. Plan, evaluate, and revise curricula, course content, and course materials and methods of instruction. Maintain student attendance records, grades, and other required records. Maintain regularly scheduled office hours to advise and assist students. Conduct research in a particular field of knowledge and publish findings in professional journals, books, or electronic media. Select and obtain materials and supplies such as textbooks. Advise students on academic and vocational curricula and on career issues. Collaborate with colleagues to address teaching and research issues. Serve on academic or administrative committees that deal with institutional policies, departmental matters, and academic issues. Participate in campus and community events. Act as advisers to student organizations. Participate in student recruitment, registration, and placement activities. Compile bibliographies of specialized materials for outside reading assignments. Supervise undergraduate and graduate teaching, internship, and research work. Perform administrative duties such as serving as department head. Write grant proposals to procure external research funding. Provide professional consulting services to government, educational institutions, and industry.

Personality Type: Social-Investigative-Artistic. Social occupations frequently involve working with, communicating with, and teaching people. These occupations often involve helping or providing service to others.

Career Cluster: 15 Science, Technology, Engineering, and Mathematics. **Career Pathway:** 15.3 Science and Mathematics.

Skills—Writing: Communicating effectively in writing as appropriate for the needs of the audience. **Instructing:** Teaching others how to do something. **Learning Strategies:** Selecting and using training/instructional methods and procedures appropriate for the situation when learning or teaching new things. **Reading Comprehension:** Understanding written sentences and

paragraphs in work-related documents. **Speaking:** Talking to others to convey information effectively. **Persuasion:** Persuading others to change their minds or behavior.

Related Knowledge/Courses—History and Archeology: Historical events and their causes, indicators, and impact on particular civilizations and cultures. **Philosophy and Theology:** Different philosophical systems and religions, including their basic principles, values, ethics, ways of thinking, customs, and practices and their impact on human culture. **Geography:** Various methods for describing the location and distribution of land, sea, and air masses, including their physical locations, relationships, and characteristics. **Sociology and Anthropology:** Group behavior and dynamics; societal trends and influences; and cultures and their history, migrations, ethnicity, and origins. **Education and Training:** Instructional methods and training techniques, including curriculum design principles, learning theory, group and individual teaching techniques, design of individual development plans, and test design principles. **English Language:** The structure and content of the English language, including the meaning and spelling of words, rules of composition, and grammar.

Work Environment: Indoors; sitting.

Home Economics Teachers, Postsecondary

Related Major: Graduate Study for College Teaching

- ❋ Education/Training Required: Master's degree
- ❋ Annual Earnings: $58,170
- ❋ Beginning Wage: $29,510
- ❋ Earnings Growth Potential: High (49.3%)
- ❋ Growth: 22.9%
- ❋ Annual Job Openings: 820
- ❋ Self-Employed: 0.4%
- ❋ Part-Time: 27.8%

Industries with Greatest Employment: Educational Services, Public and Private (97.3%).

Highest-Growth Industries (Projected Growth for This Job): Administrative and Support Services (48.3%); Amusement, Gambling, and Recreation Industries (45.2%); Social Assistance (38.6%); Support Activities for Transportation (32.8%); Religious, Grantmaking, Civic, Professional, and Similar Organizations (29.9%); Professional, Scientific, and Technical Services (28.8%); Management of Companies and Enterprises (26.8%); Local Government (23.5%); Educational Services, Public and Private (22.8%); Hospitals, Public and Private (21.4%).

Lowest-Growth Industries (Projected Growth for This Job): Other Information Services (7.4%); State Government (7.9%); Sporting Goods, Hobby, Book, and Music Stores (13.3%); Performing Arts, Spectator Sports, and Related Industries (13.4%); Insurance Carriers and Related Activities (13.8%).

Fastest-Growing Metropolitan Areas (Recent Growth for This Job): Riverside–San Bernardino–Ontario, CA (50.0%); Los Angeles–Long Beach–Santa Ana, CA (14.3%).

Other Considerations for Job Security: Retirements of current postsecondary teachers should create numerous openings for all types of postsecondary teachers, so job opportunities are generally expected to be very good. One of the main reasons why students attend postsecondary institutions is to prepare themselves for careers, so the best job prospects for postsecondary teachers are likely to be in rapidly growing fields that offer many nonacademic career options. Many home economics majors, such as textiles and culinary arts, are very career-oriented. Community colleges and other institutions offering career and technical education have been among the most rapidly growing, and these institutions are expected to offer some of the best opportunities for postsecondary teachers.

Teach courses in child care, family relations, finance, nutrition, and related subjects as pertaining to home management. Evaluate and grade students' classwork, laboratory work, projects, assignments, and papers. Initiate, facilitate, and moderate classroom discussions. Prepare and deliver lectures to undergraduate or graduate students on topics such as food science, nutrition, and child care. Prepare course materials such as syllabi, homework assignments, and handouts. Keep abreast of developments in their field by reading current literature, talking with colleagues, and participating in professional conferences. Maintain student attendance records, grades, and other required records. Plan, evaluate, and revise curricula, course content, and course materials and methods of instruction. Compile, administer, and grade examinations or assign this work to others. Advise students on academic and vocational curricula and on career issues. Maintain regularly scheduled office hours to advise and assist students. Supervise undergraduate or graduate teaching, internship, and research work. Select and obtain materials and supplies such as textbooks. Conduct research in a particular field of knowledge and publish findings in professional journals, books, and/or electronic media. Collaborate with colleagues to address teaching and research issues. Act as advisers to student organizations. Participate in student recruitment, registration, and placement activities. Serve on academic or administrative committees that deal with institutional policies, departmental matters, and academic issues. Participate in campus and community events. Compile bibliographies of specialized materials for outside reading assignments. Perform administrative duties such as serving as department head. Write grant proposals to procure external research funding. Provide professional consulting services to government and industry.

Personality Type: No data available.

Career Clusters: 08 Health Science; 10 Human Services. **Career Pathways:** 08.4 Support Services; 10.1 Early Childhood Development and Services; 10.3 Family and Community Services; 10.5 Consumer Services Career.

Skills—Writing: Communicating effectively in writing as appropriate for the needs of the audience. **Instructing:** Teaching others how to do something. **Learning Strategies:** Selecting and using training/instructional methods and procedures appropriate for the situation when learning or teaching new things. **Service Orientation:** Actively looking for ways to help people. **Active Learning:** Understanding the implications of new information for both current and future problem-solving and decision-making.

Operations Analysis: Analyzing needs and product requirements to create a design.

Related Knowledge/Courses—Sociology and Anthropology: Group behavior and dynamics; societal trends and influences; and cultures and their history, migrations, ethnicity, and origins. **Philosophy and Theology:** Different philosophical systems and religions, including their basic principles, values, ethics, ways of thinking, customs, and practices and their impact on human culture. **Education and Training:** Instructional methods and training techniques, including curriculum design principles, learning theory, group and individual teaching techniques, design of individual development plans, and test design principles. **Therapy and Counseling:** Information and techniques needed to rehabilitate physical and mental ailments and to provide career guidance, including alternative treatments, rehabilitation equipment and its proper use, and methods to evaluate treatment effects. **Psychology:** Human behavior and performance, mental processes, psychological research methods, and the assessment and treatment of behavioral and affective disorders. **English Language:** The structure and content of the English language, including the meaning and spelling of words, rules of composition, and grammar.

Work Environment: Indoors; sitting.

Hydrologists

Related Majors: Geology; Oceanography

- ❀ Education/Training Required: Master's degree
- ❀ Annual Earnings: $68,140
- ❀ Beginning Wage: $42,450
- ❀ Earnings Growth Potential: Medium (37.7%)
- ❀ Growth: 24.3%
- ❀ Annual Job Openings: 687
- ❀ Self-Employed: 2.4%
- ❀ Part-Time: 5.3%

Industries with Greatest Employment: Professional, Scientific, and Technical Services (46.7%); Federal Government (28.0%); State Government (15.4%); Local Government (5.4%).

Highest-Growth Industries (Projected Growth for This Job): Professional, Scientific, and Technical Services (53.9%).

Lowest-Growth Industries (Projected Growth for This Job): Federal Government (–5.5%); State Government (–1.9%); Educational Services, Public and Private (11.5%); Local Government (12.4%).

Fastest-Growing Metropolitan Areas (Recent Growth for This Job): Baltimore-Towson, MD (57.1%); Madison, WI (36.4%); Raleigh-Cary, NC (28.6%); Los Angeles–Long Beach–Santa Ana, CA (27.3%); Columbus, OH (25.0%).

Other Considerations for Job Security: Job prospects for hydrologists should be favorable, particularly for those with field experience. Demand for hydrologists who understand both the scientific and engineering aspects of waste remediation should be strong. Few colleges and universities offer programs in hydrology, so the number of qualified workers may be limited.

Funding for federal and state geological surveys depend largely on the political climate and the current budget. Thus, job security for hydrologists may vary. During periods of economic recession, layoffs of hydrologists may occur in consulting firms; layoffs are much less likely in government.

Research the distribution, circulation, and physical properties of underground and surface waters; study the form and intensity of precipitation, its rate of infiltration into the soil, its movement through the earth, and its return to the ocean and atmosphere. Study and document quantities, distribution, disposition, and development of underground and surface waters. Draft final reports describing research results, including illustrations, appendices, maps, and other attachments. Coordinate and supervise the work of professional and technical staff, including research assistants, technologists, and technicians. Prepare hydrogeologic evaluations of known or suspected hazardous waste sites and land treatment and feedlot facilities. Design and conduct scientific hydrogeological investigations to ensure that accurate and appropriate information is available for use in water resource management decisions. Study public water supply issues, including flood and drought risks, water quality, wastewater, and impacts on wetland habitats. Collect and analyze water samples as part of field investigations and/or to validate data from automatic monitors. Apply research findings to help minimize the environmental impacts of pollution, water-borne diseases, erosion, and sedimentation. Measure and graph phenomena such as lake levels, stream flows, and changes in water volumes. Investigate complaints or conflicts related to the alteration of public waters, gathering information, recommending alternatives, informing participants of progress, and preparing draft orders. Develop or modify methods of conducting hydrologic studies. Answer questions and provide technical assistance and information to contractors and/or the public regarding issues such as well drilling, code requirements, hydrology, and geology. Install, maintain, and calibrate instruments such as those that monitor water levels, rainfall, and sediments. Evaluate data and provide recommendations regarding the feasibility of municipal projects such as hydroelectric power plants, irrigation systems, flood warning systems, and waste treatment facilities. Conduct short-term and long-term climate assessments and study storm occurrences. Study and analyze the physical aspects of the Earth in terms of the hydrological components, including atmosphere, hydrosphere, and interior structure. Conduct research and communicate information to promote the conservation and preservation of water resources.

Personality Type: Investigative-Realistic. Investigative occupations frequently involve working with ideas and require an extensive amount of thinking. These occupations can involve searching for facts and figuring out problems mentally.

Career Cluster: 15 Science, Technology, Engineering, and Mathematics. **Career Pathway:** 15.3 Science and Mathematics.

Skills—Science: Using scientific rules and methods to solve problems. **Programming:** Writing computer programs for various purposes. **Management of Financial Resources:** Determining how money will be spent to get the work done and accounting for these expenditures. **Mathematics:** Using mathematics to solve problems. **Management of Personnel Resources:** Motivating, developing, and directing people as they work, identifying the best people for the job. **Complex Problem Solving:** Identifying complex problems and reviewing related information to develop and evaluate options and implement solutions.

Related Knowledge/Courses—Geography: Various methods for describing the location and distribution of land, sea, and air masses, including their physical locations, relationships, and characteristics. **Physics:** Physical principles, laws, and applications, including air, water, material dynamics, light, atomic principles, heat, electric theory, earth formations, and meteorological and related natural phenomena. **Engineering and Technology:** Equipment, tools, and mechanical devices and their uses to produce motion, light, power, technology, and other applications. **Biology:** Plant and animal living tissue, cells, organisms, and entities, including their functions, interdependencies, and interactions with each other and the environment. **Chemistry:** The composition, structure, and properties of substances and of the chemical processes and transformations that they undergo. This includes uses of chemicals and their interactions, danger signs, production techniques, and disposal methods. **Mathematics:** Numbers and their operations and interrelationships, including arithmetic, algebra, geometry, calculus, and statistics and their applications.

Work Environment: More often indoors than outdoors; sitting.

Immigration and Customs Inspectors

Related Major: Criminal Justice/Law Enforcement

* Education/Training Required: Work experience in a related occupation
* Annual Earnings: $59,930
* Beginning Wage: $35,600
* Earnings Growth Potential: High (40.6%)
* Growth: 17.3%
* Annual Job Openings: 14,746
* Self-Employed: 0.3%
* Part-Time: 2.2%

Industries with Greatest Employment: Local Government (47.3%); Federal Government (37.2%); State Government (14.9%).

Highest-Growth Industries (Projected Growth for This Job): Local Government (23.6%).

Lowest-Growth Industries (Projected Growth for This Job): State Government (7.9%); Educational Services, Public and Private (11.9%); Federal Government (13.3%).

Fastest-Growing Metropolitan Areas (Recent Growth for This Job): Davenport–Moline–Rock Island, IA-IL (100.0%); Harrisburg-Carlisle, PA (69.2%); Anniston-Oxford, AL (66.7%); Springfield, IL (66.7%); Springfield, MA-CT (50.0%).

Other Considerations for Job Security: The level of government spending determines the level of employment for immigration and customs inspectors. The number of job opportunities, therefore, can vary from year to year. Concerns about homeland security may create a need for additional inspectors. Layoffs are rare because retirements enable most staffing cuts to be handled through attrition.

Investigate and inspect persons, common carriers, goods, and merchandise arriving in or departing from the United States or moving between states to detect violations of immigration and customs laws and regulations. Examine immigration applications, visas, and passports and interview persons to determine eligibility for admission, residence, and travel in U.S. Detain persons found to be in violation of customs or immigration laws and arrange for legal action such as deportation. Locate and seize contraband or undeclared merchandise and vehicles, aircraft, or boats that contain such merchandise. Interpret and explain laws and regulations to travelers, prospective immigrants, shippers, and manufacturers. Inspect cargo, baggage, and personal articles entering or leaving U.S. for compliance with revenue laws and U.S. Customs Service regulations. Record and report job-related activities, findings, transactions, violations, discrepancies, and decisions. Institute civil and criminal prosecutions and cooperate with other law enforcement agencies in the investigation and prosecution of those in violation of immigration or customs laws. Testify regarding decisions at immigration appeals or in federal court. Determine duty and taxes to be paid on goods. Collect samples of merchandise for examination, appraisal, or testing. Investigate applications for duty refunds and petition for remission or mitigation of penalties when warranted.

Personality Type: Conventional-Enterprising-Realistic. Conventional occupations frequently involve following set procedures and routines. These occupations can include working with data and details more than with ideas. Usually there is a clear line of authority to follow.

Career Cluster: 12 Law, Public Safety, Corrections, and Security. **Career Pathway:** 12.4 Law Enforcement Services.

Skills—Persuasion: Persuading others to change their minds or behavior. **Operations Analysis:** Analyzing needs and product requirements to create a design. **Equipment Selection:** Determining the kind of tools and equipment needed to do a job. **Negotiation:** Bringing others together and trying to reconcile differences. **Speaking:** Talking to others to convey information effectively. **Social Perceptiveness:** Being aware of others' reactions and understanding why they react as they do.

Related Knowledge/Courses—Public Safety and Security: Weaponry; public safety; security operations, rules, regulations, precautions, and prevention; and the protection of people, data, and property. **Law and Government:** Laws, legal codes, court procedures, precedents, government regulations, executive orders, agency rules, and the democratic political process. **Foreign Language:** The structure and content of a foreign (non-English) language, including the meaning and spelling of words, rules of composition and grammar, and pronunciation. **Geography:** Various methods for describing the location and distribution of land, sea, and air masses, including their physical locations, relationships, and characteristics. **Customer and Personal Service:** Principles and processes for providing customer and personal services, including needs assessment techniques, quality service standards, alternative delivery systems, and customer satisfaction evaluation techniques. **Philosophy and Theology:** Different philosophical systems and religions, including their basic principles, values, ethics, ways of thinking, customs, and practices and their impact on human culture.

Work Environment: More often outdoors than indoors; noisy; contaminants; radiation; hazardous equipment.

Industrial-Organizational Psychologists

Related Major: Psychology

- ❋ Education/Training Required: Master's degree
- ❋ Annual Earnings: $80,820
- ❋ Beginning Wage: $38,910
- ❋ Earnings Growth Potential: Very high (51.9%)
- ❋ Growth: 21.3%
- ❋ Annual Job Openings: 118
- ❋ Self-Employed: 39.3%
- ❋ Part-Time: 24.0%

Industries with Greatest Employment: Professional, Scientific, and Technical Services (29.7%); Educational Services, Public and Private (6.0%).

Highest-Growth Industries (Projected Growth for This Job): Professional, Scientific, and Technical Services (49.6%).

Lowest-Growth Industries (Projected Growth for This Job): Educational Services, Public and Private (10.3%).

Fastest-Growing Metropolitan Areas (Recent Growth for This Job): Boston-Cambridge-Quincy, MA-NH (66.7%); New York–Northern New Jersey–Long Island, NY-NJ-PA (21.4%).

Other Considerations for Job Security: Industrial-organizational psychologists will be in demand to help to boost worker productivity and retention rates in a wide range of businesses.

Industrial-organizational psychologists will help companies deal with issues such as workplace diversity and antidiscrimination policies. Companies also will use psychologists' expertise in survey design, analysis, and research to develop tools for marketing evaluation and statistical analysis. Job prospects should be the best for people who have a doctoral degree from a leading university. Psychologists with extensive training in quantitative research methods and computer science may have a competitive edge over applicants without such background.

Apply principles of psychology to personnel, administration, management, sales, and marketing problems. Activities may include policy planning; employee screening, training, and development; and organizational development and analysis. May work with management to reorganize the work setting to improve worker productivity. Develop and implement employee selection and placement programs. Analyze job requirements and content to establish criteria for classification, selection, training, and other related personnel functions. Develop interview techniques, rating scales, and psychological tests used to assess skills, abilities, and interests for the purpose of employee selection, placement, and promotion. Advise management concerning personnel, managerial, and marketing policies and practices and their potential effects on organizational effectiveness and efficiency. Analyze data, using statistical methods and applications, to evaluate the outcomes and effectiveness of workplace programs. Assess employee performance. Observe and interview workers to obtain information about the physical, mental, and educational requirements of jobs as well as information about aspects such as job satisfaction. Write reports on research findings and implications to contribute to general knowledge and to suggest potential changes in organizational functioning. Facilitate organizational development and change. Identify training and development needs. Formulate and implement training programs, applying principles of learning and individual differences. Study organizational effectiveness, productivity, and efficiency, including the nature of workplace supervision and leadership. Conduct research studies of physical work environments, organizational structures, communication systems, group interactions, morale, and motivation to assess organizational functioning. Counsel workers about job and career-related issues. Study consumers' reactions to new products and package designs, and to advertising efforts, using surveys and tests. Participate in mediation and dispute resolution.

Personality Type: Investigative-Enterprising-Artistic. Investigative occupations frequently involve working with ideas and require an extensive amount of thinking. These occupations can involve searching for facts and figuring out problems mentally.

Career Cluster: 08 Health Science. **Career Pathway:** 08.1 Therapeutic Services.

Skills—Science: Using scientific rules and methods to solve problems. **Systems Evaluation:** Identifying measures or indicators of system performance and the actions needed to improve or correct performance relative to the goals of the system. **Judgment and Decision Making:** Considering the relative costs and benefits of potential actions to choose the most appropriate one. **Writing:** Communicating effectively in writing as appropriate for the needs of the audience. **Monitoring:** Monitoring/assessing your performance or that of other individuals or organizations to make improvements or take corrective action. **Time Management:** Managing one's own time and the time of others.

Related Knowledge/Courses—Personnel and Human Resources: Principles and procedures for personnel recruitment; selection; training; compensation and benefits; labor relations and negotiation; and personnel information systems. **Psychology:** Human behavior and performance, mental processes, psychological research methods, and the assessment and treatment of behavioral and affective disorders. **Sociology and Anthropology:** Group behavior and dynamics; societal trends and influences; and cultures and their history, migrations, ethnicity, and origins. **Education and Training:** Instructional methods and training techniques, including curriculum design principles, learning theory, group and individual teaching techniques, design of individual development plans, and test design principles. **Therapy and Counseling:** Information and techniques needed to rehabilitate physical and mental ailments and to provide career guidance, including alternative treatments, rehabilitation equipment and its proper use, and methods to evaluate treatment effects. **Mathematics:** Numbers and their operations and interrelationships, including arithmetic, algebra, geometry, calculus, and statistics and their applications.

Work Environment: Indoors; sitting.

Internists, General

Related Major: Medicine

- ✳ Education/Training Required: First professional degree
- ✳ Annual Earnings: More than $145,600
- ✳ Beginning Wage: $89,130
- ✳ Earnings Growth Potential: Cannot be calculated
- ✳ Growth: 14.2%
- ✳ Annual Job Openings: 38,027
- ✳ Self-Employed: 14.7%
- ✳ Part-Time: 8.1%

Industries with Greatest Employment: Ambulatory Health Care Services (55.9%); Hospitals, Public and Private (17.8%).

Highest-Growth Industries (Projected Growth for This Job): Social Assistance (58.6%); Administrative and Support Services (26.8%); Professional, Scientific, and Technical Services (22.6%); Nursing and Residential Care Facilities (21.0%); Ambulatory Health Care Services (19.4%); Religious, Grantmaking, Civic, Professional, and Similar Organizations (16.7%); Management of Companies and Enterprises (15.3%).

Lowest-Growth Industries (Projected Growth for This Job): Federal Government (–5.5%); State Government (–1.9%); Insurance Carriers and Related Activities (4.6%); Health and Personal Care Stores (5.3%); Hospitals, Public and Private (9.9%); Educational Services, Public and Private (11.8%); Local Government (12.3%).

Fastest-Growing Metropolitan Areas (Recent Growth for This Job): Winston-Salem, NC (137.5%); Oklahoma City, OK (112.5%); Bakersfield, CA (111.1%); Sacramento–Arden-Arcade–Roseville, CA (110.0%); Modesto, CA (85.7%).

Other Considerations for Job Security: Opportunities for individuals interested in becoming physicians and surgeons are expected to be very good. Unlike their predecessors, new physicians are much less likely to enter solo practice and more likely to take salaried jobs in group medical practices, clinics, and health networks. Reports of shortages in some specialties, such as general or family practice, internal medicine, and OB/GYN, or in rural or low-income areas should attract new entrants, encouraging schools to expand programs and hospitals to increase available residency slots. However, because physician training is so lengthy, employment change happens gradually. Opportunities should be particularly good in rural and low-income areas, as some physicians find these areas unattractive because of less control over work hours, isolation from medical colleagues, or other reasons.

Diagnose and provide non-surgical treatment of diseases and injuries of internal organ systems. Provide care mainly for adults who have a wide range of problems associated with the internal organs. Treat internal disorders, such as hypertension; heart disease; diabetes; and problems of the lung, brain, kidney, and gastrointestinal tract. Analyze records, reports, test results, or examination information to diagnose medical condition of patient. Prescribe or administer medication, therapy, and other specialized medical care to treat or prevent illness, disease, or injury. Provide and manage long-term, comprehensive medical care, including diagnosis and non-surgical treatment of diseases, for adult patients in an office or hospital. Manage and treat common health problems, such as infections, influenza and pneumonia, as well as serious, chronic, and complex illnesses, in adolescents, adults, and the elderly. Monitor patients' conditions and progress and re-evaluate treatments as necessary. Collect, record, and maintain patient information, such as medical history, reports, and examination results. Make diagnoses when different illnesses occur together or in situations where the diagnosis may be obscure. Explain procedures and discuss test results or prescribed treatments with patients. Advise patients and community members concerning diet, activity, hygiene, and disease prevention. Refer patient to medical specialist or other practitioner when necessary. Immunize patients to protect them from preventable diseases. Advise surgeon of a patient's risk status and recommend appropriate intervention to minimize risk. Direct and coordinate activities of nurses, students, assistants, specialists, therapists, and other medical staff. Provide consulting services to other doctors caring for patients with special or difficult problems. Operate on patients to remove, repair, or improve functioning of diseased or injured body parts and systems. Plan, implement, or administer health programs in hospitals, businesses, or communities for prevention and treatment of injuries or illnesses. Conduct research to develop or test medications, treatments, or procedures to prevent or control disease or injury. Prepare government or organizational reports on birth, death, and disease statistics; workforce evaluations; or the medical status of individuals.

Personality Type: Investigative. Investigative occupations frequently involve working with ideas and require an extensive amount of thinking. These occupations can involve searching for facts and figuring out problems mentally.

Career Cluster: 08 Health Science. **Career Pathway:** 08.1 Therapeutic Services.

Skills—Science: Using scientific rules and methods to solve problems. **Judgment and Decision Making:** Considering the relative costs and benefits of potential actions to choose the most appropriate one. **Complex Problem Solving:**

Identifying complex problems and reviewing related information to develop and evaluate options and implement solutions. **Reading Comprehension:** Understanding written sentences and paragraphs in work-related documents. **Social Perceptiveness:** Being aware of others' reactions and understanding why they react as they do. **Service Orientation:** Actively looking for ways to help people.

Related Knowledge/Courses—Medicine and Dentistry: The information and techniques needed to diagnose and treat injuries, diseases, and deformities. This includes symptoms, treatment alternatives, drug properties and interactions, and preventive health-care measures. **Biology:** Plant and animal living tissue, cells, organisms, and entities, including their functions, interdependencies, and interactions with each other and the environment. **Therapy and Counseling:** Information and techniques needed to rehabilitate physical and mental ailments and to provide career guidance, including alternative treatments, rehabilitation equipment and its proper use, and methods to evaluate treatment effects. **Psychology:** Human behavior and performance, mental processes, psychological research methods, and the assessment and treatment of behavioral and affective disorders. **Chemistry:** The composition, structure, and properties of substances and of the chemical processes and transformations that they undergo. This includes uses of chemicals and their interactions, danger signs, production techniques, and disposal methods. **Education and Training:** Instructional methods and training techniques, including curriculum design principles, learning theory, group and individual teaching techniques, design of individual development plans, and test design principles.

Work Environment: Indoors; disease or infections; standing.

Interpreters and Translators

Related Majors: Chinese; Classics; French; German; Japanese; Modern Foreign Language; Russian; Spanish

- Education/Training Required: Long-term on-the-job training
- Annual Earnings: $37,490
- Beginning Wage: $21,500
- Earnings Growth Potential: High (42.7%)
- Growth: 23.6%
- Annual Job Openings: 6,630
- Self-Employed: 21.6%
- Part-Time: 28.5%

Industries with Greatest Employment: Educational Services, Public and Private (32.8%); Professional, Scientific, and Technical Services (14.2%); Hospitals, Public and Private (5.9%); Local Government (5.8%).

Highest-Growth Industries (Projected Growth for This Job): Social Assistance (62.8%); Museums, Historical Sites, and Similar Institutions (49.8%); Administrative and Support Services (44.3%); Ambulatory Health Care Services (39.2%); Professional, Scientific, and Technical Services (37.4%); Nursing and Residential Care Facilities (33.3%); Religious, Grantmaking, Civic, Professional, and Similar Organizations (30.9%); Management of Companies and Enterprises (27.4%); Local Government (23.6%); Hospitals, Public and Private (21.8%); Educational Services, Public and Private (18.9%); Insurance Carriers and Related Activities (15.7%).

Lowest-Growth Industries (Projected Growth for This Job): Transportation Equipment Manufacturing (–7.1%); Federal Government (4.0%); Telecommunications (5.1%); State Government (7.9%); Publishing Industries (Except Internet) (9.7%).

Fastest-Growing Metropolitan Areas (Recent Growth for This Job): Raleigh-Cary, NC (142.9%); Orlando-Kissimmee, FL (100.0%); Riverside–San Bernardino–Ontario, CA (86.7%); Philadelphia-Camden-Wilmington, PA-NJ-DE-MD (84.2%); Virginia Beach–Norfolk–Newport News, VA-NC (83.3%).

Other Considerations for Job Security: Growth in demand will be driven partly by strong demand in health-care settings and work related to homeland security. Job prospects for interpreters and translators vary by specialty. There should be demand for specialists in localization (adapting language content of products so they can be used in foreign countries), driven by imports and exports and the expansion of the Internet; however, demand may be dampened somewhat by outsourcing of localization work to other countries. Demand is expected to be strong in other technical areas, such as medicine and law. Given the shortage of interpreters and translators meeting the desired skill level of employers, interpreters for the deaf will continue to have favorable employment prospects. On the other hand, job opportunities are expected to be limited for both conference interpreters and literary translators.

Translate or interpret written, oral, or sign language text into another language for others. Follow ethical codes that protect the confidentiality of information. Identify and resolve conflicts related to the meanings of words, concepts, practices, or behaviors. Proofread, edit, and revise translated materials. Translate messages simultaneously or consecutively into specified languages orally or by using hand signs, maintaining message content, context, and style as much as possible. Check translations of technical terms and terminology to ensure that they are accurate and remain consistent throughout translation revisions. Read written materials such as legal documents, scientific works, or news reports and rewrite material into specified languages. Refer to reference materials such as dictionaries, lexicons, encyclopedias, and computerized terminology banks as needed to ensure translation accuracy. Compile terminology and information to be used in translations, including technical terms such as those for legal or medical material. Adapt translations to students' cognitive and grade levels, collaborating with educational team members as necessary. Listen to speakers' statements to determine meanings and to prepare translations, using electronic listening systems as necessary. Check original texts or confer with authors to ensure that translations retain the content, meaning, and feeling of the original material. Compile information about the content and context of information to be translated, as well as details of the groups for whom translation or interpretation is being performed. Discuss translation requirements with clients and determine any fees to be charged for services provided. Adapt software and accompanying technical documents to another language and culture. Educate students, parents, staff, and teachers about the roles and functions of educational interpreters. Train and supervise other translators/interpreters. Travel with or guide tourists who speak another language.

Personality Type: Artistic-Social-Investigative. Artistic occupations frequently involve working with forms, designs, and patterns. They often require self-expression, and the work can be done without following a clear set of rules.

Career Clusters: 05 Education and Training; 10 Human Services. **Career Pathways:** 05.3 Teaching/Training; 10.5 Consumer Services Career.

Skills—No data available.

Related Knowledge/Courses—Foreign Language: The structure and content of a foreign (non-English) language, including the meaning and spelling of words, rules of composition and grammar, and pronunciation. **English Language:** The structure and content of the English language, including the meaning and spelling of words, rules of composition, and grammar. **Geography:** Various methods for describing the location and distribution of land, sea, and air masses, including their physical locations, relationships, and characteristics. **Sociology and Anthropology:** Group behavior and dynamics; societal trends and influences; and cultures and their history, migrations, ethnicity, and origins. **Computers and Electronics:** Electric circuit boards, processors, chips, and computer hardware and software, including applications and programming. **Communications and Media:** Media production, communication, and dissemination techniques and methods, including alternative ways to inform and entertain via written, oral, and visual media.

Work Environment: Indoors; sitting; repetitive motions.

Kindergarten Teachers, Except Special Education

Related Major: Early Childhood Education

- ❋ Education/Training Required: Bachelor's degree
- ❋ Annual Earnings: $45,120
- ❋ Beginning Wage: $29,300
- ❋ Earnings Growth Potential: Medium (35.1%)
- ❋ Growth: 16.3%
- ❋ Annual Job Openings: 27,603
- ❋ Self-Employed: 1.1%
- ❋ Part-Time: 25.1%

Industries with Greatest Employment: Educational Services, Public and Private (92.9%).

Highest-Growth Industries (Projected Growth for This Job): Social Assistance (25.8%); Religious, Grantmaking, Civic, Professional, and Similar Organizations (18.8%); Educational Services, Public and Private (15.9%).

Lowest-Growth Industries (Projected Growth for This Job): Local Government (12.5%).

Fastest-Growing Metropolitan Areas (Recent Growth for This Job): Madera, CA (154.5%); Killeen–Temple–Fort Hood, TX (107.7%); Bismarck, ND (100.0%); El Centro, CA (100.0%); Tuscaloosa, AL (100.0%).

Other Considerations for Job Security: Job prospects are expected to be favorable, with particularly good prospects for teachers in less desirable urban or rural school districts and for those with licensure in more than one subject. Fast-growing states in the South and West— led by Nevada, Arizona, Texas, and Georgia— will experience the largest enrollment increases. Enrollments in the Midwest are expected to hold relatively steady, while those in the Northeast are expected to decline. The number of teachers employed is dependent on state and local expenditures for education and on the enactment of legislation to increase the quality and scope of public education. At the federal level, there has been a large increase in funding for education, particularly for the hiring of qualified teachers in lower-income areas. Also, some states are instituting programs to improve early childhood education, such as offering full-day kindergarten and universal preschool.

Teach elemental natural and social science, personal hygiene, music, art, and literature to children from 4 to 6 years old. Promote physical, mental, and social development. May be required to hold state certification. Teach basic skills such as color, shape, number, and letter recognition; personal hygiene; and social skills. Establish and enforce rules for behavior and policies and procedures to maintain order among students. Observe and evaluate children's performance, behavior, social development, and physical health. Instruct students individually and in groups, adapting teaching methods to meet students' varying needs and interests. Read books to entire classes or to small groups. Demonstrate activities to children. Provide a variety of materials and resources for children to explore, manipulate, and use, both in learning activities and in imaginative play. Plan and conduct activities for a balanced program of instruction, demonstration, and work time that provides students with opportunities to observe, question, and investigate. Confer with parents or guardians, other teachers, counselors, and administrators to resolve students' behavioral and academic problems. Prepare children for later grades by encouraging them to explore learning opportunities and to persevere with challenging tasks. Establish clear objectives for all lessons, units, and projects

and communicate those objectives to children. Prepare and implement remedial programs for students requiring extra help. Meet with parents and guardians to discuss their children's progress and to determine their priorities for their children and their resource needs. Prepare objectives and outlines for courses of study, following curriculum guidelines or requirements of states and schools. Organize and lead activities designed to promote physical, mental, and social development such as games, arts and crafts, music, and storytelling. Guide and counsel students with adjustment or academic problems or special academic interests. Identify children showing signs of emotional, developmental, or health-related problems and discuss them with supervisors, parents or guardians, and child development specialists. Instruct and monitor students in the use and care of equipment and materials to prevent injuries and damage. Assimilate arriving children to the school environment by greeting them, helping them remove outerwear, and selecting activities of interest to them.

Personality Type: Social-Artistic. Social occupations frequently involve working with, communicating with, and teaching people. These occupations often involve helping or providing service to others.

Career Cluster: 05 Education and Training. **Career Pathway:** 05.3 Teaching/Training.

Skills—Learning Strategies: Selecting and using training/instructional methods and procedures appropriate for the situation when learning or teaching new things. **Instructing:** Teaching others how to do something. **Monitoring:** Monitoring/assessing your performance or that of other individuals or organizations to make improvements or take corrective action. **Social Perceptiveness:** Being aware of others' reactions and understanding why they react as they do.

Writing: Communicating effectively in writing as appropriate for the needs of the audience. **Time Management:** Managing one's own time and the time of others.

Related Knowledge/Courses—History and Archeology: Historical events and their causes, indicators, and impact on particular civilizations and cultures. **Geography:** Various methods for describing the location and distribution of land, sea, and air masses, including their physical locations, relationships, and characteristics. **Sociology and Anthropology:** Group behavior and dynamics; societal trends and influences; and cultures and their history, migrations, ethnicity, and origins. **Philosophy and Theology:** Different philosophical systems and religions, including their basic principles, values, ethics, ways of thinking, customs, and practices and their impact on human culture. **Psychology:** Human behavior and performance, mental processes, psychological research methods, and the assessment and treatment of behavioral and affective disorders. **Education and Training:** Instructional methods and training techniques, including curriculum design principles, learning theory, group and individual teaching techniques, design of individual development plans, and test design principles.

Work Environment: Indoors; disease or infections; standing.

Law Teachers, Postsecondary

Related Major: Graduate Study for College Teaching

- ❋ Education/Training Required: First professional degree
- ❋ Annual Earnings: $87,730
- ❋ Beginning Wage: $39,670
- ❋ Earnings Growth Potential: Very high (54.8%)
- ❋ Growth: 22.9%
- ❋ Annual Job Openings: 2,169
- ❋ Self-Employed: 0.4%
- ❋ Part-Time: 27.8%

Industries with Greatest Employment: Educational Services, Public and Private (97.3%).

Highest-Growth Industries (Projected Growth for This Job): Administrative and Support Services (48.3%); Amusement, Gambling, and Recreation Industries (45.2%); Social Assistance (38.6%); Support Activities for Transportation (32.8%); Religious, Grantmaking, Civic, Professional, and Similar Organizations (29.9%); Professional, Scientific, and Technical Services (28.8%); Management of Companies and Enterprises (26.8%); Local Government (23.5%); Educational Services, Public and Private (22.8%); Hospitals, Public and Private (21.4%).

Lowest-Growth Industries (Projected Growth for This Job): Other Information Services (7.4%); State Government (7.9%); Sporting Goods, Hobby, Book, and Music Stores (13.3%); Performing Arts, Spectator Sports, and Related Industries (13.4%); Insurance Carriers and Related Activities (13.8%).

Fastest-Growing Metropolitan Areas (Recent Growth for This Job): Washington-Arlington-Alexandria, DC-VA-MD-WV (29.5%).

Other Considerations for Job Security: Retirements of current postsecondary teachers should create numerous openings for all types of postsecondary teachers, so job opportunities are generally expected to be very good. One of the main reasons why students attend postsecondary institutions is to prepare themselves for careers, so the best job prospects for postsecondary teachers are likely to be in rapidly growing fields that offer many nonacademic career options. Enrollments in law schools seem likely to remain high.

Teach courses in law. Evaluate and grade students' classwork, assignments, papers, and oral presentations. Compile, administer, and grade examinations or assign this work to others. Prepare and deliver lectures to undergraduate or graduate students on topics such as civil procedure, contracts, and torts. Initiate, facilitate, and moderate classroom discussions. Prepare course materials such as syllabi, homework assignments, and handouts. Keep abreast of developments in their field by reading current literature, talking with colleagues, and participating in professional conferences. Plan, evaluate, and revise curricula, course content, and course materials and methods of instruction. Maintain regularly scheduled office hours to advise and assist students. Conduct research in a particular field of knowledge and publish findings in professional journals, books, or electronic media. Advise students on academic and vocational curricula and on career issues. Supervise undergraduate and/or graduate teaching, internship, and research work. Select and obtain materials and supplies such as textbooks. Maintain student attendance records, grades, and other required records. Serve on academic or administrative committees that deal with institutional policies, departmental matters, and academic issues. Perform administrative duties such as serving as department head. Collaborate with colleagues to address

teaching and research issues. Participate in student recruitment, registration, and placement activities. Compile bibliographies of specialized materials for outside reading assignments. Participate in campus and community events. Act as advisers to student organizations. Assign cases for students to hear and try. Provide professional consulting services to government or industry. Write grant proposals to procure external research funding.

Personality Type: No data available.

Career Cluster: 12 Law, Public Safety, Corrections, and Security. **Career Pathway:** 12.5 Legal Services.

Skills—Instructing: Teaching others how to do something. **Critical Thinking:** Using logic and reasoning to identify the strengths and weaknesses of alternative solutions, conclusions, or approaches to problems. **Writing:** Communicating effectively in writing as appropriate for the needs of the audience. **Reading Comprehension:** Understanding written sentences and paragraphs in work-related documents. **Persuasion:** Persuading others to change their minds or behavior. **Speaking:** Talking to others to convey information effectively.

Related Knowledge/Courses—Law and Government: Laws, legal codes, court procedures, precedents, government regulations, executive orders, agency rules, and the democratic political process. **English Language:** The structure and content of the English language, including the meaning and spelling of words, rules of composition, and grammar. **History and Archeology:** Historical events and their causes, indicators, and impact on particular civilizations and cultures. **Education and Training:** Instructional methods and training techniques, including curriculum design principles, learning theory, group and individual teaching techniques, design of individual development plans, and test design principles. **Philosophy and Theology:** Different philosophical systems and religions, including their basic principles, values, ethics, ways of thinking, customs, and practices and their impact on human culture. **Communications and Media:** Media production, communication, and dissemination techniques and methods, including alternative ways to inform and entertain via written, oral, and visual media.

Work Environment: Indoors; sitting.

Librarians

Related Major: Library Science

- ✴ Education/Training Required: Master's degree
- ✴ Annual Earnings: $50,970
- ✴ Beginning Wage: $31,960
- ✴ Earnings Growth Potential: Medium (37.3%)
- ✴ Growth: 3.6%
- ✴ Annual Job Openings: 18,945
- ✴ Self-Employed: 0.6%
- ✴ Part-Time: 21.2%

Industries with Greatest Employment: Educational Services, Public and Private (59.7%); Local Government (26.7%).

Highest-Growth Industries (Projected Growth for This Job): Securities, Commodity Contracts, and Other Financial Investments and Related Activities (48.1%); Social Assistance (36.8%); Museums, Historical Sites, and Similar Institutions (36.1%); Administrative and Support Services (28.5%); Chemical Manufacturing (25.1%); Ambulatory Health Care Services (25.0%); Religious, Grantmaking, Civic, Professional, and Similar Organizations (18.5%); Professional, Scientific, and Technical Services (18.3%); Motion Picture, Video, and Sound Recording Industries (17.0%); Management of Companies and Enterprises (15.2%).

Lowest-Growth Industries (Projected Growth for This Job): Computer and Electronic Product Manufacturing (–9.1%); Publishing Industries (Except Internet) (–7.3%); Federal Government (–5.4%); Other Information Services (–2.1%); State Government (–1.9%); Transportation Equipment Manufacturing (0.0%); Local Government (1.1%); Educational Services, Public and Private (3.9%); Performing Arts, Spectator Sports, and Related Industries (4.0%); Credit Intermediation and Related Activities (8.0%); others.

Fastest-Growing Metropolitan Areas (Recent Growth for This Job): Lebanon, PA (100.0%); Fort Smith, AR-OK (83.3%); Decatur, IL (75.0%); Logan, UT-ID (66.7%); Salisbury, MD (60.0%).

Other Considerations for Job Security: More than 2 out of 3 librarians are aged 45 or older, which will result in many job openings over the next decade as many librarians retire. However, recent increases in enrollments in MLS programs will prepare a sufficient number of new librarians to fill these positions. Opportunities for public school librarians, who are usually drawn from the ranks of teachers, should be particularly favorable.

Administer libraries and perform related library services. Work in a variety of settings, including public libraries, schools, colleges and universities, museums, corporations, government agencies, law firms, non-profit organizations, and health-care providers. Tasks may include selecting, acquiring,

cataloguing, classifying, circulating, and maintaining library materials and furnishing reference, bibliographical, and readers' advisory services. May perform in-depth, strategic research and synthesize, analyze, edit, and filter information. May set up or work with databases and information systems to catalogue and access information. Search standard reference materials, including online sources and the Internet, to answer patrons' reference questions. Analyze patrons' requests to determine needed information and assist in furnishing or locating that information. Teach library patrons to search for information by using databases. Keep records of circulation and materials. Supervise budgeting, planning, and personnel activities. Check books in and out of the library. Explain use of library facilities, resources, equipment, and services and provide information about library policies. Review and evaluate resource material, such as book reviews and catalogs, to select and order print, audiovisual, and electronic resources. Code, classify, and catalog books, publications, films, audiovisual aids, and other library materials based on subject matter or standard library classification systems. Locate unusual or unique information in response to specific requests. Direct and train library staff in duties such as receiving, shelving, researching, cataloguing, and equipment use. Respond to customer complaints, taking action as necessary. Organize collections of books, publications, documents, audiovisual aids, and other reference materials for convenient access. Develop library policies and procedures. Evaluate materials to determine outdated or unused items to be discarded. Develop information access aids such as indexes and annotated bibliographies, Web pages, electronic pathfinders, and online tutorials. Plan and deliver client-centered programs and services such as special services for corporate clients, storytelling for children, newsletters, or programs for special groups. Compile lists of books, periodicals, articles, and audiovisual materials on particular subjects. Arrange for interlibrary loans of materials not available in a particular library. Assemble and arrange display materials. Confer with teachers, parents, and community organizations to develop, plan, and conduct programs in reading, viewing, and communication skills. Compile lists of overdue materials and notify borrowers that their materials are overdue.

Personality Type: Artistic-Conventional. Artistic occupations frequently involve working with forms, designs, and patterns. They often require self-expression, and the work can be done without following a clear set of rules.

Career Cluster: 05 Education and Training. **Career Pathways:** 05.2 Professional Support Services; 05.3 Teaching/Training.

Skills—Management of Financial Resources: Determining how money will be spent to get the work done and accounting for these expenditures. **Management of Material Resources:** Obtaining and seeing to the appropriate use of equipment, facilities, and materials needed to do certain work. **Learning Strategies:** Selecting and using training/instructional methods and procedures appropriate for the situation when learning or teaching new things. **Equipment Selection:** Determining the kind of tools and equipment needed to do a job. **Service Orientation:** Actively looking for ways to help people. **Systems Evaluation:** Identifying measures or indicators of system performance and the actions needed to improve or correct performance relative to the goals of the system.

Related Knowledge/Courses—Communications and Media: Media production, communication, and dissemination techniques and methods, including alternative ways to inform and entertain via written, oral, and visual media. **Clerical Practices:** Administrative and clerical procedures and systems such as word-processing systems, filing and records management systems, stenography and transcription, forms, design principles, and other office procedures and terminology. **Customer and Personal Service:** Principles and processes for providing customer and personal services, including needs assessment techniques, quality service standards, alternative delivery systems, and customer satisfaction evaluation techniques. **Personnel and Human Resources:** Principles and procedures for personnel recruitment; selection; training; compensation and benefits; labor relations and negotiation; and personnel information systems. **English Language:** The structure and content of the English language, including the meaning and spelling of words, rules of composition, and grammar. **Computers and Electronics:** Electric circuit boards, processors, chips, and computer hardware and software, including applications and programming.

Work Environment: Indoors; sitting; using hands on objects, tools, or controls; repetitive motions.

Library Science Teachers, Postsecondary

Related Major: Graduate Study for College Teaching

* Education/Training Required: Master's degree
* Annual Earnings: $56,810
* Beginning Wage: $34,850
* Earnings Growth Potential: Medium (38.7%)
* Growth: 22.9%
* Annual Job Openings: 702
* Self-Employed: 0.4%
* Part-Time: 27.8%

Industries with Greatest Employment: Educational Services, Public and Private (97.3%).

Highest-Growth Industries (Projected Growth for This Job): Administrative and Support Services (48.3%); Amusement, Gambling, and Recreation Industries (45.2%); Social Assistance (38.6%); Support Activities for Transportation (32.8%); Religious, Grantmaking, Civic, Professional, and Similar Organizations (29.9%); Professional, Scientific, and Technical Services (28.8%); Management of Companies and Enterprises (26.8%); Local Government (23.5%); Educational Services, Public and Private (22.8%); Hospitals, Public and Private (21.4%).

Lowest-Growth Industries (Projected Growth for This Job): Other Information Services (7.4%); State Government (7.9%); Sporting Goods, Hobby, Book, and Music Stores (13.3%); Performing Arts, Spectator Sports, and Related Industries (13.4%); Insurance Carriers and Related Activities (13.8%).

Fastest-Growing Metropolitan Areas (Recent Growth for This Job): New York–Northern New Jersey–Long Island, NY-NJ-PA (50.0%); Tampa–St. Petersburg–Clearwater, FL (33.3%); St. Louis, MO-IL (20.0%).

Other Considerations for Job Security: Retirements of current postsecondary teachers should create numerous openings for all types of postsecondary teachers. However, one of the main reasons why students attend postsecondary institutions is to prepare themselves for careers, so the best job prospects for postsecondary teachers are likely to be in rapidly growing fields that offer many nonacademic career options. Community colleges and other institutions offering career and technical education have been among the most rapidly growing, and these institutions are expected to offer some of the best opportunities for postsecondary teachers.

Teach courses in library science. Prepare course materials such as syllabi, homework assignments, and handouts. Prepare and deliver lectures to undergraduate or graduate students on topics such as collection development, archival methods, and indexing and abstracting. Evaluate and grade students' classwork, assignments, and papers. Keep abreast of developments in their field by reading current literature, talking with colleagues, and participating in professional conferences. Initiate, facilitate, and moderate classroom discussions. Plan, evaluate, and revise curricula, course content, and course materials and methods of instruction. Conduct research in a particular field of knowledge and publish findings in professional journals, books, and/or electronic media. Maintain student attendance records, grades, and other required records. Collaborate with colleagues to address teaching and research issues. Advise students on academic and vocational curricula and on career issues.

Compile, administer, and grade examinations or assign this work to others. Supervise undergraduate or graduate teaching, internship, and research work. Maintain regularly scheduled office hours in order to advise and assist students. Write grant proposals to procure external research funding. Select and obtain materials and supplies such as textbooks. Serve on academic or administrative committees that deal with institutional policies, departmental matters, and academic issues. Compile bibliographies of specialized materials for outside reading assignments. Participate in student recruitment, registration, and placement activities. Perform administrative duties such as serving as department head. Participate in campus and community events. Act as advisers to student organizations. Provide professional consulting services to government and/or industry.

Personality Type: No data available.

Career Cluster: 05 Education and Training. **Career Pathways:** 05.2 Professional Support Services; 05.3 Teaching/Training.

Skills—Writing: Communicating effectively in writing as appropriate for the needs of the audience. **Learning Strategies:** Selecting and using training/instructional methods and procedures appropriate for the situation when learning or teaching new things. **Instructing:** Teaching others how to do something. **Reading Comprehension:** Understanding written sentences and paragraphs in work-related documents. **Active Learning:** Understanding the implications of new information for both current and future problem-solving and decision-making. **Monitoring:** Monitoring/assessing your performance or that of other individuals or organizations to make improvements or take corrective action.

Related Knowledge/Courses—Education and Training: Instructional methods and training techniques, including curriculum design principles, learning theory, group and individual teaching techniques, design of individual development plans, and test design principles. **Sociology and Anthropology:** Group behavior and dynamics; societal trends and influences; and cultures and their history, migrations, ethnicity, and origins. **English Language:** The structure and content of the English language, including the meaning and spelling of words, rules of composition, and grammar. **Communications and Media:** Media production, communication, and dissemination techniques and methods, including alternative ways to inform and entertain via written, oral, and visual media. **History and Archeology:** Historical events and their causes, indicators, and impact on particular civilizations and cultures. **Philosophy and Theology:** Different philosophical systems and religions, including their basic principles, values, ethics, ways of thinking, customs, and practices and their impact on human culture.

Work Environment: Indoors; sitting.

Marriage and Family Therapists

Related Major: Social Work

- ✸ Education/Training Required: Master's degree
- ✸ Annual Earnings: $43,600
- ✸ Beginning Wage: $26,080
- ✸ Earnings Growth Potential: High (40.2%)
- ✸ Growth: 29.8%
- ✸ Annual Job Openings: 5,953
- ✸ Self-Employed: 6.2%
- ✸ Part-Time: 15.4%

Industries with Greatest Employment: Social Assistance (35.6%); Ambulatory Health Care Services (19.4%); State Government (18.1%); Local Government (7.1%); Religious, Grantmaking, Civic, Professional, and Similar Organizations (6.6%).

Highest-Growth Industries (Projected Growth for This Job): Social Assistance (63.4%); Nursing and Residential Care Facilities (23.6%); Ambulatory Health Care Services (20.4%); Religious, Grantmaking, Civic, Professional, and Similar Organizations (19.8%); Management of Companies and Enterprises (15.6%).

Lowest-Growth Industries (Projected Growth for This Job): State Government (–1.9%); Hospitals, Public and Private (4.7%); Educational Services, Public and Private (9.9%); Local Government (12.4%).

Fastest-Growing Metropolitan Areas (Recent Growth for This Job): Oklahoma City, OK (140.0%); St. Louis, MO-IL (92.3%); Cincinnati-Middletown, OH-KY-IN (88.9%); Hartford–West Hartford–East Hartford, CT (60.0%); San Diego–Carlsbad–San Marcos, CA (50.0%).

Other Considerations for Job Security: Marriage and family therapists will experience fast growth in part because of an increased recognition of the field. It is more common for people to seek help for their marital and family problems than it was in the past. Job prospects should be good due to growth and the need to replace people leaving the field.

Diagnose and treat mental and emotional disorders, whether cognitive, affective, or behavioral, within the context of marriage and family systems. Apply psychotherapeutic and family systems theories and techniques in the delivery of professional services

to individuals, couples, and families for the purpose of treating such diagnosed nervous and mental disorders. Ask questions that will help clients identify their feelings and behaviors. Counsel clients on concerns such as unsatisfactory relationships, divorce and separation, child rearing, home management, and financial difficulties. Encourage individuals and family members to develop and use skills and strategies for confronting their problems in a constructive manner. Maintain case files that include activities, progress notes, evaluations, and recommendations. Collect information about clients, using techniques such as testing, interviewing, discussion, and observation. Develop and implement individualized treatment plans addressing family relationship problems. Determine whether clients should be counseled or referred to other specialists in such fields as medicine, psychiatry, and legal aid. Confer with clients in order to develop plans for post-treatment activities. Confer with other counselors to analyze individual cases and to coordinate counseling services. Follow up on results of counseling programs and clients' adjustments to determine effectiveness of programs. Provide instructions to clients on how to obtain help with legal, financial, and other personal issues. Contact doctors, schools, social workers, juvenile counselors, law enforcement personnel, and others to gather information in order to make recommendations to courts for the resolution of child custody or visitation disputes. Provide public education and consultation to other professionals or groups regarding counseling services, issues, and methods. Supervise other counselors, social service staff, and assistants. Provide family counseling and treatment services to inmates participating in substance abuse programs. Write evaluations of parents and children for use by courts deciding divorce and custody cases, testifying in court if necessary.

Personality Type: No data available.

Career Cluster: 10 Human Services. **Career Pathways:** 10.2 Counseling and Mental Health Services; 10.3 Family and Community Services.

Skills—Social Perceptiveness: Being aware of others' reactions and understanding why they react as they do. **Negotiation:** Bringing others together and trying to reconcile differences. **Active Listening:** Giving full attention to what other people are saying, taking time to understand the points being made, asking questions as appropriate, and not interrupting at inappropriate times. **Persuasion:** Persuading others to change their minds or behavior. **Service Orientation:** Actively looking for ways to help people. **Monitoring:** Monitoring/assessing your performance or that of other individuals or organizations to make improvements or take corrective action.

Related Knowledge/Courses—Therapy and Counseling: Information and techniques needed to rehabilitate physical and mental ailments and to provide career guidance, including alternative treatments, rehabilitation equipment and its proper use, and methods to evaluate treatment effects. **Psychology:** Human behavior and performance, mental processes, psychological research methods, and the assessment and treatment of behavioral and affective disorders. **Philosophy and Theology:** Different philosophical systems and religions, including their basic principles, values, ethics, ways of thinking, customs, and practices and their impact on human culture. **Sociology and Anthropology:** Group behavior and dynamics; societal trends and influences; and cultures and their history, migrations, ethnicity, and origins. **Medicine and Dentistry:** The information and techniques needed to diagnose and treat injuries, diseases, and deformities. This includes symptoms, treatment alternatives,

M

drug properties and interactions, and preventive health-care measures. **Customer and Personal Service:** Principles and processes for providing customer and personal services, including needs assessment techniques, quality service standards, alternative delivery systems, and customer satisfaction evaluation techniques.

Work Environment: Indoors; sitting.

Mathematical Science Teachers, Postsecondary

Related Major: Graduate Study for College Teaching

- ✳ Education/Training Required: Master's degree
- ✳ Annual Earnings: $58,560
- ✳ Beginning Wage: $32,690
- ✳ Earnings Growth Potential: High (44.2%)
- ✳ Growth: 22.9%
- ✳ Annual Job Openings: 7,663
- ✳ Self-Employed: 0.4%
- ✳ Part-Time: 27.8%

Industries with Greatest Employment: Educational Services, Public and Private (97.3%).

Highest-Growth Industries (Projected Growth for This Job): Administrative and Support Services (48.3%); Amusement, Gambling, and Recreation Industries (45.2%); Social Assistance (38.6%); Support Activities for Transportation (32.8%); Religious, Grantmaking, Civic, Professional, and Similar Organizations (29.9%); Professional, Scientific, and Technical Services (28.8%); Management of Companies and Enterprises (26.8%); Local Government (23.5%); Educational Services, Public and Private (22.8%); Hospitals, Public and Private (21.4%).

Lowest-Growth Industries (Projected Growth for This Job): Other Information Services (7.4%); State Government (7.9%); Sporting Goods, Hobby, Book, and Music Stores (13.3%); Performing Arts, Spectator Sports, and Related Industries (13.4%); Insurance Carriers and Related Activities (13.8%).

Fastest-Growing Metropolitan Areas (Recent Growth for This Job): Des Moines–West Des Moines, IA (150.0%); New Haven, CT (100.0%); Syracuse, NY (62.5%); Little Rock–North Little Rock, AR (40.0%); Los Angeles–Long Beach–Santa Ana, CA (34.2%).

Other Considerations for Job Security: Retirements of current postsecondary teachers should create numerous openings for all types of postsecondary teachers, so job opportunities are generally expected to be very good. However, one of the main reasons why students attend postsecondary institutions is to prepare themselves for careers, so the best job prospects for postsecondary teachers are likely to be in rapidly growing fields that offer many nonacademic career options. Community colleges and other institutions offering career and technical education have been among the most rapidly growing, and these institutions are expected to offer some of the best opportunities for postsecondary teachers.

Teach courses pertaining to mathematical concepts, statistics, and actuarial science and to the application of original and standardized mathematical techniques in solving specific problems and situations. Evaluate and grade students' classwork, assignments, and papers. Compile, administer, and grade examinations or assign this work to others. Prepare and deliver lectures to undergraduate and/or graduate students on topics such as linear algebra, differential equations, and discrete mathematics. Prepare course materials such as syllabi, homework assignments, and handouts. Maintain student attendance records, grades, and other required records. Maintain regularly scheduled office hours to advise and assist students. Plan, evaluate, and revise curricula, course content, and course materials and methods of instruction. Initiate, facilitate, and moderate classroom discussions. Select and obtain materials and supplies such as textbooks. Keep abreast of developments in their field by reading current literature, talking with colleagues, and participating in professional conferences. Advise students on academic and vocational curricula and on career issues. Collaborate with colleagues to address teaching and research issues. Serve on academic or administrative committees that deal with institutional policies, departmental matters, and academic issues. Participate in student recruitment, registration, and placement activities. Perform administrative duties such as serving as department head. Conduct research in a particular field of knowledge and publish findings in books, professional journals, and/or electronic media. Supervise undergraduate and/or graduate teaching, internship, and research work. Act as advisers to student organizations. Participate in campus and community events. Write grant proposals to procure external research funding. Compile bibliographies of specialized materials for outside reading assignments. Provide professional consulting services to government and/or industry.

Personality Type: Investigative-Social-Conventional. Investigative occupations frequently involve working with ideas and require an extensive amount of thinking. These occupations can involve searching for facts and figuring out problems mentally.

Career Clusters: 04 Business, Management, and Administration; 10 Human Services; 15 Science,

Technology, Engineering, and Mathematics. **Career Pathways:** 04.2 Business Financial Management and Accounting; 10.2 Counseling and Mental Health Services; 15.3 Science and Mathematics.

Skills—Mathematics: Using mathematics to solve problems. **Instructing:** Teaching others how to do something. **Science:** Using scientific rules and methods to solve problems. **Learning Strategies:** Selecting and using training/instructional methods and procedures appropriate for the situation when learning or teaching new things. **Critical Thinking:** Using logic and reasoning to identify the strengths and weaknesses of alternative solutions, conclusions, or approaches to problems. **Complex Problem Solving:** Identifying complex problems and reviewing related information to develop and evaluate options and implement solutions.

Related Knowledge/Courses—Mathematics: Numbers and their operations and interrelationships, including arithmetic, algebra, geometry, calculus, and statistics and their applications. **Education and Training:** Instructional methods and training techniques, including curriculum design principles, learning theory, group and individual teaching techniques, design of individual development plans, and test design principles. **Physics:** Physical principles, laws, and applications, including air, water, material dynamics, light, atomic principles, heat, electric theory, earth formations, and meteorological and related natural phenomena. **Computers and Electronics:** Electric circuit boards, processors, chips, and computer hardware and software, including applications and programming. **English Language:** The structure and content of the English language, including the meaning and spelling of words, rules of composition, and grammar. **Communications and Media:** Media production, communication, and dissemination techniques and methods, including alternative ways to inform and entertain via written, oral, and visual media.

Work Environment: Indoors; more often standing than sitting.

Mathematicians

Related Majors: Mathematics; Statistics

- ✺ Education/Training Required: Doctoral degree
- ✺ Annual Earnings: $90,870
- ✺ Beginning Wage: $51,240
- ✺ Earnings Growth Potential: High (43.6%)
- ✺ Growth: 10.2%
- ✺ Annual Job Openings: 473
- ✺ Self-Employed: 0.0%
- ✺ Part-Time: 5.6%

Industries with Greatest Employment: Professional, Scientific, and Technical Services (38.1%); Federal Government (36.8%); Educational Services, Public and Private (13.6%); State Government (6.0%).

Highest-Growth Industries (Projected Growth for This Job): Professional, Scientific, and Technical Services (26.3%).

Lowest-Growth Industries (Projected Growth for This Job): Federal Government (–5.5%); State Government (–1.7%); Educational Services, Public and Private (10.0%).

Fastest-Growing Metropolitan Areas (Recent Growth for This Job): New York–Northern New Jersey–Long Island, NY-NJ-PA (140.0%); Baltimore-Towson, MD (50.0%).

Other Considerations for Job Security: Keen competition for jobs is expected because employment in this occupation is relatively small and few new jobs are expected. Master's degree and Ph.D. holders with a strong background in mathematics and a related discipline, such as engineering or computer science, who apply mathematical theory to real-world problems will have the best job prospects in related occupations. Employment in theoretical mathematical research is sensitive to general economic fluctuations and to changes in government spending. Job prospects will be greatly influenced by changes in public and private funding for research and development.

Conduct research in fundamental mathematics or in application of mathematical techniques to science, management, and other fields. Solve or direct solutions to problems in various fields by mathematical methods. Apply mathematical theories and techniques to the solution of practical problems in business, engineering, the sciences, or other fields. Develop computational methods for solving problems that occur in areas of science and engineering or that come from applications in business or industry. Maintain knowledge in the field by reading professional journals, talking with other mathematicians, and attending professional conferences. Perform computations and apply methods of numerical analysis to data. Develop mathematical or statistical models of phenomena to be used for analysis or for computational simulation. Assemble sets of assumptions and explore the consequences of each set. Address the relationships of quantities, magnitudes, and forms through the use of numbers and symbols. Develop new principles and new relationships between existing mathematical principles to advance mathematical science. Design, analyze, and decipher encryption systems designed to transmit military, political, financial, or law-enforcement-related information in code. Conduct research to extend mathematical knowledge in traditional areas, such as algebra, geometry, probability, and logic.

Personality Type: Investigative-Conventional. Investigative occupations frequently involve working with ideas and require an extensive amount of thinking. These occupations can involve searching for facts and figuring out problems mentally.

Career Clusters: 10 Human Services; 15 Science, Technology, Engineering, and Mathematics. **Career Pathways:** 10.2 Counseling and Mental Health Services; 15.3 Science and Mathematics.

Skills—Programming: Writing computer programs for various purposes. **Science:** Using scientific rules and methods to solve problems. **Mathematics:** Using mathematics to solve problems. **Complex Problem Solving:** Identifying complex problems and reviewing related information to develop and evaluate options and implement solutions. **Operations Analysis:** Analyzing needs and product requirements to create a design. **Reading Comprehension:** Understanding written sentences and paragraphs in work-related documents.

Related Knowledge/Courses—Mathematics: Numbers and their operations and interrelationships, including arithmetic, algebra, geometry, calculus, and statistics and their applications. **Physics:** Physical principles, laws, and applications, including air, water, material dynamics, light, atomic principles, heat, electric theory, earth formations, and meteorological and related natural phenomena. **Computers and Electronics:** Electric circuit boards, processors, chips, and computer hardware and software, including

applications and programming. **Engineering and Technology:** Equipment, tools, and mechanical devices and their uses to produce motion, light, power, technology, and other applications. **English Language:** The structure and content of the English language, including the meaning and spelling of words, rules of composition, and grammar.

Work Environment: Indoors; sitting.

Medical and Clinical Laboratory Technologists

Related Major: Medical Technology

- ❋ Education/Training Required: Bachelor's degree
- ❋ Annual Earnings: $51,720
- ❋ Beginning Wage: $35,460
- ❋ Earnings Growth Potential: Low (31.4%)
- ❋ Growth: 12.4%
- ❋ Annual Job Openings: 11,457
- ❋ Self-Employed: 0.7%
- ❋ Part-Time: 14.3%

Industries with Greatest Employment: Hospitals, Public and Private (60.6%); Ambulatory Health Care Services (25.3%); Educational Services, Public and Private (5.2%).

Highest-Growth Industries (Projected Growth for This Job): Social Assistance (46.7%); Ambulatory Health Care Services (36.8%); Professional, Scientific, and Technical Services (27.1%); Administrative and Support Services (26.5%); Chemical Manufacturing (26.1%); Nursing and Residential Care Facilities (15.7%); Management of Companies and Enterprises (15.3%).

Lowest-Growth Industries (Projected Growth for This Job): Federal Government (–5.5%); State Government (–1.9%); Miscellaneous Manufacturing (2.4%); Hospitals, Public and Private (3.1%); Educational Services, Public and Private (11.9%); Local Government (12.3%).

Fastest-Growing Metropolitan Areas (Recent Growth for This Job): Albuquerque, NM (136.1%); Salisbury, MD (133.3%); Albany, GA (120.0%); Boulder, CO (80.0%); Charleston, WV (78.6%).

Other Considerations for Job Security: Job opportunities are expected to be excellent because the number of job openings is expected to continue to exceed the number of job seekers. Although significant, job growth will not be the only source of opportunities. As in most occupations, many additional openings will result from the need to replace workers who transfer to other occupations, retire, or stop working for some other reason. The volume of laboratory tests continues to increase with both population growth and the development of new types of tests. Technological advances will continue to have opposing effects on employment. On the one hand, new, increasingly powerful diagnostic tests will encourage additional testing and spur employment. On the other, research and development efforts targeted at simplifying routine testing procedures may enhance the ability of nonlaboratory personnel—physicians and patients in particular—to perform tests now conducted in laboratories.

Perform complex medical laboratory tests for diagnosis, treatment, and prevention of disease. May train or supervise staff. Conduct chemical analysis of bodily fluids, including blood, urine, and spinal fluid, to determine presence of normal and abnormal components. Analyze laboratory findings to check the accuracy of the results. Enter data from analysis of medical tests and clinical results into computer for storage. Operate, calibrate, and maintain equipment used in quantitative and qualitative analysis, such as spectrophotometers, calorimeters, flame photometers, and computer-controlled analyzers. Establish and monitor quality assurance programs and activities to ensure the accuracy of laboratory results. Set up, clean, and maintain laboratory equipment. Provide technical information about test results to physicians, family members, and researchers. Supervise, train, and direct lab assistants, medical and clinical laboratory technicians and technologists, and other medical laboratory workers engaged in laboratory testing. Collect and study blood samples to determine the number of cells, their morphology, or their blood group, blood type, and compatibility for transfusion purposes, using microscopic techniques. Analyze samples of biological material for chemical content or reaction. Cultivate, isolate, and assist in identifying microbial organisms, and perform various tests on these microorganisms. Obtain, cut, stain, and mount biological material on slides for microscopic study and diagnosis, following standard laboratory procedures. Select and prepare specimen and media for cell culture, using aseptic technique and knowledge of medium components and cell requirements. Develop, standardize, evaluate, and modify procedures, techniques, and tests used in the analysis of specimens and in medical laboratory experiments. Harvest cell cultures at optimum time based on knowledge of cell cycle differences and culture conditions. Conduct medical research under direction of microbiologist or biochemist.

Personality Type: Investigative-Realistic. Investigative occupations frequently involve working with ideas and require an extensive amount of thinking. These occupations can involve searching for facts and figuring out problems mentally.

Career Cluster: 08 Health Science. **Career Pathway:** 08.2 Diagnostics Services.

Skills—No data available.

Related Knowledge/Courses—Biology: Plant and animal living tissue, cells, organisms, and entities, including their functions, interdependencies, and interactions with each other and the environment. **Chemistry:** The composition, structure, and properties of substances and of the chemical processes and transformations that they undergo. This includes uses of chemicals and their interactions, danger signs, production techniques, and disposal methods. **Medicine and Dentistry:** The information and techniques needed to diagnose and treat injuries, diseases, and deformities. This includes symptoms, treatment alternatives, drug properties and interactions, and preventive health-care measures. **Mechanical Devices:** Machines and tools, including their designs, uses, benefits, repair, and maintenance. **Clerical Practices:** Administrative and clerical procedures and systems such as word-processing systems, filing and records management systems, stenography and transcription, forms, design principles, and other office procedures and terminology. **Mathematics:** Numbers and their operations and interrelationships, including arithmetic, algebra, geometry, calculus, and statistics and their applications.

Work Environment: Indoors; noisy; contaminants; disease or infections; standing; using hands on objects, tools, or controls.

Medical and Health Services Managers

Related Majors: Health Information Systems Administration; Hospital/Health Facilities Administration

- ✹ Education/Training Required: Work experience plus degree
- ✹ Annual Earnings: $76,990
- ✹ Beginning Wage: $46,860
- ✹ Earnings Growth Potential: Medium (39.1%)
- ✹ Growth: 16.4%
- ✹ Annual Job Openings: 31,877
- ✹ Self-Employed: 8.2%
- ✹ Part-Time: 5.5%

Industries with Greatest Employment: Hospitals, Public and Private (37.3%); Ambulatory Health Care Services (21.7%); Nursing and Residential Care Facilities (11.7%).

Highest-Growth Industries (Projected Growth for This Job): Social Assistance (51.7%); Professional, Scientific, and Technical Services (35.2%); Ambulatory Health Care Services (31.0%); Administrative and Support Services (28.5%); Funds, Trusts, and Other Financial Vehicles (23.2%); Nonstore Retailers (22.8%); Nursing and Residential Care Facilities (22.1%); Merchant Wholesalers, Nondurable Goods (18.8%); Religious, Grantmaking, Civic, Professional, and Similar Organizations (18.1%); Management of Companies and Enterprises (15.3%).

Lowest-Growth Industries (Projected Growth for This Job): Computer and Electronic Product Manufacturing (–6.5%); Federal Government (–5.5%); State Government (–1.9%); Transportation Equipment Manufacturing (–1.8%);

Miscellaneous Manufacturing (2.2%); Insurance Carriers and Related Activities (4.9%); Health and Personal Care Stores (8.3%); Rental and Leasing Services (9.6%); Hospitals, Public and Private (10.3%); Educational Services, Public and Private (11.6%); others.

Fastest-Growing Metropolitan Areas (Recent Growth for This Job): Albany, GA (133.3%); Palm Bay–Melbourne–Titusville, FL (111.1%); Bay City, MI (100.0%); Redding, CA (81.8%); Missoula, MT (75.0%).

Other Considerations for Job Security: Job opportunities for medical and health services managers should be good, especially for applicants with work experience in the health-care field and strong business management skills. Hospitals will continue to employ the most medical and health services managers, but the number of new jobs created is expected to increase at a slower rate in hospitals than in many other industries because of the growing use of clinics and other outpatient care sites. Despite relatively slow employment growth, a large number of new jobs will be created because of the industry's large size. Employment will grow fastest in practitioners' offices and in home health-care agencies. Medical and health services managers also will be employed by HMOs. Competition for jobs at the highest management levels will be keen because of the high pay and prestige.

Plan, direct, or coordinate medicine and health services in hospitals, clinics, managed care organizations, public health agencies, or similar organizations. Conduct and administer fiscal operations, including accounting, planning budgets, authorizing expenditures, establishing rates for services, and coordinating financial reporting. Direct, supervise, and evaluate work activities of medical, nursing, technical, clerical, service, maintenance, and other personnel. Maintain communication between governing boards, medical staff, and department heads by attending board meetings and coordinating interdepartmental functioning. Review and analyze facility activities and data to aid planning and cash and risk management and to improve service utilization. Plan, implement, and administer programs and services in a health-care or medical facility, including personnel administration, training, and coordination of medical, nursing, and physical plant staff. Direct or conduct recruitment, hiring, and training of personnel. Establish work schedules and assignments for staff, according to workload, space, and equipment availability. Maintain awareness of advances in medicine, computerized diagnostic and treatment equipment, data processing technology, government regulations, health insurance changes, and financing options. Monitor the use of diagnostic services, inpatient beds, facilities, and staff to ensure effective use of resources and assess the need for additional staff, equipment, and services. Develop and maintain computerized record management systems to store and process data such as personnel activities and information and to produce reports. Establish and evaluative objectives and evaluative operational criteria for units they manage. Prepare activity reports to inform management of the status and implementation plans of programs, services, and quality initiatives. Inspect facilities and recommend building or equipment modifications to ensure emergency readiness and compliance to access, safety, and sanitation regulations. Develop and implement organizational policies and procedures for the facility or medical unit. Manage change in integrated health care delivery systems such as work restructuring, technological innovations, and shifts in the focus of care.

Personality Type: Enterprising-Social. Enterprising occupations frequently involve starting up and carrying out projects. These occupations can involve leading people and making many decisions. They sometimes require risk taking and often deal with business.

Career Cluster: 08 Health Science. **Career Pathways:** 08.1 Therapeutic Services; 08.2 Diagnostics Services; 08.3 Health Informatics.

Skills—Management of Financial Resources: Determining how money will be spent to get the work done and accounting for these expenditures. **Management of Personnel Resources:** Motivating, developing, and directing people as they work, identifying the best people for the job. **Systems Analysis:** Determining how a system should work and how changes in conditions, operations, and the environment will affect outcomes. **Systems Evaluation:** Identifying measures or indicators of system performance and the actions needed to improve or correct performance relative to the goals of the system. **Management of Material Resources:** Obtaining and seeing to the appropriate use of equipment, facilities, and materials needed to do certain work. **Negotiation:** Bringing others together and trying to reconcile differences.

Related Knowledge/Courses—Economics and Accounting: Economic and accounting principles and practices, the financial markets, banking, and the analysis and reporting of financial data. **Personnel and Human Resources:** Principles and procedures for personnel recruitment; selection; training; compensation and benefits; labor relations and negotiation; and personnel information systems. **Administration and Management:** Principles and processes involved in business and organizational planning, coordination, and execution. This includes strategic

planning, resource allocation, manpower modeling, leadership techniques, and production methods. **Sales and Marketing:** Principles and methods involved in showing, promoting, and selling products or services. This includes marketing strategies and tactics, product demonstration and sales techniques, and sales control systems. **Medicine and Dentistry:** The information and techniques needed to diagnose and treat injuries, diseases, and deformities. This includes symptoms, treatment alternatives, drug properties and interactions, and preventive health-care measures. **Law and Government:** Laws, legal codes, court procedures, precedents, government regulations, executive orders, agency rules, and the democratic political process.

Work Environment: Indoors; disease or infections; sitting.

Middle School Teachers, Except Special and Vocational Education

Related Majors: Family and Consumer Sciences; Physical Education

- ✲ Education/Training Required: Bachelor's degree
- ✲ Annual Earnings: $47,900
- ✲ Beginning Wage: $32,630
- ✲ Earnings Growth Potential: Low (31.9%)
- ✲ Growth: 11.2%
- ✲ Annual Job Openings: 75,270
- ✲ Self-Employed: 0.0%
- ✲ Part-Time: 9.5%

Industries with Greatest Employment: Educational Services, Public and Private (98.8%).

Highest-Growth Industries (Projected Growth for This Job): Social Assistance (27.7%); Administrative and Support Services (26.6%); Nursing and Residential Care Facilities (22.4%); Religious, Grantmaking, Civic, Professional, and Similar Organizations (20.0%).

Lowest-Growth Industries (Projected Growth for This Job): Educational Services, Public and Private (11.1%); Local Government (12.4%).

Fastest-Growing Metropolitan Areas (Recent Growth for This Job): San Luis Obispo–Paso Robles, CA (107.1%); Greenville, SC (71.4%); Huntsville, AL (68.8%); Fort Wayne, IN (63.3%); Corvallis, OR (50.0%).

Other Considerations for Job Security: Job prospects are expected to be favorable, with particularly good prospects for teachers in high-demand fields such as math, science, and bilingual education or in less desirable urban or rural school districts. Fast-growing states in the South and West—led by Nevada, Arizona, Texas, and Georgia—will experience the largest enrollment increases. Enrollments in the Midwest are expected to hold relatively steady, while those in the Northeast are expected to decline. The number of teachers employed is dependent on state and local expenditures for education and on the enactment of legislation to increase the quality and scope of public education. At the federal level, there has been a large increase in funding for education, particularly for the hiring of qualified teachers in lower-income areas.

Teach students in public or private schools in one or more subjects at the middle, intermediate, or junior high level, which falls between elementary and senior high school as defined by applicable state laws and regulations. Establish and enforce rules for behavior and procedures for maintaining order among the students for whom they are responsible. Adapt teaching methods and instructional materials to meet students' varying needs and interests. Instruct through lectures, discussions, and demonstrations in one or more subjects such as English, mathematics, or social studies. Prepare, administer, and grade tests and assignments to evaluate students' progress. Establish clear objectives for all lessons, units, and projects and communicate these objectives to students. Plan and conduct activities for a balanced program of instruction, demonstration, and work time that provides students with opportunities to observe, question, and investigate. Maintain accurate, complete, and correct student records as required by laws, district policies, and administrative regulations. Observe and evaluate students' performance, behavior, social development, and physical health. Assign lessons and correct homework. Prepare materials and classrooms for class activities. Enforce all administration policies and rules governing students. Confer with parents or guardians, other teachers, counselors, and administrators to resolve students' behavioral and academic problems. Prepare students for later grades by encouraging them to explore learning opportunities and to persevere with challenging tasks. Prepare objectives and outlines for courses of study, following curriculum guidelines or requirements of states and schools. Guide and counsel students with adjustment or academic problems or special academic interests. Meet with parents and guardians to discuss their children's progress and to determine their priorities for their children and their resource needs. Meet with other professionals to discuss individual students' needs and progress. Prepare and implement remedial programs for students requiring extra help. Prepare for assigned classes and show written evidence of preparation upon request of immediate supervisors. Instruct and monitor students in the use and care of equipment and materials to prevent injury and damage.

Personality Type: Social-Artistic-Investigative. Social occupations frequently involve working with, communicating with, and teaching people. These occupations often involve helping or providing service to others.

Career Cluster: 05 Education and Training. **Career Pathway:** 05.3 Teaching/Training.

Skills—Learning Strategies: Selecting and using training/instructional methods and procedures appropriate for the situation when learning or teaching new things. **Instructing:** Teaching others how to do something. **Monitoring:** Monitoring/assessing your performance or that of other individuals or organizations to make improvements or take corrective action. **Social Perceptiveness:** Being aware of others' reactions and understanding why they react as they do. **Time Management:** Managing one's own time and the time of others. **Persuasion:** Persuading others to change their minds or behavior.

Related Knowledge/Courses—Sociology and Anthropology: Group behavior and dynamics; societal trends and influences; and cultures and their history, migrations, ethnicity, and origins. **History and Archeology:** Historical events and their causes, indicators, and impact on particular civilizations and cultures. **Philosophy and Theology:** Different philosophical systems and religions, including their basic principles, values, ethics, ways of thinking, customs, and practices and their impact on human culture. **Education and Training:** Instructional methods and training techniques, including curriculum design principles, learning theory, group and individual teaching techniques, design of individual development plans, and test design

principles. **Geography:** Various methods for describing the location and distribution of land, sea, and air masses, including their physical locations, relationships, and characteristics. **Therapy and Counseling:** Information and techniques needed to rehabilitate physical and mental ailments and to provide career guidance, including alternative treatments, rehabilitation equipment and its proper use, and methods to evaluate treatment effects.

Work Environment: Indoors; noisy; standing.

Museum Technicians and Conservators

Related Major: Art History

- ✸ Education/Training Required: Bachelor's degree
- ✸ Annual Earnings: $35,350
- ✸ Beginning Wage: $21,630
- ✸ Earnings Growth Potential: Medium (38.8%)
- ✸ Growth: 15.9%
- ✸ Annual Job Openings: 1,341
- ✸ Self-Employed: 1.3%
- ✸ Part-Time: 18.4%

Industries with Greatest Employment: Museums, Historical Sites, and Similar Institutions (37.6%); Federal Government (26.1%); Educational Services, Public and Private (11.9%); Local Government (11.4%); State Government (7.3%).

Highest-Growth Industries (Projected Growth for This Job): Performing Arts, Spectator Sports, and Related Industries (39.4%); Museums, Historical Sites, and Similar Institutions (36.2%).

Lowest-Growth Industries (Projected Growth for This Job): Federal Government (–5.5%); Other Information Services (–2.2%); State Government (–1.9%); Educational Services, Public and Private (12.2%); Local Government (12.4%); Religious, Grantmaking, Civic, Professional, and Similar Organizations (12.6%).

Fastest-Growing Metropolitan Areas (Recent Growth for This Job): Atlanta–Sandy Springs–Marietta, GA (50.0%); Los Angeles–Long Beach–Santa Ana, CA (46.7%); San Francisco–Oakland–Fremont, CA (31.0%); Baltimore-Towson, MD (25.0%); Milwaukee–Waukesha–West Allis, WI (25.0%).

Other Considerations for Job Security: Keen competition is expected because qualified applicants generally outnumber job openings. Competition is stiff for the limited number of openings in conservation graduate programs, and applicants need a technical background. Conservation program graduates with knowledge of a foreign language and a willingness to relocate will have an advantage over less-qualified candidates. Public interest in science, art, history, and technology will continue, creating opportunities for curators, conservators, and museum technicians. Museum attendance has held steady in recent years, many museums are financially healthy, and many have pursued building and renovation projects. There has been an increase in self-employment among conservators, as many museums move toward hiring these workers on contract rather than keeping them permanently on staff. This trend is expected to continue.

Prepare specimens, such as fossils, skeletal parts, lace, and textiles, for museum collection and exhibits. May restore documents or install, arrange, and exhibit materials. Install, arrange, assemble, and prepare artifacts for exhibition, ensuring the artifacts' safety, reporting their status and condition, and identifying and correcting any problems with the setup. Coordinate exhibit installations, assisting with design; constructing displays, dioramas, display cases, and models; and ensuring the availability of necessary materials. Determine whether objects need repair and choose the safest and most effective method of repair. Clean objects, such as paper, textiles, wood, metal, glass, rock, pottery, and furniture, using cleansers, solvents, soap solutions, and polishes. Prepare artifacts for storage and shipping. Supervise and work with volunteers. Present public programs and tours. Specialize in particular materials or types of object, such as documents and books, paintings, decorative arts, textiles, metals, or architectural materials. Recommend preservation procedures, such as control of temperature and humidity, to curatorial and building staff. Classify and assign registration numbers to artifacts and supervise inventory control. Direct and supervise curatorial and technical staff in the handling, mounting, care, and storage of art objects. Perform on-site fieldwork, which may involve interviewing people, inspecting and identifying artifacts, note-taking, viewing sites and collections, and repainting exhibition spaces. Repair, restore, and reassemble artifacts, designing and fabricating missing or broken parts, to restore them to their original appearance and prevent deterioration. Prepare reports on the operation of conservation laboratories, documenting the condition of artifacts, treatment options, and the methods of preservation and repair used. Study object documentation or conduct standard chemical and physical tests to ascertain the object's age, composition, original appearance, need for treatment or restoration, and appropriate preservation method. Cut and weld metal sections in reconstruction or renovation of exterior structural sections and accessories of exhibits. Perform tests and examinations to establish storage and conservation requirements, policies, and procedures.

Personality Type: Artistic-Realistic. Artistic occupations frequently involve working with forms, designs, and patterns. They often require self-expression, and the work can be done without following a clear set of rules.

Career Clusters: 03 Arts, Audio/Video Technology, and Communications; 15 Science, Technology, Engineering, and Mathematics. **Career Pathways:** 03.1 Audio and Video Technology and Film; 15.3 Science and Mathematics.

Skills—Management of Material Resources: Obtaining and seeing to the appropriate use of equipment, facilities, and materials needed to do certain work. **Repairing:** Repairing machines or systems using the needed tools. **Installation:** Installing equipment, machines, wiring, or programs to meet specifications. **Technology Design:** Generating or adapting equipment and technology to serve user needs. **Equipment Maintenance:** Performing routine maintenance on equipment and determining when and what kind of maintenance is needed. **Equipment Selection:** Determining the kind of tools and equipment needed to do a job.

Related Knowledge/Courses—History and Archeology: Historical events and their causes, indicators, and impact on particular civilizations and cultures. **Fine Arts:** Theory and techniques required to produce, compose, and perform works of music, dance, visual arts, drama, and sculpture. **Sociology and Anthropology:** Group behavior and dynamics; societal trends and influences; and cultures and their history, migrations, ethnicity, and origins. **Design:** Design techniques, principles, tools, and instruments involved in the production and use of precision technical plans, blueprints, drawings, and

models. **Clerical Practices:** Administrative and clerical procedures and systems such as word-processing systems, filing and records management systems, stenography and transcription, forms, design principles, and other office procedures and terminology. **Building and Construction:** Materials, methods, and the appropriate tools to construct objects, structures, and buildings.

Work Environment: Indoors; standing; using hands on objects, tools, or controls.

Nursing Instructors and Teachers, Postsecondary

Related Major: Graduate Study for College Teaching

- ❋ Education/Training Required: Master's degree
- ❋ Annual Earnings: $57,500
- ❋ Beginning Wage: $36,020
- ❋ Earnings Growth Potential: Medium (37.4%)
- ❋ Growth: 22.9%
- ❋ Annual Job Openings: 7,337
- ❋ Self-Employed: 0.4%
- ❋ Part-Time: 27.8%

Industries with Greatest Employment: Educational Services, Public and Private (97.3%).

Highest-Growth Industries (Projected Growth for This Job): Administrative and Support Services (48.3%); Amusement, Gambling, and Recreation Industries (45.2%); Social Assistance (38.6%); Support Activities for Transportation (32.8%); Religious, Grantmaking, Civic, Professional, and Similar Organizations (29.9%); Professional, Scientific, and Technical Services (28.8%); Management of Companies and Enterprises (26.8%); Local Government

(23.5%); Educational Services, Public and Private (22.8%); Hospitals, Public and Private (21.4%).

Lowest-Growth Industries (Projected Growth for This Job): Other Information Services (7.4%); State Government (7.9%); Sporting Goods, Hobby, Book, and Music Stores (13.3%); Performing Arts, Spectator Sports, and Related Industries (13.4%); Insurance Carriers and Related Activities (13.8%).

Fastest-Growing Metropolitan Areas (Recent Growth for This Job): Harrisburg-Carlisle, PA (133.3%); Memphis, TN-MS-AR (120.0%); Augusta–Richmond County, GA-SC (100.0%); Worcester, MA-CT (100.0%); Syracuse, NY (71.4%).

Other Considerations for Job Security: Retirements of current postsecondary teachers should create numerous openings for all types of postsecondary teachers. However, one of the main reasons why students attend postsecondary institutions is to prepare themselves for careers, so the best job prospects for postsecondary teachers are likely to be in rapidly growing fields that offer many nonacademic career options, such as nursing. The demand for nurses continues to grow, and many who are qualified to teach are finding work outside of education, so job opportunities should be excellent. Community colleges and other institutions offering career and technical education have been among the most rapidly growing, and these institutions are expected to offer some of the best opportunities for postsecondary teachers.

Demonstrate and teach patient care in classroom and clinical units to nursing students. Includes both teachers primarily engaged in teaching and those who do a combination of both teaching and research. Initiate, facilitate, and moderate classroom discussions. Prepare and deliver lectures to undergraduate or graduate students on topics such as pharmacology, mental health nursing, and community health-care practices. Keep abreast of developments in their field by reading current literature, talking with colleagues, and participating in professional conferences. Prepare course materials such as syllabi, homework assignments, and handouts. Supervise students' laboratory and clinical work. Evaluate and grade students' classwork, laboratory and clinic work, assignments, and papers. Collaborate with colleagues to address teaching and research issues. Plan, evaluate, and revise curricula, course content, and course materials and methods of instruction. Assess clinical education needs and patient and client teaching needs, utilizing a variety of methods. Compile, administer, and grade examinations or assign this work to others. Advise students on academic and vocational curricula and on career issues. Maintain student attendance records, grades, and other required records. Maintain regularly scheduled office hours to advise and assist students. Supervise undergraduate or graduate teaching, internship, and research work. Conduct research in a particular field of knowledge and publish findings in professional journals, books, and/or electronic media. Participate in student recruitment, registration, and placement activities. Serve on academic or administrative committees that deal with institutional policies, departmental matters, and academic issues. Coordinate training programs with area universities, clinics, hospitals, health agencies, and/or vocational schools. Compile bibliographies of specialized materials for outside reading assignments. Select and obtain materials and supplies such as textbooks and laboratory equipment. Participate in campus and community events. Write grant proposals to procure external research funding. Act as advisers to student organizations. Demonstrate patient care in clinical units of hospitals. Perform administrative duties such as serving as department head.

Personality Type: Social-Investigative. Social occupations frequently involve working with, communicating with, and teaching people. These occupations often involve helping or providing service to others.

Career Cluster: 08 Health Science. **Career Pathway:** 08.1 Therapeutic Services.

Skills—Science: Using scientific rules and methods to solve problems. **Instructing:** Teaching others how to do something. **Writing:** Communicating effectively in writing as appropriate for the needs of the audience. **Social Perceptiveness:** Being aware of others' reactions and understanding why they react as they do. **Reading Comprehension:** Understanding written sentences and paragraphs in work-related documents. **Learning Strategies:** Selecting and using training/instructional methods and procedures appropriate for the situation when learning or teaching new things.

Related Knowledge/Courses—Therapy and Counseling: Information and techniques needed to rehabilitate physical and mental ailments and to provide career guidance, including alternative treatments, rehabilitation equipment and its proper use, and methods to evaluate treatment effects. **Biology:** Plant and animal living tissue, cells, organisms, and entities, including their functions, interdependencies, and interactions with each other and the environment. **Sociology and Anthropology:** Group behavior and dynamics; societal trends and influences; and cultures and their history, migrations, ethnicity, and origins. **Medicine and Dentistry:** The information and techniques needed to diagnose and treat injuries, diseases, and deformities. This includes symptoms, treatment alternatives, drug properties and interactions, and preventive health-care measures. **Philosophy and Theology:** Different philosophical systems and religions, including their basic principles, values, ethics, ways of thinking, customs, and practices and their impact on human culture. **Psychology:** Human behavior and performance, mental processes, psychological research methods, and the assessment and treatment of behavioral and affective disorders.

Work Environment: Indoors; disease or infections; sitting.

Obstetricians and Gynecologists

Related Major: Medicine

- ❋ Education/Training Required: First professional degree
- ❋ Annual Earnings: More than $145,600
- ❋ Beginning Wage: $100,770
- ❋ Earnings Growth Potential: Cannot be calculated
- ❋ Growth: 14.2%
- ❋ Annual Job Openings: 38,027
- ❋ Self-Employed: 14.7%
- ❋ Part-Time: 8.1%

Industries with Greatest Employment: Ambulatory Health Care Services (55.9%); Hospitals, Public and Private (17.8%).

Highest-Growth Industries (Projected Growth for This Job): Social Assistance (58.6%); Administrative and Support Services (26.8%); Professional, Scientific, and Technical Services (22.6%); Nursing and Residential

Care Facilities (21.0%); Ambulatory Health Care Services (19.4%); Religious, Grantmaking, Civic, Professional, and Similar Organizations (16.7%); Management of Companies and Enterprises (15.3%).

Lowest-Growth Industries (Projected Growth for This Job): Federal Government (–5.5%); State Government (–1.9%); Insurance Carriers and Related Activities (4.6%); Health and Personal Care Stores (5.3%); Hospitals, Public and Private (9.9%); Educational Services, Public and Private (11.8%); Local Government (12.3%).

Fastest-Growing Metropolitan Areas (Recent Growth for This Job): Milwaukee–Waukesha–West Allis, WI (140.0%); Birmingham-Hoover, AL (75.0%); Austin–Round Rock, TX (60.0%); Indianapolis-Carmel, IN (60.0%); Oklahoma City, OK (42.9%).

Other Considerations for Job Security: Opportunities for individuals interested in becoming physicians and surgeons are expected to be very good. Unlike their predecessors, new physicians are much less likely to enter solo practice and more likely to take salaried jobs in group medical practices, clinics, and health networks. Reports of shortages in some specialties, such as general or family practice, internal medicine, and OB/GYN, or in rural or low-income areas should attract new entrants, encouraging schools to expand programs and hospitals to increase available residency slots. However, because physician training is so lengthy, employment change happens gradually. Opportunities should be particularly good in rural and low-income areas, as some physicians find these areas unattractive because of less control over work hours, isolation from medical colleagues, or other reasons.

Diagnose, treat, and help prevent diseases of women, especially those affecting the reproductive system and the process of childbirth. Care for and treat women during prenatal, natal, and post-natal periods. Explain procedures and discuss test results or prescribed treatments with patients. Treat diseases of female organs. Monitor patients' condition and progress and re-evaluate treatments as necessary. Perform cesarean sections or other surgical procedures as needed to preserve patients' health and deliver babies safely. Prescribe or administer therapy, medication, and other specialized medical care to treat or prevent illness, disease, or injury. Analyze records, reports, test results, or examination information to diagnose medical condition of patient. Collect, record, and maintain patient information, such as medical histories, reports, and examination results. Advise patients and community members concerning diet, activity, hygiene, and disease prevention. Refer patient to medical specialist or other practitioner when necessary. Consult with, or provide consulting services to, other physicians. Direct and coordinate activities of nurses, students, assistants, specialists, therapists, and other medical staff. Plan, implement, or administer health programs in hospitals, businesses, or communities for prevention and treatment of injuries or illnesses. Prepare government and organizational reports on birth, death, and disease statistics; workforce evaluations; or the medical status of individuals. Conduct research to develop or test medications, treatments, or procedures to prevent or control disease or injury.

Personality Type: Investigative. Investigative occupations frequently involve working with ideas and require an extensive amount of thinking. These occupations can involve searching for facts and figuring out problems mentally.

Career Cluster: 08 Health Science. **Career Pathway:** 08.1 Therapeutic Services.

Skills—Science: Using scientific rules and methods to solve problems. **Judgment and Decision Making:** Considering the relative costs and benefits of potential actions to choose the most appropriate one. **Reading Comprehension:** Understanding written sentences and paragraphs in work-related documents. **Complex Problem Solving:** Identifying complex problems and reviewing related information to develop and evaluate options and implement solutions. **Active Learning:** Understanding the implications of new information for both current and future problem-solving and decision-making. **Social Perceptiveness:** Being aware of others' reactions and understanding why they react as they do.

Related Knowledge/Courses—Medicine and Dentistry: The information and techniques needed to diagnose and treat injuries, diseases, and deformities. This includes symptoms, treatment alternatives, drug properties and interactions, and preventive health-care measures. **Therapy and Counseling:** Information and techniques needed to rehabilitate physical and mental ailments and to provide career guidance, including alternative treatments, rehabilitation equipment and its proper use, and methods to evaluate treatment effects. **Biology:** Plant and animal living tissue, cells, organisms, and entities, including their functions, interdependencies, and interactions with each other and the environment. **Psychology:** Human behavior and performance, mental processes, psychological research methods, and the assessment and treatment of behavioral and affective disorders. **Sociology and Anthropology:** Group behavior and dynamics; societal trends and influences; and cultures and their history, migrations, ethnicity, and origins. **Chemistry:** The composition, structure, and properties of substances and of the chemical processes and transformations that they undergo. This includes uses of chemicals and their interactions, danger signs, production techniques, and disposal methods.

Work Environment: Indoors; disease or infections; standing; using hands on objects, tools, or controls.

Occupational Therapists

Related Major: Occupational Therapy

- ✸ Education/Training Required: Master's degree
- ✸ Annual Earnings: $63,790
- ✸ Beginning Wage: $42,330
- ✸ Earnings Growth Potential: Low (33.6%)
- ✸ Growth: 23.1%
- ✸ Annual Job Openings: 8,338
- ✸ Self-Employed: 8.6%
- ✸ Part-Time: 29.8%

Industries with Greatest Employment: Hospitals, Public and Private (29.2%); Ambulatory Health Care Services (27.8%); Educational Services, Public and Private (12.7%); Nursing and Residential Care Facilities (9.9%); Social Assistance (5.2%).

Highest-Growth Industries (Projected Growth for This Job): Professional, Scientific, and Technical Services (64.0%); Social Assistance (38.0%); Ambulatory Health Care Services (37.2%); Administrative and Support Services (26.6%); Nursing and Residential Care Facilities (23.9%); Hospitals, Public and Private (21.5%); Management of Companies and Enterprises (15.3%).

Lowest-Growth Industries (Projected Growth for This Job): Federal Government (–5.5%); State Government (–1.9%); Insurance Carriers and

Related Activities (3.5%); Educational Services, Public and Private (6.5%); Local Government (12.4%); Religious, Grantmaking, Civic, Professional, and Similar Organizations (14.7%).

Fastest-Growing Metropolitan Areas (Recent Growth for This Job): Chattanooga, TN-GA (250.0%); Chico, CA (166.7%); Panama City–Lynn Haven, FL (125.0%); Fayetteville, NC (100.0%); Texarkana-Texarkana, TX-AR (100.0%).

Other Considerations for Job Security: Job opportunities should be good for licensed occupational therapists in all settings, particularly in acute hospital, rehabilitation, and orthopedic settings because the elderly receive most of their treatment in these settings. Occupational therapists with specialized knowledge in a treatment area also will have increased job prospects. Driver rehabilitation and fall-prevention training for the elderly are emerging practice areas for occupational therapy.

Assess, plan, organize, and participate in rehabilitative programs that help restore vocational, homemaking, and daily living skills, as well as general independence, to disabled persons. Plan, organize, and conduct occupational therapy programs in hospital, institutional, or community settings to help rehabilitate those impaired because of illness, injury, or psychological or developmental problems. Test and evaluate patients' physical and mental abilities and analyze medical data to determine realistic rehabilitation goals for patients. Select activities that will help individuals learn work and life-management skills within limits of their mental and physical capabilities. Evaluate patients' progress and prepare reports that detail progress. Complete and maintain necessary records. Train caregivers to provide for the needs of patients during and after therapies. Recommend changes in patients' work or living environments, consistent with their needs and capabilities. Develop and participate in health promotion programs, group activities, or discussions to promote client health, facilitate social adjustment, alleviate stress, and prevent physical or mental disability. Consult with rehabilitation team to select activity programs and coordinate occupational therapy with other therapeutic activities. Plan and implement programs and social activities to help patients learn work and school skills and adjust to handicaps. Design and create, or requisition, special supplies and equipment such as splints, braces, and computer-aided adaptive equipment. Conduct research in occupational therapy. Provide training and supervision in therapy techniques and objectives for students and nurses and other medical staff. Help clients improve decision making, abstract reasoning, memory, sequencing, coordination, and perceptual skills, using computer programs. Advise on health risks in the workplace and on health-related transition to retirement. Lay out materials such as puzzles, scissors, and eating utensils for use in therapy, and clean and repair these tools after therapy sessions. Provide patients with assistance in locating and holding jobs.

Personality Type: Social-Realistic. Social occupations frequently involve working with, communicating with, and teaching people. These occupations often involve helping or providing service to others.

Career Cluster: 08 Health Science. **Career Pathway:** 08.3 Health Informatics.

Skills—No data available.

Related Knowledge/Courses—Therapy and Counseling: Information and techniques needed to rehabilitate physical and mental ailments and to provide career guidance, including alternative treatments, rehabilitation equipment and its proper use, and methods to evaluate treatment effects. Psychology: Human behavior and performance, mental processes, psychological research methods, and the assessment and treatment of behavioral and affective disorders. Sociology and Anthropology: Group behavior and dynamics; societal trends and influences; and cultures and their history, migrations, ethnicity, and origins. Medicine and Dentistry: The information and techniques needed to diagnose and treat injuries, diseases, and deformities. This includes symptoms, treatment alternatives, drug properties and interactions, and preventive health-care measures. Biology: Plant and animal living tissue, cells, organisms, and entities, including their functions, interdependencies, and interactions with each other and the environment. Education and Training: Instructional methods and training techniques, including curriculum design principles, learning theory, group and individual teaching techniques, design of individual development plans, and test design principles.

Work Environment: Indoors; disease or infections; standing; using hands on objects, tools, or controls; bending or twisting the body.

Optometrists

Related Major: Optometry

- ❋ Education/Training Required: First professional degree
- ❋ Annual Earnings: $93,800
- ❋ Beginning Wage: $47,980
- ❋ Earnings Growth Potential: High (48.8%)
- ❋ Growth: 11.3%
- ❋ Annual Job Openings: 1,789
- ❋ Self-Employed: 25.5%
- ❋ Part-Time: 20.8%

Industries with Greatest Employment: Ambulatory Health Care Services (62.4%); Health and Personal Care Stores (7.8%).

Highest-Growth Industries (Projected Growth for This Job): Administrative and Support Services (23.6%); Ambulatory Health Care Services (16.4%).

Lowest-Growth Industries (Projected Growth for This Job): Federal Government (–8.4%); Miscellaneous Manufacturing (–1.6%); Health and Personal Care Stores (–0.4%); General Merchandise Stores (4.3%); Educational Services, Public and Private (7.9%); Hospitals, Public and Private (8.2%); Management of Companies and Enterprises (11.6%).

Fastest-Growing Metropolitan Areas (Recent Growth for This Job): Trenton-Ewing, NJ (100.0%); San Jose–Sunnyvale–Santa Clara, CA (85.0%); Colorado Springs, CO (83.3%); Phoenix-Mesa-Scottsdale, AZ (76.0%); Lansing–East Lansing, MI (60.0%).

Other Considerations for Job Security: Job opportunities for optometrists should be very good over the next decade. Demand is expected to be much higher, and because there are only 16 schools of optometry, the number of students who can get a degree in optometry is limited. In addition to growth, the need to replace optometrists who retire or leave the occupation for other reasons will create more employment opportunities.

Diagnose, manage, and treat conditions and diseases of the human eye and visual system. Examine eyes and visual systems, diagnose problems or impairments, prescribe corrective lenses, and provide treatment. May prescribe therapeutic drugs to treat specific eye conditions. Examine eyes, using observation, instruments, and pharmaceutical agents, to determine visual acuity and perception, focus, and coordination and to diagnose diseases and other abnormalities such as glaucoma or color blindness. Prescribe medications to treat eye diseases if state laws permit. Analyze test results and develop treatment plans. Prescribe, supply, fit, and adjust eyeglasses, contact lenses, and other vision aids. Educate and counsel patients on contact lens care, visual hygiene, lighting arrangements, and safety factors. Remove foreign bodies from eyes. Consult with and refer patients to ophthalmologist or other health-care practitioners if additional medical treatment is determined necessary. Provide patients undergoing eye surgeries such as cataract and laser vision correction, with pre- and post-operative care. Prescribe therapeutic procedures to correct or conserve vision. Provide vision therapy and low vision rehabilitation.

Personality Type: Investigative-Realistic. Investigative occupations frequently involve working with ideas and require an extensive amount of thinking. These occupations can involve searching for facts and figuring out problems mentally.

Career Cluster: 08 Health Science. **Career Pathway:** 08.1 Therapeutic Services.

Skills—No data available.

Related Knowledge/Courses—Medicine and Dentistry: The information and techniques needed to diagnose and treat injuries, diseases, and deformities. This includes symptoms, treatment alternatives, drug properties and interactions, and preventive health-care measures. **Biology:** Plant and animal living tissue, cells, organisms, and entities, including their functions, interdependencies, and interactions with each other and the environment. **Therapy and Counseling:** Information and techniques needed to rehabilitate physical and mental ailments and to provide career guidance, including alternative treatments, rehabilitation equipment and its proper use, and methods to evaluate treatment effects. **Physics:** Physical principles, laws, and applications, including air, water, material dynamics, light, atomic principles, heat, electric theory, earth formations, and meteorological and related natural phenomena. **Sales and Marketing:** Principles and methods involved in showing, promoting, and selling products or services. This includes marketing strategies and tactics, product demonstration and sales techniques, and sales control systems. **Economics and Accounting:** Economic and accounting principles and practices, the financial markets, banking, and the analysis and reporting of financial data.

Work Environment: Indoors; disease or infections; sitting; using hands on objects, tools, or controls.

Pediatricians, General

Related Major: Medicine

* ❋ Education/Training Required: First professional degree
* ❋ Annual Earnings: $140,690
* ❋ Beginning Wage: $67,430
* ❋ Earnings Growth Potential: Very high (52.1%)
* ❋ Growth: 14.2%
* ❋ Annual Job Openings: 38,027
* ❋ Self-Employed: 14.7%
* ❋ Part-Time: 8.1%

Industries with Greatest Employment: Ambulatory Health Care Services (55.9%); Hospitals, Public and Private (17.8%).

Highest-Growth Industries (Projected Growth for This Job): Social Assistance (58.6%); Administrative and Support Services (26.8%); Professional, Scientific, and Technical Services (22.6%); Nursing and Residential Care Facilities (21.0%); Ambulatory Health Care Services (19.4%); Religious, Grantmaking, Civic, Professional, and Similar Organizations (16.7%); Management of Companies and Enterprises (15.3%).

Lowest-Growth Industries (Projected Growth for This Job): Federal Government (–5.5%); State Government (–1.9%); Insurance Carriers and Related Activities (4.6%); Health and Personal Care Stores (5.3%); Hospitals, Public and Private (9.9%); Educational Services, Public and Private (11.8%); Local Government (12.3%).

Fastest-Growing Metropolitan Areas (Recent Growth for This Job): Sacramento–Arden-Arcade–Roseville, CA (114.3%); Milwaukee–Waukesha–West Allis, WI (83.3%); Memphis, TN-MS-AR (68.8%); Dallas–Fort Worth–Arlington, TX (53.3%); San Francisco–Oakland–Fremont, CA (47.5%).

Other Considerations for Job Security: Opportunities for individuals interested in becoming physicians and surgeons are expected to be very good. Unlike their predecessors, new physicians are much less likely to enter solo practice and more likely to take salaried jobs in group medical practices, clinics, and health networks. Reports of shortages in some specialties, such as general or family practice, internal medicine, and OB/GYN, or in rural or low-income areas should attract new entrants, encouraging schools to expand programs and hospitals to increase available residency slots. However, because physician training is so lengthy, employment change happens gradually. Opportunities should be particularly good in rural and low-income areas, as some physicians find these areas unattractive because of less control over work hours, isolation from medical colleagues, or other reasons.

Diagnose, treat, and help prevent children's diseases and injuries. Examine patients or order, perform, and interpret diagnostic tests to obtain information on medical condition and determine diagnosis. Examine children regularly to assess their growth and development. Prescribe or administer treatment, therapy, medication, vaccination, and other specialized medical care to treat or prevent illness, disease, or injury in infants and children. Collect, record, and maintain patient information, such as medical history, reports, and examination results. Advise patients, parents or guardians, and community members concerning diet, activity, hygiene, and disease prevention. Treat children who have minor illnesses, acute and chronic health problems, and growth and development concerns. Explain procedures and discuss test results or prescribed treatments with patients and parents or guardians. Monitor patients' condition and progress and re-evaluate treatments as necessary. Plan and execute medical care programs to aid in the mental and physical growth and development of children and adolescents. Refer patients to medical specialists or other practitioners when necessary. Direct and coordinate activities of nurses, students, assistants, specialists, therapists, and other medical staff. Provide consulting services to other physicians. Plan, implement, or administer health programs or standards in hospital, business, or community for information, prevention, or treatment of injury or illness. Operate on patients to remove, repair, or improve functioning of diseased or injured body parts and systems. Conduct research to study anatomy and develop or test medications, treatments, or procedures to prevent or control disease or injury. Prepare reports for government or management of birth, death, and disease statistics; workforce evaluations; or medical status of individuals.

Personality Type: Investigative. Investigative occupations frequently involve working with ideas and require an extensive amount of thinking. These occupations can involve searching for facts and figuring out problems mentally.

Career Cluster: 08 Health Science. **Career Pathway:** 08.1 Therapeutic Services.

Skills—Science: Using scientific rules and methods to solve problems. **Social Perceptiveness:** Being aware of others' reactions and understanding why they react as they do. **Active Learning:** Understanding the implications of new information for both current and future problem-solving and decision-making. **Reading Comprehension:** Understanding written

sentences and paragraphs in work-related documents. **Persuasion:** Persuading others to change their minds or behavior. **Critical Thinking:** Using logic and reasoning to identify the strengths and weaknesses of alternative solutions, conclusions, or approaches to problems.

Related Knowledge/Courses—Medicine and Dentistry: The information and techniques needed to diagnose and treat injuries, diseases, and deformities. This includes symptoms, treatment alternatives, drug properties and interactions, and preventive health-care measures. **Therapy and Counseling:** Information and techniques needed to rehabilitate physical and mental ailments and to provide career guidance, including alternative treatments, rehabilitation equipment and its proper use, and methods to evaluate treatment effects. **Biology:** Plant and animal living tissue, cells, organisms, and entities, including their functions, interdependencies, and interactions with each other and the environment. **Psychology:** Human behavior and performance, mental processes, psychological research methods, and the assessment and treatment of behavioral and affective disorders. **Chemistry:** The composition, structure, and properties of substances and of the chemical processes and transformations that they undergo. This includes uses of chemicals and their interactions, danger signs, production techniques, and disposal methods. **Sociology and Anthropology:** Group behavior and dynamics; societal trends and influences; and cultures and their history, migrations, ethnicity, and origins.

Work Environment: Indoors; disease or infections; standing; using hands on objects, tools, or controls.

Pharmacists

Related Major: Pharmacy

- ❋ Education/Training Required: First professional degree
- ❋ Annual Earnings: $100,480
- ❋ Beginning Wage: $73,010
- ❋ Earnings Growth Potential: Low (27.3%)
- ❋ Growth: 21.7%
- ❋ Annual Job Openings: 16,358
- ❋ Self-Employed: 0.5%
- ❋ Part-Time: 18.1%

Industries with Greatest Employment: Health and Personal Care Stores (44.1%); Hospitals, Public and Private (23.2%); General Merchandise Stores (9.6%); Food and Beverage Stores (8.3%).

Highest-Growth Industries (Projected Growth for This Job): Social Assistance (62.8%); Nonstore Retailers (50.1%); Professional, Scientific, and Technical Services (48.3%); Warehousing and Storage (33.7%); Ambulatory Health Care Services (31.7%); Administrative and Support Services (27.8%); General Merchandise Stores (26.2%); Chemical Manufacturing (26.0%); Health and Personal Care Stores (22.1%); Hospitals, Public and Private (21.1%); Food and Beverage Stores (20.0%); Merchant Wholesalers, Nondurable Goods (18.9%); Religious, Grantmaking, Civic, Professional, and Similar Organizations (18.8%); Nursing and Residential Care Facilities (17.2%); Merchant Wholesalers, Durable Goods (16.6%); Management of Companies and Enterprises (15.2%).

Lowest-Growth Industries (Projected Growth for This Job): Federal Government (–5.5%); State Government (–1.9%); Rental and Leasing Services (11.0%); Educational Services, Public and Private (11.9%); Local Government (12.3%); Wholesale Electronic Markets and Agents and Brokers (13.5%).

Fastest-Growing Metropolitan Areas (Recent Growth for This Job): Abilene, TX (100.0%); Grand Forks, ND-MN (66.7%); Sheboygan, WI (66.7%); Oshkosh-Neenah, WI (62.5%); Ames, IA (50.0%).

Other Considerations for Job Security: Excellent opportunities are expected for pharmacists over the 2006 to 2016 period. Job openings will result from rapid employment growth and from the need to replace workers who retire or leave the occupation for other reasons. As the use of prescription drugs increases, demand for pharmacists will grow in most practice settings, such as community pharmacies, hospital pharmacies, and mail-order pharmacies. As the population ages, assisted living facilities and home care organizations should see particularly rapid growth. Demand will also increase as cost-conscious insurers, in an attempt to improve preventative care, use pharmacists in areas such as patient education and vaccination administration.

Compound and dispense medications, following prescriptions issued by physicians, dentists, or other authorized medical practitioners. Review prescriptions to assure accuracy, to ascertain the needed ingredients, and to evaluate their suitability. Provide information and advice regarding drug interactions, side effects, dosage, and proper medication storage. Analyze prescribing trends to monitor patient compliance and to prevent excessive usage or harmful interactions. Order and purchase pharmaceutical supplies, medical supplies, and drugs, maintaining stock and storing and handling it properly.

P

Maintain records, such as pharmacy files; patient profiles; charge system files; inventories; control records for radioactive nuclei; and registries of poisons, narcotics, and controlled drugs. Provide specialized services to help patients manage conditions such as diabetes, asthma, smoking cessation, or high blood pressure. Advise customers on the selection of medication brands, medical equipment, and health-care supplies. Collaborate with other health-care professionals to plan, monitor, review, and evaluate the quality and effectiveness of drugs and drug regimens, providing advice on drug applications and characteristics. Compound and dispense medications as prescribed by doctors and dentists by calculating, weighing, measuring, and mixing ingredients or oversee these activities. Offer health promotion and prevention activities—for example, training people to use devices such as blood-pressure or diabetes monitors. Refer patients to other health professionals and agencies when appropriate. Prepare sterile solutions and infusions for use in surgical procedures, emergency rooms, or patients' homes. Plan, implement, and maintain procedures for mixing, packaging, and labeling pharmaceuticals according to policy and legal requirements to ensure quality, security, and proper disposal. Assay radiopharmaceuticals, verify rates of disintegration, and calculate the volume required to produce the desired results to ensure proper dosages. Manage pharmacy operations, hiring and supervising staff, performing administrative duties, and buying and selling nonpharmaceutical merchandise. Work in hospitals, clinics, or for health maintenance organizations (HMOs), dispensing prescriptions, serving as a medical team consultant, or specializing in specific drug therapy areas such as oncology or nuclear pharmacotherapy.

Personality Type: Investigative-Conventional-Realistic. Investigative occupations frequently involve working with ideas and require an extensive amount of thinking. These occupations can involve searching for facts and figuring out problems mentally.

Career Cluster: 08 Health Science. **Career Pathways:** 08.1 Therapeutic Services; 08.5 Biotechnology Research and Development.

Skills—Science: Using scientific rules and methods to solve problems. **Reading Comprehension:** Understanding written sentences and paragraphs in work-related documents. **Social Perceptiveness:** Being aware of others' reactions and understanding why they react as they do. **Active Listening:** Giving full attention to what other people are saying, taking time to understand the points being made, asking questions as appropriate, and not interrupting at inappropriate times. **Instructing:** Teaching others how to do something. **Mathematics:** Using mathematics to solve problems.

Related Knowledge/Courses—Medicine and Dentistry: The information and techniques needed to diagnose and treat injuries, diseases, and deformities. This includes symptoms, treatment alternatives, drug properties and interactions, and preventive health-care measures. **Chemistry:** The composition, structure, and properties of substances and of the chemical processes and transformations that they undergo. This includes uses of chemicals and their interactions, danger signs, production techniques, and disposal methods. **Therapy and Counseling:** Information and techniques needed to rehabilitate physical and mental ailments and to provide career guidance, including alternative treatments, rehabilitation equipment and its proper use, and methods to evaluate treatment effects. **Biology:** Plant and animal living tissue, cells, organisms, and entities, including their functions, interdependencies, and interactions with each other and the environment. **Psychology:** Human behavior and performance, mental processes, psychological research methods, and the assessment and treatment of behavioral and affective disorders. **Mathematics:** Numbers and their operations and interrelationships, including arithmetic, algebra, geometry, calculus, and statistics and their applications.

Work Environment: Indoors; disease or infections; standing; repetitive motions.

Philosophy and Religion Teachers, Postsecondary

Related Major: Graduate Study for College Teaching

- ※ Education/Training Required: Master's degree
- ※ Annual Earnings: $56,380
- ※ Beginning Wage: $32,640
- ※ Earnings Growth Potential: High (42.1%)
- ※ Growth: 22.9%
- ※ Annual Job Openings: 3,120
- ※ Self-Employed: 0.4%
- ※ Part-Time: 27.8%

Industries with Greatest Employment: Educational Services, Public and Private (97.3%).

Highest-Growth Industries (Projected Growth for This Job): Administrative and Support Services (48.3%); Amusement, Gambling, and Recreation Industries (45.2%); Social Assistance (38.6%); Support Activities for Transportation (32.8%); Religious, Grantmaking, Civic, Professional, and Similar Organizations (29.9%); Professional, Scientific, and Technical Services (28.8%); Management of Companies and Enterprises (26.8%); Local Government (23.5%); Educational Services, Public and Private (22.8%); Hospitals, Public and Private (21.4%).

Lowest-Growth Industries (Projected Growth for This Job): Other Information Services (7.4%); State Government (7.9%); Sporting Goods, Hobby, Book, and Music Stores (13.3%); Performing Arts, Spectator Sports, and Related Industries (13.4%); Insurance Carriers and Related Activities (13.8%).

Fastest-Growing Metropolitan Areas (Recent Growth for This Job): Phoenix-Mesa-Scottsdale, AZ (80.0%); New York–Northern New Jersey–Long Island, NY-NJ-PA (51.9%); San Antonio, TX (50.0%); Detroit-Warren-Livonia, MI (42.9%); Riverside–San Bernardino–Ontario, CA (42.9%).

Other Considerations for Job Security: Retirements of current postsecondary teachers should create numerous openings for all types of postsecondary teachers, so job opportunities are generally expected to be very good. However, one of the main reasons why students attend postsecondary institutions is to prepare themselves for careers, so the best job prospects for postsecondary teachers are likely to be in rapidly growing fields that offer many nonacademic career options, unlike philosophy and religious studies. Community colleges and other institutions offering career and technical education have been among the most rapidly growing, and these institutions are expected to offer some of the best opportunities for postsecondary teachers.

Teach courses in philosophy, religion, and theology. Evaluate and grade students' classwork, assignments, and papers. Initiate, facilitate, and moderate classroom discussions. Prepare and deliver lectures to undergraduate and graduate students on topics such as ethics, logic, and contemporary religious thought. Prepare course materials such as syllabi, homework assignments, and handouts. Compile, administer, and grade examinations or assign this work to others. Keep abreast of developments in their field by reading current literature, talking with colleagues, and participating in professional conferences. Maintain student attendance records, grades, and other required records. Plan, evaluate, and revise curricula, course content, and course materials and methods of instruction. Maintain regularly scheduled office hours to advise and assist students. Select and obtain materials and supplies such as textbooks. Advise students on academic and vocational curricula and on career issues. Conduct research in a particular field of knowledge and publish findings in professional journals, books, or electronic media. Perform administrative duties such as serving as department head. Serve on academic or administrative committees that deal with institutional policies, departmental matters, and academic issues. Collaborate with colleagues to address teaching and research issues. Participate in campus and community events. Participate in student recruitment, registration, and placement activities. Compile bibliographies of specialized materials for outside reading assignments. Supervise undergraduate and graduate teaching, internship, and research work. Act as advisers to student organizations. Write grant proposals to procure external research funding. Provide professional consulting services to government or industry.

Personality Type: No data available.

Career Clusters: 10 Human Services; 15 Science, Technology, Engineering, and Mathematics. **Career Pathways:** 10.2 Counseling and Mental Health Services; 15.3 Science and Mathematics.

Skills—Writing: Communicating effectively in writing as appropriate for the needs of the audience. **Instructing:** Teaching others how to do something. **Reading Comprehension:** Understanding written sentences and paragraphs in work-related documents. **Critical Thinking:** Using logic and reasoning to identify the strengths and weaknesses of alternative solutions, conclusions, or approaches to problems. **Speaking:** Talking to others to convey information effectively. **Learning Strategies:** Selecting and using training/instructional methods and procedures appropriate for the situation when learning or teaching new things.

Related Knowledge/Courses—Philosophy and Theology: Different philosophical systems and religions, including their basic principles, values, ethics, ways of thinking, customs, and practices and their impact on human culture. **History and Archeology:** Historical events and their causes, indicators, and impact on particular civilizations and cultures. **Sociology and Anthropology:** Group behavior and dynamics; societal trends and influences; and cultures and their history, migrations, ethnicity, and origins. **Foreign Language:** The structure and content of a foreign (non-English) language, including the meaning and spelling of words, rules of composition and grammar, and pronunciation. **English Language:** The structure and content of the English language, including the meaning and spelling of words, rules of composition, and grammar. **Education and Training:** Instructional methods and training techniques, including curriculum design principles, learning theory, group and individual teaching techniques, design of individual development plans, and test design principles.

Work Environment: Indoors; sitting.

Physical Therapists

Related Major: Physical Therapy

- ⊛ Education/Training Required: Master's degree
- ⊛ Annual Earnings: $69,760
- ⊛ Beginning Wage: $48,530
- ⊛ Earnings Growth Potential: Low (30.4%)
- ⊛ Growth: 27.1%
- ⊛ Annual Job Openings: 12,072
- ⊛ Self-Employed: 8.4%
- ⊛ Part-Time: 22.7%

Industries with Greatest Employment: Ambulatory Health Care Services (44.2%); Hospitals, Public and Private (30.5%); Nursing and Residential Care Facilities (6.9%).

Highest-Growth Industries (Projected Growth for This Job): Social Assistance (39.7%); Ambulatory Health Care Services (37.2%); Amusement, Gambling, and Recreation Industries (33.0%); Administrative and Support Services (26.6%); Nursing and Residential Care Facilities (23.8%); Hospitals, Public and Private (22.1%); Management of Companies and Enterprises (15.2%).

Lowest-Growth Industries (Projected Growth for This Job): Federal Government (–5.5%); State Government (–1.8%); Educational Services, Public and Private (7.5%); Local Government (12.4%).

Fastest-Growing Metropolitan Areas (Recent Growth for This Job): Lawrence, KS (125.0%); Valdosta, GA (125.0%); Harrisonburg, VA (100.0%); Honolulu, HI (89.2%); Kingsport-Bristol, TN-VA (87.5%).

Other Considerations for Job Security: Job opportunities will be good for licensed physical therapists in all settings. Job opportunities should be particularly good in acute hospital, rehabilitation, and orthopedic settings, where the elderly are most often treated. Physical therapists with specialized knowledge of particular types of treatment also will have excellent job prospects. The increasing elderly population will drive growth in the demand for physical therapy services. The elderly population is particularly vulnerable to chronic and debilitating conditions that require therapeutic services. Also, the baby-boom generation is entering the prime age for heart attacks and strokes, increasing the demand for cardiac and physical rehabilitation. And increasing numbers of children will need physical therapy as technological advances save the lives of a larger proportion of newborns with severe birth defects.

Assess, plan, organize, and participate in rehabilitative programs that improve mobility, relieve pain, increase strength, and decrease or prevent deformity of patients suffering from disease or injury. Perform and document initial exams, evaluating data to identify problems and determine diagnoses prior to interventions. Plan, prepare, and carry out individually designed programs of physical treatment to maintain, improve, or restore physical functioning; alleviate pain; and prevent physical dysfunction in patients. Record prognoses, treatments, responses, and progresses in patients' charts or enter information into computers. Identify and document goals, anticipated progresses, and plans for reevaluation. Evaluate effects of treatments at various stages and adjust treatments to achieve maximum benefits. Administer manual exercises, massages, or traction to help relieve pain, increase patient strength, or decrease or prevent deformity or crippling. Test and measure patients' strength, motor development and function, sensory perception, functional capacity, and respiratory and circulatory efficiency and record data. Instruct patients and families in treatment procedures to be continued at home. Confer with patients, medical practitioners, and appropriate others to plan, implement, and assess intervention programs. Review physicians' referrals and patients' medical records to help determine diagnoses and physical therapy treatments required. Obtain patients' informed consent to proposed interventions. Discharge patients from physical therapy when goals or projected outcomes have been attained and provide for appropriate follow-up care or referrals. Provide information to patients about proposed interventions, material risks, and expected benefits and any reasonable alternatives. Inform patients when diagnoses reveal findings outside the scope of physical therapy to treat and refer to appropriate practitioners. Direct, supervise, assess, and communicate with supportive personnel. Provide educational information about physical therapy and physical therapists, injury prevention, ergonomics, and ways to promote health. Refer clients to community resources and services. Administer treatment involving application of physical agents, using equipment, moist packs, ultraviolet and infrared lamps, and ultrasound machines.

Personality Type: Social-Realistic-Investigative. Social occupations frequently involve working with, communicating with, and teaching people. These occupations often involve helping or providing service to others.

Career Cluster: 08 Health Science. **Career Pathway:** 08.3 Health Informatics.

Skills—No data available.

Related Knowledge/Courses—Therapy and Counseling: Information and techniques needed to rehabilitate physical and mental ailments and to provide career guidance, including alternative treatments, rehabilitation equipment and its proper use, and methods to evaluate treatment effects. **Medicine and Dentistry:** The information and techniques needed to diagnose and treat injuries, diseases, and deformities. This includes symptoms, treatment alternatives, drug properties and interactions, and preventive healthcare measures. **Psychology:** Human behavior and performance, mental processes, psychological research methods, and the assessment and treatment of behavioral and affective disorders. **Education and Training:** Instructional methods and training techniques, including curriculum design principles, learning theory, group and individual teaching techniques, design of individual development plans, and test design principles. **Biology:** Plant and animal living tissue, cells, organisms, and entities, including their functions, interdependencies, and interactions with each other and the environment. **Customer and Personal Service:** Principles and processes for providing customer and personal services, including needs assessment techniques, quality service standards, alternative delivery systems, and customer satisfaction evaluation techniques.

Work Environment: Indoors; disease or infections; standing.

Physician Assistants

Related Major: Physician Assisting

- ❋ Education/Training Required: Bachelor's degree
- ❋ Annual Earnings: $78,450
- ❋ Beginning Wage: $46,750
- ❋ Earnings Growth Potential: High (40.4%)
- ❋ Growth: 27.0%
- ❋ Annual Job Openings: 7,147
- ❋ Self-Employed: 1.8%
- ❋ Part-Time: 15.6%

Industries with Greatest Employment: Ambulatory Health Care Services (64.0%); Hospitals, Public and Private (23.6%).

Highest-Growth Industries (Projected Growth for This Job): Ambulatory Health Care Services (36.5%); Administrative and Support Services (26.9%); Management of Companies and Enterprises (15.2%).

Lowest-Growth Industries (Projected Growth for This Job): Federal Government (–5.5%); State Government (–2.0%); Hospitals, Public and Private (10.7%); Educational Services, Public and Private (11.9%); Local Government (12.4%); Professional, Scientific, and Technical Services (13.4%).

Fastest-Growing Metropolitan Areas (Recent Growth for This Job): San Luis Obispo–Paso Robles, CA (175.0%); Champaign-Urbana, IL (166.7%); Provo-Orem, UT (150.0%); Knoxville, TN (106.7%); Johnson City, TN (100.0%).

Other Considerations for Job Security: Job opportunities for PAs should be good, particularly in rural and inner-city clinics because those settings have difficulty attracting physicians.

In addition to job openings from employment growth, openings will result from the need to replace physician assistants who retire or leave the occupation permanently during the 2006–2016 decade. Opportunities will be best in states that allow PAs a wider scope of practice, such as allowing PAs to prescribe medications. Physicians and institutions are expected to employ more PAs to provide primary care and to assist with medical and surgical procedures because PAs are cost-effective and productive members of the health-care team. Physician assistants can relieve physicians of routine duties and procedures. Telemedicine—using technology to facilitate interactive consultations between physicians and physician assistants—also will expand the use of physician assistants.

Under the supervision of physicians, provide health-care services typically performed by a physician. Conduct complete physicals, provide treatment, and counsel patients. May, in some cases, prescribe medication. Must graduate from an accredited educational program for physician assistants. Examine patients to obtain information about their physical conditions. Obtain, compile, and record patient medical data, including health history, progress notes, and results of physical examinations. Interpret diagnostic test results for deviations from normal. Make tentative diagnoses and decisions about management and treatment of patients. Prescribe therapy or medication with physician approval. Administer or order diagnostic tests, such as X-ray, electrocardiogram, and laboratory tests. Instruct and counsel patients about prescribed therapeutic regimens, normal growth and development, family planning, emotional problems of daily living, and health maintenance. Perform therapeutic procedures such as injections, immunizations, suturing and wound care, and infection management. Provide physicians with assistance during surgery or complicated medical procedures. Visit and observe patients on hospital rounds or house calls, updating charts, ordering therapy, and reporting back to physicians. Supervise and coordinate activities of technicians and technical assistants. Order medical and laboratory supplies and equipment.

Personality Type: Investigative-Social. Investigative occupations frequently involve working with ideas and require an extensive amount of thinking. These occupations can involve searching for facts and figuring out problems mentally.

Career Cluster: 08 Health Science. **Career Pathway:** 08.2 Diagnostics Services.

Skills—Social Perceptiveness: Being aware of others' reactions and understanding why they react as they do. **Systems Analysis:** Determining how a system should work and how changes in conditions, operations, and the environment will affect outcomes. **Systems Evaluation:** Identifying measures or indicators of system performance and the actions needed to improve or correct performance relative to the goals of the system. **Persuasion:** Persuading others to change their minds or behavior. **Complex Problem Solving:** Identifying complex problems and reviewing related information to develop and evaluate options and implement solutions. **Reading Comprehension:** Understanding written sentences and paragraphs in work-related documents.

Related Knowledge/Courses—Medicine and Dentistry: The information and techniques needed to diagnose and treat injuries, diseases, and deformities. This includes symptoms, treatment alternatives, drug properties and interactions, and preventive health-care measures.

Biology: Plant and animal living tissue, cells, organisms, and entities, including their functions, interdependencies, and interactions with each other and the environment. **Therapy and Counseling:** Information and techniques needed to rehabilitate physical and mental ailments and to provide career guidance, including alternative treatments, rehabilitation equipment and its proper use, and methods to evaluate treatment effects. **Psychology:** Human behavior and performance, mental processes, psychological research methods, and the assessment and treatment of behavioral and affective disorders. **Chemistry:** The composition, structure, and properties of substances and of the chemical processes and transformations that they undergo. This includes uses of chemicals and their interactions, danger signs, production techniques, and disposal methods. **Sociology and Anthropology:** Group behavior and dynamics; societal trends and influences; and cultures and their history, migrations, ethnicity, and origins.

Work Environment: Indoors; disease or infections; standing; using hands on objects, tools, or controls.

Physicians and Surgeons, All Other

Related Major: Medicine

- ✱ Education/Training Required: First professional degree
- ✱ Annual Earnings: More than $145,600
- ✱ Beginning Wage: $47,930
- ✱ Earnings Growth Potential: Cannot be calculated
- ✱ Growth: 14.2%
- ✱ Annual Job Openings: 38,027
- ✱ Self-Employed: 14.7%
- ✱ Part-Time: 8.1%

Industries with Greatest Employment: Ambulatory Health Care Services (55.9%); Hospitals, Public and Private (17.8%).

Highest-Growth Industries (Projected Growth for This Job): Social Assistance (58.6%); Administrative and Support Services (26.8%); Professional, Scientific, and Technical Services (22.6%); Nursing and Residential Care Facilities (21.0%); Ambulatory Health Care Services (19.4%); Religious, Grantmaking, Civic, Professional, and Similar Organizations (16.7%); Management of Companies and Enterprises (15.3%).

Lowest-Growth Industries (Projected Growth for This Job): Federal Government (–5.5%); State Government (–1.9%); Insurance Carriers and Related Activities (4.6%); Health and Personal Care Stores (5.3%); Hospitals, Public and Private (9.9%); Educational Services, Public and Private (11.8%); Local Government (12.3%).

Fastest-Growing Metropolitan Areas (Recent Growth for This Job): Lubbock, TX (525.0%); Tyler, TX (300.0%); Raleigh-Cary, NC (206.7%); Peoria, IL (164.3%); McAllen-Edinburg-Mission, TX (160.0%).

Other Considerations for Job Security: Opportunities for individuals interested in becoming physicians and surgeons are expected to be very good. Unlike their predecessors, new physicians are much less likely to enter solo practice and more likely to take salaried jobs in group medical practices, clinics, and health networks. Reports of shortages in some specialties, such as general or family practice, internal medicine, and OB/GYN, or in rural or low-income areas should attract new entrants, encouraging schools to expand programs and hospitals to increase available residency slots. However, because physician training is so lengthy, employment change happens gradually. Opportunities should be particularly good in rural and low-income areas, as some physicians find these areas unattractive because of less control over work hours, isolation from medical colleagues, or other reasons.

All physicians and surgeons not listed separately. No task data available.

Personality Type: No data available.

Career Cluster: 08 Health Science. **Career Pathway:** 08.1 Therapeutic Services.

Skills—No data available.

Related Knowledge/Courses—No data available.

Work Environment: No data available.

P

Physics Teachers, Postsecondary

Related Major: Graduate Study for College Teaching

- ❈ Education/Training Required: Master's degree
- ❈ Annual Earnings: $70,090
- ❈ Beginning Wage: $40,580
- ❈ Earnings Growth Potential: High (42.1%)
- ❈ Growth: 22.9%
- ❈ Annual Job Openings: 2,155
- ❈ Self-Employed: 0.4%
- ❈ Part-Time: 27.8%

Industries with Greatest Employment: Educational Services, Public and Private (97.3%).

Highest-Growth Industries (Projected Growth for This Job): Administrative and Support Services (48.3%); Amusement, Gambling, and Recreation Industries (45.2%); Social Assistance (38.6%); Support Activities for Transportation (32.8%); Religious, Grantmaking, Civic, Professional, and Similar Organizations (29.9%); Professional, Scientific, and Technical Services (28.8%); Management of Companies and Enterprises (26.8%); Local Government (23.5%); Educational Services, Public and Private (22.8%); Hospitals, Public and Private (21.4%).

Lowest-Growth Industries (Projected Growth for This Job): Other Information Services (7.4%); State Government (7.9%); Sporting Goods, Hobby, Book, and Music Stores (13.3%); Performing Arts, Spectator Sports, and Related Industries (13.4%); Insurance Carriers and Related Activities (13.8%).

Fastest-Growing Metropolitan Areas (Recent Growth for This Job): Indianapolis-Carmel, IN (33.3%); Virginia Beach–Norfolk–Newport News, VA-NC (27.3%); Washington-Arlington-Alexandria, DC-VA-MD-WV (25.6%); Harrisburg-Carlisle, PA (25.0%); New York–Northern New Jersey–Long Island, NY-NJ-PA (22.9%).

Other Considerations for Job Security: Retirements of current postsecondary teachers should create numerous openings for all types of postsecondary teachers, so job opportunities are generally expected to be very good. One of the main reasons why students attend postsecondary institutions is to prepare themselves for careers, so the best job prospects for postsecondary teachers are likely to be in rapidly growing fields that offer many nonacademic career options. Physics is a key part of the curriculum for many technician majors and some health-care majors. Community colleges and other institutions offering career and technical education have been among the most rapidly growing, and these institutions are expected to offer some of the best opportunities for postsecondary teachers.

Teach courses pertaining to the laws of matter and energy. Includes both teachers primarily engaged in teaching and those who do a combination of both teaching and research. Evaluate and grade students' classwork, laboratory work, assignments, and papers. Prepare and deliver lectures to undergraduate and/or graduate students on topics such as quantum mechanics, particle physics, and optics. Compile, administer, and grade examinations or assign this work to others. Maintain student attendance records, grades, and other required records. Supervise students' laboratory work. Prepare course materials such as syllabi, homework assignments, and handouts. Maintain regularly scheduled office hours to advise and assist students. Supervise undergraduate and/or graduate teaching, internship, and research work. Keep abreast of developments in their field by reading current literature, talking with colleagues, and participating in professional conferences. Plan, evaluate, and revise curricula, course content, and course materials and methods of instruction. Initiate, facilitate, and moderate classroom discussions. Conduct research in a particular field of knowledge and publish findings in professional journals, books, and/or electronic media. Advise students on academic and vocational curricula and on career issues. Select and obtain materials and supplies such as textbooks and laboratory equipment. Collaborate with colleagues to address teaching and research issues. Participate in student recruitment, registration, and placement activities. Serve on academic or administrative committees that deal with institutional policies, departmental matters, and academic issues. Write grant proposals to procure external research funding. Perform administrative duties such as serving as department head. Act as advisers to student organizations. Provide professional consulting services to government and/or industry. Compile bibliographies of specialized materials for outside reading assignments. Participate in campus and community events.

Personality Type: Investigative-Social-Realistic. Investigative occupations frequently involve working with ideas and require an extensive amount of thinking. These occupations can involve searching for facts and figuring out problems mentally.

Career Cluster: 15 Science, Technology, Engineering, and Mathematics. **Career Pathway:** 15.3 Science and Mathematics.

Skills—Science: Using scientific rules and methods to solve problems. **Programming:** Writing computer programs for various purposes. **Mathematics:** Using mathematics to solve problems. **Instructing:** Teaching others how to do something. **Writing:** Communicating effectively in writing as appropriate for the needs of the audience. **Reading Comprehension:** Understanding written sentences and paragraphs in work-related documents.

Related Knowledge/Courses—Physics: Physical principles, laws, and applications, including air, water, material dynamics, light, atomic principles, heat, electric theory, earth formations, and meteorological and related natural phenomena. **Mathematics:** Numbers and their operations and interrelationships, including arithmetic, algebra, geometry, calculus, and statistics and their applications. **Chemistry:** The composition, structure, and properties of substances and of the chemical processes and transformations that they undergo. This includes uses of chemicals and their interactions, danger signs, production techniques, and disposal methods. **Engineering and Technology:** Equipment, tools, and mechanical devices and their uses to produce motion, light, power, technology, and other applications. **Education and Training:** Instructional methods and training techniques, including curriculum design principles, learning theory, group and individual teaching techniques, design of individual development plans, and test design principles. **Computers and Electronics:** Electric circuit boards, processors, chips, and computer hardware and software, including applications and programming.

Work Environment: Indoors; sitting.

Podiatrists

Related Major: Podiatry

- ❀ Education/Training Required: First professional degree
- ❀ Annual Earnings: $110,510
- ❀ Beginning Wage: $45,260
- ❀ Earnings Growth Potential: Very high (59.0%)
- ❀ Growth: 9.5%
- ❀ Annual Job Openings: 648
- ❀ Self-Employed: 23.9%
- ❀ Part-Time: 23.6%

Industries with Greatest Employment: Ambulatory Health Care Services (67.0%); Federal Government (5.0%).

Highest-Growth Industries (Projected Growth for This Job): None met the criteria.

Lowest-Growth Industries (Projected Growth for This Job): Federal Government (–5.5%); Ambulatory Health Care Services (4.4%); Hospitals, Public and Private (9.5%).

Fastest-Growing Metropolitan Areas (Recent Growth for This Job): Tucson, AZ (233.3%); Scranton–Wilkes-Barre, PA (80.0%); Boston-Cambridge-Quincy, MA-NH (75.0%); Nashville–Davidson County–Murfreesboro, TN (75.0%); Virginia Beach–Norfolk–Newport News, VA-NC (75.0%).

Other Considerations for Job Security: Although the occupation is small and most podiatrists continue to practice until retirement, job opportunities should be good for entry-level graduates of accredited podiatric medicine programs. Job growth and replacement needs should create enough job openings for the supply of new podiatric medicine graduates. Opportunities will be better for board-certified podiatrists because many managed-care organizations require board certification. Newly trained podiatrists will find more opportunities in group medical practices, clinics, and health networks than in traditional solo practices. Establishing a practice will be most difficult in the areas surrounding colleges of podiatric medicine, where podiatrists concentrate.

Diagnose and treat diseases and deformities of the human foot. Treat bone, muscle, and joint disorders affecting the feet. Diagnose diseases and deformities of the foot, using medical histories, physical examinations, X rays, and laboratory test results. Prescribe medications, corrective devices, physical therapy, or surgery. Treat conditions such as corns, calluses, ingrown nails, tumors, shortened tendons, bunions, cysts, and abscesses by surgical methods. Advise patients about treatments and foot care techniques necessary for prevention of future problems. Refer patients to physicians when symptoms indicative of systemic disorders, such as arthritis or diabetes, are observed in feet and legs. Correct deformities by means of plaster casts and strapping. Make and fit prosthetic appliances. Perform administrative duties such as hiring employees, ordering supplies, and keeping records. Educate the public about the benefits of foot care through techniques such as speaking engagements, advertising, and other forums. Treat deformities, using mechanical methods, such as whirlpool or paraffin baths, and electrical methods, such as short-wave and low-voltage currents.

Personality Type: Social-Investigative. Social occupations frequently involve working with, communicating with, and teaching people. These occupations often involve helping or providing service to others.

Career Cluster: 08 Health Science. **Career Pathway:** 08.1 Therapeutic Services.

Skills—Science: Using scientific rules and methods to solve problems. **Active Listening:** Giving full attention to what other people are saying, taking time to understand the points being made, asking questions as appropriate, and not interrupting at inappropriate times. **Complex Problem Solving:** Identifying complex problems and reviewing related information to develop and evaluate options and implement solutions. **Management of Financial Resources:** Determining how money will be spent to get the work done and accounting for these expenditures. **Reading Comprehension:** Understanding written sentences and paragraphs in work-related documents. **Equipment Selection:** Determining the kind of tools and equipment needed to do a job.

Related Knowledge/Courses—Medicine and Dentistry: The information and techniques needed to diagnose and treat injuries, diseases, and deformities. This includes symptoms, treatment alternatives, drug properties and interactions, and preventive health-care measures. **Biology:** Plant and animal living tissue, cells, organisms, and entities, including their functions, interdependencies, and interactions with each other and the environment. **Therapy and Counseling:** Information and techniques needed to rehabilitate physical and mental ailments and to provide career guidance, including alternative treatments, rehabilitation equipment and its proper use, and methods to evaluate treatment effects. **Sales and Marketing:** Principles and methods involved in showing, promoting, and selling products or services. This includes marketing strategies and tactics, product demonstration and sales techniques, and sales control systems. **Chemistry:** The composition, structure, and properties of substances and of the chemical processes and transformations that they undergo. This includes uses of chemicals and their interactions, danger signs, production techniques, and disposal methods. **Psychology:** Human behavior and performance, mental processes, psychological research methods, and the assessment and treatment of behavioral and affective disorders.

Work Environment: Indoors; contaminants; disease or infections; sitting; using hands on objects, tools, or controls; repetitive motions.

Police Detectives

Related Major: Criminal Justice/Law Enforcement

- Education/Training Required: Work experience in a related occupation
- Annual Earnings: $59,930
- Beginning Wage: $35,600
- Earnings Growth Potential: High (40.6%)
- Growth: 17.3%
- Annual Job Openings: 14,746
- Self-Employed: 0.3%
- Part-Time: 2.2%

Industries with Greatest Employment: Local Government (47.3%); Federal Government (37.2%); State Government (14.9%).

Highest-Growth Industries (Projected Growth for This Job): Local Government (23.6%).

Lowest-Growth Industries (Projected Growth for This Job): State Government (7.9%); Educational Services, Public and Private (11.9%); Federal Government (13.3%).

P

Fastest-Growing Metropolitan Areas (Recent Growth for This Job): Davenport–Moline–Rock Island, IA-IL (100.0%); Harrisburg-Carlisle, PA (69.2%); Anniston-Oxford, AL (66.7%); Springfield, IL (66.7%); Springfield, MA-CT (50.0%).

Other Considerations for Job Security: Overall opportunities in local police departments will be excellent for individuals who meet the psychological, personal, and physical qualifications. There will be more competition for jobs in federal and state law enforcement agencies than for jobs in local agencies. Less competition for jobs will occur in departments that offer relatively low salaries or those in urban communities where the crime rate is relatively high. Applicants with military experience or college training in police science will have the best opportunities in local and state departments. Applicants with a bachelor's degree and several years of law enforcement or military experience, especially investigative experience, will have the best opportunities in federal agencies. The level of government spending determines the level of employment for police and detectives, but layoffs are rare because retirements enable most staffing cuts to be handled through attrition.

Conduct investigations to prevent crimes or solve criminal cases. Provide testimony as witnesses in court. Secure deceased bodies and obtain evidence from them, preventing bystanders from tampering with bodies prior to medical examiners' arrival. Examine crime scenes to obtain clues and evidence such as loose hairs, fibers, clothing, or weapons. Obtain evidence from suspects. Record progress of investigations, maintain informational files on suspects, and submit reports to commanding officers or magistrates to authorize warrants. Check victims for signs of life such as breathing and pulse. Prepare charges or responses to charges, or information for court cases, according to formalized procedures. Obtain facts or statements from complainants, witnesses, and accused persons and record interviews, using recording devices. Prepare and serve search and arrest warrants. Note, mark, and photograph locations of objects found such as footprints, tire tracks, bullets, and bloodstains, and take measurements of each scene. Question individuals or observe persons and establishments to confirm information given to patrol officers. Preserve, process, and analyze items of evidence obtained from crime scenes and suspects, placing them in proper containers and destroying evidence no longer needed. Secure persons at scenes, keeping witnesses from conversing or leaving scenes before investigators arrive. Take photographs from all angles of relevant parts of crime scenes, including entrance and exit routes and streets and intersections. Analyze completed police reports to determine what additional information and investigative work is needed. Obtain summary of incidents from officers in charge at crime scenes, taking care to avoid disturbing evidence. Provide information to lab personnel concerning the source of each item of evidence and tests to be performed. Examine records and governmental agency files to find identifying data about suspects. Block or rope off scenes and check perimeters to ensure that scenes are completely secured. Summon medical help for injured individuals and alert medical personnel to take statements from them. Observe and photograph narcotic purchase transactions to compile evidence and protect undercover investigators.

Personality Type: Enterprising-Social. Enterprising occupations frequently involve starting up and carrying out projects. These occupations can involve leading people and making many decisions. They sometimes require risk taking and often deal with business.

Career Cluster: 12 Law, Public Safety, Corrections, and Security. **Career Pathway:** 12.4 Law Enforcement Services.

Skills—No data available.

Related Knowledge/Courses—Public Safety and Security: Weaponry; public safety; security operations, rules, regulations, precautions, and prevention; and the protection of people, data, and property. **Law and Government:** Laws, legal codes, court procedures, precedents, government regulations, executive orders, agency rules, and the democratic political process. **Psychology:** Human behavior and performance, mental processes, psychological research methods, and the assessment and treatment of behavioral and affective disorders. **Therapy and Counseling:** Information and techniques needed to rehabilitate physical and mental ailments and to provide career guidance, including alternative treatments, rehabilitation equipment and its proper use, and methods to evaluate treatment effects. **Customer and Personal Service:** Principles and processes for providing customer and personal services, including needs assessment techniques, quality service standards, alternative delivery systems, and customer satisfaction evaluation techniques. **Philosophy and Theology:** Different philosophical systems and religions, including their basic principles, values, ethics, ways of thinking, customs, and practices and their impact on human culture.

Work Environment: More often outdoors than indoors; noisy; very hot or cold; contaminants; sitting.

Police Identification and Records Officers

Related Major: Criminal Justice/Law Enforcement

- ✳ Education/Training Required: Work experience in a related occupation
- ✳ Annual Earnings: $59,930
- ✳ Beginning Wage: $35,600
- ✳ Earnings Growth Potential: High (40.6%)
- ✳ Growth: 17.3%
- ✳ Annual Job Openings: 14,746
- ✳ Self-Employed: 0.3%
- ✳ Part-Time: 2.2%

Industries with Greatest Employment: Local Government (47.3%); Federal Government (37.2%); State Government (14.9%).

Highest-Growth Industries (Projected Growth for This Job): Local Government (23.6%).

Lowest-Growth Industries (Projected Growth for This Job): State Government (7.9%); Educational Services, Public and Private (11.9%); Federal Government (13.3%).

Fastest-Growing Metropolitan Areas (Recent Growth for This Job): Davenport–Moline–Rock Island, IA-IL (100.0%); Harrisburg-Carlisle, PA (69.2%); Anniston-Oxford, AL (66.7%); Springfield, IL (66.7%); Springfield, MA-CT (50.0%).

Other Considerations for Job Security: Overall opportunities in local police departments will be excellent for individuals who meet the psychological, personal, and physical qualifications. There will be more competition for jobs in federal and state law enforcement agencies than for jobs in local agencies. Less competition for jobs will occur in departments that offer relatively low salaries or those in urban communities where the crime rate is relatively high. Applicants with military experience or college training in police science will have the best opportunities in local and state departments. Applicants with a bachelor's degree and several years of law enforcement or military experience, especially investigative experience, will have the best opportunities in federal agencies. The level of government spending determines the level of employment for police and detectives, but layoffs are rare because retirements enable most staffing cuts to be handled through attrition.

Collect evidence at crime scene, classify and identify fingerprints, and photograph evidence for use in criminal and civil cases. Photograph crime or accident scenes for evidence records. Analyze and process evidence at crime scenes and in the laboratory, wearing protective equipment and using powders and chemicals. Look for trace evidence, such as fingerprints, hairs, fibers, or shoe impressions, using alternative light sources when necessary. Dust selected areas of crime scene and lift latent fingerprints, adhering to proper preservation procedures. Testify in court and present evidence. Package, store, and retrieve evidence. Serve as technical advisor and coordinate with other law enforcement workers to exchange information on crime scene collection activities. Perform emergency work during off-hours. Submit evidence to supervisors. Process film and prints from crime or accident scenes. Identify, classify, and file fingerprints, using systems such as the Henry Classification system.

Personality Type: Conventional-Realistic. Conventional occupations frequently involve following set procedures and routines. These occupations can include working with data and details more than with ideas. Usually there is a clear line of authority to follow.

Career Cluster: 12 Law, Public Safety, Corrections, and Security. **Career Pathway:** 12.4 Law Enforcement Services.

Skills—Persuasion: Persuading others to change their minds or behavior. **Judgment and Decision Making:** Considering the relative costs and benefits of potential actions to choose the most appropriate one. **Negotiation:** Bringing others together and trying to reconcile differences. **Service Orientation:** Actively looking for ways to help people. **Social Perceptiveness:** Being aware of others' reactions and understanding why they react as they do. **Critical Thinking:** Using logic and reasoning to identify the strengths and weaknesses of alternative solutions, conclusions, or approaches to problems.

Related Knowledge/Courses—Law and Government: Laws, legal codes, court procedures, precedents, government regulations, executive orders, agency rules, and the democratic political process. **Public Safety and Security:** Weaponry; public safety; security operations, rules, regulations, precautions, and prevention; and the protection of people, data, and property. **Telecommunications:** Transmission, broadcasting, switching, control, and operation of telecommunications systems. **Customer and Personal Service:** Principles and processes for providing customer and personal services, including needs assessment techniques, quality service standards, alternative delivery systems, and customer satisfaction evaluation techniques. **Psychology:** Human behavior and performance, mental processes, psychological research methods, and the assessment and treatment of behavioral and affective disorders. **Computers and Electronics:** Electric circuit boards, processors, chips, and computer hardware and software, including applications and programming.

Work Environment: More often outdoors than indoors; noisy; very hot or cold; contaminants; using hands on objects, tools, or controls.

Police Patrol Officers

Related Major: Criminal Justice/Law Enforcement

- ⊛ Education/Training Required: Long-term on-the-job training
- ⊛ Annual Earnings: $49,630
- ⊛ Beginning Wage: $28,820
- ⊛ Earnings Growth Potential: High (41.9%)
- ⊛ Growth: 10.8%
- ⊛ Annual Job Openings: 37,842
- ⊛ Self-Employed: 0.0%
- ⊛ Part-Time: 1.1%

Industries with Greatest Employment: Local Government (85.8%); State Government (9.5%).

Highest-Growth Industries (Projected Growth for This Job): None met the criteria.

Lowest-Growth Industries (Projected Growth for This Job): State Government (–1.9%); Federal Government (3.8%); Hospitals, Public and Private (11.3%); Educational Services, Public and Private (11.7%); Local Government (12.3%).

Fastest-Growing Metropolitan Areas (Recent Growth for This Job): Nashville–Davidson County–Murfreesboro, TN (95.2%); Brunswick, GA (78.6%); Hagerstown-Martinsburg, MD-WV (68.4%); Erie, PA (52.4%); Fond du Lac, WI (41.2%).

Other Considerations for Job Security: Overall opportunities in local police departments will be excellent for individuals who meet the psychological, personal, and physical qualifications. There will be more competition for jobs in federal and state law enforcement agencies than for jobs in local agencies. Less competition for jobs will occur in departments that offer relatively low salaries or those in urban communities where the crime rate is relatively high. Applicants with military experience or college training in police science will have the best opportunities in local and state departments. Applicants with a bachelor's degree and several years of law enforcement or military experience, especially investigative experience, will have the best opportunities in federal agencies. The level of government spending determines the level of employment for police and detectives, but layoffs are rare because retirements enable most staffing cuts to be handled through attrition.

Patrol assigned areas to enforce laws and ordinances, regulate traffic, control crowds, prevent crime, and arrest violators. Provide for public safety by maintaining order, responding to emergencies, protecting people and property, enforcing motor vehicle and criminal laws, and promoting good community relations. Monitor, note, report, and investigate suspicious persons and situations, safety hazards, and unusual or illegal activity in patrol area. Record facts to prepare reports that document incidents and activities. Identify, pursue, and arrest suspects and perpetrators of criminal acts. Patrol specific areas on foot, horseback, or motorized conveyance, responding promptly to calls for assistance. Review facts of incidents to determine whether criminal acts or statute violations were involved. Investigate traffic accidents and other accidents to determine causes and to determine whether crimes have been committed. Render aid to accident victims and other persons requiring first aid for physical injuries. Testify in court to present evidence or act as witness in traffic and criminal cases. Photograph or draw diagrams of crime or accident scenes and interview principals and eyewitnesses. Relay complaint and emergency-request information to appropriate agency dispatchers. Evaluate complaint and emergency-request information to determine response requirements. Process prisoners and prepare and maintain records of prisoner bookings and prisoner statuses during booking and pre-trial processes. Monitor traffic to ensure motorists observe traffic regulations and exhibit safe driving procedures. Issue citations or warnings to violators of motor vehicle ordinances. Direct traffic flow and reroute traffic during emergencies. Inform citizens of community services and recommend options to facilitate longer-term problem resolution. Provide road information to assist motorists. Inspect public establishments to ensure compliance with rules and regulations. Act as official escorts at times, such as when leading funeral processions or firefighters.

Personality Type: Social-Realistic-Enterprising. Social occupations frequently involve working with, communicating with, and teaching people. These occupations often involve helping or providing service to others.

Career Cluster: 12 Law, Public Safety, Corrections, and Security. **Career Pathway:** 12.4 Law Enforcement Services.

Skills—No data available.

Related Knowledge/Courses—Psychology: Human behavior and performance, mental processes, psychological research methods, and the assessment and treatment of behavioral and affective disorders. **Public Safety and Security:** Weaponry; public safety; security operations, rules, regulations, precautions, and prevention; and the protection of people, data, and property. **Law and Government:** Laws, legal codes, court procedures, precedents, government regulations, executive orders, agency rules, and the democratic political process. **Customer and Personal Service:** Principles and processes for providing customer and personal services, including needs assessment techniques, quality service standards, alternative delivery systems, and customer satisfaction evaluation techniques. **Therapy and Counseling:** Information and techniques needed to rehabilitate physical and mental ailments and to provide career guidance, including alternative treatments, rehabilitation equipment and its proper use, and methods to evaluate treatment effects. **Sociology and Anthropology:** Group behavior and dynamics; societal trends and influences; and cultures and their history, migrations, ethnicity, and origins.

Work Environment: More often outdoors than indoors; noisy; very hot or cold; hazardous equipment; sitting.

Political Science Teachers, Postsecondary

Related Major: Graduate Study for College Teaching

- ⊛ Education/Training Required: Master's degree
- ⊛ Annual Earnings: $63,100
- ⊛ Beginning Wage: $35,600
- ⊛ Earnings Growth Potential: High (43.6%)
- ⊛ Growth: 22.9%
- ⊛ Annual Job Openings: 2,435
- ⊛ Self-Employed: 0.4%
- ⊛ Part-Time: 27.8%

Industries with Greatest Employment: Educational Services, Public and Private (97.3%).

Highest-Growth Industries (Projected Growth for This Job): Administrative and Support Services (48.3%); Amusement, Gambling, and Recreation Industries (45.2%); Social Assistance (38.6%); Support Activities for Transportation (32.8%); Religious, Grantmaking, Civic, Professional, and Similar Organizations (29.9%); Professional, Scientific, and Technical Services (28.8%); Management of Companies and Enterprises (26.8%); Local Government (23.5%); Educational Services, Public and Private (22.8%); Hospitals, Public and Private (21.4%).

Lowest-Growth Industries (Projected Growth for This Job): Other Information Services (7.4%); State Government (7.9%); Sporting Goods, Hobby, Book, and Music Stores (13.3%); Performing Arts, Spectator Sports, and Related Industries (13.4%); Insurance Carriers and Related Activities (13.8%).

Fastest-Growing Metropolitan Areas (Recent Growth for This Job): Greenville, SC (50.0%); Oklahoma City, OK (50.0%); Cleveland-Elyria-Mentor, OH (42.9%); Los Angeles–Long Beach–Santa Ana, CA (33.3%); Springfield, MO (33.3%).

Other Considerations for Job Security: Retirements of current postsecondary teachers should create numerous openings for all types of postsecondary teachers, so job opportunities are generally expected to be very good. However, one of the main reasons why students attend postsecondary institutions is to prepare themselves for careers, so the best job prospects for postsecondary teachers are likely to be in rapidly growing fields that offer many nonacademic career options—unlike political science. Community colleges and other institutions offering career and technical education have been among the most rapidly growing, and these institutions are expected to offer some of the best opportunities for postsecondary teachers.

Teach courses in political science, international affairs, and international relations. Initiate, facilitate, and moderate classroom discussions. Prepare and deliver lectures to undergraduate or graduate students on topics such as classical political thought, international relations, and democracy and citizenship. Evaluate and grade students' classwork, assignments, and papers. Compile, administer, and grade examinations or assign this work to others. Prepare course materials such as syllabi, homework assignments, and handouts. Keep abreast of developments in their field by reading current literature, talking with colleagues, and participating in professional conferences. Plan, evaluate, and revise curricula, course content, and course materials and methods of instruction.

P

Maintain student attendance records, grades, and other required records. Maintain regularly scheduled office hours in order to advise and assist students. Advise students on academic and vocational curricula and on career issues. Select and obtain materials and supplies such as textbooks. Conduct research in a particular field of knowledge and publish findings in professional journals, books, and electronic media. Supervise undergraduate and graduate teaching, internship, and research work. Collaborate with colleagues to address teaching and research issues. Serve on academic or administrative committees that deal with institutional policies, departmental matters, and academic issues. Participate in student recruitment, registration, and placement activities. Participate in campus and community events. Compile bibliographies of specialized materials for outside reading assignments. Act as advisers to student organizations. Perform administrative duties such as serving as department head. Write grant proposals to procure external research funding. Provide professional consulting services to government and industry.

Personality Type: Social-Investigative-Artistic. Social occupations frequently involve working with, communicating with, and teaching people. These occupations often involve helping or providing service to others.

Career Clusters: 07 Government and Public Administration; 15 Science, Technology, Engineering, and Mathematics. **Career Pathways:** 07.1 Governance; 07.4 Planning; 15.3 Science and Mathematics.

Skills—Writing: Communicating effectively in writing as appropriate for the needs of the audience. **Instructing:** Teaching others how to do something. **Reading Comprehension:** Understanding written sentences and paragraphs in work-related documents. **Learning Strategies:** Selecting and using training/instructional methods and procedures appropriate for the situation when learning or teaching new things. **Persuasion:** Persuading others to change their minds or behavior. **Critical Thinking:** Using logic and reasoning to identify the strengths and weaknesses of alternative solutions, conclusions, or approaches to problems.

Related Knowledge/Courses—History and Archeology: Historical events and their causes, indicators, and impact on particular civilizations and cultures. **Philosophy and Theology:** Different philosophical systems and religions, including their basic principles, values, ethics, ways of thinking, customs, and practices and their impact on human culture. **Sociology and Anthropology:** Group behavior and dynamics; societal trends and influences; and cultures and their history, migrations, ethnicity, and origins. **Geography:** Various methods for describing the location and distribution of land, sea, and air masses, including their physical locations, relationships, and characteristics. **Law and Government:** Laws, legal codes, court procedures, precedents, government regulations, executive orders, agency rules, and the democratic political process. **English Language:** The structure and content of the English language, including the meaning and spelling of words, rules of composition, and grammar.

Work Environment: Indoors; sitting.

Political Scientists

Related Major: Political Science

- ✸ Education/Training Required: Master's degree
- ✸ Annual Earnings: $91,580
- ✸ Beginning Wage: $37,960
- ✸ Earnings Growth Potential: Very high (58.5%)
- ✸ Growth: 5.3%
- ✸ Annual Job Openings: 318
- ✸ Self-Employed: 7.5%
- ✸ Part-Time: 20.1%

Industries with Greatest Employment: Federal Government (50.8%); Professional, Scientific, and Technical Services (21.2%); Religious, Grantmaking, Civic, Professional, and Similar Organizations (10.5%); Educational Services, Public and Private (5.8%).

Highest-Growth Industries (Projected Growth for This Job): Professional, Scientific, and Technical Services (21.0%); Religious, Grantmaking, Civic, Professional, and Similar Organizations (20.0%).

Lowest-Growth Industries (Projected Growth for This Job): Federal Government (–5.5%); Educational Services, Public and Private (11.7%); Local Government (12.2%).

Fastest-Growing Metropolitan Areas (Recent Growth for This Job): None met the criteria.

Other Considerations for Job Security: Political scientists will mainly find jobs in policy or research. Demand for political science research is growing because of increasing interest about politics and foreign affairs, including social and environmental policy issues and immigration. Political scientists will use their knowledge of political institutions to further the interests of nonprofit, political lobbying, and social organizations. Those with higher educational attainment will have the best prospects. There will be keen competition for tenured college-teaching positions.

Study the origin, development, and operation of political systems. Research a wide range of subjects, such as relations between the United States and foreign countries, the beliefs and institutions of foreign nations, or the politics of small towns or a major metropolis. May study topics such as public opinion, political decision making, and ideology. May analyze the structure and operation of governments, as well as various political entities. May conduct public opinion surveys, analyze election results, or analyze public documents. Teach political science. Disseminate research results through academic publications, written reports, or public presentations. Identify issues for research and analysis. Develop and test theories, using information from interviews, newspapers, periodicals, case law, historical papers, polls, and/or statistical sources. Maintain current knowledge of government policy decisions. Collect, analyze, and interpret data such as election results and public opinion surveys; report on findings, recommendations, and conclusions. Interpret and analyze policies; public issues; legislation; and the operations of governments, businesses, and organizations. Evaluate programs and policies and make related recommendations to institutions and organizations. Write drafts of legislative proposals and prepare speeches, correspondence, and policy papers for governmental use. Forecast political, economic, and social trends. Consult with and advise government officials, civic bodies, research agencies, the media, political parties, and others concerned with

P

political issues. Provide media commentary and/or criticism related to public policy and political issues and events.

Personality Type: Investigative-Artistic. Investigative occupations frequently involve working with ideas and require an extensive amount of thinking. These occupations can involve searching for facts and figuring out problems mentally.

Career Clusters: 07 Government and Public Administration; 10 Human Services; 15 Science, Technology, Engineering, and Mathematics. **Career Pathways:** 07.1 Governance; 10.3 Family and Community Services; 15.3 Science and Mathematics.

Skills—Writing: Communicating effectively in writing as appropriate for the needs of the audience. **Reading Comprehension:** Understanding written sentences and paragraphs in work-related documents. **Critical Thinking:** Using logic and reasoning to identify the strengths and weaknesses of alternative solutions, conclusions, or approaches to problems. **Speaking:** Talking to others to convey information effectively. **Active Learning:** Understanding the implications of new information for both current and future problem-solving and decision-making. **Instructing:** Teaching others how to do something.

Related Knowledge/Courses—History and Archeology: Historical events and their causes, indicators, and impact on particular civilizations and cultures. **Law and Government:** Laws, legal codes, court procedures, precedents, government regulations, executive orders, agency rules, and the democratic political process. **Philosophy and Theology:** Different philosophical systems and religions, including their basic principles, values, ethics, ways of thinking, customs, and practices and their impact on human

culture. **Sociology and Anthropology:** Group behavior and dynamics; societal trends and influences; and cultures and their history, migrations, ethnicity, and origins. **Foreign Language:** The structure and content of a foreign (non-English) language, including the meaning and spelling of words, rules of composition and grammar, and pronunciation. **Geography:** Various methods for describing the location and distribution of land, sea, and air masses, including their physical locations, relationships, and characteristics.

Work Environment: Indoors; sitting.

Postsecondary Teachers, All Other

Related Major: Graduate Study for College Teaching

- ✴ Education/Training Required: Master's degree
- ✴ Annual Earnings: $62,760
- ✴ Beginning Wage: $32,870
- ✴ Earnings Growth Potential: High (47.6%)
- ✴ Growth: 22.9%
- ✴ Annual Job Openings: 45,660
- ✴ Self-Employed: 0.4%
- ✴ Part-Time: 27.8%

Industries with Greatest Employment: Educational Services, Public and Private (97.3%).

Highest-Growth Industries (Projected Growth for This Job): Administrative and Support Services (48.3%); Amusement, Gambling, and Recreation Industries (45.2%); Social Assistance (38.6%); Support Activities for Transportation (32.8%); Religious, Grantmaking, Civic, Professional, and Similar Organizations (29.9%); Professional, Scientific, and Technical Services

(28.8%); Management of Companies and Enterprises (26.8%); Local Government (23.5%); Educational Services, Public and Private (22.8%); Hospitals, Public and Private (21.4%).

Lowest-Growth Industries (Projected Growth for This Job): Other Information Services (7.4%); State Government (7.9%); Sporting Goods, Hobby, Book, and Music Stores (13.3%); Performing Arts, Spectator Sports, and Related Industries (13.4%); Insurance Carriers and Related Activities (13.8%).

Fastest-Growing Metropolitan Areas (Recent Growth for This Job): Billings, MT (166.7%); Chattanooga, TN-GA (150.0%); Harrisburg-Carlisle, PA (150.0%); Boulder, CO (93.9%); Madison, WI (85.3%).

Other Considerations for Job Security: Retirements of current postsecondary teachers should create numerous openings for all types of postsecondary teachers, so job opportunities are generally expected to be very good. One of the main reasons why students attend postsecondary institutions is to prepare themselves for careers, so the best job prospects for postsecondary teachers are likely to be in rapidly growing fields that offer many nonacademic career options. Business is one of the most rapidly growing of these fields. Community colleges and other institutions offering career and technical education have been among the most rapidly growing, and these institutions are expected to offer some of the best opportunities for postsecondary teachers.

All postsecondary teachers not listed separately. No task data available.

Personality Type: No data available.

Career Cluster: 05 Education and Training. **Career Pathway:** 05.3 Teaching/Training.

Skills—No data available.

Related Knowledge/Courses—No data available.

Work Environment: No data available.

Preschool Teachers, Except Special Education

Related Major: Early Childhood Education

* Education/Training Required: Postsecondary vocational training
* Annual Earnings: $23,130
* Beginning Wage: $15,380
* Earnings Growth Potential: Low (33.5%)
* Growth: 26.3%
* Annual Job Openings: 78,172
* Self-Employed: 1.1%
* Part-Time: 25.1%

Industries with Greatest Employment: Social Assistance (63.0%); Religious, Grantmaking, Civic, Professional, and Similar Organizations (17.9%); Educational Services, Public and Private (15.9%).

Highest-Growth Industries (Projected Growth for This Job): Amusement, Gambling, and Recreation Industries (32.2%); Social Assistance (31.8%); Administrative and Support Services (26.8%); Professional, Scientific, and Technical Services (26.2%); Ambulatory Health Care Services (26.2%); Nursing and Residential Care Facilities (19.6%); Religious, Grantmaking, Civic, Professional, and Similar Organizations (18.5%); Educational Services, Public and Private (16.0%); Management of Companies and Enterprises (15.2%).

Lowest-Growth Industries (Projected Growth for This Job): Sporting Goods, Hobby, Book, and Music Stores (–19.1%); Hospitals, Public and Private (10.6%); Local Government (12.3%).

Fastest-Growing Metropolitan Areas (Recent Growth for This Job): Dalton, GA (180.0%); Provo-Orem, UT (88.2%); Panama City–Lynn Haven, FL (85.7%); Killeen–Temple–Fort Hood, TX (84.0%); Michigan City–La Porte, IN (80.0%).

Other Considerations for Job Security: Job prospects are expected to be favorable, with particularly good prospects for teachers in less desirable urban or rural school districts and for those with licensure in more than one subject. Fast-growing states in the South and West—led by Nevada, Arizona, Texas, and Georgia—will experience the largest enrollment increases. Enrollments in the Midwest are expected to hold relatively steady, while those in the Northeast are expected to decline. The number of teachers employed is dependent on state and local expenditures for education and on the enactment of legislation to increase the quality and scope of public education. At the federal level, there has been a large increase in funding for education, particularly for the hiring of qualified teachers in lower-income areas. Also, some states are instituting programs to improve early childhood education.

Instruct children (normally up to 5 years of age) in activities designed to promote social, physical, and intellectual growth needed for primary school in preschool, day care center, or other child development facility. May be required to hold state certification. Provide a variety of materials and resources for children to explore, manipulate, and use, both in learning activities and in imaginative play. Attend to children's basic needs by feeding them, dressing them, and changing their diapers. Establish and enforce rules for behavior and procedures for maintaining order. Read books to entire classes or to small groups. Teach basic skills such as color, shape, number, and letter recognition; personal hygiene; and social skills. Organize and lead activities designed to promote physical, mental, and social development, such as games, arts and crafts, music, storytelling, and field trips. Observe and evaluate children's performance, behavior, social development, and physical health. Meet with parents and guardians to discuss their children's progress and needs, determine their priorities for their children, and suggest ways that they can promote learning and development. Identify children showing signs of emotional, developmental, or health-related problems and discuss them with supervisors, parents or guardians, and child development specialists. Enforce all administration policies and rules governing students. Prepare materials and classrooms for class activities. Serve meals and snacks in accordance with nutritional guidelines. Teach proper eating habits and personal hygiene. Assimilate arriving children to the school environment by greeting them, helping them remove outerwear, and selecting activities of interest to them. Adapt teaching methods and instructional materials to meet students' varying needs and interests. Establish clear objectives for all lessons, units, and projects and communicate those objectives to children. Demonstrate activities to children. Arrange indoor and outdoor space to facilitate creative play, motor-skill activities, and safety. Plan and conduct activities for a balanced program of instruction, demonstration, and work time that provides students with opportunities to observe, question, and investigate. Maintain accurate and complete student records as required by laws, district policies, and administrative regulations.

Personality Type: Social-Artistic. Social occupations frequently involve working with, communicating with, and teaching people. These occupations often involve helping or providing service to others.

Career Clusters: 05 Education and Training; 10 Human Services. **Career Pathways:** 05.3 Teaching/Training; 10.1 Early Childhood Development and Services.

Skills—No data available.

Related Knowledge/Courses—Philosophy and Theology: Different philosophical systems and religions, including their basic principles, values, ethics, ways of thinking, customs, and practices and their impact on human culture. **Sociology and Anthropology:** Group behavior and dynamics; societal trends and influences; and cultures and their history, migrations, ethnicity, and origins. **Psychology:** Human behavior and performance, mental processes, psychological research methods, and the assessment and treatment of behavioral and affective disorders. **Customer and Personal Service:** Principles and processes for providing customer and personal services, including needs assessment techniques, quality service standards, alternative delivery systems, and customer satisfaction evaluation techniques. **Education and Training:** Instructional methods and training techniques, including curriculum design principles, learning theory, group and individual teaching techniques, design of individual development plans, and test design principles.

Work Environment: Indoors; standing; walking and running; bending or twisting the body.

Private Detectives and Investigators

Related Major: Criminal Justice/Law Enforcement

⚹ Education/Training Required: Work experience in a related occupation

⚹ Annual Earnings: $37,640

⚹ Beginning Wage: $20,990

⚹ Earnings Growth Potential: High (44.2%)

⚹ Growth: 18.2%

⚹ Annual Job Openings: 7,329

⚹ Self-Employed: 29.7%

⚹ Part-Time: 11.1%

Industries with Greatest Employment: Administrative and Support Services (36.7%).

Highest-Growth Industries (Projected Growth for This Job): Amusement, Gambling, and Recreation Industries (62.3%); Administrative and Support Services (32.5%); Professional, Scientific, and Technical Services (29.8%); Accommodation, Including Hotels and Motels (16.9%); Management of Companies and Enterprises (15.3%).

Lowest-Growth Industries (Projected Growth for This Job): Utilities (–11.7%); State Government (–1.9%); Telecommunications (1.5%); Transportation Equipment Manufacturing (1.9%); Electronics and Appliance Stores (3.2%); Clothing and Clothing Accessories Stores (4.4%); Hospitals, Public and Private (5.9%); Internet Service Providers, Web Search Portals, and Data Processing Services (6.6%); Sporting Goods, Hobby, Book, and Music Stores (7.2%); Educational Services, Public and Private (8.1%); others.

P

Fastest-Growing Metropolitan Areas (Recent Growth for This Job): Raleigh-Cary, NC (153.8%); Buffalo–Niagara Falls, NY (137.5%); Fresno, CA (125.0%); Dayton, OH (108.3%); Ann Arbor, MI (100.0%).

Other Considerations for Job Security: Keen competition is expected for most jobs because private detective and investigator careers attract many qualified people, including relatively young retirees from law enforcement and military careers. The best opportunities for new job-seekers will be in entry-level jobs in detective agencies or stores, particularly large chain and discount stores that hire detectives on a part-time basis. Opportunities are expected to be excellent for qualified computer forensic investigators. Increased demand for private detectives and investigators will result from heightened security concerns, increased litigation, and the need to protect confidential information and property of all kinds.

Detect occurrences of unlawful acts or infractions of rules in private establishments or seek, examine, and compile information for clients. Question persons to obtain evidence for cases of divorce, child custody, or missing persons or information about an individual's character or financial status. Conduct private investigations on a paid basis. Confer with establishment officials, security departments, police, or postal officials to identify problems, provide information, and receive instructions. Observe and document activities of individuals to detect unlawful acts or to obtain evidence for cases, using binoculars and still or video cameras. Investigate companies' financial standings or locate funds stolen by embezzlers, using accounting skills. Monitor industrial or commercial properties to enforce conformance to establishment rules and to protect people or property. Search computer databases, credit reports, public records, tax and legal filings, and other resources to locate persons or to compile information for investigations. Write reports and case summaries to document investigations. Count cash and review transactions, sales checks, and register tapes to verify amounts and to identify shortages. Perform undercover operations such as evaluating employee performance and honesty by posing as customers or employees. Expose fraudulent insurance claims or stolen funds. Alert appropriate personnel to suspects' locations. Conduct background investigations of individuals, such as pre-employment checks, to obtain information about each individual's character, financial status, or personal history. Testify at hearings and court trials to present evidence. Warn troublemakers causing problems on establishment premises and eject them from premises when necessary. Obtain and analyze information on suspects, crimes, and disturbances to solve cases, identify criminal activity, and gather information for court cases. Apprehend suspects and release them to law-enforcement authorities or security personnel.

Personality Type: Enterprising-Social-Realistic. Enterprising occupations frequently involve starting up and carrying out projects. These occupations can involve leading people and making many decisions. They sometimes require risk taking and often deal with business.

Career Cluster: 12 Law, Public Safety, Corrections, and Security. **Career Pathway:** 12.3 Security and Protective Services.

Skills—Management of Financial Resources: Determining how money will be spent to get the work done and accounting for these expenditures. **Persuasion:** Persuading others to change their minds or behavior. **Time Management:** Managing one's own time and the time of others.

Writing: Communicating effectively in writing as appropriate for the needs of the audience. **Service Orientation:** Actively looking for ways to help people. **Technology Design:** Generating or adapting equipment and technology to serve user needs.

Related Knowledge/Courses—Clerical Practices: Administrative and clerical procedures and systems such as word-processing systems, filing and records management systems, stenography and transcription, forms, design principles, and other office procedures and terminology. **Law and Government:** Laws, legal codes, court procedures, precedents, government regulations, executive orders, agency rules, and the democratic political process. **Customer and Personal Service:** Principles and processes for providing customer and personal services, including needs assessment techniques, quality service standards, alternative delivery systems, and customer satisfaction evaluation techniques. **Computers and Electronics:** Electric circuit boards, processors, chips, and computer hardware and software, including applications and programming. **Sales and Marketing:** Principles and methods involved in showing, promoting, and selling products or services. This includes marketing strategies and tactics, product demonstration and sales techniques, and sales control systems. **Mathematics:** Numbers and their operations and interrelationships, including arithmetic, algebra, geometry, calculus, and statistics and their applications.

Work Environment: Outdoors; noisy; very hot or cold; very bright or dim lighting; sitting; using hands on objects, tools, or controls.

Probation Officers and Correctional Treatment Specialists

Related Major: Social Work

- ❋ Education/Training Required: Bachelor's degree
- ❋ Annual Earnings: $44,510
- ❋ Beginning Wage: $28,400
- ❋ Earnings Growth Potential: Medium (36.2%)
- ❋ Growth: 10.9%
- ❋ Annual Job Openings: 18,335
- ❋ Self-Employed: 0.1%
- ❋ Part-Time: 12.0%

Industries with Greatest Employment: State Government (54.8%); Local Government (42.2%).

Highest-Growth Industries (Projected Growth for This Job): Social Assistance (65.6%); Administrative and Support Services (47.5%); Nursing and Residential Care Facilities (19.8%); Religious, Grantmaking, Civic, Professional, and Similar Organizations (15.3%).

Lowest-Growth Industries (Projected Growth for This Job): Hospitals, Public and Private (–1.4%); State Government (7.9%); Educational Services, Public and Private (12.2%); Local Government (12.3%); Ambulatory Health Care Services (14.8%).

Fastest-Growing Metropolitan Areas (Recent Growth for This Job): Boulder, CO (80.0%); Johnson City, TN (60.0%); Cleveland-Elyria-Mentor, OH (55.3%); Indianapolis-Carmel, IN (48.6%); Birmingham-Hoover, AL (45.0%).

Other Considerations for Job Security: Job outlook depends primarily on the amount of government funding that is allocated to corrections, and especially to probation systems. Although community supervision is far less expensive than keeping offenders in prison, a change in political trends toward more imprisonment and away from community supervision could result in reduced employment opportunities. In addition to openings due to growth, many openings will be created by replacement needs, especially openings due to the large number of these workers who are expected to retire. This occupation is not attractive to some potential entrants due to relatively low earnings, heavy workloads, and high stress. For these reasons, job opportunities are expected to be excellent.

Provide social services to assist in rehabilitation of law offenders in custody or on probation or parole. Make recommendations for actions involving formulation of rehabilitation plan and treatment of offender, including conditional release and education and employment stipulations. Prepare and maintain case folder for each assigned inmate or offender. Write reports describing offenders' progress. Inform offenders or inmates of requirements of conditional release, such as office visits, restitution payments, or educational and employment stipulations. Discuss with offenders how such issues as drug and alcohol abuse and anger management problems might have played roles in their criminal behavior. Gather information about offenders' backgrounds by talking to offenders, their families and friends, and other people who have relevant information. Develop rehabilitation programs for assigned offenders or inmates, establishing rules of conduct, goals, and objectives. Develop liaisons and networks with other parole officers, community agencies, staff in correctional institutions, psychiatric facilities, and after-care agencies to make plans for helping offenders with life adjustments. Arrange for medical, mental health, or substance abuse treatment services according to individual needs and court orders. Provide offenders or inmates with assistance in matters concerning detainers, sentences in other jurisdictions, writs, and applications for social assistance. Arrange for post-release services such as employment, housing, counseling, education, and social activities. Recommend remedial action or initiate court action when terms of probation or parole are not complied with. Interview probationers and parolees regularly to evaluate their progress in accomplishing goals and maintaining the terms specified in their probation contracts and rehabilitation plans. Supervise people on community-based sentences, including people on electronically monitored home detention. Assess the suitability of penitentiary inmates for release under parole and statutory release programs and submit recommendations to parole boards. Investigate alleged parole violations, using interviews, surveillance, and search and seizure. Conduct prehearing and presentencing investigations and testify in court regarding offenders' backgrounds and recommended sentences and sentencing conditions.

Personality Type: Social-Conventional. Social occupations frequently involve working with, communicating with, and teaching people. These occupations often involve helping or providing service to others.

Career Cluster: 10 Human Services. **Career Pathway:** 10.3 Family and Community Services.

Skills—Social Perceptiveness: Being aware of others' reactions and understanding why they react as they do. **Persuasion:** Persuading others to change their minds or behavior. **Negotiation:** Bringing others together and trying to reconcile differences. **Management of Personnel Resources:** Motivating, developing, and directing people as they work, identifying the best people for the job. **Time Management:** Managing one's own time and the time of others. **Monitoring:** Monitoring/assessing your performance or that of other individuals or organizations to make improvements or take corrective action.

Related Knowledge/Courses—Therapy and Counseling: Information and techniques needed to rehabilitate physical and mental ailments and to provide career guidance, including alternative treatments, rehabilitation equipment and its proper use, and methods to evaluate treatment effects. **Psychology:** Human behavior and performance, mental processes, psychological research methods, and the assessment and treatment of behavioral and affective disorders. **Sociology and Anthropology:** Group behavior and dynamics; societal trends and influences; and cultures and their history, migrations, ethnicity, and origins. **Philosophy and Theology:** Different philosophical systems and religions, including their basic principles, values, ethics, ways of thinking, customs, and practices and their impact on human culture. **Law and Government:** Laws, legal codes, court procedures, precedents, government regulations, executive orders, agency rules, and the democratic political process. **Public Safety and Security:** Weaponry; public safety; security operations, rules, regulations, precautions, and prevention; and the protection of people, data, and property.

Work Environment: More often indoors than outdoors; very hot or cold; disease or infections; sitting.

Psychiatrists

Related Major: Medicine

- ❋ Education/Training Required: First professional degree
- ❋ Annual Earnings: More than $145,600
- ❋ Beginning Wage: $59,090
- ❋ Earnings Growth Potential: Cannot be calculated
- ❋ Growth: 14.2%
- ❋ Annual Job Openings: 38,027
- ❋ Self-Employed: 14.7%
- ❋ Part-Time: 8.1%

Industries with Greatest Employment: Ambulatory Health Care Services (55.9%); Hospitals, Public and Private (17.8%).

Highest-Growth Industries (Projected Growth for This Job): Social Assistance (58.6%); Administrative and Support Services (26.8%); Professional, Scientific, and Technical Services (22.6%); Nursing and Residential Care Facilities (21.0%); Ambulatory Health Care Services (19.4%); Religious, Grantmaking, Civic, Professional, and Similar Organizations (16.7%); Management of Companies and Enterprises (15.3%).

Lowest-Growth Industries (Projected Growth for This Job): Federal Government (–5.5%); State Government (–1.9%); Insurance Carriers and Related Activities (4.6%); Health and Personal Care Stores (5.3%); Hospitals, Public and Private (9.9%); Educational Services, Public and Private (11.8%); Local Government (12.3%).

Fastest-Growing Metropolitan Areas (Recent Growth for This Job): Tampa–St. Petersburg–Clearwater, FL (114.3%); Atlanta–Sandy Springs–Marietta, GA (100.0%); Birmingham-Hoover, AL (100.0%); Toledo, OH (66.7%); Albuquerque, NM (50.0%).

P

Other Considerations for Job Security: Opportunities for individuals interested in becoming physicians and surgeons are expected to be very good. Unlike their predecessors, new physicians are much less likely to enter solo practice and more likely to take salaried jobs in group medical practices, clinics, and health networks. Reports of shortages in some specialties, such as general or family practice, internal medicine, and OB/GYN, or in rural or low-income areas should attract new entrants, encouraging schools to expand programs and hospitals to increase available residency slots. However, because physician training is so lengthy, employment change happens gradually. Opportunities should be particularly good in rural and low-income areas, as some physicians find these areas unattractive because of less control over work hours, isolation from medical colleagues, or other reasons.

Diagnose, treat, and help prevent disorders of the mind. Prescribe, direct, and administer psychotherapeutic treatments or medications to treat mental, emotional, or behavioral disorders. Analyze and evaluate patient data and test findings to diagnose nature and extent of mental disorders. Collaborate with physicians, psychologists, social workers, psychiatric nurses, or other professionals to discuss treatment plans and progress. Gather and maintain patient information and records, including social and medical histories obtained from patients, relatives, and other professionals. Design individualized care plans, using a variety of treatments. Counsel outpatients and other patients during office visits. Examine or conduct laboratory or diagnostic tests on patients to provide information on general physical conditions and mental disorders. Advise and inform guardians, relatives, and significant others of patients' conditions and treatments. Teach, take continuing education classes, attend conferences and seminars, and conduct research and publish findings to increase understanding of mental, emotional, and behavioral states and disorders. Review and evaluate treatment procedures and outcomes of other psychiatrists and medical professionals. Prepare and submit case reports and summaries to government and mental health agencies. Serve on committees to promote and maintain community mental health services and delivery systems.

Personality Type: Investigative-Artistic-Social. Investigative occupations frequently involve working with ideas and require an extensive amount of thinking. These occupations can involve searching for facts and figuring out problems mentally.

Career Cluster: 08 Health Science. **Career Pathway:** 08.1 Therapeutic Services.

Skills—Social Perceptiveness: Being aware of others' reactions and understanding why they react as they do. **Systems Evaluation:** Identifying measures or indicators of system performance and the actions needed to improve or correct performance relative to the goals of the system. **Systems Analysis:** Determining how a system should work and how changes in conditions, operations, and the environment will affect outcomes. **Active Listening:** Giving full attention to what other people are saying, taking time to understand the points being made, asking questions as appropriate, and not interrupting at inappropriate times. **Writing:** Communicating effectively in writing as appropriate for the needs of the audience. **Speaking:** Talking to others to convey information effectively.

Related Knowledge/Courses—Therapy and Counseling: Information and techniques needed to rehabilitate physical and mental ailments and to provide career guidance, including alternative treatments, rehabilitation equipment and its proper use, and methods to evaluate treatment effects. **Medicine and Dentistry:** The information and techniques needed to diagnose and treat injuries, diseases, and deformities. This includes symptoms, treatment alternatives, drug properties and interactions, and preventive health-care measures. **Psychology:** Human behavior and performance, mental processes, psychological research methods, and the assessment and treatment of behavioral and affective disorders. **Biology:** Plant and animal living tissue, cells, organisms, and entities, including their functions, interdependencies, and interactions with each other and the environment. **Sociology and Anthropology:** Group behavior and dynamics; societal trends and influences; and cultures and their history, migrations, ethnicity, and origins. **Philosophy and Theology:** Different philosophical systems and religions, including their basic principles, values, ethics, ways of thinking, customs, and practices and their impact on human culture.

Work Environment: Indoors; disease or infections; sitting.

Psychology Teachers, Postsecondary

Related Major: Graduate Study for College Teaching

- ❋ Education/Training Required: Master's degree
- ❋ Annual Earnings: $60,610
- ❋ Beginning Wage: $34,030
- ❋ Earnings Growth Potential: High (43.9%)
- ❋ Growth: 22.9%
- ❋ Annual Job Openings: 5,261
- ❋ Self-Employed: 0.4%
- ❋ Part-Time: 27.8%

Industries with Greatest Employment: Educational Services, Public and Private (97.3%).

Highest-Growth Industries (Projected Growth for This Job): Administrative and Support Services (48.3%); Amusement, Gambling, and Recreation Industries (45.2%); Social Assistance (38.6%); Support Activities for Transportation (32.8%); Religious, Grantmaking, Civic, Professional, and Similar Organizations (29.9%); Professional, Scientific, and Technical Services (28.8%); Management of Companies and Enterprises (26.8%); Local Government (23.5%); Educational Services, Public and Private (22.8%); Hospitals, Public and Private (21.4%).

Lowest-Growth Industries (Projected Growth for This Job): Other Information Services (7.4%); State Government (7.9%); Sporting Goods, Hobby, Book, and Music Stores (13.3%); Performing Arts, Spectator Sports, and Related Industries (13.4%); Insurance Carriers and Related Activities (13.8%).

Fastest-Growing Metropolitan Areas (Recent Growth for This Job): Denver-Aurora, CO (117.6%); Phoenix-Mesa-Scottsdale, AZ (83.3%); Los Angeles–Long Beach–Santa Ana, CA (70.7%); Springfield, MO (60.0%); San Diego–Carlsbad–San Marcos, CA (56.0%).

Other Considerations for Job Security: Retirements of current postsecondary teachers should create numerous openings for all types of postsecondary teachers, so job opportunities are generally expected to be very good. However, one of the main reasons why students attend postsecondary institutions is to prepare themselves for careers, so the best job prospects for postsecondary teachers are likely to be in rapidly growing fields that offer many nonacademic career options. Psychology is a course requirement in many health-care majors. Community colleges

P

and other institutions offering career and technical education have been among the most rapidly growing, and these institutions are expected to offer some of the best opportunities for post-secondary teachers.

Teach courses in psychology, such as child, clinical, and developmental psychology, and psychological counseling. Prepare and deliver lectures to undergraduate and/or graduate students on topics such as abnormal psychology, cognitive processes, and work motivation. Evaluate and grade students' classwork, laboratory work, assignments, and papers. Initiate, facilitate, and moderate classroom discussions. Compile, administer, and grade examinations or assign this work to others. Keep abreast of developments in their field by reading current literature, talking with colleagues, and participating in professional conferences. Prepare course materials such as syllabi, homework assignments, and handouts. Plan, evaluate, and revise curricula, course content, and course materials and methods of instruction. Maintain student attendance records, grades, and other required records. Supervise undergraduate and/or graduate teaching, internship, and research work. Maintain regularly scheduled office hours to advise and assist students. Conduct research in a particular field of knowledge and publish findings in professional journals, books, and electronic media. Advise students on academic and vocational curricula and on career issues. Select and obtain materials and supplies such as textbooks. Collaborate with colleagues to address teaching and research issues. Serve on academic or administrative committees that deal with institutional policies, departmental matters, and academic issues. Compile bibliographies of specialized materials for outside reading assignments. Participate in student recruitment, registration, and placement activities. Supervise students' laboratory work.

Perform administrative duties such as serving as department head. Act as advisers to student organizations. Write grant proposals to procure external research funding. Participate in campus and community events. Provide professional consulting services to government and industry.

Personality Type: Social-Investigative-Artistic. Social occupations frequently involve working with, communicating with, and teaching people. These occupations often involve helping or providing service to others.

Career Clusters: 05 Education and Training; 08 Health Science; 10 Human Services; 12 Law, Public Safety, Corrections, and Security. **Career Pathways:** 05.3 Teaching/Training; 08.1 Therapeutic Services; 10.2 Counseling and Mental Health Services; 12.1 Correction Services.

Skills—Science: Using scientific rules and methods to solve problems. **Learning Strategies:** Selecting and using training/instructional methods and procedures appropriate for the situation when learning or teaching new things. **Instructing:** Teaching others how to do something. **Social Perceptiveness:** Being aware of others' reactions and understanding why they react as they do. **Writing:** Communicating effectively in writing as appropriate for the needs of the audience. **Reading Comprehension:** Understanding written sentences and paragraphs in work-related documents.

Related Knowledge/Courses—Therapy and Counseling: Information and techniques needed to rehabilitate physical and mental ailments and to provide career guidance, including alternative treatments, rehabilitation equipment and its proper use, and methods to evaluate treatment effects. **Psychology:** Human behavior and performance, mental processes, psychological research methods, and the assessment and treatment of behavioral and affective disorders. **Sociology and Anthropology:** Group behavior and dynamics; societal trends and influences; and cultures and their history, migrations, ethnicity, and origins. **Philosophy and Theology:** Different philosophical systems and religions, including their basic principles, values, ethics, ways of thinking, customs, and practices and their impact on human culture. **Education and Training:** Instructional methods and training techniques, including curriculum design principles, learning theory, group and individual teaching techniques, design of individual development plans, and test design principles. **English Language:** The structure and content of the English language, including the meaning and spelling of words, rules of composition, and grammar.

Work Environment: Indoors; sitting.

Public Address System and Other Announcers

Related Major: Communications Studies/ Speech

- ⚜ Education/Training Required: Long-term on-the-job training
- ⚜ Annual Earnings: $25,860
- ⚜ Beginning Wage: $14,960
- ⚜ Earnings Growth Potential: High (42.2%)
- ⚜ Growth: –0.2%
- ⚜ Annual Job Openings: 1,351
- ⚜ Self-Employed: 30.0%
- ⚜ Part-Time: 35.9%

Industries with Greatest Employment: Performing Arts, Spectator Sports, and Related Industries (28.7%); Food Services and Drinking Places (26.1%); Broadcasting (Except Internet) (5.3%); Amusement, Gambling, and Recreation Industries (5.2%).

Highest-Growth Industries (Projected Growth for This Job): Amusement, Gambling, and Recreation Industries (20.5%); Performing Arts, Spectator Sports, and Related Industries (16.6%).

Lowest-Growth Industries (Projected Growth for This Job): Food Services and Drinking Places (–14.4%); Broadcasting (Except Internet) (–8.2%); Educational Services, Public and Private (2.3%).

Fastest-Growing Metropolitan Areas (Recent Growth for This Job): Miami–Fort Lauderdale–Miami Beach, FL (100.0%); Chicago-Naperville-Joliet, IL-IN-WI (65.3%); Dallas–Fort Worth–Arlington, TX (41.2%); Omaha–Council Bluffs, NE-IA (25.0%); Memphis, TN-MS-AR (20.0%).

Other Considerations for Job Security: No data available.

Make announcements over loudspeaker at sporting or other public events. May act as master of ceremonies or disc jockey at weddings, parties, clubs, or other gathering places. Greet attendees and serve as masters of ceremonies at banquets, store openings, and other events. Preview any music intended to be broadcast over the public address system. Inform patrons of coming events at a specific venue. Meet with event directors to review schedules and exchange information about details, such as national anthem performers and starting line-ups. Announce programs and player substitutions or other changes to patrons. Read prepared scripts describing acts or tricks presented during performances. Improvise commentary on items of interest, such as background and history of

P

an event or past records of participants. Instruct and calm crowds during emergencies. Learn to pronounce the names of players, coaches, institutional personnel, officials, and other individuals involved in an event. Study the layout of an event venue in order to be able to give accurate directions in the event of an emergency. Review and announce crowd control procedures before the beginning of each event. Provide running commentaries of event activities, such as play-by-play descriptions or explanations of official decisions. Organize team information, such as statistics and tournament records, to ensure accessibility for use during events. Furnish information concerning plays to scoreboard operators.

Personality Type: Social-Artistic-Enterprising. Social occupations frequently involve working with, communicating with, and teaching people. These occupations often involve helping or providing service to others.

Career Cluster: 03 Arts, Audio/Video Technology, and Communications. **Career Pathway:** 03.5 Journalism and Broadcasting.

Skills—Management of Material Resources: Obtaining and seeing to the appropriate use of equipment, facilities, and materials needed to do certain work. **Social Perceptiveness:** Being aware of others' reactions and understanding why they react as they do. **Operation and Control:** Controlling operations of equipment or systems. **Equipment Selection:** Determining the kind of tools and equipment needed to do a job. **Installation:** Installing equipment, machines, wiring, or programs to meet specifications. **Operation Monitoring:** Watching gauges, dials, or other indicators to make sure a machine is working properly.

Related Knowledge/Courses—Sales and Marketing: Principles and methods involved in showing, promoting, and selling products or services. This includes marketing strategies and tactics, product demonstration and sales techniques, and sales control systems. **Computers and Electronics:** Electric circuit boards, processors, chips, and computer hardware and software, including applications and programming. **Customer and Personal Service:** Principles and processes for providing customer and personal services, including needs assessment techniques, quality service standards, alternative delivery systems, and customer satisfaction evaluation techniques. **Communications and Media:** Media production, communication, and dissemination techniques and methods, including alternative ways to inform and entertain via written, oral, and visual media.

Work Environment: Indoors; standing; using hands on objects, tools, or controls.

Public Relations Specialists

Related Majors: Communications Studies/Speech; Family and Consumer Sciences; Public Relations

- ❋ Education/Training Required: Bachelor's degree
- ❋ Annual Earnings: $49,800
- ❋ Beginning Wage: $29,580
- ❋ Earnings Growth Potential: High (40.6%)
- ❋ Growth: 17.6%
- ❋ Annual Job Openings: 51,216
- ❋ Self-Employed: 4.9%
- ❋ Part-Time: 13.9%

Industries with Greatest Employment: Religious, Grantmaking, Civic, Professional, and Similar Organizations (19.8%); Professional, Scientific, and Technical Services (18.9%);

Educational Services, Public and Private (10.0%).

Highest-Growth Industries (Projected Growth for This Job): Social Assistance (44.1%); Securities, Commodity Contracts, and Other Financial Investments and Related Activities (42.9%); Internet Publishing and Broadcasting (40.3%); Amusement, Gambling, and Recreation Industries (38.6%); Museums, Historical Sites, and Similar Institutions (36.1%); Ambulatory Health Care Services (35.0%); Warehousing and Storage (34.0%); Funds, Trusts, and Other Financial Vehicles (32.0%); Professional, Scientific, and Technical Services (30.8%); Lessors of Nonfinancial Intangible Assets (Except Copyrighted Works) (27.6%); Nursing and Residential Care Facilities (26.8%); Waste Management and Remediation Services (26.7%); Administrative and Support Services (25.1%); Building Material and Garden Equipment and Supplies Dealers (22.6%); Personal and Laundry Services (22.5%); Performing Arts, Spectator Sports, and Related Industries (21.6%); Support Activities for Transportation (20.8%); Real Estate (19.8%); Nonstore Retailers (19.5%); Religious, Grantmaking, Civic, Professional, and Similar Organizations (17.6%); Repair and Maintenance (17.3%); Accommodation, Including Hotels and Motels (15.5%); Management of Companies and Enterprises (15.3%).

Lowest-Growth Industries (Projected Growth for This Job): Crop Production (–33.5%); Petroleum and Coal Products Manufacturing (–24.3%); Electrical Equipment, Appliance, and Component Manufacturing (–21.8%); Printing and Related Support Activities (–20.8%); Computer and Electronic Product Manufacturing (–18.9%); Rail Transportation (–13.6%); Machinery Manufacturing (–12.5%); Fabricated Metal Product Manufacturing (–12.3%);

Monetary Authorities—Central Bank (–12.3%); Furniture and Related Product Manufacturing (–12.2%); others.

Fastest-Growing Metropolitan Areas (Recent Growth for This Job): Laredo, TX (183.3%); Rochester-Dover, NH-ME (150.0%); Waco, TX (142.9%); Columbus, IN (133.3%); State College, PA (120.0%).

Other Considerations for Job Security: Keen competition likely will continue for entry-level public relations jobs, as the number of qualified applicants is expected to exceed the number of job openings. Many people are attracted to this profession because of the high-profile nature of the work. Opportunities should be best for college graduates who combine a degree in journalism, public relations, advertising, or another communications-related field with a public relations internship or other related work experience. Applicants without the appropriate educational background or work experience will face the toughest obstacles.

Engage in promoting or creating goodwill for individuals, groups, or organizations by writing or selecting favorable publicity material and releasing it through various communications media. May prepare and arrange displays and make speeches. Prepare or edit organizational publications for internal and external audiences, including employee newsletters and stockholders' reports. Respond to requests for information from the media or designate another appropriate spokesperson or information source. Establish and maintain cooperative relationships with representatives of community, consumer, employee, and public interest groups. Plan and direct development and communication of informational programs to maintain favorable public and stockholder perceptions of an organization's accomplishments and agenda. Confer with production and support personnel to produce or coordinate production of advertisements and promotions. Arrange public appearances, lectures, contests, or exhibits for clients to increase product and service awareness and to promote goodwill. Study the objectives, promotional policies, and needs of organizations to develop public relations strategies that will influence public opinion or promote ideas, products, and services. Consult with advertising agencies or staff to arrange promotional campaigns in all types of media for products, organizations, or individuals. Confer with other managers to identify trends and key group interests and concerns or to provide advice on business decisions. Coach client representatives in effective communication with the public and with employees. Prepare and deliver speeches to further public relations objectives. Purchase advertising space and time as required to promote client's product or agenda. Plan and conduct market and public opinion research to test products or determine potential for product success, communicating results to client or management.

Personality Type: Enterprising-Artistic-Social. Enterprising occupations frequently involve starting up and carrying out projects. These occupations can involve leading people and making many decisions. They sometimes require risk taking and often deal with business.

Career Clusters: 03 Arts, Audio/Video Technology, and Communications; 04 Business, Management, and Administration; 07 Government and Public Administration; 08 Health Science; 10 Human Services. **Career Pathways:** 03.5 Journalism and Broadcasting; 04.1 Management; 07.1 Governance; 08.3 Health Informatics; 10.5 Consumer Services Career.

Skills—Service Orientation: Actively looking for ways to help people. **Management of Financial Resources:** Determining how money will be spent to get the work done and accounting for these expenditures. **Persuasion:** Persuading others to change their minds or behavior. **Writing:** Communicating effectively in writing as appropriate for the needs of the audience. **Negotiation:** Bringing others together and trying to reconcile differences. **Social Perceptiveness:** Being aware of others' reactions and understanding why they react as they do.

Related Knowledge/Courses—Sales and Marketing: Principles and methods involved in showing, promoting, and selling products or services. This includes marketing strategies and tactics, product demonstration and sales techniques, and sales control systems. **Communications and Media:** Media production, communication, and dissemination techniques and methods, including alternative ways to inform and entertain via written, oral, and visual media. **Customer and Personal Service:** Principles and processes for providing customer and personal services, including needs assessment techniques, quality service standards, alternative delivery systems, and customer satisfaction evaluation techniques. **Sociology and Anthropology:** Group behavior and dynamics; societal trends and influences; and cultures and their history, migrations, ethnicity, and origins. **Clerical Practices:** Administrative and clerical procedures and systems such as word-processing systems, filing and records management systems, stenography and transcription, forms, design principles, and other office procedures and terminology. **Administration and Management:** Principles and processes involved in business and organizational planning, coordination, and execution. This includes strategic planning, resource allocation, manpower modeling, leadership techniques, and production methods.

Work Environment: Indoors; sitting.

Recreation and Fitness Studies Teachers, Postsecondary

Related Major: Graduate Study for College Teaching

⚙ Education/Training Required: Master's degree

⚙ Annual Earnings: $52,170

⚙ Beginning Wage: $26,790

⚙ Earnings Growth Potential: High (48.6%)

⚙ Growth: 22.9%

⚙ Annual Job Openings: 3,010

⚙ Self-Employed: 0.4%

⚙ Part-Time: 27.8%

Industries with Greatest Employment: Educational Services, Public and Private (97.3%).

Highest-Growth Industries (Projected Growth for This Job): Administrative and Support Services (48.3%); Amusement, Gambling, and Recreation Industries (45.2%); Social Assistance (38.6%); Support Activities for Transportation (32.8%); Religious, Grantmaking, Civic, Professional, and Similar Organizations (29.9%); Professional, Scientific, and Technical Services (28.8%); Management of Companies and Enterprises (26.8%); Local Government (23.5%); Educational Services, Public and Private (22.8%); Hospitals, Public and Private (21.4%).

Lowest-Growth Industries (Projected Growth for This Job): Other Information Services (7.4%); State Government (7.9%); Sporting Goods, Hobby, Book, and Music Stores (13.3%); Performing Arts, Spectator Sports, and Related Industries (13.4%); Insurance Carriers and Related Activities (13.8%).

Fastest-Growing Metropolitan Areas (Recent Growth for This Job): Spokane, WA (133.3%); Harrisburg-Carlisle, PA (33.3%); Phoenix-Mesa-Scottsdale, AZ (33.3%); Riverside–San Bernardino–Ontario, CA (30.8%); Oklahoma City, OK (25.0%).

Other Considerations for Job Security: Retirements of current postsecondary teachers should create numerous openings for all types of postsecondary teachers, so job opportunities are generally expected to be very good. However, one of the main reasons why students attend postsecondary institutions is to prepare themselves for careers, so the best job prospects for postsecondary teachers are likely to be in rapidly growing fields that offer many nonacademic career options, such as recreation and fitness studies. Community colleges and other institutions offering career and technical education have been among the most rapidly growing, and these institutions are expected to offer some of the best opportunities for postsecondary teachers.

Teach courses pertaining to recreation, leisure, and fitness studies, including exercise physiology and facilities management. Evaluate and grade students' classwork, assignments, and papers. Maintain student attendance records, grades, and other required records. Prepare and deliver lectures to undergraduate and graduate students on topics such as anatomy, therapeutic recreation, and conditioning theory. Prepare course materials such as syllabi, homework assignments, and handouts. Maintain regularly scheduled office hours to advise and assist students. Compile, administer, and grade examinations or assign this work to others. Plan, evaluate, and revise curricula, course content, and

R

course materials and methods of instruction. Initiate, facilitate, and moderate classroom discussions. Keep abreast of developments in their field by reading current literature, talking with colleagues, and participating in professional conferences. Advise students on academic and vocational curricula and on career issues. Participate in student recruitment, registration, and placement activities. Collaborate with colleagues to address teaching and research issues. Select and obtain materials and supplies such as textbooks. Participate in campus and community events. Serve on academic or administrative committees that deal with institutional policies, departmental matters, and academic issues. Compile bibliographies of specialized materials for outside reading assignments. Supervise undergraduate or graduate teaching, internship, and research work. Perform administrative duties such as serving as department heads. Prepare students to act as sports coaches. Conduct research in a particular field of knowledge and publish findings in professional journals, books, or electronic media. Act as advisers to student organizations. Write grant proposals to procure external research funding. Provide professional consulting services to government or industry.

Personality Type: No data available.

Career Clusters: 01 Agriculture, Food, and Natural Resources; 05 Education and Training. **Career Pathways:** 01.5 Natural Resources Systems; 05.1 Administration and Administrative Support; 05.3 Teaching/Training.

Skills—Instructing: Teaching others how to do something. **Learning Strategies:** Selecting and using training/instructional methods and procedures appropriate for the situation when learning or teaching new things. **Science:** Using scientific rules and methods to solve problems. **Social Perceptiveness:** Being aware of others' reactions and understanding why they react as they do. **Persuasion:** Persuading others to change their minds or behavior. **Time Management:** Managing one's own time and the time of others.

Related Knowledge/Courses—Education and Training: Instructional methods and training techniques, including curriculum design principles, learning theory, group and individual teaching techniques, design of individual development plans, and test design principles. **Philosophy and Theology:** Different philosophical systems and religions, including their basic principles, values, ethics, ways of thinking, customs, and practices and their impact on human culture. **Psychology:** Human behavior and performance, mental processes, psychological research methods, and the assessment and treatment of behavioral and affective disorders. **Therapy and Counseling:** Information and techniques needed to rehabilitate physical and mental ailments and to provide career guidance, including alternative treatments, rehabilitation equipment and its proper use, and methods to evaluate treatment effects. **Medicine and Dentistry:** The information and techniques needed to diagnose and treat injuries, diseases, and deformities. This includes symptoms, treatment alternatives, drug properties and interactions, and preventive health-care measures. **Sociology and Anthropology:** Group behavior and dynamics; societal trends and influences; and cultures and their history, migrations, ethnicity, and origins.

Work Environment: More often indoors than outdoors; standing.

Registered Nurses

Related Major: Nursing (R.N. Training)

- ❋ Education/Training Required: Associate degree
- ❋ Annual Earnings: $60,010
- ❋ Beginning Wage: $42,020
- ❋ Earnings Growth Potential: Low (30.0%)
- ❋ Growth: 23.5%
- ❋ Annual Job Openings: 233,499
- ❋ Self-Employed: 0.8%
- ❋ Part-Time: 21.8%

Industries with Greatest Employment: Hospitals, Public and Private (59.0%); Ambulatory Health Care Services (17.3%); Nursing and Residential Care Facilities (6.5%).

Highest-Growth Industries (Projected Growth for This Job): Social Assistance (51.0%); Professional, Scientific, and Technical Services (44.8%); Ambulatory Health Care Services (37.5%); Internet Service Providers, Web Search Portals, and Data Processing Services (34.3%); Amusement, Gambling, and Recreation Industries (32.5%); Administrative and Support Services (26.7%); Nursing and Residential Care Facilities (25.2%); Nonstore Retailers (25.0%); Funds, Trusts, and Other Financial Vehicles (23.6%); Performing Arts, Spectator Sports, and Related Industries (23.3%); Hospitals, Public and Private (21.6%); Religious, Grantmaking, Civic, Professional, and Similar Organizations (19.3%); Real Estate (18.8%); Merchant Wholesalers, Nondurable Goods (18.8%); Personal and Laundry Services (15.5%); Management of Companies and Enterprises (15.3%).

Lowest-Growth Industries (Projected Growth for This Job): Primary Metal Manufacturing (–29.7%); Paper Manufacturing (–26.3%); Electrical Equipment, Appliance, and Component Manufacturing (–16.8%); Fabricated Metal Product Manufacturing (–13.3%); Computer and Electronic Product Manufacturing (–11.4%); Machinery Manufacturing (–9.6%); Transportation Equipment Manufacturing (–8.0%); Publishing Industries (Except Internet) (–5.1%); State Government (–1.9%); Miscellaneous Manufacturing (0.0%); others.

Fastest-Growing Metropolitan Areas (Recent Growth for This Job): Flagstaff, AZ (109.4%); Lawrence, KS (108.0%); Cape Coral–Fort Myers, FL (40.2%); Oxnard–Thousand Oaks–Ventura, CA (37.9%); Charleston–North Charleston, SC (33.7%).

Other Considerations for Job Security: Overall job opportunities are expected to be excellent for registered nurses, but they can vary by employment setting. Generally, RNs with at least a bachelor's degree will have better job prospects than those without a bachelor's. In addition, all four advanced practice specialties—clinical nurse specialists, nurse practitioners, nurse-midwives, and nurse anesthetists—will be in high demand, particularly in medically underserved areas such as inner cities and rural areas. Relative to physicians, these RNs increasingly serve as lower-cost primary care providers.

Assess patient health problems and needs, develop and implement nursing care plans, and maintain medical records. Administer nursing care to ill, injured, convalescent, or disabled patients. May advise patients on health maintenance and disease prevention or provide case management. Licensing or registration required. Includes advance practice nurses such as nurse practitioners, clinical nurse specialists, certified nurse midwives, and certified registered nurse anesthetists.

R

Advanced practice nursing is practiced by RNs who have specialized formal, post-basic education and who function in highly autonomous and specialized roles. Monitor, record, and report symptoms and changes in patients' conditions. Maintain accurate, detailed reports and records. Record patients' medical information and vital signs. Order, interpret, and evaluate diagnostic tests to identify and assess patients' conditions. Modify patient treatment plans as indicated by patients' responses and conditions. Direct and supervise less skilled nursing or health-care personnel or supervise particular units. Consult and coordinate with health-care team members to assess, plan, implement, and evaluate patient care plans. Monitor all aspects of patient care, including diet and physical activity. Instruct individuals, families, and other groups on topics such as health education, disease prevention, and childbirth and develop health improvement programs. Prepare patients for, and assist with, examinations and treatments. Assess the needs of individuals, families, or communities, including assessment of individuals' home or work environments to identify potential health or safety problems. Provide health care, first aid, immunizations, and assistance in convalescence and rehabilitation in locations such as schools, hospitals, and industry. Prepare rooms, sterile instruments, equipment, and supplies and ensure that stock of supplies is maintained. Inform physicians of patients' conditions during anesthesia. Administer local, inhalation, intravenous, and other anesthetics. Perform physical examinations, make tentative diagnoses, and treat patients en route to hospitals or at disaster site triage centers. Observe nurses and visit patients to ensure proper nursing care. Conduct specified laboratory tests. Direct and coordinate infection control programs, advising and consulting with specified personnel about

necessary precautions. Prescribe or recommend drugs; medical devices; or other forms of treatment such as physical therapy, inhalation therapy, or related therapeutic procedures. Perform administrative and managerial functions such as taking responsibility for a unit's staff, budget, planning, and long-range goals. Hand items to surgeons during operations.

Personality Type: Social-Investigative. Social occupations frequently involve working with, communicating with, and teaching people. These occupations often involve helping or providing service to others.

Career Cluster: 08 Health Science. **Career Pathway:** 08.1 Therapeutic Services.

Skills—No data available.

Related Knowledge/Courses—Medicine and Dentistry: The information and techniques needed to diagnose and treat injuries, diseases, and deformities. This includes symptoms, treatment alternatives, drug properties and interactions, and preventive health-care measures. **Psychology:** Human behavior and performance, mental processes, psychological research methods, and the assessment and treatment of behavioral and affective disorders. **Therapy and Counseling:** Information and techniques needed to rehabilitate physical and mental ailments and to provide career guidance, including alternative treatments, rehabilitation equipment and its proper use, and methods to evaluate treatment effects. **Biology:** Plant and animal living tissue, cells, organisms, and entities, including their functions, interdependencies, and interactions with each other and the environment. **Philosophy and Theology:** Different philosophical systems and religions, including their basic principles, values, ethics, ways of thinking, customs, and practices and their impact on human culture.

Sociology and Anthropology: Group behavior and dynamics; societal trends and influences; and cultures and their history, migrations, ethnicity, and origins.

Work Environment: Indoors; disease or infections; standing; walking and running; using hands on objects, tools, or controls.

Religious Workers, All Other

Related Major: Philosophy

* Education/Training Required: Bachelor's degree
* Annual Earnings: $26,660
* Beginning Wage: $15,420
* Earnings Growth Potential: High (42.2%)
* Growth: 19.7%
* Annual Job Openings: 7,924
* Self-Employed: 0.4%
* Part-Time: 33.1%

Industries with Greatest Employment: Religious, Grantmaking, Civic, Professional, and Similar Organizations (96.1%).

Highest-Growth Industries (Projected Growth for This Job): Ambulatory Health Care Services (44.6%); Social Assistance (31.4%); Nursing and Residential Care Facilities (22.9%); Religious, Grantmaking, Civic, Professional, and Similar Organizations (20.0%).

Lowest-Growth Industries (Projected Growth for This Job): Private Households; Primary and Secondary Jobs (4.0%); Educational Services, Public and Private (9.0%); Hospitals, Public and Private (9.6%); Local Government (13.1%).

Fastest-Growing Metropolitan Areas (Recent Growth for This Job): Baltimore-Towson, MD (28.6%).

Other Considerations for Job Security: No data available.

All religious workers not listed separately. No task data available.

Personality Type: No data available.

Career Cluster: 10 Human Services. **Career Pathway:** 10.2 Counseling and Mental Health Services.

Skills—No data available.

Related Knowledge/Courses—No data available.

Work Environment: No data available.

School Psychologists

Related Major: Psychology

* Education/Training Required: Doctoral degree
* Annual Earnings: $62,210
* Beginning Wage: $37,300
* Earnings Growth Potential: High (40.0%)
* Growth: 15.8%
* Annual Job Openings: 8,309
* Self-Employed: 34.2%
* Part-Time: 24.0%

Industries with Greatest Employment: Educational Services, Public and Private (30.4%); Ambulatory Health Care Services (13.2%); Hospitals, Public and Private (6.0%); Social Assistance (5.9%).

Highest-Growth Industries (Projected Growth for This Job): Social Assistance (56.2%); Professional, Scientific, and Technical Services (34.6%); Ambulatory Health Care Services (26.8%); Nursing and Residential Care

Facilities (24.8%); Funds, Trusts, and Other Financial Vehicles (23.3%); Religious, Grant-making, Civic, Professional, and Similar Organizations (19.4%); Management of Companies and Enterprises (15.2%).

Lowest-Growth Industries (Projected Growth for This Job): Hospitals, Public and Private (–3.5%); State Government (–1.9%); Educational Services, Public and Private (6.9%); Local Government (12.3%).

Fastest-Growing Metropolitan Areas (Recent Growth for This Job): Hattiesburg, MS (300.0%); Albuquerque, NM (171.4%); Little Rock–North Little Rock, AR (82.4%); Fayetteville-Springdale-Rogers, AR-MO (75.0%); Boise City–Nampa, ID (70.6%).

Other Considerations for Job Security: Growing awareness of how students' mental health and behavioral problems, such as bullying, affect learning will increase demand for school psychologists to offer student counseling and mental health services. Job prospects should be the best for people with a specialist or doctoral degree in school psychology. Opportunities directly related to psychology will be limited for bachelor's degree holders. Those who meet state certification requirements may become high school psychology teachers.

Investigate processes of learning and teaching and develop psychological principles and techniques applicable to educational problems. Compile and interpret students' test results, along with information from teachers and parents, to diagnose conditions and to help assess eligibility for special services. Report any pertinent information to the proper authorities in cases of child endangerment, neglect, or abuse. Assess an individual child's needs, limitations, and potential, using observation, review

of school records, and consultation with parents and school personnel. Select, administer, and score psychological tests. Provide consultation to parents, teachers, administrators, and others on topics such as learning styles and behavior modification techniques. Promote an understanding of child development and its relationship to learning and behavior. Collaborate with other educational professionals to develop teaching strategies and school programs. Counsel children and families to help solve conflicts and problems in learning and adjustment. Develop individualized educational plans in collaboration with teachers and other staff members. Maintain student records, including special education reports, confidential records, records of services provided, and behavioral data. Serve as a resource to help families and schools deal with crises, such as separation and loss. Attend workshops, seminars, or professional meetings to remain informed of new developments in school psychology. Design classes and programs to meet the needs of special students. Refer students and their families to appropriate community agencies for medical, vocational, or social services. Initiate and direct efforts to foster tolerance, understanding, and appreciation of diversity in school communities. Collect and analyze data to evaluate the effectiveness of academic programs and other services, such as behavioral management systems. Provide educational programs on topics such as classroom management, teaching strategies, or parenting skills. Conduct research to generate new knowledge that can be used to address learning and behavior issues.

Personality Type: Investigative-Social. Investigative occupations frequently involve working with ideas and require an extensive amount of thinking. These occupations can involve searching for facts and figuring out problems mentally.

Career Clusters: 08 Health Science; 10 Human Services. **Career Pathways:** 08.1 Therapeutic Services; 10.2 Counseling and Mental Health Services.

Skills—Social Perceptiveness: Being aware of others' reactions and understanding why they react as they do. **Negotiation:** Bringing others together and trying to reconcile differences. **Learning Strategies:** Selecting and using training/instructional methods and procedures appropriate for the situation when learning or teaching new things. **Persuasion:** Persuading others to change their minds or behavior. **Writing:** Communicating effectively in writing as appropriate for the needs of the audience. **Active Listening:** Giving full attention to what other people are saying, taking time to understand the points being made, asking questions as appropriate, and not interrupting at inappropriate times.

Related Knowledge/Courses—Therapy and Counseling: Information and techniques needed to rehabilitate physical and mental ailments and to provide career guidance, including alternative treatments, rehabilitation equipment and its proper use, and methods to evaluate treatment effects. **Psychology:** Human behavior and performance, mental processes, psychological research methods, and the assessment and treatment of behavioral and affective disorders. **Sociology and Anthropology:** Group behavior and dynamics; societal trends and influences; and cultures and their history, migrations, ethnicity, and origins. **Philosophy and Theology:** Different philosophical systems and religions, including their basic principles, values, ethics, ways of thinking, customs, and practices and their impact on human culture. **Education and Training:** Instructional methods and training techniques, including curriculum design principles, learning theory, group and individual

teaching techniques, design of individual development plans, and test design principles. **Medicine and Dentistry:** The information and techniques needed to diagnose and treat injuries, diseases, and deformities. This includes symptoms, treatment alternatives, drug properties and interactions, and preventive health-care measures.

Work Environment: Indoors; sitting.

Secondary School Teachers, Except Special and Vocational Education

Related Majors: Business Education; Family and Consumer Sciences; Physical Education; Secondary Education

- ✹ Education/Training Required: Bachelor's degree
- ✹ Annual Earnings: $49,420
- ✹ Beginning Wage: $32,920
- ✹ Earnings Growth Potential: Low (33.4%)
- ✹ Growth: 5.6%
- ✹ Annual Job Openings: 93,166
- ✹ Self-Employed: 0.0%
- ✹ Part-Time: 7.8%

Industries with Greatest Employment: Educational Services, Public and Private (99.0%).

Highest-Growth Industries (Projected Growth for This Job): Social Assistance (50.4%); Administrative and Support Services (26.7%); Nursing and Residential Care Facilities (21.6%).

Lowest-Growth Industries (Projected Growth for This Job): Hospitals, Public and Private (–10.1%); State Government (–1.9%);

Educational Services, Public and Private (5.5%); Local Government (12.4%).

Fastest-Growing Metropolitan Areas (Recent Growth for This Job): Napa, CA (96.6%); Macon, GA (88.2%); Rochester-Dover, NH-ME (71.4%); Visalia-Porterville, CA (70.8%); Birmingham-Hoover, AL (68.1%).

Other Considerations for Job Security: Job prospects are expected to be favorable, with particularly good prospects for teachers in high-demand fields like math, science, and bilingual education, in less desirable urban or rural school districts, and who obtain licensure in more than one subject. Fast-growing states in the South and West—led by Nevada, Arizona, Texas, and Georgia—will experience the largest enrollment increases. Enrollments in the Midwest are expected to hold relatively steady, while those in the Northeast are expected to decline. Teachers who are geographically mobile and who obtain licensure in more than one subject should have a distinct advantage in finding a job. The number of teachers employed is dependent on state and local expenditures for education and on the enactment of legislation to increase the quality and scope of public education. At the federal level, there has been a large increase in funding for education, particularly for the hiring of qualified teachers in lower-income areas.

Instruct students in secondary public or private schools in one or more subjects at the secondary level, such as English, mathematics, or social studies. May be designated according to subject matter specialty, such as typing instructors, commercial teachers, or English teachers. Establish and enforce rules for behavior and procedures for maintaining order among the students for whom they are responsible. Instruct through lectures, discussions, and demonstrations in one or more subjects such as English, mathematics, or social studies. Establish clear objectives for all lessons, units, and projects and communicate those objectives to students. Prepare, administer, and grade tests and assignments to evaluate students' progress. Prepare materials and classrooms for class activities. Adapt teaching methods and instructional materials to meet students' varying needs and interests. Assign and grade classwork and homework. Maintain accurate and complete student records as required by laws, district policies, and administrative regulations. Enforce all administration policies and rules governing students. Observe and evaluate students' performance, behavior, social development, and physical health. Plan and conduct activities for a balanced program of instruction, demonstration, and work time that provides students with opportunities to observe, question, and investigate. Prepare students for later grades by encouraging them to explore learning opportunities and to persevere with challenging tasks. Guide and counsel students with adjustment and/or academic problems or special academic interests. Instruct and monitor students in the use and care of equipment and materials to prevent injuries and damage. Prepare for assigned classes and show written evidence of preparation upon request of immediate supervisors. Meet with parents and guardians to discuss their children's progress and to determine their priorities for their children and their resource needs. Confer with parents or guardians, other teachers, counselors, and administrators in order to resolve students' behavioral and academic problems. Use computers, audio-visual aids, and other equipment and materials to supplement presentations. Prepare objectives and outlines for courses of study, following curriculum guidelines or requirements of states and schools. Meet with other professionals to discuss individual students' needs and progress.

Personality Type: Social-Artistic-Investigative. Social occupations frequently involve working with, communicating with, and teaching people. These occupations often involve helping or providing service to others.

Career Cluster: 05 Education and Training. **Career Pathway:** 05.3 Teaching/Training.

Skills—Learning Strategies: Selecting and using training/instructional methods and procedures appropriate for the situation when learning or teaching new things. **Social Perceptiveness:** Being aware of others' reactions and understanding why they react as they do. **Persuasion:** Persuading others to change their minds or behavior. **Monitoring:** Monitoring/assessing your performance or that of other individuals or organizations to make improvements or take corrective action. **Instructing:** Teaching others how to do something. **Time Management:** Managing one's own time and the time of others.

Related Knowledge/Courses—History and Archeology: Historical events and their causes, indicators, and impact on particular civilizations and cultures. **Philosophy and Theology:** Different philosophical systems and religions, including their basic principles, values, ethics, ways of thinking, customs, and practices and their impact on human culture. **Sociology and Anthropology:** Group behavior and dynamics; societal trends and influences; and cultures and their history, migrations, ethnicity, and origins. **Education and Training:** Instructional methods and training techniques, including curriculum design principles, learning theory, group and individual teaching techniques, design of individual development plans, and test design principles. **Geography:** Various methods for describing the location and distribution of land, sea, and air masses, including their physical locations, relationships, and characteristics. **Therapy and Counseling:** Information and techniques needed to rehabilitate physical and mental ailments and to provide career guidance, including alternative treatments, rehabilitation equipment and its proper use, and methods to evaluate treatment effects.

Work Environment: Indoors; noisy; standing.

Sheriffs and Deputy Sheriffs

Related Major: Criminal Justice/Law Enforcement

- Education/Training Required: Long-term on-the-job training
- Annual Earnings: $49,630
- Beginning Wage: $28,820
- Earnings Growth Potential: High (41.9%)
- Growth: 10.8%
- Annual Job Openings: 37,842
- Self-Employed: 0.0%
- Part-Time: 1.1%

Industries with Greatest Employment: Local Government (85.8%); State Government (9.5%).

Highest-Growth Industries (Projected Growth for This Job): None met the criteria.

Lowest-Growth Industries (Projected Growth for This Job): State Government (–1.9%); Federal Government (3.8%); Hospitals, Public and Private (11.3%); Educational Services, Public and Private (11.7%); Local Government (12.3%).

Fastest-Growing Metropolitan Areas (Recent Growth for This Job): Nashville–Davidson County–Murfreesboro, TN (95.2%); Brunswick, GA (78.6%); Hagerstown-Martinsburg, MD-WV (68.4%); Erie, PA (52.4%); Fond du Lac, WI (41.2%).

Other Considerations for Job Security: Overall opportunities in local police departments will be excellent for individuals who meet the psychological, personal, and physical qualifications. There will be more competition for jobs in federal and state law enforcement agencies than for jobs in local agencies. Less competition for jobs will occur in departments that offer relatively low salaries or those in urban communities where the crime rate is relatively high. Applicants with military experience or college training in police science will have the best opportunities in local and state departments. Applicants with a bachelor's degree and several years of law enforcement or military experience, especially investigative experience, will have the best opportunities in federal agencies. The level of government spending determines the level of employment for police and detectives, but layoffs are rare because retirements enable most staffing cuts to be handled through attrition.

Enforce law and order in rural or unincorporated districts or serve legal processes of courts. May patrol courthouse, guard court or grand jury, or escort defendants. Drive vehicles or patrol specific areas to detect law violators, issue citations, and make arrests. Investigate illegal or suspicious activities. Verify that the proper legal charges have been made against law offenders. Execute arrest warrants, locating and taking persons into custody. Record daily activities and submit logs and other related reports and paperwork to appropriate authorities. Patrol and guard courthouses, grand jury rooms, or assigned areas to provide security, enforce laws, maintain order, and arrest violators. Notify patrol units to take violators into custody or to provide needed assistance or medical aid. Place people in protective custody. Serve statements of claims, subpoenas, summonses, jury summonses, orders to pay alimony, and other court orders. Take control of accident scenes to maintain traffic flow, to assist accident victims, and to investigate causes. Question individuals entering secured areas to determine their business, directing and rerouting individuals as necessary. Transport or escort prisoners and defendants en route to courtrooms, prisons or jails, attorneys' offices, or medical facilities. Locate and confiscate real or personal property, as directed by court order. Manage jail operations and tend to jail inmates.

Personality Type: Social-Enterprising-Realistic. Social occupations frequently involve working with, communicating with, and teaching people. These occupations often involve helping or providing service to others.

Career Cluster: 12 Law, Public Safety, Corrections, and Security. **Career Pathways:** 12.3 Security and Protective Services; 12.4 Law Enforcement Services.

Skills—Negotiation: Bringing others together and trying to reconcile differences. **Persuasion:** Persuading others to change their minds or behavior. **Social Perceptiveness:** Being aware of others' reactions and understanding why they react as they do. **Service Orientation:** Actively looking for ways to help people. **Equipment Selection:** Determining the kind of tools and equipment needed to do a job. **Complex Problem Solving:** Identifying complex problems and reviewing related information to develop and evaluate options and implement solutions.

Related Knowledge/Courses—Public Safety and Security: Weaponry; public safety; security operations, rules, regulations, precautions, and prevention; and the protection of people, data, and property. **Law and Government:** Laws, legal codes, court procedures, precedents, government regulations, executive orders, agency rules, and the democratic political process. **Telecommunications:** Transmission, broadcasting, switching, control, and operation of telecommunications systems. **Psychology:** Human behavior and performance, mental processes, psychological research methods, and the assessment and treatment of behavioral and affective disorders. **Therapy and Counseling:** Information and techniques needed to rehabilitate physical and mental ailments and to provide career guidance, including alternative treatments, rehabilitation equipment and its proper use, and methods to evaluate treatment effects. **Philosophy and Theology:** Different philosophical systems and religions, including their basic principles, values, ethics, ways of thinking, customs, and practices and their impact on human culture.

Work Environment: More often outdoors than indoors; very hot or cold; contaminants; disease or infections; sitting.

Social Work Teachers, Postsecondary

Related Major: Graduate Study for College Teaching

- ✳ Education/Training Required: Master's degree
- ✳ Annual Earnings: $56,240
- ✳ Beginning Wage: $33,840
- ✳ Earnings Growth Potential: Medium (39.8%)
- ✳ Growth: 22.9%
- ✳ Annual Job Openings: 1,292
- ✳ Self-Employed: 0.4%
- ✳ Part-Time: 27.8%

Industries with Greatest Employment: Educational Services, Public and Private (97.3%).

Highest-Growth Industries (Projected Growth for This Job): Administrative and Support Services (48.3%); Amusement, Gambling, and Recreation Industries (45.2%); Social Assistance (38.6%); Support Activities for Transportation (32.8%); Religious, Grantmaking, Civic, Professional, and Similar Organizations (29.9%); Professional, Scientific, and Technical Services (28.8%); Management of Companies and Enterprises (26.8%); Local Government (23.5%); Educational Services, Public and Private (22.8%); Hospitals, Public and Private (21.4%).

Lowest-Growth Industries (Projected Growth for This Job): Other Information Services (7.4%); State Government (7.9%); Sporting Goods, Hobby, Book, and Music Stores (13.3%); Performing Arts, Spectator Sports, and Related Industries (13.4%); Insurance Carriers and Related Activities (13.8%).

Fastest-Growing Metropolitan Areas (Recent Growth for This Job): Portland-Vancouver-Beaverton, OR-WA (33.3%); New York–Northern New Jersey–Long Island, NY-NJ-PA (23.1%); Chicago-Naperville-Joliet, IL-IN-WI (15.2%); Boston-Cambridge-Quincy, MA-NH (13.0%).

Other Considerations for Job Security: Retirements of current postsecondary teachers should create numerous openings for all types of postsecondary teachers, so job opportunities are generally expected to be very good. One of the main reasons why students attend postsecondary institutions is to prepare themselves for careers, so the best job prospects for postsecondary teachers are likely to be in rapidly growing fields that offer many nonacademic career options. Community colleges and other institutions offering career and technical education have been among the most rapidly growing, and these institutions are expected to offer some of the best opportunities for postsecondary teachers.

Teach courses in social work. Initiate, facilitate, and moderate classroom discussions. Evaluate and grade students' classwork, assignments, and papers. Prepare and deliver lectures to undergraduate or graduate students on topics such as family behavior, child and adolescent mental health, and social intervention evaluation. Keep abreast of developments in their field by reading current literature, talking with colleagues, and participating in professional conferences. Supervise students' laboratory work and fieldwork. Conduct research in a particular field of knowledge and publish findings in professional journals, books, or electronic media. Prepare course materials such as syllabi, homework assignments, and handouts. Maintain regularly scheduled office hours to advise and assist students. Supervise undergraduate or graduate teaching, internship, and research work. Plan, evaluate, and revise curricula, course content, and course materials and methods of instruction. Collaborate with colleagues and with community agencies to address teaching and research issues. Compile, administer, and grade examinations or assign this work to others. Advise students on academic and vocational curricula and on career issues. Maintain student attendance records, grades, and other required records. Write grant proposals to procure external research funding. Serve on academic or administrative committees that deal with institutional policies, departmental matters, and academic issues. Perform administrative duties such as serving as department head. Compile bibliographies of specialized materials for outside reading assignments. Select and obtain materials and supplies such as textbooks and laboratory equipment. Participate in student recruitment, registration, and placement activities. Participate in campus and community events. Provide professional consulting services to government and industry. Act as advisers to student organizations.

Personality Type: No data available.

Career Clusters: 05 Education and Training; 10 Human Services. **Career Pathways:** 05.3 Teaching/Training; 10.2 Counseling and Mental Health Services; 10.3 Family and Community Services.

Skills—Social Perceptiveness: Being aware of others' reactions and understanding why they react as they do. **Service Orientation:** Actively looking for ways to help people. **Instructing:** Teaching others how to do something. **Learning Strategies:** Selecting and using training/instructional methods and procedures appropriate for the situation when learning or teaching new things. **Writing:** Communicating effectively in writing as appropriate for the needs of the audience. **Complex Problem Solving:** Identifying complex problems and reviewing related information to develop and evaluate options and implement solutions.

Related Knowledge/Courses—Therapy and Counseling: Information and techniques needed to rehabilitate physical and mental ailments and to provide career guidance, including alternative treatments, rehabilitation equipment and its proper use, and methods to evaluate treatment effects. **Sociology and Anthropology:** Group behavior and dynamics; societal trends and influences; and cultures and their history, migrations, ethnicity, and origins. **Psychology:** Human behavior and performance, mental processes, psychological research methods, and the assessment and treatment of behavioral and affective disorders. **Philosophy and Theology:** Different philosophical systems and religions, including their basic principles, values, ethics, ways of thinking, customs, and practices and their impact on human culture. **Education and Training:** Instructional methods and training techniques, including curriculum design principles, learning theory, group and individual teaching techniques, design of individual development plans, and test design principles. **English Language:** The structure and content of the English language, including the meaning and spelling of words, rules of composition, and grammar.

Work Environment: Indoors; sitting.

Sociology Teachers, Postsecondary

Related Major: Graduate Study for College Teaching

- ✻ Education/Training Required: Master's degree
- ✻ Annual Earnings: $58,160
- ✻ Beginning Wage: $31,310
- ✻ Earnings Growth Potential: High (46.2%)
- ✻ Growth: 22.9%
- ✻ Annual Job Openings: 2,774
- ✻ Self-Employed: 0.4%
- ✻ Part-Time: 27.8%

Industries with Greatest Employment: Educational Services, Public and Private (97.3%).

Highest-Growth Industries (Projected Growth for This Job): Administrative and Support Services (48.3%); Amusement, Gambling, and Recreation Industries (45.2%); Social Assistance (38.6%); Support Activities for Transportation (32.8%); Religious, Grantmaking, Civic, Professional, and Similar Organizations (29.9%); Professional, Scientific, and Technical Services

(28.8%); Management of Companies and Enterprises (26.8%); Local Government (23.5%); Educational Services, Public and Private (22.8%); Hospitals, Public and Private (21.4%).

Lowest-Growth Industries (Projected Growth for This Job): Other Information Services (7.4%); State Government (7.9%); Sporting Goods, Hobby, Book, and Music Stores (13.3%); Performing Arts, Spectator Sports, and Related Industries (13.4%); Insurance Carriers and Related Activities (13.8%).

Fastest-Growing Metropolitan Areas (Recent Growth for This Job): Detroit-Warren-Livonia, MI (257.1%); Milwaukee–Waukesha–West Allis, WI (100.0%); Sacramento–Arden-Arcade–Roseville, CA (57.1%); Virginia Beach–Norfolk–Newport News, VA-NC (42.9%); Miami–Fort Lauderdale–Miami Beach, FL (36.4%).

Other Considerations for Job Security: Retirements of current postsecondary teachers should create numerous openings for all types of postsecondary teachers. However, one of the main reasons why students attend postsecondary institutions is to prepare themselves for careers, so the best job prospects for postsecondary teachers are likely to be in rapidly growing fields that offer many nonacademic career options, unlike sociology. Community colleges and other institutions offering career and technical education have been among the most rapidly growing, and these institutions are expected to offer some of the best opportunities for postsecondary teachers.

Teach courses in sociology. Evaluate and grade students' classwork, assignments, and papers. Prepare and deliver lectures to undergraduate and graduate students on topics such as race and ethnic relations, measurement and data collection, and workplace social relations. Initiate, facilitate, and moderate classroom discussions.

Prepare course materials such as syllabi, homework assignments, and handouts. Compile, administer, and grade examinations or assign this work to others. Keep abreast of developments in their field by reading current literature, talking with colleagues, and participating in professional conferences. Maintain student attendance records, grades, and other required records. Maintain regularly scheduled office hours in order to advise and assist students. Plan, evaluate, and revise curricula, course content, and course materials and methods of instruction. Advise students on academic and vocational curricula and on career issues. Collaborate with colleagues to address teaching and research issues. Conduct research in a particular field of knowledge and publish findings in professional journals, books, or electronic media. Select and obtain materials and supplies such as textbooks and laboratory equipment. Supervise undergraduate and graduate teaching, internship, and research work. Serve on academic or administrative committees that deal with institutional policies, departmental matters, and academic issues. Participate in student recruitment, registration, and placement activities. Perform administrative duties such as serving as department head. Supervise students' laboratory work and fieldwork. Write grant proposals to procure external research funding. Act as advisers to student organizations. Compile bibliographies of specialized materials for outside reading assignments. Participate in campus and community events. Provide professional consulting services to government and industry.

Personality Type: Social-Investigative-Artistic. Social occupations frequently involve working with, communicating with, and teaching people. These occupations often involve helping or providing service to others.

Career Cluster: 02 Architecture and Construction. **Career Pathway:** 02.2 Construction.

Skills—Science: Using scientific rules and methods to solve problems. **Instructing:** Teaching others how to do something. **Writing:** Communicating effectively in writing as appropriate for the needs of the audience. **Learning Strategies:** Selecting and using training/instructional methods and procedures appropriate for the situation when learning or teaching new things. **Social Perceptiveness:** Being aware of others' reactions and understanding why they react as they do. **Critical Thinking:** Using logic and reasoning to identify the strengths and weaknesses of alternative solutions, conclusions, or approaches to problems.

Related Knowledge/Courses—Sociology and Anthropology: Group behavior and dynamics; societal trends and influences; and cultures and their history, migrations, ethnicity, and origins. **Philosophy and Theology:** Different philosophical systems and religions, including their basic principles, values, ethics, ways of thinking, customs, and practices and their impact on human culture. **History and Archeology:** Historical events and their causes, indicators, and impact on particular civilizations and cultures. **Education and Training:** Instructional methods and training techniques, including curriculum design principles, learning theory, group and individual teaching techniques, design of individual development plans, and test design principles. **English Language:** The structure and content of the English language, including the meaning and spelling of words, rules of composition, and grammar. **Geography:** Various methods for describing the location and distribution of land, sea, and air masses, including their physical locations, relationships, and characteristics.

Work Environment: Indoors; sitting.

Special Education Teachers, Middle School

Related Major: Special Education

⊛ Education/Training Required: Bachelor's degree

⊛ Annual Earnings: $48,940

⊛ Beginning Wage: $33,690

⊛ Earnings Growth Potential: Low (31.2%)

⊛ Growth: 15.8%

⊛ Annual Job Openings: 8,846

⊛ Self-Employed: 0.3%

⊛ Part-Time: 9.6%

Industries with Greatest Employment: Educational Services, Public and Private (98.1%).

Highest-Growth Industries (Projected Growth for This Job): Social Assistance (39.2%); Nursing and Residential Care Facilities (26.9%); Ambulatory Health Care Services (18.2%); Educational Services, Public and Private (16.0%).

Lowest-Growth Industries (Projected Growth for This Job): State Government (–1.9%); Local Government (12.5%).

Fastest-Growing Metropolitan Areas (Recent Growth for This Job): Fort Wayne, IN (112.5%); Sacramento–Arden-Arcade–Roseville, CA (100.0%); Grand Rapids–Wyoming, MI (87.5%); Milwaukee–Waukesha–West Allis, WI (80.0%); Pittsburgh, PA (67.3%).

Other Considerations for Job Security: Special education teachers should have excellent job prospects. The job outlook does vary by geographic area and specialty. Although most areas of the country report difficulty finding qualified applicants, positions in inner cities and rural areas usually are more plentiful than job openings in suburban or wealthy urban areas. Student population growth will be highest in the South and West. In addition, job opportunities may be better in certain specialties—such as teachers who work with children with multiple disabilities or severe disabilities like autism. Bilingual special education teachers and those with multicultural experience also are needed.

Teach middle school subjects to educationally and physically handicapped students. Includes teachers who specialize and work with audibly and visually handicapped students and those who teach basic academic and life processes skills to the mentally impaired. Establish and enforce rules for behavior and policies and procedures to maintain order among students. Maintain accurate and complete student records and prepare reports on children and activities as required by laws, district policies, and administrative regulations. Prepare materials and classrooms for class activities. Confer with parents, administrators, testing specialists, social workers, and professionals to develop individual educational plans designed to promote students' educational, physical, and social development. Develop and implement strategies to meet the needs of students with a variety of handicapping conditions. Teach socially acceptable behavior, employing techniques such as behavior modification and positive reinforcement. Modify the general education curriculum for special-needs students based upon a variety of instructional techniques and instructional technology. Employ special educational strategies and techniques during instruction to improve the development of sensory- and perceptual-motor skills, language, cognition, and memory. Confer with parents or guardians, other teachers, counselors, and administrators to resolve students' behavioral and academic problems. Instruct through lectures, discussions, and demonstrations in one or more subjects such as English, mathematics, or social studies. Coordinate placement of students with special needs into mainstream classes. Meet with parents and guardians to discuss their children's progress and to determine their priorities for their children and their resource needs. Guide and counsel students with adjustment or academic problems or special academic interests. Prepare, administer, and grade tests and assignments to evaluate students' progress. Observe and evaluate students' performance, behavior, social development, and physical health. Establish clear objectives for all lessons, units, and projects and communicate those objectives to students. Teach students personal development skills such as goal setting, independence, and self-advocacy. Plan and conduct activities for a balanced program of instruction, demonstration, and work time that provides students with opportunities to observe, question, and investigate.

Personality Type: Social-Artistic. Social occupations frequently involve working with, communicating with, and teaching people. These occupations often involve helping or providing service to others.

Career Cluster: 05 Education and Training. **Career Pathway:** 05.3 Teaching/Training.

Skills—Learning Strategies: Selecting and using training/instructional methods and procedures appropriate for the situation when learning or teaching new things. **Social Perceptiveness:** Being aware of others' reactions and understanding why they react as they do. **Instructing:** Teaching others how to do something. **Monitoring:** Monitoring/assessing your performance or that of other individuals or organizations to make improvements or take corrective action. **Persuasion:** Persuading others to change their minds or behavior. **Writing:** Communicating effectively in writing as appropriate for the needs of the audience.

Related Knowledge/Courses—Geography: Various methods for describing the location and distribution of land, sea, and air masses, including their physical locations, relationships, and characteristics. **History and Archeology:** Historical events and their causes, indicators, and impact on particular civilizations and cultures. **Psychology:** Human behavior and performance, mental processes, psychological research methods, and the assessment and treatment of behavioral and affective disorders. **Therapy and Counseling:** Information and techniques needed to rehabilitate physical and mental ailments and to provide career guidance, including alternative treatments, rehabilitation equipment and its proper use, and methods to evaluate treatment effects. **Sociology and Anthropology:** Group behavior and dynamics; societal trends and influences; and cultures and their history, migrations, ethnicity, and origins. **Education and Training:** Instructional methods and training techniques, including curriculum design principles, learning theory, group and individual teaching techniques, design of individual development plans, and test design principles.

Work Environment: Indoors; noisy; standing.

Special Education Teachers, Secondary School

Related Major: Special Education

* Education/Training Required: Bachelor's degree
* Annual Earnings: $49,640
* Beginning Wage: $33,930
* Earnings Growth Potential: Low (31.6%)
* Growth: 8.5%
* Annual Job Openings: 10,601
* Self-Employed: 0.3%
* Part-Time: 9.6%

Industries with Greatest Employment: Educational Services, Public and Private (96.2%).

Highest-Growth Industries (Projected Growth for This Job): Social Assistance (48.1%); Nursing and Residential Care Facilities (25.8%); Ambulatory Health Care Services (23.1%).

Lowest-Growth Industries (Projected Growth for This Job): Hospitals, Public and Private (−14.3%); State Government (−1.9%); Educational Services, Public and Private (8.1%); Local Government (12.4%).

Fastest-Growing Metropolitan Areas (Recent Growth for This Job): Monroe, LA (183.3%); Visalia-Porterville, CA (150.0%); Charleston, WV (130.0%); Vallejo-Fairfield, CA (87.5%); Birmingham-Hoover, AL (85.7%).

Other Considerations for Job Security: Special education teachers should have excellent job prospects. The job outlook does vary by geographic area and specialty. Although most areas of the country report difficulty finding qualified applicants, positions in inner cities and rural areas usually are more plentiful than job openings in suburban or wealthy urban areas. Student population growth will be highest in the South and West. In addition, job opportunities may be better in certain specialties—such as teachers who work with children with multiple disabilities or severe disabilities like autism. Bilingual special education teachers and those with multicultural experience also are needed.

Teach secondary school subjects to educationally and physically handicapped students. Includes teachers who specialize and work with audibly and visually handicapped students and those who teach basic academic and life processes skills to the mentally impaired. Maintain accurate and complete student records and prepare reports on children and activities as required by laws, district policies, and administrative regulations. Prepare materials and classrooms for class activities. Teach socially acceptable behavior, employing techniques such as behavior modification and positive reinforcement. Establish and enforce rules for behavior and policies and procedures to maintain order among students. Confer with parents, administrators, testing specialists, social workers, and professionals to develop individual educational plans designed to promote students' educational, physical, and social development. Instruct through lectures, discussions, and demonstrations in one or more subjects such as English, mathematics, or social studies. Employ special educational strategies and techniques during instruction to improve the development of sensory- and perceptual-motor skills, language, cognition, and memory. Plan and conduct activities for a balanced program of instruction, demonstration, and work time that provides students with opportunities to observe, question, and investigate. Prepare students for later grades by encouraging them to explore learning opportunities and to persevere with challenging tasks.

Teach personal development skills such as goal setting, independence, and self-advocacy. Establish clear objectives for all lessons, units, and projects and communicate those objectives to students. Develop and implement strategies to meet the needs of students with a variety of handicapping conditions. Modify the general education curriculum for special-needs students based upon a variety of instructional techniques and technologies. Meet with other professionals to discuss individual students' needs and progress. Confer with parents or guardians, other teachers, counselors, and administrators to resolve students' behavioral and academic problems. Meet with parents and guardians to discuss their children's progress and to determine their priorities for their children and their resource needs. Guide and counsel students with adjustment or academic problems or special academic interests.

Personality Type: Social-Artistic. Social occupations frequently involve working with, communicating with, and teaching people. These occupations often involve helping or providing service to others.

Career Cluster: 05 Education and Training. **Career Pathway:** 05.3 Teaching/Training.

Skills—Learning Strategies: Selecting and using training/instructional methods and procedures appropriate for the situation when learning or teaching new things. **Social Perceptiveness:** Being aware of others' reactions and understanding why they react as they do. **Negotiation:** Bringing others together and trying to reconcile differences. **Instructing:** Teaching others how to do something. **Persuasion:** Persuading others to change their minds or behavior. **Service Orientation:** Actively looking for ways to help people.

Related Knowledge/Courses—Therapy and Counseling: Information and techniques needed to rehabilitate physical and mental ailments and to provide career guidance, including alternative treatments, rehabilitation equipment and its proper use, and methods to evaluate treatment effects. **History and Archeology:** Historical events and their causes, indicators, and impact on particular civilizations and cultures. **Geography:** Various methods for describing the location and distribution of land, sea, and air masses, including their physical locations, relationships, and characteristics. **Psychology:** Human behavior and performance, mental processes, psychological research methods, and the assessment and treatment of behavioral and affective disorders. **Philosophy and Theology:** Different philosophical systems and religions, including their basic principles, values, ethics, ways of thinking, customs, and practices and their impact on human culture. **Sociology and Anthropology:** Group behavior and dynamics; societal trends and influences; and cultures and their history, migrations, ethnicity, and origins.

Work Environment: Indoors; noisy; standing.

Speech-Language Pathologists

Related Major: Speech-Language Pathology and Audiology

- ❋ Education/Training Required: Master's degree
- ❋ Annual Earnings: $60,690
- ❋ Beginning Wage: $40,200
- ❋ Earnings Growth Potential: Low (33.8%)
- ❋ Growth: 10.6%
- ❋ Annual Job Openings: 11,160
- ❋ Self-Employed: 8.8%
- ❋ Part-Time: 24.6%

Industries with Greatest Employment: Educational Services, Public and Private (48.0%); Ambulatory Health Care Services (18.1%); Hospitals, Public and Private (12.8%).

Highest-Growth Industries (Projected Growth for This Job): Social Assistance (40.5%); Administrative and Support Services (26.5%); Ambulatory Health Care Services (16.2%); Nursing and Residential Care Facilities (15.5%); Management of Companies and Enterprises (15.2%); Religious, Grantmaking, Civic, Professional, and Similar Organizations (15.1%).

Lowest-Growth Industries (Projected Growth for This Job): Federal Government (–5.5%); State Government (–1.9%); Educational Services, Public and Private (6.2%); Local Government (12.3%); Hospitals, Public and Private (13.6%).

Fastest-Growing Metropolitan Areas (Recent Growth for This Job): Las Cruces, NM (100.0%); Greensboro–High Point, NC (80.0%); York-Hanover, PA (77.8%); Chico, CA (75.0%); Pueblo, CO (75.0%).

Other Considerations for Job Security: The combination of growth in the occupation and an expected increase in retirements over the coming years should create excellent job opportunities for speech-language pathologists. Opportunities should be particularly favorable for those with the ability to speak a second language, such as Spanish. Job prospects also are expected to be especially favorable for those who are willing to relocate, particularly to areas experiencing difficulty in attracting and hiring speech-language pathologists.

Assess and treat persons with speech, language, voice, and fluency disorders. May select alternative communication systems and teach their use. May perform research related to speech and language problems. Monitor patients' progress and adjust treatments accordingly. Evaluate hearing and speech/language test results and medical or background information to diagnose and plan treatment for speech, language, fluency, voice, and swallowing disorders. Administer hearing or speech and language evaluations, tests, or examinations to patients to collect information on type and degree of impairments, using written and oral tests and special instruments. Record information on the initial evaluation, treatment, progress, and discharge of clients. Develop and implement treatment plans for problems such as stuttering, delayed language, swallowing disorders, and inappropriate pitch or harsh voice problems, based on own assessments and recommendations of physicians, psychologists, or social workers. Develop individual or group programs in schools to deal with speech or language problems. Instruct clients in techniques for more effective communication, including sign language, lip reading, and voice improvement. Teach clients to control or strengthen tongue, jaw, face muscles, and breathing mechanisms. Develop speech exercise programs to reduce disabilities. Consult with and advise educators or medical staff on speech or hearing topics, such as communication strategies or speech and language stimulation. Instruct patients and family members in strategies to cope with or avoid communication-related misunderstandings. Design, develop, and employ alternative diagnostic or communication devices and strategies. Conduct lessons and direct educational or therapeutic games to assist teachers dealing with speech problems. Refer clients to additional medical or educational services if needed. Participate in conferences or training, or publish research results, to share knowledge of new hearing or speech disorder treatment methods or technologies. Communicate with non-speaking students, using sign language or computer technology. Provide communication instruction to dialect speakers or students with limited English proficiency. Use computer applications to identify and assist with communication disabilities.

Personality Type: Social-Investigative. Social occupations frequently involve working with, communicating with, and teaching people. These occupations often involve helping or providing service to others.

Career Cluster: 08 Health Science. **Career Pathway:** 08.1 Therapeutic Services.

Skills—Learning Strategies: Selecting and using training/instructional methods and procedures appropriate for the situation when learning or teaching new things. **Instructing:** Teaching others how to do something. **Social Perceptiveness:** Being aware of others' reactions and understanding why they react as they do. **Speaking:** Talking to others to convey information effectively. **Monitoring:** Monitoring/assessing your

performance or that of other individuals or organizations to make improvements or take corrective action. **Service Orientation:** Actively looking for ways to help people.

Related Knowledge/Courses—Therapy and Counseling: Information and techniques needed to rehabilitate physical and mental ailments and to provide career guidance, including alternative treatments, rehabilitation equipment and its proper use, and methods to evaluate treatment effects. **Psychology:** Human behavior and performance, mental processes, psychological research methods, and the assessment and treatment of behavioral and affective disorders. **Sociology and Anthropology:** Group behavior and dynamics; societal trends and influences; and cultures and their history, migrations, ethnicity, and origins. **Medicine and Dentistry:** The information and techniques needed to diagnose and treat injuries, diseases, and deformities. This includes symptoms, treatment alternatives, drug properties and interactions, and preventive health-care measures. **Education and Training:** Instructional methods and training techniques, including curriculum design principles, learning theory, group and individual teaching techniques, design of individual development plans, and test design principles. **English Language:** The structure and content of the English language, including the meaning and spelling of words, rules of composition, and grammar.

Work Environment: Indoors; disease or infections; sitting.

Statisticians

Related Majors: Mathematics; Statistics

- ✸ Education/Training Required: Master's degree
- ✸ Annual Earnings: $69,900
- ✸ Beginning Wage: $38,140
- ✸ Earnings Growth Potential: High (45.4%)
- ✸ Growth: 8.5%
- ✸ Annual Job Openings: 3,433
- ✸ Self-Employed: 6.0%
- ✸ Part-Time: 13.1%

Industries with Greatest Employment: Professional, Scientific, and Technical Services (21.0%); Federal Government (20.2%); Educational Services, Public and Private (11.5%); State Government (8.7%); Insurance Carriers and Related Activities (7.4%).

Highest-Growth Industries (Projected Growth for This Job): Social Assistance (47.1%); Securities, Commodity Contracts, and Other Financial Investments and Related Activities (42.4%); Ambulatory Health Care Services (27.2%); Chemical Manufacturing (25.7%); Administrative and Support Services (23.8%); Professional, Scientific, and Technical Services (19.9%); Religious, Grantmaking, Civic, Professional, and Similar Organizations (18.8%); Management of Companies and Enterprises (15.2%).

Lowest-Growth Industries (Projected Growth for This Job): Computer and Electronic Product Manufacturing (–12.6%); Fabricated Metal Product Manufacturing (–11.7%); Federal Government (–5.2%); State Government (–1.9%); Publishing Industries (Except Internet) (1.4%); Miscellaneous Manufacturing (1.6%); Insurance Carriers and Related Activities (5.2%); Internet Service Providers, Web Search Portals, and Data Processing Services (10.0%); Hospitals, Public and Private (11.9%); Educational Services, Public and Private (12.1%); others.

Fastest-Growing Metropolitan Areas (Recent Growth for This Job): Providence–Fall River–Warwick, RI-MA (166.7%); Cincinnati-Middletown, OH-KY-IN (80.0%); Atlanta–Sandy Springs–Marietta, GA (41.4%); Louisville–Jefferson County, KY-IN (33.3%); Madison, WI (33.3%).

Other Considerations for Job Security: Individuals with a degree in statistics should have opportunities in a variety of fields. Among graduates with a master's degree in statistics, those with a strong background in an allied field, such as finance, biology, engineering, or computer science, should have the best prospects of finding jobs related to their field of study.

Engage in the development of mathematical theory or apply statistical theory and methods to collect, organize, interpret, and summarize numerical data to provide usable information. May specialize in fields such as bio-statistics, agricultural statistics, business statistics, economic statistics, or other fields. Report results of statistical analyses, including information in the form of graphs, charts, and tables. Process large amounts of data for statistical modeling and graphic analysis, using computers. Identify relationships and trends in data, as well as any factors that could affect the results of research. Analyze and interpret statistical data in order to identify significant differences in relationships among sources of information. Prepare data for processing by organizing information, checking for any inaccuracies, and adjusting and weighting the raw data. Evaluate the statistical methods and procedures used to obtain data in order to ensure validity, applicability, efficiency, and accuracy. Evaluate sources of information in order to determine any limitations in terms of reliability or usability. Plan data collection methods for specific projects and determine the types and sizes of sample groups to be used. Design research projects that apply valid scientific techniques and utilize information obtained from baselines or historical data in order to structure uncompromised and efficient analyses. Develop an understanding of fields to which statistical methods are to be applied in order to determine whether methods and results are appropriate. Supervise and provide instructions for workers collecting and tabulating data. Apply sampling techniques or utilize complete enumeration bases in order to determine and define groups to be surveyed. Adapt statistical methods in order to solve specific problems in many fields, such as economics, biology, and engineering. Develop and test experimental designs, sampling techniques, and analytical methods. Examine theories, such as those of probability and inference, in order to discover mathematical bases for new or improved methods of obtaining and evaluating numerical data.

Personality Type: Investigative-Conventional. Investigative occupations frequently involve working with ideas and require an extensive amount of thinking. These occupations can involve searching for facts and figuring out problems mentally.

Career Clusters: 04 Business, Management, and Administration; 15 Science, Technology, Engineering, and Mathematics. **Career Pathways:** 04.2 Business Financial Management and Accounting; 15.3 Science and Mathematics.

Skills—Programming: Writing computer programs for various purposes. **Science:** Using scientific rules and methods to solve problems. **Mathematics:** Using mathematics to solve problems. **Writing:** Communicating effectively in writing as appropriate for the needs of the audience. **Active Learning:** Understanding the implications of new information for both current and future problem-solving and decision-making. **Negotiation:** Bringing others together and trying to reconcile differences.

Related Knowledge/Courses—Mathematics: Numbers and their operations and interrelationships, including arithmetic, algebra, geometry, calculus, and statistics and their applications. **Computers and Electronics:** Electric circuit boards, processors, chips, and computer hardware and software, including applications and programming. **English Language:** The structure and content of the English language, including the meaning and spelling of words, rules of composition, and grammar. **Law and Government:** Laws, legal codes, court procedures, precedents, government regulations, executive orders, agency rules, and the democratic political process. **Education and Training:** Instructional methods and training techniques, including curriculum design principles, learning theory, group and individual teaching techniques, design of individual development plans, and test design principles.

Work Environment: Indoors; sitting; using hands on objects, tools, or controls; repetitive motions.

Surgeons

Related Major: Medicine

- ✳ Education/Training Required: First professional degree
- ✳ Annual Earnings: More than $145,600
- ✳ Beginning Wage: $104,410
- ✳ Earnings Growth Potential: Cannot be calculated
- ✳ Growth: 14.2%
- ✳ Annual Job Openings: 38,027
- ✳ Self-Employed: 14.7%
- ✳ Part-Time: 8.1%

Industries with Greatest Employment: Ambulatory Health Care Services (55.9%); Hospitals, Public and Private (17.8%).

Highest-Growth Industries (Projected Growth for This Job): Social Assistance (58.6%); Administrative and Support Services (26.8%); Professional, Scientific, and Technical Services (22.6%); Nursing and Residential Care Facilities (21.0%); Ambulatory Health Care Services (19.4%); Religious, Grantmaking, Civic, Professional, and Similar Organizations (16.7%); Management of Companies and Enterprises (15.3%).

Lowest-Growth Industries (Projected Growth for This Job): Federal Government (–5.5%); State Government (–1.9%); Insurance Carriers and Related Activities (4.6%); Health and Personal Care Stores (5.3%); Hospitals, Public and Private (9.9%); Educational Services, Public and Private (11.8%); Local Government (12.3%).

Fastest-Growing Metropolitan Areas (Recent Growth for This Job): Memphis, TN-MS-AR (150.0%); Albuquerque, NM (100.0%); Jackson, MS (100.0%); Louisville–Jefferson County, KY-IN (74.2%); Tucson, AZ (71.4%).

Other Considerations for Job Security: Opportunities for individuals interested in becoming physicians and surgeons are expected to be very good. Unlike their predecessors, new physicians are much less likely to enter solo practice and more likely to take salaried jobs in group medical practices, clinics, and health networks. Reports of shortages in some specialties, such as general or family practice, internal medicine, and OB/GYN, or in rural or low-income areas should attract new entrants, encouraging schools to expand programs and hospitals to increase available residency slots. However, because physician training is so lengthy, employment change happens gradually. Opportunities should be particularly good in rural and low-income areas, as some physicians find these areas unattractive because of less control over work hours, isolation from medical colleagues, or other reasons.

Treat diseases, injuries, and deformities by invasive methods, such as manual manipulation, or by using instruments and appliances. Analyze patient's medical history, medication allergies, physical condition, and examination results to verify operation's necessity and to determine best procedure. Operate on patients to correct deformities, repair injuries, prevent and treat diseases, or improve or restore patients' functions. Follow established surgical techniques during the operation. Prescribe preoperative and postoperative treatments and procedures, such as sedatives, diets, antibiotics, and preparation and treatment of the patient's operative area. Examine patient to provide information on medical condition and surgical risk. Diagnose bodily disorders and orthopedic conditions and provide treatments, such as medicines and surgeries, in clinics, hospital wards, and operating rooms. Direct and coordinate activities of nurses, assistants, specialists, residents, and other medical staff. Provide consultation and surgical assistance to other physicians and surgeons. Refer patient to medical specialist or other practitioners when necessary. Examine instruments, equipment, and operating room to ensure sterility. Prepare case histories. Manage surgery services, including planning, scheduling and coordination, determination of procedures, and procurement of supplies and equipment. Conduct research to develop and test surgical techniques that can improve operating procedures and outcomes.

Personality Type: Investigative-Realistic. Investigative occupations frequently involve working with ideas and require an extensive amount of thinking. These occupations can involve searching for facts and figuring out problems mentally.

Career Cluster: 08 Health Science. **Career Pathway:** 08.1 Therapeutic Services.

Skills—Science: Using scientific rules and methods to solve problems. **Reading Comprehension:** Understanding written sentences and paragraphs in work-related documents. **Judgment and Decision Making:** Considering the relative costs and benefits of potential actions to choose the most appropriate one. **Complex Problem Solving:** Identifying complex problems and reviewing related information to develop and evaluate options and implement solutions. **Management of Financial Resources:** Determining how money will be spent to get the work done and accounting for these expenditures. **Critical Thinking:** Using logic and reasoning to identify the strengths and weaknesses of alternative solutions, conclusions, or approaches to problems.

Related Knowledge/Courses—Medicine and Dentistry: The information and techniques needed to diagnose and treat injuries, diseases, and deformities. This includes symptoms, treatment alternatives, drug properties and interactions, and preventive health-care measures. **Biology:** Plant and animal living tissue, cells, organisms, and entities, including their functions, interdependencies, and interactions with each other and the environment. **Therapy and Counseling:** Information and techniques needed to rehabilitate physical and mental ailments and to provide career guidance, including alternative treatments, rehabilitation equipment and its proper use, and methods to evaluate treatment effects. **Psychology:** Human behavior and performance, mental processes, psychological research methods, and the assessment and treatment of behavioral and affective disorders. **Chemistry:** The composition, structure, and properties of substances and of the chemical processes and transformations that they undergo. This includes uses of chemicals and their interactions, danger signs, production techniques, and disposal methods. **Customer and Personal Service:** Principles and processes for providing customer and personal services, including needs assessment techniques, quality service standards, alternative delivery systems, and customer satisfaction evaluation techniques.

Work Environment: Indoors; contaminants; radiation; disease or infections; standing; using hands on objects, tools, or controls.

Teachers and Instructors, All Other

Related Majors: Early Childhood Education; Secondary Education

- ❋ Education/Training Required: Bachelor's degree
- ❋ Annual Earnings: $30,020
- ❋ Beginning Wage: $16,900
- ❋ Earnings Growth Potential: High (43.7%)
- ❋ Growth: 8.7%
- ❋ Annual Job Openings: 161,191
- ❋ Self-Employed: 18.8%
- ❋ Part-Time: 41.3%

Industries with Greatest Employment: Educational Services, Public and Private (70.9%).

Highest-Growth Industries (Projected Growth for This Job): Social Assistance (38.0%); Museums, Historical Sites, and Similar Institutions (36.2%); Amusement, Gambling, and Recreation Industries (31.8%); Administrative and Support Services (27.3%); Ambulatory Health Care Services (26.4%); Publishing Industries (Except Internet) (24.5%); Professional, Scientific, and Technical Services (24.3%); Nursing and Residential Care Facilities (21.6%); Religious, Grantmaking, Civic, Professional, and Similar Organizations (17.2%); Management of Companies and Enterprises (15.3%); Merchant Wholesalers, Durable Goods (15.1%).

Lowest-Growth Industries (Projected Growth for This Job): Computer and Electronic Product Manufacturing (–5.7%); Federal Government (–5.5%); State Government (–1.9%); Private Households; Primary and Secondary Jobs (4.2%); Hospitals, Public and Private (4.4%); Insurance Carriers and Related Activities (6.7%); Educational Services, Public and Private (9.0%); Air Transportation (11.9%); Merchant Wholesalers, Nondurable Goods (12.3%); others.

Fastest-Growing Metropolitan Areas (Recent Growth for This Job): Boise City–Nampa, ID (457.9%); Iowa City, IA (400.0%); Cumberland, MD-WV (225.0%); Florence–Muscle Shoals, AL (154.5%); State College, PA (150.0%).

Other Considerations for Job Security: Job prospects are expected to be favorable, with particularly good prospects for teachers in less desirable urban or rural school districts and for those with licensure in more than one subject. Fast-growing states in the South and West—led by Nevada, Arizona, Texas, and Georgia—will experience the largest enrollment increases. Enrollments in the Midwest are expected to hold relatively steady, while those in the Northeast are expected to decline. The number of teachers employed is dependent on state and local expenditures for education and on the enactment of legislation to increase the quality and scope of public education. At the federal level, there has been a large increase in funding for education, particularly for the hiring of qualified teachers in lower-income areas.

All teachers and instructors not listed separately. No task data available.

Personality Type: No data available.

Career Cluster: 05 Education and Training. **Career Pathway:** 05.3 Teaching/Training.

Skills—No data available.

Related Knowledge/Courses—No data available.

Work Environment: No data available.

Veterinarians

Related Major: Veterinary Medicine

- ✸ Education/Training Required: First professional degree
- ✸ Annual Earnings: $75,230
- ✸ Beginning Wage: $44,150
- ✸ Earnings Growth Potential: High (41.3%)
- ✸ Growth: 35.0%
- ✸ Annual Job Openings: 5,301
- ✸ Self-Employed: 17.1%
- ✸ Part-Time: 13.4%

Industries with Greatest Employment: Professional, Scientific, and Technical Services (74.5%).

Highest-Growth Industries (Projected Growth for This Job): Professional, Scientific, and Technical Services (45.1%); Amusement, Gambling, and Recreation Industries (38.8%); Museums, Historical Sites, and Similar Institutions (36.8%); Personal and Laundry Services (31.9%); Chemical Manufacturing (26.1%); Performing Arts, Spectator Sports, and Related Industries (23.6%); Religious, Grantmaking, Civic, Professional, and Similar Organizations (15.5%).

Lowest-Growth Industries (Projected Growth for This Job): Animal Production (–11.3%); Federal Government (–5.5%); State Government (–1.9%); Educational Services, Public and Private (11.9%); Local Government (12.1%).

Fastest-Growing Metropolitan Areas (Recent Growth for This Job): Prescott, AZ (66.7%); St. Cloud, MN (50.0%); Birmingham-Hoover, AL (45.0%); Albuquerque, NM (44.4%); Boulder, CO (41.7%).

Other Considerations for Job Security: Excellent job opportunities are expected because there are only 28 accredited schools of veterinary medicine in the United States, resulting in a limited number of graduates—about 2,700— each year. However, applicants face keen competition for admission to veterinary school. New graduates continue to be attracted to companion-animal medicine. Employment opportunities are good in cities and suburbs, but even better in rural areas because fewer veterinarians compete to work there. The number of jobs for large-animal veterinarians is likely to grow more slowly than jobs for companion-animal veterinarians. Nevertheless, job prospects should be better for veterinarians who specialize in farm animals. Veterinarians with training in food safety and security, animal health and welfare, and public health and epidemiology should have the best opportunities for a career in the federal government.

Diagnose and treat diseases and dysfunctions of animals. May engage in a particular function, such as research and development, consultation, administration, technical writing, sale or production of commercial products, or rendering of technical services to commercial firms or other organizations. Includes veterinarians who inspect livestock. Examine animals to detect and determine the nature of diseases or injuries. Treat sick or injured animals by prescribing medication, setting bones, dressing wounds, or performing surgery. Inoculate animals against various diseases such as rabies and distemper. Collect body tissue, feces, blood, urine, or other body fluids for examination and analysis. Operate diagnostic equipment such as radiographic and ultrasound equipment and interpret the resulting images. Advise animal owners regarding sanitary measures, feeding, and general care necessary to promote health of animals. Educate the public about diseases that can be spread from animals to humans. Train and supervise workers who handle and care for animals. Provide care to a wide range of animals or specialize in a particular species, such as horses or exotic birds. Euthanize animals. Establish and conduct quarantine and testing procedures that prevent the spread of diseases to other animals or to humans and that comply with applicable government regulations. Conduct postmortem studies and analyses to determine the causes of animals' deaths. Perform administrative duties such as scheduling appointments, accepting payments from clients, and maintaining business records. Drive mobile clinic vans to farms so that health problems can be treated or prevented. Direct the overall operations of animal hospitals, clinics, or mobile services to farms. Specialize in a particular type of treatment such as dentistry, pathology, nutrition, surgery, microbiology, or internal medicine. Inspect and test horses, sheep, poultry, and other animals to detect the presence of communicable diseases. Research diseases to which animals could be susceptible. Plan and execute animal nutrition and reproduction programs. Inspect animal housing facilities to determine their cleanliness and adequacy. Determine the effects of drug therapies, antibiotics, or new surgical techniques by testing them on animals.

Personality Type: Investigative-Realistic. Investigative occupations frequently involve working with ideas and require an extensive amount of thinking. These occupations can involve searching for facts and figuring out problems mentally.

Career Cluster: 08 Health Science. **Career Pathway:** 08.1 Therapeutic Services.

Skills—Science: Using scientific rules and methods to solve problems. **Management of**

Financial Resources: Determining how money will be spent to get the work done and accounting for these expenditures. **Reading Comprehension:** Understanding written sentences and paragraphs in work-related documents. **Judgment and Decision Making:** Considering the relative costs and benefits of potential actions to choose the most appropriate one. **Complex Problem Solving:** Identifying complex problems and reviewing related information to develop and evaluate options and implement solutions. **Management of Personnel Resources:** Motivating, developing, and directing people as they work, identifying the best people for the job.

Related Knowledge/Courses—Biology: Plant and animal living tissue, cells, organisms, and entities, including their functions, interdependencies, and interactions with each other and the environment. **Medicine and Dentistry:** The information and techniques needed to diagnose and treat injuries, diseases, and deformities. This includes symptoms, treatment alternatives, drug properties and interactions, and preventive health-care measures. **Chemistry:** The composition, structure, and properties of substances and of the chemical processes and transformations that they undergo. This includes uses of chemicals and their interactions, danger signs, production techniques, and disposal methods. **Therapy and Counseling:** Information and techniques needed to rehabilitate physical and mental ailments and to provide career guidance, including alternative treatments, rehabilitation equipment and its proper use, and methods to evaluate treatment effects. **Sales and Marketing:** Principles and methods involved in showing, promoting, and selling products or services. This includes marketing strategies and tactics, product demonstration and sales techniques, and sales control systems. **Customer and Personal Service:** Principles and processes for providing customer and personal services, including needs assessment techniques, quality service standards, alternative delivery systems, and customer satisfaction evaluation techniques.

Work Environment: Indoors; noisy; contaminants; disease or infections; standing; using hands on objects, tools, or controls.

Vocational Education Teachers, Postsecondary

Related Major: Graduate Study for College Teaching

- ⊛ Education/Training Required: Work experience in a related occupation
- ⊛ Annual Earnings: $45,850
- ⊛ Beginning Wage: $26,380
- ⊛ Earnings Growth Potential: High (42.5%)
- ⊛ Growth: 22.9%
- ⊛ Annual Job Openings: 19,313
- ⊛ Self-Employed: 0.4%
- ⊛ Part-Time: 27.8%

Industries with Greatest Employment: Educational Services, Public and Private (97.3%).

Highest-Growth Industries (Projected Growth for This Job): Administrative and Support Services (48.3%); Amusement, Gambling, and Recreation Industries (45.2%); Social Assistance (38.6%); Support Activities for Transportation (32.8%); Religious, Grantmaking, Civic, Professional, and Similar Organizations (29.9%); Professional, Scientific, and Technical Services (28.8%); Management of Companies and Enterprises (26.8%); Local Government (23.5%); Educational Services, Public and Private (22.8%); Hospitals, Public and Private (21.4%).

Lowest-Growth Industries (Projected Growth for This Job): Other Information Services (7.4%); State Government (7.9%); Sporting Goods, Hobby, Book, and Music Stores (13.3%); Performing Arts, Spectator Sports, and Related Industries (13.4%); Insurance Carriers and Related Activities (13.8%).

Fastest-Growing Metropolitan Areas (Recent Growth for This Job): Lexington-Fayette, KY (164.0%); New Haven, CT (150.0%); Springfield, MO (140.0%); Des Moines–West Des Moines, IA (127.3%); Virginia Beach–Norfolk–Newport News, VA-NC (90.4%).

Other Considerations for Job Security: Retirements of current postsecondary teachers should create numerous openings for all types of postsecondary teachers, so job opportunities are generally expected to be very good. However, one of the main reasons why students attend postsecondary institutions is to prepare themselves for careers, so the best job prospects for postsecondary teachers are likely to be in rapidly growing fields that offer many nonacademic career options. Community colleges and other institutions offering career and technical education have been among the most rapidly growing, and these institutions are expected to offer some of the best opportunities for postsecondary teachers.

Teach or instruct vocational or occupational subjects at the postsecondary level (but at less than the baccalaureate) to students who have graduated or left high school. Includes correspondence school instructors; industrial, commercial, and government training instructors; and adult education teachers and instructors who prepare persons to operate industrial machinery and equipment and transportation and communications equipment. Teaching may take place in public or

private schools whose primary business is education or in a school associated with an organization whose primary business is other than education. Supervise and monitor students' use of tools and equipment. Observe and evaluate students' work to determine progress, provide feedback, and make suggestions for improvement. Present lectures and conduct discussions to increase students' knowledge and competence, using visual aids such as graphs, charts, videotapes, and slides. Administer oral, written, or performance tests to measure progress and to evaluate training effectiveness. Prepare reports and maintain records such as student grades, attendance rolls, and training activity details. Supervise independent or group projects, field placements, laboratory work, or other training. Determine training needs of students or workers. Provide individualized instruction and tutorial or remedial instruction. Conduct on-the-job training, classes, or training sessions to teach and demonstrate principles, techniques, procedures, and methods of designated subjects. Develop curricula and plan course content and methods of instruction. Prepare outlines of instructional programs and training schedules and establish course goals. Integrate academic and vocational curricula so that students can obtain a variety of skills. Develop teaching aids such as instructional software, multimedia visual aids, or study materials. Select and assemble books, materials, supplies, and equipment for training, courses, or projects. Advise students on course selection, career decisions, and other academic and vocational concerns. Participate in conferences, seminars, and training sessions to keep abreast of developments in the field and integrate relevant information into training programs. Serve on faculty and school committees concerned with budgeting, curriculum revision, and course and diploma requirements. Review enrollment applications and correspond with applicants to obtain additional information. Arrange for lectures by experts in designated fields.

Personality Type: Social-Realistic. Social occupations frequently involve working with, communicating with, and teaching people. These occupations often involve helping or providing service to others.

Career Cluster: 05 Education and Training. **Career Pathway:** 05.3 Teaching/Training.

Skills—Instructing: Teaching others how to do something. **Learning Strategies:** Selecting and using training/instructional methods and procedures appropriate for the situation when learning or teaching new things. **Social Perceptiveness:** Being aware of others' reactions and understanding why they react as they do. **Service Orientation:** Actively looking for ways to help people. **Speaking:** Talking to others to convey information effectively. **Time Management:** Managing one's own time and the time of others.

Related Knowledge/Courses—Education and Training: Instructional methods and training techniques, including curriculum design principles, learning theory, group and individual teaching techniques, design of individual development plans, and test design principles. **Psychology:** Human behavior and performance, mental processes, psychological research methods, and the assessment and treatment of behavioral and affective disorders. **Therapy and Counseling:** Information and techniques needed to rehabilitate physical and mental ailments and to provide career guidance, including alternative treatments, rehabilitation equipment and its proper use, and methods to evaluate treatment effects. **Computers and Electronics:** Electric circuit boards, processors, chips, and computer hardware and software, including applications and programming. **Sales and Marketing:** Principles and methods involved in showing, promoting, and selling products or services. This includes marketing strategies and tactics, product demonstration and sales techniques, and sales control systems. **Design:** Design techniques, principles, tools, and instruments involved in the production and use of precision technical plans, blueprints, drawings, and models.

Work Environment: Indoors; standing; using hands on objects, tools, or controls.

APPENDIX

Resources for Further Exploration

The facts and pointers in this book provide a good beginning to the subject of college majors and their related secure jobs. If you want additional details, we suggest you consult some of the resources listed here.

Facts About College Majors

A good source of facts is the *College Majors Handbook with Real Career Paths and Payoffs: The Actual Jobs, Earnings, and Trends for Graduates of 60 College Majors,* by Neeta P. Fogg, Ph.D., Paul E. Harrington, Ed.D., and Thomas F. Harrington, Ph.D. (JIST).

The College Board's Web site has information about a large number of college majors at www.collegeboard.com/csearch/majors_careers/profiles.

Facts About Careers

The *Occupational Outlook Handbook* (or the *OOH*) (JIST): Updated every two years by the U.S. Department of Labor, this book provides descriptions for 270 major jobs covering more than 85 percent of the workforce.

The *Enhanced Occupational Outlook Handbook* (JIST): Includes all descriptions in the *OOH* plus descriptions of more than 6,300 more-specialized jobs related to them.

The *O*NET Dictionary of Occupational Titles* (JIST): The only printed source of the 950 jobs described in the U.S. Department of Labor's Occupational Information Network database. It covers all the jobs in the book you're now reading, including the recession-sensitive jobs that are not described here, and it offers more topics than we were able to fit here.

The *New Guide for Occupational Exploration* (JIST): An important career reference that allows you to explore all major O*NET jobs based on your interests.

America's Career InfoNet: This Web site, maintained by the Minnesota Department of Employment Security for the U.S. Department of Labor, includes information on state and local earnings. Go to www.careerinfonet.org.

Index

The 20 High-Security Majors with the Best Income Potential, 26

The 20 High-Security Majors with the Best Job-Growth Potential, 27

The 20 High-Security Majors with the Best Job-Opening Potential, 28

The 50 Best High-Security Majors Overall, 24–25

A

Actuarial Science, 24, 26–27, 38–39, 41, 47, 55, 63, 65–66, 68, 75, 139

Actuaries, 75, 139–140

Advertising and Promotions Managers, 125

African-American Studies, 75–77

Agricultural Sciences Teachers, Postsecondary, 98, 140–142

Agriculture, Food, and Natural Resources career cluster, 49, 53

American Studies, 77–78

America's Career InfoNet, 330

Anesthesiologists, 110, 142–144

Anthropologists, 78–79, 144–146

Anthropology, 25, 31, 47, 58, 60–61, 65–66, 68–69, 78–79, 144, 148

Anthropology and Archeology Teachers, Postsecondary, 98, 104, 146–148

Archeologists, 79, 148–150

Archeology, 25, 31, 47, 58, 60–61, 65–66, 68–69, 79–80, 144, 148

Architecture and Construction career cluster, 49–50, 53

Architecture Teachers, Postsecondary, 98, 150–152

Archivists, 82, 152–153

Area, Ethnic, and Cultural Studies Teachers, Postsecondary, 76, 78, 81, 98, 104, 136, 153–155

Area Studies, 80–81

Art, Drama, and Music Teachers, Postsecondary, 98, 104, 155–157

Art History, 25, 31, 35, 40, 46–47, 54, 58, 60–62, 67, 81–82, 152, 189, 251

Artistic personality type, 59, 61–62

Arts, Audio/Video Technology, and Communications career cluster, 50, 54

Atmospheric, Earth, Marine, and Space Sciences Teachers, Postsecondary, 98, 157–159

Audiologists, 132, 159–161

B

bachelor's degree, 45–46

Bailiffs, 88, 161–162

Best High-Security Majors for People with a Conventional Personality Type, 63

Best High-Security Majors for People with a Realistic Personality Type, 60

Best High-Security Majors for People with a Social Personality Type, 62

Best High-Security Majors for People with an Artistic Personality Type, 61–62

Best High-Security Majors for People with an Enterprising Personality Type, 63

Best High-Security Majors for People with an Investigative Personality Type, 61

Best High-Security Majors in the Agriculture, Food and Natural Resources Cluster, 53

Best High-Security Majors in the Architecture and Construction Cluster, 53

Best High-Security Majors in the Arts, Audio/ Video Technology, and Communications Cluster, 54

Best High-Security Majors in the Business, Management, and Administration Cluster, 54

Best High-Security Majors in the Education and Training Cluster, 54–55

Best High-Security Majors in the Finance Cluster, 55

Best High-Security Majors in the Government and Public Administration Cluster, 55

Best High-Security Majors in the Health Science Cluster, 56

Best High-Security Majors in the Human Services Cluster, 56–57

Best High-Security Majors in the Information Technology Cluster, 57

Best High-Security Majors in the Law, Public Safety, Corrections, and Security Cluster, 57

Best High-Security Majors in the Marketing, Sales, and Service Cluster, 58

Best High-Security Majors in the Science, Technology, Engineering, and Mathematics Cluster, 58

Best High-Security Majors Related to Jobs Employing a High Percentage of Men, 38

Best High-Security Majors Related to Jobs Employing a High Percentage of Rural Workers, 43

Best High-Security Majors Related to Jobs Employing a High Percentage of Urban Workers, 41

Best High-Security Majors Related to Jobs Employing a High Percentage of Women, 36–37

Best High-Security Majors Related to Jobs Employing the Highest Percentage of Men, 38

Best High-Security Majors Related to Jobs Employing the Highest Percentage of Rural Workers, 42

Best High-Security Majors Related to Jobs Employing the Highest Percentage of Urban Workers, 39–40

Best High-Security Majors Related to Jobs Employing the Highest Percentage of Women, 35–36

Best High-Security Majors Related to Jobs Requiring a Bachelor's Degree or Less, 46

Best High-Security Majors Related to Jobs Requiring a Doctoral Degree, 48

Best High-Security Majors Related to Jobs Requiring a First Professional Degree, 48

Best High-Security Majors Related to Jobs Requiring a Master's Degree, 47

Best High-Security Majors Related to Jobs Requiring Work Experience Plus Degree, 47

Best High-Security Majors Related to Jobs that Require a High Level of Math Skills, 68–69

Best High-Security Majors Related to Jobs that Require a High Level of Verbal Skills, 66

Best High-Security Majors Related to Jobs that Require a Lower Level of Math Skills, 70

Best High-Security Majors Related to Jobs that Require a Lower Level of Verbal Skills, 67

Best High-Security Majors Related to Jobs with a High Percentage of Part-Time Workers, 31–32

Best High-Security Majors Related to Jobs with a High Percentage of Self-Employed Workers, 34

Best High-Security Majors Related to Jobs with the Highest Percentage of Part-Time Workers, 30–31

Best High-Security Majors Related to Jobs with the Highest Percentage of Self-Employed Workers, 33

Biological Science Teachers, Postsecondary, 98, 162–164

Broadcast News Analysts, 106

business cycle, 15

Business Education, 24, 28, 42–43, 46, 55, 62, 65–66, 82–83, 305

Business, Management, and Administration career cluster, 50, 54

Business Teachers, Postsecondary, 98, 164–166

C

Calculus (course), 71

career clusters

Agriculture, Food, and Natural Resources, 53
Architecture and Construction, 53
Arts, Audio/Video Technology, and Communications, 54
Business, Management, and Administration, 54
Education and Training, 54–55
Finance, 55
Government and Public Administration, 55
Health Science, 56
Human Services, 56–57
Information Technology, 57
Law, Public Safety, Corrections, and Security, 57
list of, 49–53
Marketing, Sales, and Service, 58
Science, Technology, Engineering, and Mathematics, 58

Chemistry Teachers, Postsecondary, 99, 166–168

Child, Family, and School Social Workers, 129, 168–170

Chinese, 24, 27, 30–31, 33–36, 39, 41, 46, 54, 56, 61, 67, 70, 83–84, 230

Chiropractic, 25–26, 30, 32–34, 38, 48, 56, 60–61, 67, 70, 84–85, 171

Chiropractors, 85, 171–172

Classics, 24, 27, 30–31, 33–35, 37, 39, 41, 46, 54, 56, 61, 67, 70, 85–86, 230

Clergy, 118, 126, 172–174

Clinical Psychologists, 123, 174–176

Coaches and Scouts, 119, 176–178

College Algebra (course), 71

The College Board Web site, 329

College Majors Handbook with Real Career Paths and Payoffs: The Actual Jobs, Earnings, and Trends for Graduates of 60 College Majors (Fogg, Harrington, and Harrington), 329

Communications Studies/Speech, 24, 28, 36–37, 39, 46, 54–57, 62–63, 65–66, 70, 86–87, 184, 295–296

Communications Teachers, Postsecondary, 99, 104, 178–180

Computer Science Teachers, Postsecondary, 99, 180–182

Conventional personality type, 60, 63

Copy Writers, 87, 90, 93, 106

Counseling Psychologists, 123, 182–183

courses, important for future, 71

Court Reporters, 87, 106, 184–185

Criminal Investigators and Special Agents, 88, 185–187

Criminal Justice and Law Enforcement Teachers, Postsecondary, 99, 187–189

Criminal Justice/Law Enforcement, 24, 28, 38, 42–43, 46, 57, 60, 62–63, 67, 70, 87–89, 161, 185, 225, 275, 277, 279, 287, 307

Curators, 82, 189–191

D

demographics
    men, 38
    part-time workers, 30–32
    rural workers, 42–44
    self-employed workers, 33–34
    urban workers, 39–41
    women, 35–37
Directors, Religious Activities and Education, 118

doctoral degree, 45, 48

E

Early Childhood Education, 25, 28, 30, 32–35, 42–43, 46, 55–56, 62, 67, 70, 89–90, 232, 285, 323

Economics Teachers, Postsecondary, 99, 104, 191–193

Editors, 90, 93, 106, 193–195

Education and Training career cluster, 50, 54–55

education levels
    bachelor's degree, 46
    doctoral degree, 48
    first professional degree, 48
    list of, 45
    master's degree, 47
    work experience plus degree, 47
Education Teachers, Postsecondary, 99, 104, 195–197

Engineering Teachers, Postsecondary, 99, 197–199

English, 25, 28, 33–34, 39, 46, 54, 56–57, 62, 65, 90, 193

English Composition (course), 71

English Language and Literature Teachers, Postsecondary, 99, 104, 199–201

Enhanced Occupational Outlook Handbook, 329

Enterprising personality type, 60, 63

Environmental Science, 24, 27, 38, 40–41, 47, 53, 60–61, 67, 91, 203

Environmental Science and Protection Technicians, Including Health, 91

Environmental Science Teachers, Postsecondary, 99, 201–203

Environmental Scientists and Specialists, Including Health, 91, 203–205

F

Family and Consumer Sciences, 24, 28, 36–37, 40–42, 46, 54–57, 62–63, 65–66, 92–93, 193, 249, 296, 305

Family and General Practitioners, 110, 205–206

Farm and Home Management Advisors, 93

female workers, 35–37

Finance career cluster, 50, 55

First-Line Supervisors/Managers of Retail Sales Workers, 93

first professional degree, 45, 48

Fitness Trainers and Aerobics Instructors, 119

Fogg, Neeta P., 329

forecasts, limitations of, 17–18

Foreign Language and Literature Teachers, Postsecondary, 99, 104, 207–208

Foreign Language (course), 71

Forestry and Conservation Science Teachers, Postsecondary, 99, 209–210

French, 24, 27, 30–31, 33–35, 37, 39, 41, 46, 54, 56, 61, 67, 70, 93–94, 230

G

General Biology (course), 71

General Chemistry (course), 71

General Microbiology (course), 71

Geography Teachers, Postsecondary, 99, 104, 211–212

Geology, 24, 26–27, 38–39, 47, 58, 60–61, 67–69, 94–95, 213, 223

Geophysics, 24, 26–27, 38–39, 41, 47, 58, 60–61, 67, 95–96, 213

Geoscientists, Except Hydrologists and Geographers, 95–96, 115, 213–215

German, 24, 27, 30–31, 33–34, 36–37, 39, 41, 46, 55, 57, 61, 67, 70, 96–97, 230

Government and Public Administration career cluster, 51, 55

Graduate Study for College Teaching, 24, 27–28, 30–31, 46, 48, 53–58, 60–62, 65–66, 68–69, 97–100, 140, 146, 150, 153, 155, 157, 162, 164, 166, 178, 180, 187, 191, 195, 197, 199, 201, 207, 209, 211, 215, 217, 219, 221, 234, 238, 242, 253, 265, 272, 281, 284, 293, 299, 309, 311, 326

Graduate Teaching Assistants, 99, 215–216

H

Harrington, Paul E., 329

Harrington, Thomas F., 329

Health Information Systems Administration, 24, 26, 28, 33–34, 36, 40–43, 47, 56, 63, 67, 100–101, 247

Health Science career cluster, 51, 56

Health Specialties Teachers, Postsecondary, 99, 217–219

High-Security Majors Related to Jobs that Require the Highest Level of Math Skills, 68

High-Security Majors Related to Jobs that Require the Highest Level of Verbal Skills, 65

History Teachers, Postsecondary, 99, 104, 219–220

Holland, John L., 58

Home Economics Teachers, Postsecondary, 99, 221–222

Hospital/Health Facilities Administration, 24, 26, 28, 33–34, 36, 40–43, 47, 56, 63, 67, 101–102, 247

Hospitality and Tourism career cluster, 51

Human Services career cluster, 51, 56–57

Humanities, 102–104

Hydrologists, 115, 223–224

I

Immigration and Customs Inspectors, 88, 225–226

Industrial-Organizational Psychologists, 124, 226–228

industries with relatively high job security, 15–17

Information Technology career cluster, 51, 57

Internists, General, 110, 228–230

Interpreters and Translators, 84, 86, 94, 97, 105, 112, 127, 130, 230–232

Introduction to Biochemisty (course), 71

Introduction to Computer Science (course), 71

Introduction to Psychology (course), 71

Investigative personality type, 59, 61

irreplaceable workers, work habits for, 18–19

J–K

Japanese, 24, 27, 30–31, 33–34, 36–37, 39, 41, 46, 55, 57, 61, 67, 70, 104–105, 230

job security

considering when job hunting, 17

limitations of forecasts, 17–18

reasons for, 15–17

work habits for, 18–19

Journalism and Mass Communications, 25, 33–34, 39, 46, 54, 56–57, 62, 65, 105–106, 184, 193

Kindergarten Teachers, Except Special Education, 89, 232–234

L

Law, Public Safety, Corrections, and Security career cluster, 52, 57

Law Teachers, Postsecondary, 100, 234–236

Librarians, 107, 236–238

Library Science, 25, 28, 30, 32, 35, 40, 42–43, 47, 55, 62, 65, 106–107, 236

Library Science Teachers, Postsecondary, 100, 238–240

lists

The 20 High-Security Majors with the Best Income Potential, 26

The 20 High-Security Majors with the Best Job-Growth Potential, 27

The 20 High-Security Majors with the Best Job-Opening Potential, 28

The 50 Best High-Security Majors Overall, 24–25

Best High-Security Majors for People with a Conventional Personality Type, 63

Best High-Security Majors for People with a Realistic Personality Type, 60

Best High-Security Majors for People with a Social Personality Type, 62

Best High-Security Majors for People with an Artistic Personality Type, 61–62

Best High-Security Majors for People with an Enterprising Personality Type, 63

Best High-Security Majors for People with an Investigative Personality Type, 61

Best High-Security Majors in the Agriculture, Food and Natural Resources Cluster, 53

Best High-Security Majors in the Architecture and Construction Cluster, 53

Best High-Security Majors in the Arts, Audio/Video Technology, and Communications Cluster, 54

Best High-Security Majors in the Business, Management, and Administration Cluster, 54

Best High-Security Majors in the Education and Training Cluster, 54–55

Best High-Security Majors in the Finance Cluster, 55

Best High-Security Majors in the Government and Public Administration Cluster, 55

Best High-Security Majors in the Health Science Cluster, 56

Best High-Security Majors in the Human Services Cluster, 56–57

Best High-Security Majors in the Information Technology Cluster, 57

Best High-Security Majors in the Law, Public Safety, Corrections, and Security Cluster, 57

Best High-Security Majors in the Marketing, Sales, and Service Cluster, 58

Best High-Security Majors in the Science, Technology, Engineering, and Mathematics Cluster, 58

Best High-Security Majors Related to Jobs Employing a High Percentage of Men, 38

Best High-Security Majors Related to Jobs Employing a High Percentage of Rural Workers, 43

Best High-Security Majors Related to Jobs Employing a High Percentage of Urban Workers, 41

Best High-Security Majors Related to Jobs Employing a High Percentage of Women, 36–37

Best High-Security Majors Related to Jobs Employing the Highest Percentage of Men, 38

Best High-Security Majors Related to Jobs Employing the Highest Percentage of Rural Workers, 42

Best High-Security Majors Related to Jobs Employing the Highest Percentage of Urban Workers, 39–40

Best High-Security Majors Related to Jobs Employing the Highest Percentage of Women, 35–36

Best High-Security Majors Related to Jobs Requiring a Bachelor's Degree or Less, 46

Best High-Security Majors Related to Jobs Requiring a Doctoral Degree, 48

Best High-Security Majors Related to Jobs Requiring a First Professional Degree, 48

Best High-Security Majors Related to Jobs Requiring a Master's Degree, 47

Best High-Security Majors Related to Jobs Requiring Work Experience Plus Degree, 47

Best High-Security Majors Related to Jobs that Require a High Level of Math Skills, 68–69

Best High-Security Majors Related to Jobs that Require a High Level of Verbal Skills, 66

Best High-Security Majors Related to Jobs that Require a Lower Level of Math Skills, 70

Best High-Security Majors Related to Jobs that Require a Lower Level of Verbal Skills, 67

Best High-Security Majors Related to Jobs with a High Percentage of Part-Time Workers, 31–32

Best High-Security Majors Related to Jobs with a High Percentage of Self-Employed Workers, 34

Best High-Security Majors Related to Jobs with the Highest Percentage of Part-Time Workers, 30–31

Best High-Security Majors Related to Jobs with the Highest Percentage of Self-Employed Workers, 33

High-Security Majors Related to Jobs that Require the Highest Level of Math Skills, 68

High-Security Majors Related to Jobs that Require the Highest Level of Verbal Skills, 65

The Most Important Courses for a Secure Future, 71

M

male workers, 38

Manufacturing career cluster, 52

Marketing Managers, 93

Marketing, Sales, and Service career cluster, 52, 58

Marriage and Family Therapists, 129, 240–242

master's degree, 45, 47

math skills, 68–70

Mathematical Science Teachers, Postsecondary, 100, 242–244

Mathematicians, 108, 133, 244–245

Mathematics, 25–26, 39, 47–48, 54, 57–58, 61, 65–66, 68–69, 107–108, 244, 319

Medical and Clinical Laboratory Technologists, 109, 245–247

Medical and Health Services Managers, 101, 102, 247–249

Medical Technology, 24, 35, 37, 39, 42–43, 46, 56, 60–61, 67, 70, 108–109, 245

Medicine, 24, 26, 28, 33–34, 38, 48, 56, 58, 60–61, 65–66, 109–110, 142, 205, 228, 255, 261, 271, 291, 321

men workers, 38

Middle School Teachers, Except Special and Vocational Education, 93, 119, 249–251

Modern Foreign Language, 24, 27, 30–31, 33–34, 36–37, 40–41, 46, 55, 57, 62, 67, 70, 111–112, 230

The Most Important Courses for a Secure Future, 71

Museum Technicians and Conservators, 82, 251–253

N

Natural Sciences Managers, 95–96, 108, 115, 134

New Guide for Occupational Exploration, 330

Nursing Instructors and Teachers, Postsecondary, 100, 253–255

Nursing (R.N. Training), 24, 27–28, 30–31, 35–36, 40–43, 46, 56, 62, 67, 70, 112–113, 301

O

Obstetricians and Gynecologists, 110, 255–257

Occupational Outlook Handbook (OOH), 329

Occupational Therapists, 114, 257–259

Occupational Therapy, 24, 26–27, 30–31, 33–36, 40–41, 47, 56, 60, 62, 67, 70, 113–114, 257

occupations with relatively high job security, 15–17

Oceanography, 24, 26–27, 38–39, 47, 58, 60–61, 67–69, 114–115, 213, 223

O*NET Dictionary of Occupational Titles, 329

OOH (Occupational Outlook Handbook), 329

Optometrists, 116, 259–260

Optometry, 24, 26, 30, 32–34, 38, 48, 56, 60–61, 67, 70, 115–116, 259

Oral Communication (course), 71

Organic Chemistry (course), 71

P

part-time workers, 30–32

pathways, 48

Pediatricians, General, 110, 261–262

personality types
    Artistic, 61–62
    Conventional, 63
    Enterprising, 63
    Investigative, 61
    list of, 59–60
    Realistic, 60
    Social, 62

Pharmacists, 117, 263–265

Pharmacy, 24, 26–28, 31, 40–43, 48, 56, 61, 65–66, 68, 116–117, 263

Philosophy, 24, 28, 38, 46–47, 57, 62, 65–66, 117–118, 172, 303

Philosophy and Religion Teachers, Postsecondary, 100, 104, 265–266

Physical Education, 25, 28, 36–37, 42–43, 46, 55, 60, 62–63, 65–66, 118–119, 176, 249, 305

Physical Therapists, 120, 267–268

Physical Therapy, 24, 26–28, 30–31, 33–34, 36, 40–43, 47, 56, 60, 62, 67, 119–120, 267

Physician Assistants, 121, 269–270

Physician Assisting, 24, 26–27, 31, 35–36, 47, 56, 61, 67, 70, 120–121, 269

Physicians and Surgeons, All Other, 110, 271

Physics Teachers, Postsecondary, 100, 272–273

Podiatrists, 122, 274–275

Podiatry, 25–26, 30, 33, 38, 48, 56, 62, 65–66, 68–69, 121–122, 274

Poets, Lyricists, and Creative Writers, 87, 90, 93, 106

Police Detectives, 88, 275–277

Police Identification and Records Officers, 88, 277–279

Police Patrol Officers, 88, 279–280

Political Science, 25–26, 30, 39, 47, 55, 57–58, 61, 65, 122, 283

Political Science Teachers, Postsecondary, 100, 281–282

Political Scientists, 122, 283–284

Postsecondary Teachers, All Other, 100, 104, 284–285

Preschool Teachers, Except Special Education, 89, 285–287

Private Detectives and Investigators, 88, 287–289

Probation Officers and Correctional Treatment Specialists, 129, 289–291

Psychiatrists, 110, 291–293

Psychology, 24, 26, 30, 32–34, 36, 40, 42–43, 47–48, 56–57, 61–62, 65–66, 123–124, 174, 182, 226, 303

Psychology Teachers, Postsecondary, 100, 293–295

Public Address System and Other Announcers, 87, 295–296

Public Relations, 24, 28, 36, 39, 41, 46, 54–56, 63, 65–66, 70, 124–125, 296

Public Relations Managers, 125

Public Relations Specialists, 87, 93, 125, 296–299

R

Realistic personality type, 59–60

Recreation and Fitness Studies Teachers, Postsecondary, 100, 299–300

Registered Nurses, 113, 301–303

Religion/Religious Studies, 24, 28, 38, 40–41, 47, 57, 62, 65–66, 125–126, 172

Religious Workers, All Other, 118, 303

Reporters and Correspondents, 90, 106

rural workers, 42–44

Russian, 24, 27, 30–31, 33–34, 36–37, 40–41, 46, 55, 57, 62, 67, 70, 126–127, 230

S

Sales Managers, 93

School Psychologists, 124, 303–305

Science, Technology, Engineering, and Mathematics career cluster, 52–53, 58

Secondary Education, 25, 28, 30–31, 42–43, 46, 55, 62, 65–66, 127–128, 305, 323

Secondary School Teachers, Except Special and Vocational Education, 83, 93, 119, 128, 305–307

security. *See* job security

Self-Directed Search (SDS), 58

self-employed workers, 33–34

Seminar (reporting on research) (course), 71

Sheriffs and Deputy Sheriffs, 89, 307–309

Social personality type, 60, 62

Social Work, 24, 28, 35, 37, 40, 42–43, 46–47, 57, 62, 67, 70, 128–129, 168, 240, 289

Social Work Teachers, Postsecondary, 100, 309–311

Sociology Teachers, Postsecondary, 100, 311–312

Spanish, 24, 27, 30–31, 33–34, 36–37, 40–41, 46, 55, 57, 62, 67, 70, 129–130, 230

Special Education, 25, 35, 42–43, 46, 55, 62, 67, 131–132, 313, 315

Special Education Teachers, Middle School, 131, 313–314

Special Education Teachers, Preschool, Kindergarten, and Elementary School, 132

Special Education Teachers, Secondary School, 131, 315–316

Speech-Language Pathologists, 133, 317–318

Speech-Language Pathology and Audiology, 25–26, 30, 33, 35, 42–43, 47–48, 56, 62, 65–66, 132–133, 159, 317

Statisticians, 108, 133, 319–320

Statistics, 25–26, 39, 47–48, 54, 57–58, 61, 65–66, 68–69, 133–134, 244, 319

Statistics (course), 71

Statistics for Business and Social Sciences (course), 71

Surgeons, 110, 321–322

T–V

Teachers and Instructors, All Other, 90, 128, 323

Technical Writers, 87

Transportation, Distribution, and Logistics career cluster, 53

urban workers, 39–41

verbal skills, 65–67

Veterinarians, 135, 324–326

Veterinary Medicine, 24, 26–27, 33–34, 42–43, 48, 56, 60–61, 65–66, 68, 134–135, 324

Vocational Education Teachers, Postsecondary, 100, 326–328

W–Z

women workers, 35–37

Women's Studies, 135–136

work experience plus degree, 45, 47

work habits for job security, 18–19

Writers and Authors, 87, 90, 93, 106